Managing Conflict

Managing Conflict

An Interdisciplinary Approach

Edited by
M. Afzalur Rahim

New York
Westport, Connecticut
London

Library of Congress Cataloging-in-Publication Data

Managing conflict : an interdisciplinary approach / edited by M.
  Afzalur Rahim.
        p. cm.
      Papers from the First International Conference of the CMG
(Conflict Management Group), held June 22–25, 1987, at George Mason
University.
  Bibliography: p.
  Includes index.
  ISBN 0-275-92683-4 (alk. paper)
  1.   Conflict management—Congresses. I.   Rahim, M. Afzalur.
II.   International Conference of the CMG (1st : 1987 : George Mason
University)
HD42.M36 1989
658.4—dc19   88-14104

Library of Congress Catalog Number: 88-14104
ISBN: 0-275-92683-4

First published in 1989

Praeger Publishers, One Madison Avenue, New York, NY 10010
A division of Greenwood Press, Inc.

Printed in the United States of America

∞

The paper used in this book complies with the
Permanent Paper Standard issued by the National
Information Standards Organization (Z39.48-1984).

10 9 8 7 6 5 4 3 2 1

Contents

Preface

The concept of conflict is not new and has been with us from time immemorial. In fact, it can be traced to the pre-biblical times. It has received different degrees of attention from social scientists during different periods of history. Over the years the phenomena of conflict have been studied by philosophers, sociologists, anthropologists, psychologists, political scientists, and economists. Scholars in management, communication, education, and law have become interested in studying conflict in recent years. Conflict management is undoubtedly an interdisciplinary field of study which is reflected in the subtitle of this book, *An Interdisciplinary Approach.*

In recent years, there had been a renewed interest and significant changes in the study of conflict in social and organizational contexts. As a result of these developments, the Conflict Management Group (now International Association for Conflict Management) was founded in 1984 to encourage research, teaching, and training and development on managing social and organizational conflicts. It was decided that the then CMG would encourage these purposes by facilitating the exchange of information among members by sponsoring conferences, and by providing a computer-based clearinghouse for the publications, research projects, and training and development activities of its members. To accomplish its major objective of facilitating exchange of information among members, the First International Conference of the CMG was held at George Mason University on June 22–25, 1987. The conference program contained 82 papers, symposia, and workshops. The abstracts of these were published in our *Proceedings.*

This book contains 21 chapters presented at the conference. The competitive papers were selected on the basis of their reviewers' comments and recommendations of their respective section editors. The invited papers by scholars were accepted on the basis of the recommendations of their section editors. Each chapter and section introduction was revised or rewritten according to my comments, to maintain consistency and quality. We have strictly followed the APA style guide to prepare each chapter and section introduction.

A perusal of the titles of the chapters and their sections serves to underscore the fact that conflict can occur in practically any organizational and social contexts, and that effective management of conflict is truly an interdisciplinary task. All of us, regardless of our professional orientations and training, have much to learn from one another. I hope that this book will facilitate this process of learning.

I wish to express my gratitude to the authors for their creative and expeditious responses to my editorial comments. Their cooperation made my work as editor-in-chief a lot easier and more enjoyable than I was led to believe it would be. My special thanks are due to the section editors Dean Tjosvold, Linda Putnam, Margaret Neale, and Gabriel Buntzman who devoted many hours to preparing their respective parts. My thanks are also due to Evert van de Vliert with whom I collaborated in preparing Part V.

I have enjoyed the opportunity to work with the authors on this project. The section editors and I worked hard to prepare a high quality book. Time will show to what extent we succeeded in accomplishing our goal.

PART I

Organizational Conflict

Introduction

Dean Tjosvold

People in organizations clash, quarrel, argue, and battle as they work together to get things done. An assistant complains that his boss barks out orders without explanation; the boss seethes at his assistant's errors. Employees are frustrated when co-workers fail to do their fair share of the work. Executives debate whether the company should expand into growing markets or "stick to the knitting." Surveys indicate that managers use over 20 percent of their time dealing with conflict (Thomas & Schmidt, 1976). They probably also spend a lot of time trying to avoid conflict (Argyris & Schon, 1978).

Conflict is too pervasive in organizations to be ignored. Organizational researchers are committed to helping managers appreciate the significance of conflict and realize that conflict must be managed. They want to develop knowledge so that managers and employees can sharpen their skills and sensitivities to minimize the costs of conflict and, if possible, make it productive.

These emerging attitudes toward conflict have far-reaching implications for how we design and manage organizations. Traditional principles of management are based on the assumption that conflict disrupts and disorganizes. Frederick Taylor and other early influential theorists sought efficiency and rationality, and proposed designs, values, and roles that would reduce conflict and give managers the means to end it decisively. Contemporary managers are trying to use conflict. Companies want to develop strong cultures to gain the commitment not the compliance of employees. Project teams, labor-management problem-solving groups, interdepartmental task forces, and other innovations assume that employees should discuss their ideas openly. Rather than dominate and control, contemporary managers are expected to foster participation and solicit the views and feelings of employees.

The recognition that conflict occurs in many settings has important implications for organizational research as well as practice. Conflict cuts across traditional research areas of leadership, power, task groups, strategic management, industrial relations, innovation, corporate culture, and performance appraisal (Tjosvold, 1985). There are few if any settings in which conflict does not occur in organizations. Researchers have the challenge to demonstrate that knowledge about conflict can inform our understanding of traditional research issues. They also have the challenge to use conflict research to integrate the increasingly fragmented study of organizations.

Conflict researchers share a vision that can very much alter our thinking about organizations. But it should not be assumed that conflict researchers are of one mind. They have diverse theories, approaches, and methods. There is definitely conflict in the study of conflict. This conflict is not only inevitable but potentially very constructive. Organizational conflict is a complex phenomenon that needs to be explored from a variety of perspectives.

OVERVIEW OF CHAPTERS

The chapters in Part I reflect the common commitments and diverse perspectives of conflict researchers. While the researchers emphasize the pervasiveness of conflict and the need to manage it, they draw upon theories from organizational studies, aggression, and social psychology of interdependence. They use questionnaires, experiments, secondary data analysis, and theoretical argument.

In Chapter 1 Bergmann and Volkema help us appreciate the many forms of organizational conflict. Incompatible goals, failure to accept input, vague assignments, unfair evaluations, downgrading co-workers, unfair distribution of work, personality, and many other issues were cited as reasons for conflict. These data underline that the intense interdependence among employees makes conflict so prevalent. Their evidence also underscores the fact that employees have great variety of choices to deal with the conflict. They discuss, listen, avoid, talk to outsiders, involve higher ups, and convince. Conflict is a dynamic process, and employees were found to rely on different strategies as conflict develops. When "soft" approaches did not resolve the conflict, employees would use more aggressive strategies.

Bergmann and Volkema show that how employees reacted to conflict depends upon relative status. Employees reported less intense conflicts with superiors than with co-workers, but indicated they suffered more from them. Their results on the consequences of conflict remind us that many conflicts, at least how they are presently handled, upset people and disrupt work.

Baron in Chapter 2 demonstrates that feedback, if inappropriately given, can intensify conflict. His experiment, which won the award for the best paper on the organizational conflict tract at the conference, distinguishes constructive from destructive criticism. After performing inadequately, participants in the constructive criticism condition were given specific, considerate feedback that did not attribute their performance to internal causes. Participants in the destructive criticism received feedback that was general, inconsiderate, and attributed poor performance to internal factors.

Participants who had constructive compared to destructive criticism were less angry, more accepting of the feedback as fair, more willing to discuss future conflicts collaboratively, and felt more confident and set higher goals for future performance. In addition to important direct practical implications, Baron's study documents how conflict is part of feedback and evaluations in organizations and the need to consider conflict in such areas as performance appraisal. He also shows the power and utility of carefully executed, thoughtful experiment in the study of organizational conflict.

Psenicka and Rahim (Chapter 3) found that styles of managing conflict predicted the outcomes of an actual conflict. MBA students first completed the Rahim Organizational Conflict Inventory-II that measures conflict styles. Students then formed into two-person groups to complete a research paper for the course. They were assigned to these groups so that they would have incompatible preferences and would have to negotiate their responsibility for the qualitative and quantitative parts of the assignment.

As predicted, subjects who indicated a greater use of dominating style than their partners were found to get agreements more favorable to themselves. Subjects higher on obliging than their partners had less favorable agreements, though this did not reach statistical significance. But subjects higher on dominating than obliging relative to their partners obtained more favorable agreements for themselves. Psenicka and Rahim demonstrated a link between conflict styles and outcomes in an actual conflict and supported the validity of the Rahim Organizational Conflict Inventory. They also demonstrated a creative use of a course assignment to test conflict theory in a field setting.

In Chapter 4, I argue that interdependence research provides a useful way to distinguish conflict strategies. Experimental research, including my own, on the effects of different strategies has not been very fruitful. Threats, for example, have been shown both to escalate and moderate conflict. Moreover, employees can laugh, cry, shout, plead, compromise, tease, and use many other strategies. Interdependence offers a parsimonious approach by indicating that what is critical is whether the strategy conveys an intent to cooperate or compete. A threat, even if made softly, that is interpreted as a competitive attempt to win is reacted to much differently than a threat that is experienced as an attempt to settle the dispute for mutual benefit.

The interdependence approach to conflict management emphasizes understanding the perspective of those involved in the conflict. The norms and values of the organization, the protagonists' attitudes and relationship, and their individual characteristics, all are likely to affect how employees interpret and react to each other's strategies. While I bring substantial research to support this argument, much more is needed, especially to understand how employees conclude that others are trying to manage the conflict cooperatively or competitively.

In Chapter 5, van de Vliert and Prein empirically analyze previous findings on conflict styles. Organizational researchers have relied extensively on Blake and Mouton's formulation of five conflict styles, namely: forcing, avoiding, compromising, problem solving, and accommodating. This approach is thought to reflect more accurately employee strategies than the more simple distinction of cooperation-competition or distributive-integrative.

Drawing upon social psychological research, van de Vliert and Prein make a critical distinction between styles as experienced by the actor and by an observer. Their analysis suggests that employees tend to use the five styles *when* they describe their own behavior. However, they use a simpler forcing-nonforcing dichotomy when they describe others' styles. These results pose the very interesting idea that protagonists may be quite alert to differences in their own conflict actions. However, when they consider others they use a simpler framework to interpret the other's intentions. Indeed van de Vliert and Prein suggest, as I do in Chapter 4, that conflict protagonists want to know whether others want to force their way competitively, or are working to solve the problem jointly.

The chapters in Part I demonstrate conflict researchers' commitment to develop knowledge to help organizations manage conflict productively. They also reflect our diversity of theories, methods, and findings. We hope they contribute to ongoing debates about organizational conflict and promote exploration and integration of various ideas to further our understanding and competence in managing conflict.

1

Understanding and Managing Interpersonal Conflict at Work: Its Issues, Interactive Processes, and Consequences

Thomas J. Bergmann
Roger J. Volkema

Conflict is a natural outcome of human interaction. The way a conflict is managed will determine to a great extent the degree to which the negative impact can be minimized and the positive aspects maximized (Robbins, 1978; Tjosvold, 1985; Rahim, 1986a). Conflict that is not identified, understood and managed effectively can lead to inefficient use of organizational resources, stress on the conflicting parties, and misdirection of the energies of those affected by the conflict situation. On the other hand, conflict that is effectively managed can result in increased creativity and innovation, a rethinking of goals and practices, and a better informed work group (Burke, 1970; Folger & Poole, 1984; Tjosvold, 1985; Rahim, 1986a). But effectively managing conflict so that it does not get out of control is a very difficult task requiring exceptional skill of the manager (Rahim, 1986a).

To gain a better understanding of the interpersonal conflicts that exist within business organizations, a study was designed to identify the issues underlying conflicts and to track the behavioral responses of parties in supervisor-subordinate and co-worker–co-worker conflict dyads and identify the consequences to the conflicting parties.

PROCESS MODEL OF CONFLICT

The basic process model of conflict, as presented by Thomas (1976), is the foundation for the current study. According to Thomas, the stages in the process model of dyadic conflict are frustration, conceptualization, behavior, and outcome.

Frustration occurs when one individual perceives that his or her goals, beliefs, attitudes, ideas, etc. are incongruent with those of another individual. The source of the conflict often is based either in the behavioral or structural components of the situation. That is, the behaviors and attitudes of the parties involved and/or the structure of the situation (reward structure, job design) will be the source of the interpersonal conflict (Rahim, 1986a). The level of frustration is primarily determined by the amount of perceived dependency or interdependency of the parties, together with the amount of interaction time (Folger & Poole, 1984).

Conceptualization is the crystallizing of what specifically is causing the level of frustration. The individual who is frustrated reviews the situation and mentally clarifies the specific behaviors, comments, and so on, of the other party that cause the concern (Renwick, 1975; Filley, 1978; Musser, 1982). This lack of congruence between the parties of the conflict can be present in either a super-visor-subordinate or co-worker–type relationship. The presence of the conflict in either relationship is likely to have behavioral impact on either or both of the individuals involved.

The behavior stage consists of action taken or not taken by the parties of the conflict to cope with the perceived situation. A number of typologies have been proposed to categorize the different behaviors of the parties involved. One of the most frequently cited typologies was developed by Blake and Mouton (1964) and extended by Thomas (1976). They identified five basic behavioral responses: avoiding (the person, the issue, the situation), accommodating (giving in), com-promising (both parties make adjustments), competing (forcing to satisfy one's desires) and collaborating (problem solving).

Cosier and Ruble (1981), in two experimental studies, examined what kind of categorical breakout could adequately tap conflict response behavior. They found the traditional view of conflict, that is assertiveness and cooperativeness, was insufficient to cover the situation, and suggested that more specific break-outs should be used for better analysis. In addition, they noted that as the conflict interaction continues over time the behavior of one party becomes more depen-dent on the perceived behavior of the other party to the conflict. It would be expected that behavioral responses of the parties would change as the conflict continues (Folger & Poole, 1984).

Burke (1970) found that the type of behavior with which a manager responds in a conflict situation has a significant impact on the management of the conflict. Problem solving (collaboration) was found to be an effective management tech-nique, whereas forcing and withdrawal were ineffective. Likewise, Watson (1987) found that supervisors who used a collaborative style were more effective in dealing with subordinates in a conflict situation than were supervisors who responded in a supportive or facilitating style. These supervisors were able to be effective while maintaining employee satisfaction and motivation. Actually, Robbins (1978) and Rahim (1986b) discovered that short-term avoidance may be a very effective way to deal with a conflict situation in order to permit time for one or both of the parties to regain their composure and rationally to think through the issues and circumstances of the conflict situation.

A manager's response technique to conflict is not static. Deutsch (1973, 1980) found that if individuals perceive their goals to be incongruent with the conflict person this impacts on their selected response to the conflict situation. When individuals perceive their goals to be in conflict they pursue a more competitive and confrontive behavior than if they perceive their goals to be more congruent. In addition, Rahim (1986b) found that managers will try different response styles if their original response fails to resolve the conflict. He found that at first managers used obliging with superiors and integrating with subordinates and compromising with peers but when these were not successful they tried compromising and dominating with superiors and avoiding subordinates. Based on these studies, it would appear that multiple response behaviors to conflict situations have to be tapped in order to gain a fuller understanding of the behaviors that are used to deal with conflict issues. In addition, it would be beneficial to track the behavioral responses of the respondents as the conflict continues between the parties. The review of works by Blake and Mouton (1964), Thomas (1976) and Rahim (1983b) provided excellent sources upon which items could be developed to tap the different behavioral responses of individuals involved in a conflict situation.

Musser (1982) noted that the majority of the studies of supervisor-subordinate conflict examine the management technique used by the manager to deal with the situation and suggests increased study of the actions of the subordinate. Musser developed a strong argument that subordinates do not always take on a passive posture in dealing with conflict with superiors. He indicates that subordinates will engage in competing, problem solving, compromising, and avoiding along with accommodating behaviors to manage conflicts with superiors. Likewise, he proposes that the behaviors of the individual will change depending on the situation. A study by Drake, Zammuto, and Parasuaman (1982), however, supports the belief that workers engaged in a conflict with a superior are most likely to respond in an avoidance or obliging behavior.

Finally, referring back to Thomas' model, outcome is the consequence of the conflict situation to the parties of the conflict or to other members of the organization. Outcome can lead to continued frustrations and a recycling of the conflict, or to a satisfactory resolution of the issues. The impact of the conflict on the participants of the conflict and the organization may be functional or dysfunctional. It has been hypothesized that conflict is an inverted U-shaped function. That is, low to moderate conflict is positive but after a certain point the conflict turns dysfunctional and has negative impact on the parties involved (Rahim, 1986a). Rahim (1986a) points out that there are no well controlled empirical studies that support this inverted U-shaped function and that the difficulty of obtaining valid and reliable measures of organizational effectiveness is part of the problem. One of the focuses of this study is the impact that the conflict has on the individuals themselves, not the organization. That is, what impact does the conflict have on the psychological state of the employee, at work and away from work?

To summarize, the basic objective of this study was to identify the primary issue of an interpersonal conflict, to examine the multiple behavioral responses an individual attempts to use to resolve the perceived conflict, to look at the consequences of the conflict to the conflicting parties, and to determine if there is a difference in the above for supervisor-subordinate conflicts and conflicts between coworkers.

Method

A seven-page questionnaire was designed to obtain information from individuals who were or had recently been involved in an interpersonal conflict at work. The specific questions included in the questionnaire were the result of a review of past research (Blake & Mouton, 1964; Thomas, 1976; Roloff, 1976; Rahim, 1983b) and the experiences of the authors (e.g., as mediators). A standard procedure for validating the questionnaire was used. The questionnaire was tested on a group of participants who, upon completion of the survey, entered into a discussion with the questionnaire designers to ensure that accurate interpretation of the questionnaire was occurring. Based on this feedback, the questionnaire was revised. The process was repeated a number of times until the researchers had an instrument that was clear and meaningful.

The questionnaire consisted of two sections: a demographics section and a conflict situation section. In the demographics section, participants were asked for statistical data about themselves and the other party to the conflict (age, education, sex, etc.).

The conflict situation section contained questions regarding various aspects of the situation, such as the conflict issue or issues (the major reason for the conflict), intensity of the conflict (0 to 100%), description of the consequences of the conflict (what was the outcome of the conflict), and their personal response to the conflict. Regarding personal responses to the conflict situation, the participants were given a list of specific response behaviors and asked to: (1) rank the responses in the order in which they actually responded to the conflict situation, (2) identify which response(s) they were currently using, (3) identify those they would never use, and (4) identify those they had not used but might use in the future.

Sample

The interpersonal conflict questionnaire was administered to upper-class business students at a medium-sized state university. Participants were asked to respond based on a conflict they were currently engaged in or had just been engaged in during their vacation employment. If they worked in a conflict-free environment, they were requested to skip to the demographic section at the end of the questionnaire. A conflict was defined as "a disagreement or controversy in interests, values, goals or ideas between you and another person or persons at work." Participants were guaranteed anonymity.

A total of 263 people employed in 32 job categories filled out the questionnaire. Twenty-four different industries, with an average size of 118 employees, were sampled with (a) 95 (36.1%) reporting a conflict with a supervisor, (b) 91 (34.6%) with a co-worker, (c) 15 (5.7%) with a subordinate, (d) 5 (1.9%) with a group, (e) 16 (6.1%) with other miscellaneous classifications, and (f) 41 (15.6%) reporting no conflict at work. Due to the size of the subsamples, only the supervisor-subordinate (a) and co-worker (b) conflict dyads will be reported.

The demographic profile of the respondents in these two subsamples was as follows: 90 males (43-supervisor-subordinate [SS], 47 co-worker [CW]) and 96 females (52 SS; 44 CW) a mean age of 22 and an average of three years of college for both groups. The demographic profile of the individuals who were engaged in conflict with the respondents was as follows: 101 males (60 SS; 41 CW), 84 females (35 SS; 49 CW) and 1 missing, a mean age of 35 for SS and 26 for CW, and in the supervisor-subordinate conflict a bimodel educational distribution (34% high school graduates only, 43% with four years or more of college education), whereas in the co-worker conflict a more even educational distribution was found (although 36% were high school graduates only).

RESULTS

A series of *t*-tests were computed, using a set of demographic variables, to determine if a significant difference exists between those experiencing conflict at work and those experiencing a conflict-free environment. This was done to ensure that sample differences were not the cause of any differences emerging in further analysis. There was no significant difference ($p = < .05$) between the two groups based on the following demographic and work characteristics: size of the firm, position held, full- or part-time employment status, years in the position, years in the company, sex, age, ethnic group, education, how the position fit long-term career goals, and the number of conflicts the respondent had outside the work environment.

Conflict Issues

The specific issues identified as underlying the conflict (resulting in frustration of one or both of the parties) by the subordinate in a supervisor-subordinate conflict and by a worker in a co-worker conflict are presented in Table 1.1. The underlying conflict issues that were present in greater proportions in a supervisor-subordinate than a co-worker conflict relationship were: goal conflict (10.8% vs. 6.1%), input not accepted (10.8% vs. 4.9%), task assignment too general (8.4% vs. 3.7%), unfair evaluation (8.4% vs. 2.4%), unrealistic workload (6.0% vs. 1.2%), supervisor not interacting with employees (4.8% vs. 0.0%), application of rules (4.8% vs. 2.4%), and no feedback (3.6% vs. 0.0%). Each of the above was generally identified as the main issue resulting in a feeling of frustration in a supervisor-subordinate relationship about twice as often as in a co-worker conflict situation.

Table 1.1
Issues in Supervisor-Subordinate and Co-Worker Conflict Situations

Issue	Supervisor-Subordinate (Subordinate's Perception) Frequency (%)	Co-Worker Frequency
Goal conflict	9 (10.8)	5 (6.1)
Input not accepted	9 (10.8)	4 (4.9)
Task assignment too general	7 (8.4)	3 (3.7)
Unfair evaluation	7 (8.4)	2 (2.4)
Downgrading co-worker	5 (6.0)	8 (9.8)
Poor work scheduling	5 (6.0)	4 (4.9)
Unrealistic workload	5 (6.0)	1 (1.2)
Misuse of power	5 (6.0)	4 (4.9)
Inequitable administration of rewards	4 (4.8)	3 (3.7)
Supervisor not interacting with employees	4 (4.8)	0 (0.0)
Application of rules	4 (4.8)	2 (2.4)
No feedback	3 (3.6)	0 (0.0)
Personality	3 (3.6)	13 (15.9)
Doesn't carry workload	3 (3.6)	14 (17.1)
Poor customer relations	2 (2.4)	2 (2.4)
Lack of efficiency	2 (2.4)	3 (3.7)
Different work ethic	2 (2.4)	10 (12.2)
Inadequate inventory	1 (1.2)	0 (0.0)
Won't switch work schedule	1 (1.2)	1 (1.2)
Office layout	1 (1.2)	0 (0.0)
No challenge	1 (1.2)	0 (0.0)
Employee lacks training	0 (0.0)	1 (1.2)
Undermines supervisor authority	0 (0.0)	1 (1.2)
Takes credit for others	0 (0.0)	1 (1.2)
Missing	12	9

The conflict issues upon which co-worker conflicts arose in greater proportion than supervisor-subordinate conflicts were: personality (15.9% vs. 3.6%), doesn't carry workload (17.1% vs. 3.6%), and different work ethic of the employees (12.2% vs. 2.4%).

Behavioral Responses

Table 1.2 presents the responses (behaviors) of the subordinate in each of the supervisor-subordinate conflict situations and of a worker in each of the co-

Table 1.2

Frequency of Responses in Supervisor-Subordinate and Co-Worker Conflict Situations

Response	1st Response		2nd Response		3rd Response		Now Using		Never Use		Might Use		Most Successful	
	SS	CW	SS	CW	SS	CW	SS	CW	SS	CW	SS	CW	SS	CW
Discuss	29	16	13	14	3	8	43	21	2	2	32	35	10	7
Convince	5	5	13	12	18	9	27	15	13	7	28	33	13	8
Shout	3	0	0	0	1	1	2	5	54	44	17	19	1	1
Throw	0	0	0	0	0	0	0	0	92	82	0	3	0	0
Cry	0	0	0	0	0	0	2	1	78	79	5	6	0	0
Avoid person	10	12	9	9	5	8	15	28	20	13	20	22	3	6
Listen	12	16	14	7	8	5	28	14	7	2	28	37	2	2
Sabotage	0	0	1	1	1	0	1	1	89	85	2	1	1	0
Don't talk to them	4	12	4	4	4	6	13	17	36	19	16	26	5	0
Talk behind	2	2	9	5	5	2	11	11	26	26	16	21	0	0
Drink	0	2	1	1	1	0	3	2	70	76	10	3	0	0
Talk to co-worker	22	18	21	16	13	11	46	29	1	5	11	17	3	3
Talk to outsider	9	10	11	13	10	4	36	22	6	9	17	24	2	3
Get even	1	0	1	0	0	0	1	0	78	76	6	7	0	0
Leave	1	1	1	1	0	0	5	2	42	61	33	17	1	2
Use my authority	0	0	0	2	2	0	4	2	54	33	17	31	0	1
Other leave	0	0	0	0	0	0	1	0	81	66	5	13	0	0
Transfer	0	0	1	3	0	1	1	0	53	53	27	20	0	0
Go to higher up	0	1	6	10	1	5	11	11	32	24	35	29	3	6
Push	0	0	0	0	1	0	1	0	90	84	1	3	0	0
Form alliance	0	0	2	5	1	0	7	7	40	33	21	28	0	0
Other	2	6	2	2	1	2	8	7	18	14	1	3	9	8
Let it go	0	0	0	0	0	0	0	0	0	0	0	0	9	8
Avoid issue	0	0	0	0	0	0	0	0	0	0	0	0	1	2
Uncooperative	0	0	0	0	0	0	0	0	0	0	0	0	0	0
None	0	0	0	0	0	0	0	0	0	0	0	0	10	12
	100	101	108	107	74	62	266	195	982	893	348	398	65	56

Note: SS = Supervisor-subordinate
CW = Co-worker
Multiple responses allowed

worker conflicts. The major differences between the two groups, based on their first response, was that an employee who was in conflict with a supervisor was more likely to discuss it with that person (similar to Thomas' collaborative response), whereas if the other person was a co-worker, the employee was more likely to stop talking to that person (similar to Thomas' avoiding response). It should be noted that three subordinates even resorted to shouting, while no co-workers did until their second response to the conflict. A fairly large number from each group also engaged in more passive behavior, such as listening, avoiding the person, and discussing the conflict issue with both nonconflict co-workers and outsiders.

In examining the employee's second response, there was greater commonality of responses regardless of who the conflict was with. However, the worker was more likely to stop listening to a co-worker than a supervisor and more likely to talk behind the back of the supervisor. At this stage, for both groups, requests for help from higher authorities (competing behavior response) became a more frequent response. However, the incidence was greater when the conflict was with a co-worker. This was consistent with earlier findings: When employees were engaged in conflict with co-workers they were reluctant to take on a problem-solving role (collaborating) but instead attempted to engage a third party (competing superior) to help them deal with the conflict.

The most successful responses for both groups were discussion (collaborating) and convincing (competing). It was significant to note that approximately half of the participants did not identify any response as most successful. This suggests a feeling of futility in dealing with the conflict situation, or a realization that this was a temporary job and the conflict would soon go away because the job was about to terminate.

There are some responses that were generally considered inappropriate regardless of the source of the conflict. The majority of respondents stated they would never respond by throwing objects, crying, carrying out acts of sabatoge, drinking, getting even, leaving the job, or pushing the other conflict person.

Table 1.2 also permits us to examine the issue of whether the response of the employee changes over time, what kind of change occurs, and, indirectly, why it may occur. In looking at the subordinate's response in a supervisor-subordinate relationship, the subordinate frequently modified behavior over time. In latter stages of the conflict interaction the subordinate relied more on convincing, while discussion, avoidance of the person, or talking with other co-workers became less important. For the co-worker conflict situation there was no response that became more prominent in the latter stages of the conflict. Discussion of the issue with the conflict person, avoiding the person, listening to the person, and discussing the issue with other co-workers or other outside sources all fell off as chosen responses.

In summary, the most frequent responses to conflict situations were those dealing with problem-solving behavior (discussing the issue with the individual, convincing, listening) and attempting to gain support or understanding from others (co-workers, outside sources). In addition, the problem-solving and confronting behaviors were reported by the respondents as being the most successful (Burke, 1970; Watson, 1987). It should be noted that there was variance in respondents' reported behaviors depending on whether the conflict was horizontal (peers) or vertical (employee-supervisor) and that the conflict party switched behaviors as the conflict continued (Robbins, 1978; Rahim, 1986b). Thus, even though some responses are more common and successful, a multitude of behavioral responses are engaged in depending on the conflict situation itself. It should be noted that some respondents may be answering in what the respondents perceive to be the most socially desirable way. This is partially offset by the fact that where comparison to past results is possible, the results correspond to some past findings.

Conflict Consequences

The final focus of this study was the impact of the conflict situation on the respondent. That is, according to Thomas, what are the consequences of the conflict situation to the parties of the conflict to other people associated with the conflict situation? The participants were asked to identify the intensity of the conflict, the disabling effect the conflict had on them away from work, and the number of people affected by the conflict.

The average intensity of the conflict for the subordinate in the supervisor-subordinate relationship was 48 percent ($SD = 23.4$), and 52 percent ($SD = 22.5$) for a co-worker conflict relationship (100% = very severe intensity). It was somewhat surprising to find the intensity of the conflict to be greater for the co-worker relationship than the supervisor-subordinate dyad.

The average degree of disabling affect away from work was 22 percent ($SD = 22$) for supervisor-subordinate relationships and only 13 percent ($SD = 17.7$) for co-worker conflicts (0% = no effect; 100% = can't eat, sleep, etc.). Thus, even though the intensity was greater for co-worker conflicts, the seriousness of the psychological and physiological affects (disabling affects) was believed to be greater for supervisor-subordinate conflicts. This is not surprising when one realizes the affect a supervisor can have on the needs fulfillment of the employee.

The variety of consequences for the subordinate in a supervisor-subordinate conflict was much greater than for the worker in a co-worker conflict situation (see Table 1.3). Employees in a co-worker conflict situation had a greater tendency to perceive the conflict as causing them to work harder, lower their job performance, feel guilty, or become uneasy when the conflict person was present. A reexamination of the issues that caused the conflict to occur (different work ethic, not carrying workload) provides some insight into why the worker perceived these consequences as occurring. Adjusting inputs or outcomes in actual or perceived terms is one way of managing situations of inequity.

Table 1.3
Consequences for Supervisor-Subordinate and Co-Worker Conflicts

Consequence	Supervisor-Subordinate (Subordinate's Perception) Frequency (%)	Co-Worker Frequency
Get upset	15 (19.7)	11 (14.3)
Lower motivation	7 (9.2)	5 (6.5)
Hurts job performance	6 (7.9)	13 (16.9)
Hurts relationship with conflict person	6 (7.9)	6 (7.7)
Work drags	6 (7.9)	8 (10.4)
Uneasy when conflict person present	5 (6.6)	11 (14.3)
Hurts rewards	5 (6.6)	1 (1.3)
Left job	4 (5.3)	1 (1.3)
Loss of face	3 (3.9)	2 (2.6)
Get fired	2 (2.6)	0 (0.0)
Upset family life	2 (2.6)	0 (0.0)
Involved boss	2 (2.6)	0 (0.0)
Improved status	2 (2.6)	0 (0.0)
Work harder	1 (1.3)	10 (13.0)
Not upset with company	1 (1.3)	0 (0.0)
Lose sense of humor	1 (1.3)	0 (0.0)
About to get fired	1 (1.3)	0 (0.0)
Can't sleep	1 (1.3)	0 (0.0)
Other person benefits	1 (1.3)	0 (0.0)
Hide	1 (1.3)	0 (0.0)
Learn management	1 (1.3)	1 (1.3)
Feel guilty	0 (0.0)	4 (5.2)

DISCUSSION

The issues that differentiate a supervisor-subordinate from a co-worker conflict relationship (Table 1.1) tend to revolve around the subordination of one of the parties in the relationship through an application of rules, evaluation of performance, assignment of work, and so on. Thus, a lack of perceived congruence between the subordinate's and supervisor's attitudes, beliefs, values, and goals seems to be the root of the conflict between the parties (Musser, 1982; Folger & Poole, 1984). These results support the findings of Renwick (1975), who found that the main issue of supervisor-subordinate conflicts was the application of organizational policies and procedures. One of the biggest fears of the next generation of workers is that they will find themselves working under someone they do not respect and cannot follow with real commitment (Dyer & Dyer, 1984).

On the other hand, when frustration occurs among co-workers it tends to be based on the work behaviors or personality differences of the parties. The parties of the conflict believe the perceived contributions made by the other party should be equal to their perceived contributions. When this does not seem to be occurring, a state of inequity and cognitive dissonance arises, resulting in conflict.

One possible explanation for more frequent use of problem-solving responses with supervisors than co-workers is that in a supervisor-subordinate conflict situation 72 percent of the respondents reported that they have contact with the conflict person (supervisor) at least once a day, whereas in a co-worker situation only 53 percent of the respondents reported that they had contact with the conflict co-worker at least once a day. In addition, the number of people affected by the conflict was less in a co-worker relationship (mean $= 12$) than in a supervisor-subordinate relationship (mean $= 14$). Thus, the respondents possibly felt more compelled to resolve the conflict due to the frequency of contact with the conflict person and the larger number of other people being affected. An interesting finding is the tendency of the employee to confide in some co-worker regardless of whether the conflict is with a supervisor or another co-worker. Undoubtedly, there is a need to vent anger and frustration, as well as check one's perceptions of a situation, through another worker.

In reviewing all three stages of responding, the total number of responses is about equal for the first and second stages but drops significantly by the third. Several explanations are possible: conflict was resolved, the individual perceived a reduced probability that a response on his/her part would resolve the issue, or a third response could not be recalled. In the second and third responses to the conflict situation employees become more assertive (competing) in both supervisor-subordinate and co-worker conflict situations. Employees engage in attempts at convincing, appealing to higher authority, and forming alliances with other parties. It is interesting to note the change to increasingly aggressive behavior, as it seems that more subtle behavior has failed to resolve the conflict. As the conflict persists, the employee is willing to increase personal risk to resolve the issue and adjust his/her response based on the response or lack of response by the other party (Cosier & Ruble, 1981).

The drop-off in responses was slightly more pronounced in the co-worker situation, which may suggest that (1) the situation was more easily resolved than the supervisor-subordinate conflict and ended, or (2) the situation is now viewed as unresolvable. In either case, the conflict would seem to have less importance to the individual involved. When conflict is between co-workers, either the consequences of conflict resolution or the lack of resolution may result in the situation being uncomfortable but not as devastating to the worker as in a supervisor-subordinate conflict (dismissal, monetary penalty, demotion, etc.). This is supported by the continuous increase in the "convincing" response in the supervisor-subordinate conflict. There, the subordinate felt the real need to keep trying, to convince the conflict person, to "win" or at least to reach a resolution that would feel like winning. Thus, to relate to Thomas' classification of behavioral responses, the conflict person attempts to settle the dispute through the competing response style. The inferences drawn from the data tend to support the findings of Cosier and Ruble (1981) that parties of a conflict situation tend to adjust their behavior based on their perception of successful past behaviors, implying again a need to succeed or win in the resolution of the issue.

The list of responses that individuals would never use implies a code of acceptable behavior. Whether the conflict is with another co-worker or a supervisor, this code is the same. The category of responses does not seem to fit into the Thomas model clearly and does deserve further attention even though not frequently used. An alternative explanation for the lack of use of these more drastic responses (crying, drinking, etc.) may be due to the sample. Over 75 percent of the respondents considered themselves less than full-time employees. Thus, they may not have viewed the job as essential or the conflict as threatening. This is somewhat supported by the fact that only 22 percent considered the job they were currently occupying as fitting into their long-term career plans.

IMPLICATIONS

It is evident upon examination of the data that a better understanding of the conflict situation is obtained if separate analyses are performed on supervisor-subordinate and co-worker subgroups.

In this study, subordinates identified the issues upon which the conflict (frustration) developed as being associated with the positional power and the methods by which this power is applied by the supervisor. When the conflict was with a co-worker, the issue was primarily based on interpersonal aspects (personality) of the work situation. In reviewing the specific issues resulting in conflict (for example, task assignment not specific, disagreement on application of rules or procedures), it would seem valuable for an organization to ensure that supervisors are skilled in such areas as work scheduling, goal clarification, and interpersonal communications (giving/receiving feedback). Greater care in selecting employees for work teams would be useful in managing co-worker conflicts. Where creativity and innovation are not needed, a more homogeneous mix of workers seems appropriate to avoid personality conflicts, etc. If action by the organization to reduce or eliminate some of the areas of frustration is possible, it would seem like a positive course of action for management to take.

Inevitably, conflicts will arise. Those managers who can transfer conflicts into something positive by raising the conflict parties' level of consciousness about the importance and value of designated outcomes, getting them to transcend their own self-interests for the benefit of the group or organization, will likely be the most successful (Bass, 1985). To do so, it is essential that managers be made aware of the kinds of responses that employees engage in early as well as late in a conflict situation. By being cognizant of the early behavioral signs of a conflict situation, a manager may be able to take action to deal with the issue before the positions of the parties become hardened.

The data suggest that a subordinate may initially try to discuss an issue with a supervisor with whom there is a conflict, particularly if there is significant contact between the two and if others are affected by the conflict. If the issue isn't dealt with effectively at this stage, a subordinate may be quick to begin talking behind the person's back, forming alliances and going to higher-ups. A conflict between co-workers brought to the attention of a supervisor probably indicates that the conflicting co-workers have already stopped talking to each other.

Perhaps many managers realize that a party often will try one or two responses and then "give in." The results of this study suggest that one can wait out a conflict, since the number of responses drop off significantly after the second response. The effect of an employee's capitulation on motivation and productivity, however, is unclear.

The other possibility for a latter-stage response is an increase in aggression or risk taking (for example, shouting, going to a higher-up, and so on). While this is less common, an employee with no other perceived outlet (for example, the job is vital to his/her identity or income) may turn to such behavior.

The frequency with which the employee confided in a co-worker, regardless of whether the conflict was with a supervisor or a co-worker, highlights the importance of being tied into the informal communication network (grapevine) so that the manager may become aware of conflict issues in their early stages. This permits the manager to attempt to defuse the situation early or to be prepared ahead of time to deal with it in a logical and well-thought-out manner.

2

Negative Effects of Destructive Criticism: Impact on Conflict, Self-Efficacy, and Task Performance

Robert A. Baron

Providing negative feedback to others about their past performance is a task few persons enjoy (compare, Larson, 1986). Yet, such feedback *is* necessary in many cases (Ilgen, Mitchell, & Fredrickson, 1981). How should managers and others occupying positions of authority perform this crucial task? In short, how should they administer criticism to their subordinates? Research on the nature and impact of feedback offers several suggestions (compare, Ilgen, Fisher, & Taylor, 1979). Recipients seem to prefer feedback that is specific, delivered promptly, and is considerate in nature to feedback that is general, delivered only after a delay, and not considerate in tone (see, for example, Ilgen, Mitchell, & Fredrickson, 1981; Liden & Mitchell, 1985). Thus, existing evidence suggests that managers wishing to make effective use of criticism should attempt to follow these principles when commenting unfavorably on their subordinates' performance.

Unfortunately, both informal observation and recent research indicate that frequently criticism is not delivered in this fashion (for example, Larson, 1984; Weisinger & Lobsenz, 1981). All too often, persons in authority tend to criticize subordinates only when upset, angry, and no longer able to hold their tempers in check. As a result, the negative feedback they provide is neither specific (that is, focused on particular past behaviors) nor considerate. On the contrary, because of the criticizer's strong emotions, it is typically delivered in a biting, sarcastic tone, and includes threats and other negative features. Further, such criticism often attributes poor performance by recipients to internal causes (for example, a lack of motivation or ability), and so induces further negative reactions among these persons (compare Liden & Mitchell, 1985).

The author wishes to express his sincere appreciation to Kim Allee, Rhonda Cunat, Kurt Hennelley, Donna Lopez, and Karen Perrine for their aid in collecting the data for Study 1, and to Georgette Bartholomew, Veronica Eiting, Dave Jones, and Clay Waterman, for their aid in collecting the data for Study 2.

When criticism is delivered under these conditions, it seems unlikely either to direct recipients' behavior so that their performance can be improved, or to enhance their job-related motivation (Ilgen, Fisher, & Taylor, 1979). Instead, such criticism may exert mainly negative effects upon the individuals involved and upon the functioning of their organization or work unit. For example, it may generate negative attitudes among recipients toward their supervisor or toward appraisal procedures generally (compare, Ilgen, Peterson, Martin, & Boeschen, 1981). Similarly, it may reduce recipients' level of organizational commitment and lower their job-related motivation (Ilgen, Mitchell, & Fredrickson, 1981). The present research was designed to investigate the possibility that such criticism may have other and perhaps less obvious negative effects as well. Specifically, it sought to determine whether exposure to such criticism (1) increases the likelihood or intensity of organizational conflict and (2) impairs performance on subsequent tasks. The possible existence of such effects is suggested by several considerations.

Turning first to conflict, it seems possible that the negative emotions (for example, anger, resentment) generated by destructive criticism may decrease recipients' willingness to approach disagreements with others in a conciliatory manner. On the contrary, after experiencing such criticism, they may prefer either direct confrontation (that is, competition; Thomas, 1976) or avoidance of the source of such negative feedback (Rahim, 1983b). To the extent that this is the case, ongoing conflicts may be intensified.

With respect to task performance, it seems possible that exposure to negative feedback that is harsh in tone, nonspecific in nature, and focused on internal causes of substandard performance may serve to undermine recipients' feelings of confidence or self-efficacy (compare Bandura, 1986), and reduce their self-set goals. Such effects, in turn, may impair their performance on various tasks.

In order to investigate these and other potential effects of destructive criticism, three studies were conducted. In the first, male and female participants received negative feedback on their performance from another person (an accomplice). For half of the subjects, such feedback was consistent with principles of effective feedback suggested by previous research (for example, it was specific, considerate, and avoided attributing poor performance to internal causes; Ilgen, Fisher, & Taylor, 1979; Liden & Mitchell, 1985). For the remainder, in contrast, such feedback was not consistent with these principles. Following receipt of one of these two types of criticism, subjects engaged in negotiations with the accomplice. Finally, they indicated how they would respond to such feedback, and how they would handle future disagreements with the same person (through avoidance, accommodation, compromise, collaboration, or competition; Thomas, 1976). In accordance with the reasoning outlined above, it was hypothesized that subjects exposed to destructive criticism would behave in a less conciliatory manner toward their opponent during negotiations, and would prefer less conciliatory modes of handling future conflicts with him or her than subjects exposed to constructive criticism.

Previous research on provocation and aggression indicates that verbal assaults that seem unjustified often result in greater anger than ones that seem relatively justified (Baron, 1977; Geen & Donnerstein, 1983). In view of these findings, it seemed possible that destructive criticism from a subordinate might be even more provocative than identical criticism from a supervisor. To examine this possibility, an additional factor—the role relationship between subjects and the accomplice—was also varied. One third of the participants were instructed to view the accomplice as a subordinate, one third to view him or her as a peer, and the final third to view this person as a supervisor. It was tentatively hypothesized that the negative effects of destructive criticism would be stronger or more pronounced when the source of such feedback was a subordinate or peer than when this person was a supervisor.

The second study was designed to examine the potential effects of destructive criticism on subsequent task performance. In this investigation, participants received either constructive or destructive criticism of their work from an accomplice. Then they performed one of two additional tasks (proofreading, a clerical task). Before actually working on these tasks, subjects provided information on their self-set goals and rated their ability to perform the tasks. It was hypothesized that subjects exposed to destructive criticism would report lower goals and self-efficacy and would also demonstrate lower task performance than those exposed to constructive criticism.

STUDY 1

Method

Subjects and design. Eighty-three undergraduates (42 males, 41 females) participated in the study. Subjects took part in the investigation to satisfy a course requirement.

A 2×3 factorial design based upon type of criticism (constructive, destructive), and relationship between participants and the accomplice (accomplice as subordinate, peer, or supervisor) was employed. Subjects were randomly assigned to one of the cells of this design as they appeared for their appointments.

Procedure

Task on which subjects received constructive or destructive criticism. The subject and a same-sex accomplice (who posed as another subject) were asked to imagine that they both worked in the Marketing Department of a large company. The experimenter then explained that the subject would prepare an ad campaign for a new product, and that the accomplice would evaluate this plan and provide feedback on it. At this point, the subject was taken to an adjoining room where he or she was given a special form to complete. This form explained that the subject's company was a manufacturer of health and beauty aids, and was planning to introduce a new type of shampoo. A brief description of the product followed. Subjects were then asked to plan the ad campaign by devising a name for the shampoo, a slogan for it, pinpointing its potential market, and indicating which of its features should be stressed in advertising. They were also asked to plan the timing of the ad campaign, and to specify packaging for the new product. In sum, they were asked to work on several tasks that would be part of an actual ad campaign.

Subjects were permitted to work on this task for ten minutes. After this, their output was collected and ostensibly given to the accomplice for evaluation. Five minutes later, they received this person's evaluation. In reality, they received pre-arranged feedback determined by the experimental condition to which they had been assigned. This feedback was provided by means of a special evaluation form, on which, supposedly, the accomplice rated the subjects' output on five dimensions (originality, creativity, effort, knowledge of potential market, potential for success) and also provided an over-all summary evaluation. (Ratings on all dimensions were on seven-point scales.) In addition, written comments were included underneath each of these dimensions. In both criticism conditions, the numerical ratings received by subjects were negative and identical. (The accomplice assigned them ratings of 3,4,3,4,3,3, respectively.) However, the written comments differed in the *constructive* and *destructive* criticism conditions.

In the constructive criticism condition, these remarks were specific in content, considerate in tone, made no attributions concerning the causes behind the subjects' poor performance, and contained no threats. For example, with respect to effort they stated: "Needed to give more attention to the slogans and packaging." Similarly, the summary comment stated: "I think there's a lot of room for improvement. He/she seemed unwilling to come up with new ideas. The slogans need to be more attention-getting, and there should be a clearer focus on key aspects of the product." In the destructive criticism condition, in contrast, the accomplice's remarks were general, inconsiderate in tone, attributed the poor performance to internal factors, and included threats. For example, with respect to effort, they noted: "Didn't even try; can't seem to do anything right." The summary comment noted: "I wasn't impressed at all. The whole thing needs to be fixed. I had the impression that he/she didn't try much at all. (Or maybe it's just a lack of talent.) If his/her work doesn't improve, I'd try to get someone else to do it." It is important to note that the numerical ratings assigned to subjects' work were identical in these two conditions; only the written comments differed, and these were specifically designed to be either consistent or inconsistent with the findings of previous research concerning effective feedback.

After subjects had an opportunity to examine the feedback provided by the accomplice, they were asked to complete a questionnaire containing several of the dependent measures. The first five items on this measure concerned potential reactions to criticism, and asked participants to indicate how likely they would be to respond to the evaluation they had just received in five different ways (sticking to their guns, making excuses, finding fault with the other's evaluation, leaving the room, or avoiding future contact with this person, pretending to accept the criticism while actually rejecting it; Weisinger & Lobsenz, 1981). Four additional items asked subjects to rate their feelings after receiving the accomplice's evaluation (not angry–angry, not tense–tense, not happy–happy, bad–good). An additional item asked subjects to rate the fairness of the evaluation they received from the accomplice.

Finally, subjects were asked how they would handle future conflicts with the same person. On separate questions, they rated how likely they would be to avoid this person, accommodate themselves to him, compete, compromise, or collaborate with him. These five patterns were selected for use because they have been identified by Thomas (1976, 1977) as representing basic modes of behavior in many conflict situations.

The conflict (negotiation) situation. After subjects completed the questionnaire, the conflict (negotiation) situation was introduced. Since this situation closely resembled one employed in previous research (Baron, 1985; in press [a,b]), it will not be described in detail here. Briefly, the subject and accomplice were informed that their department (Marketing) had been given a $10,000,000 advertising budget for the new shampoo, and now faced the task of deciding how to divide this sum between two potential uses: television/newspaper and magazine advertising. The subject was asked to represent the Print Media unit within the department, while the accomplice was asked to represent the Television unit. They were then instructed to attempt to reach an agreement concerning the division of these funds between their respective units. An exchange of eight offers and counteroffers (that is, eight trials) then followed. On each trial, the experimenter asked the accomplice how much of the money should go to his or her unit and why. Then, the subject was asked to provide corresponding information. The accomplice began by demanding fully $8,000,000 for his or her own unit, and made only two small concessions (of $200,000 each) during the session. Thus, this person behaved in a uniformly confrontational manner. The accomplice's concessions occurred on Trials 4 and 6.

Results

Reported reactions to constructive and destructive criticism. Analyses of variance were performed on the data for the items dealing with potential reactions to constructive and destructive criticism. These analyses yielded significant findings (on one or more independent variables) for three items: sticking to one's guns, making excuses, and leaving the room or future avoidance. The main effect of mode of criticism was significant for the first and third of these measures, $F(1,70) = 3.72, 22,81, p < .05, < .001, \omega^2 = .12, .21$, respectively. These findings reflected the fact that subjects reported being more likely to demonstrate inflexible resistance (stick to their guns) and avoidance (leave the room or avoid contact with the criticizer) in the destructive criticism than in the constructive criticism condition. In addition, the main effect of role was significant for all three items $F(2,70) = 3.26, 5.36, 3.08, p < .05., < .005, < .05\omega^2 = .07, .12, .05$, respectively. Subjects reported being more likely to make excuses when the accomplice was a subordinate than a peer or supervisor, and more likely to leave the room or avoid future contact with the criticizer when this person was a subordinate or peer than a supervisor. However, subjects also reported being more likely to stick to their guns when the criticizer was a supervisor than when he or she was a subordinate or peer.

Emotional reactions to constructive and destructive criticism. Analyses of variance on the data for the questions designed to assess subjects' emotional reactions to criticism indicated that, consistent with initial predictions, subjects reacted negatively to destructive criticism. Specifically, they reported feeling significantly angrier and more tense after receiving destructive than constructive criticism, $F(1,70) = 11.89, 9.73, p < .001, < .003, \omega^2 = .12, .11$, respectively. In addition, the interaction between mode of criticism and role relationship with the accomplice was also significant for both items, $F(2,70) = 3.85, 3.30, p < .04, < .05$, respectively. The form of these interactions was the same for both measures, and seemed to reflect the fact that subjects felt angrier and more tense after receiving destructive feedback from a subordinate than in any other condition.

An additional item completed by subjects asked them to rate the fairness of the evaluation they received from the accomplice. As expected, subjects reported that this feedback was more fair in the constructive ($M = 3.95$) than in the destructive criticism condition ($M = 2.91$), $F(1,70) = 8.69, p < .01$.

Reported strategies for dealing with future conflicts. Five items on the questionnaire asked subjects to indicate how they would handle future conflicts with the accomplice. Analyses of variance on the data for these items indicated that subjects exposed to destructive criticism reported being more likely to avoid the accomplice and less likely to collaborate with this person, $F(1,70) = 15.53, 6.87, p < .001, .01, \omega^2 = .07, .08$, than subjects exposed to constructive criticism. In addition, subjects exposed to destructive criticism were almost significantly more likely to compete with the accomplice than subjects exposed to constructive criticism, $F(1,70) = 2.88, p < .07, \omega^2 = .04$.

In addition, the effect of role relationship between the subject and accomplice was significant for the avoidance measure, $F(2,70) = 4.32, p < .02, \omega^2 = .07$. This effect reflected the fact that subjects reported being less likely to handle future conflicts through avoidance when the accomplice was a supervisor ($M = 1.85$) than when this person was a peer ($M = 2.79$) or subordinate ($M = 2.59$).

Behavior during negotiations. Three dependent measures of subjects' behavior during the negotiation session were obtained: final offers, number of concessions, and magnitude of total concessions. Analyses of variance on the data for these variables yielded significant effects for criticism for all three measures, $F(1,70) = 3.67, 4.66, 5.16, p > .05$ in all cases; $\omega^2 = .04, .06, .06$, respectively. However, the pattern of these effects was somewhat surprising: subjects exposed to destructive criticism actually made a larger final offer, more concessions, and larger total concessions to the accomplice than subjects exposed to constructive criticism.

In addition, the interaction between role relationship and criticism was significant both for number of concessions, $F(2,70) = 3.48$, $p > .05$ and total concessions, $F(2,70) = 3.16$, $p < .05$. In both cases, the pattern of this interaction was identical. In the context of constructive criticism, subjects made more and larger concessions to the accomplice when this person was a peer than when he or she was either a supervisor or subordinate. However, in the context of destructive criticism, subjects made more and larger concessions to the accomplice when this person was a subordinate than when he or she was either a peer or supervisor. Thus, although subjects reported feeling angriest and most tense when they received destructive feedback from a subordinate, they also made more and larger concessions in this condition than any other.

STUDY TWO

The results of Study One suggest that exposure to criticism that violates basic principles of effective feedback can exert several adverse effects upon recipients. Further, these effects (negative emotional reactions, tendencies to avoid or confront the source of such feedback) are ones that may, conceivably, contribute to the initiation or perseveration of organizational conflict. As noted earlier, however, such outcomes are not the only negative effects that may stem from the use of destructive criticism. It also seems possible that such feedback may undermine recipients' confidence or self-efficacy with respect to various tasks, and so reduce their subsequent performance. In order to investigate this possibility, a second study was conducted.

Method

Subjects and design. One hundred and six undergraduates (55 males, 51 females) participated in the study. A 3 × 2 design based on three types of criticism (constructive, destructive, no feedback) and two tasks (proofreading, clerical) was employed. Subjects were randomly assigned to one of the cells of this design as they reported to the laboratory.

Procedure

Criticism. The first part of the experiment was virtually identical to Study 1. Subjects worked on planning an advertising campaign for a new product, and then received feedback on their work from a same-sex accomplice. In the *constructive* and *destructive* criticism conditions, subjects received the same numerical ratings and written comments as in Study 1. In the *no feedback* condition, however, they were not told that they would receive the accomplice's evaluation of their work, and they did not, in fact, receive such information. This latter condition was included as a control against which to assess the impact of both constructive and destructive criticism. In contrast to Study 1, no information was provided about the relative status of the subject and accomplice.

Task performance and measurement of self-set goals. Following completion of the first part of the study, subjects worked on one of two different tasks. One of these was a proofreading task, in which subjects were asked to circle every error in spelling, typing, or punctuation in typewritten passages dealing with business-related matters. The other was a clerical task requiring several steps. Subjects were given a sheet containing coded orders for various products. They then had to determine the price of each item by searching for it in a code book. After this, they determined the size of the discount that should be applied to the item by consulting a price-discount schedule. Subjects were permitted to work on each task for five minutes.

Before actually working on each task, but after it had been described to them, subjects completed a brief form on which they indicated how many lines of proofreading or orders they expected to complete (self-set goals) and rated their ability to perform these tasks. (These ratings were made on seven-point scales.)

After working on one or the other of the two tasks, subjects completed a brief questionnaire on which they rated their feelings after receiving the accomplice's evaluation (e.g., not angry–angry, not tense–tense), the extent to which this evaluation was fair, helpful, and either reduced or improved their work performance. In addition, subjects completed the same measure of preferred modes of handling future conflicts with the accomplice as was employed in Study 1.

Results

Self-set goals and self-efficacy. Because the proofreading and clerical tasks were very different in nature, it seemed inappropriate to compare subjects' performance on them directly. Thus, separate analyses of variance were performed on the data for each. (Recall that subjects performed only one or the other of these tasks.) Both sets of analyses yielded highly similar results. Subjects reported lower self-set goals and reduced feelings of self-efficacy (ability to perform the task) after receiving destructive criticism than after receiving constructive criticism or no feedback on their work.

Turning first to self-set goals, the effects of type of criticism were significant both for proofreading, $F(2,54) = 3.73, p < .05, \omega^2 = .14$, and the clerical task, $F(2,50) = 4.12, p < .05, \omega^2 = .15$. In both cases, subjects set higher goals in the no feedback and constructive criticism conditions than in the destructive criticism condition. Thus, exposure to destructive criticism appeared to reduce self-set goals on two different tasks, while exposure to constructive criticism did not reduce such goals, relative to a no feedback control condition. In addition, the main effect of sex was significant for the clerical task, $F(1,50) = 7.26, p < .01, \omega^2 =$ this task ($M = 25.08$) than females ($M = 16.64$)

Similar but somewhat less consistent findings were obtained for the measure of self-efficacy. The effect of criticism was significant for the clerical task, $F(2,50) = 3.67, p < .05, \omega^2 = .02$, and approached significance for the proof-reading task, $F(2,54) = 2.75, p < .08, \omega^2 = .01$. Subjects reported lower ability to perform the clerical task after receiving destructive criticism than after receiving constructive criticism, and almost significantly lower ability than after receiving no feedback ($p < .07$). For the proofreading task they reported lower ability after receiving destructive criticism or no feedback than after receiving constructive criticism ($p < .05$).

Task performance. No significant effects were obtained for the clerical task. However, for the proofreading task, a significant interaction between sex of subject and type of criticism was observed for the percent of errors correctly identified, $F(2,54) = 3.19, p < .05$. This interaction stemmed from the fact that the effects of this type of criticism were stronger and more consistent for females than males. Specifically, among females, exposure to destructive criticism significantly reduced subjects' accuracy below that in the no feedback and constructive criticism groups ($M = 69.25$ versus 84.78 and 78.25, respectively). Among males, these differences were in the same direction, but failed to attain significance ($M = 68.20$ vs. 76.27 and 74.67, respectively).

Emotional reactions to constructive and destructive criticism. Analyses of variance on the data for subjects' reports of their emotional reactions to constructive or destructive criticism revealed findings similar to those of Study 1. Subjects exposed to destructive criticism reported feeling more angry, $F(1,67) = 11.27, p < .001, \omega^2 = .18$, and more tense, $F(1,67) = 9.71, p < .005, \omega^2 = .16$, than subjects exposed to constructive criticism. (Since these items required subjects to rate their feelings after receiving the accomplice's evaluation of their work, they were not completed by individuals in the no feedback condition.)

Reported strategies for handling future conflicts. Analyses of variance on the items dealing with preferred modes of handling future conflicts with the accomplice indicated that subjects exposed to destructive criticism reported being more likely to avoid this person, $F(2,104) = 3.26, p < .05, \omega^2 = .10$, but less likely to accommodate to $F(2,104) = 5.08, p < .01, \omega^2 = .18$, or compromise with him or her, $F(2,104) = 3.34, p < .05, \omega^2 = .12$, than subjects exposed to constructive criticism or no feedback on their work.

Checks on the experimental manipulations. Additional items dealt with subjects' perceptions of the fairness and helpfulness of the accomplice's evaluations. Analyses of variance performed on the data for these items indicated that, as expected, subjects exposed to destructive criticism rated the accomplice's evaluations of their work as less fair, $F(1,66) = 5.41, p < .02, \omega^2 = .12$, and less helpful, $F(1,66) = 5.86, p < .02, \omega^2 = .14$ than subjects exposed to constructive criticism. (Again, individuals in the no feedback condition did not complete these items, since they referred specifically to evaluations from the accomplice.)

DISCUSSION

Considered together, the results of the studies reported here suggest that destructive criticism can affect several important processes in work settings. First, such criticism appears to produce negative feelings among recipients, especially when it is delivered by a subordinate rather than a peer or supervisor. Previous research suggests that such feelings, in turn, can initiate or intensify conflict between individuals (compare Blake & Mouton, 1984; Kabanoff, 1985). Second, destructive criticism appears to reduce recipients' preferences for handling future disagreements with the source of such feedback through conciliatory means (for example, compromise, collaboration), and increases their preferences for what are often less desirable tactics (avoidance, direct competition). Third, destructive criticism exerts negative effects upon self-set goals and feelings of self-efficacy (compare Bandura, 1986). Such shifts, in turn, may adversely affect performance on at least some tasks.

Unfortunately, the use of destructive criticism appears to be far from rare in actual work settings. As noted earlier, many individuals seem to refrain from delivering negative feedback to others until their own strong emotional reactions make it all but impossible for them to withhold such information (Larson, 1984, 1986). Then, the feedback they supply is likely to prove ineffective in several ways (Ilgen, Fisher, & Taylor, 1979; Weisinger & Lobsenz, 1981), and may exact serious costs of the type described above.

Before concluding, certain limitations of the present research should be addressed. Because both investigations involved laboratory simulations conducted with undergraduate students, the generalizability of the obtained results is, of course, uncertain. However, several steps were taken to lessen such problems. First, the task on which subjects received feedback (planning an advertising campaign) was designed to be as realistic as possible. Thus, the issues they were asked to consider (potential market, timing of the campaign) were ones that would be involved in the planning of an actual ad campaign. Second, special care was taken in devising the written comments provided to subjects as feedback on their work. These were written so as to reflect the results of previous research on feedback, and were carefully refined and adjusted through pilot testing until they were perceived, by pilot subjects, as different along key dimensions (for example, specificity, considerateness). Finally, some support for the generality of the present results is provided by the findings of a recent field investigation (Baron, in press [b]), in which managers at a large food processing company were asked to rate the importance of 14 different factors as potential causes of conflict in their units. Respondents indicated that poor use of criticism (defined as "Using such feedback to embarrass or blame the recipients, or to release anger rather than helping them improve") was rated fifth in order of importance ($M = 4.32$ on a seven-point scale), ahead of many other factors traditionally reviewed as important causes of conflict (for example, competition over resources, $M = 3.28$; reward structures/systems, $M = 3.48$; loss of face, $M = 3.43$; all differences $p < .05$). Thus, it appears that destructive criticism may indeed be an important cause of organizational conflict in at least some contexts. Needless to add, neither this finding nor any of the other considerations listed above assure the generalizability of the present results. Rather, they simply provide some basis for suggesting that these findings may, in fact, possess a degree of external validity.

Taking the results of the present research and the previous field study into account, however, two tentative conclusions seem justified. First, destructive criticism can, potentially, exert several adverse effects upon its recipients. Second, to the extent this is the case, it constitutes one type of communication managers and others occupying positions of authority would do well to avoid.

3

Integrative and Distributive Dimensions of Styles of Handling Interpersonal Conflict and Bargaining Outcome

Clement Psenicka
M. Afzalur Rahim

Game theoretic models of conflict are based on rationality postulates and are normative models of behavior. They prescribe the behavior rational individuals should follow to optimize some measure of utility. The current literature on bargaining models has its roots in economic analysis and follows, in general, the rational economic model. However, conflict management cannot always be determined by these rational models. Harsanyi (1977, p. 17) identified both emotional factors and bounded rationality as major determinants of "suboptimal" behavior. This study was an attempt to explore the relationship between a person's styles of handling conflict with peers and bargaining outcome.

There are various styles of behavior by which interpersonal conflict may be handled. Follett (1940) discussed three main ways of dealing with conflict: domination, compromise, and integration. She also found other ways of handling conflict in organizations, such as avoidance and suppression. Blake and Mouton (1964) first presented a conceptual scheme for classifying the modes (styles) for handling interpersonal conflict into five types: forcing, withdrawing, smoothing, compromising, and problem solving. They described the five modes of handling conflict on the basis of the attitudes of the manager: concern for production and for people. Their scheme was reinterpreted by Thomas (1976). He considered the intentions of a party (cooperativeness, that is, attempting to satisfy the other party's concerns; and assertiveness, or attempting to satisfy one's own concerns) in classifying the modes of handling conflict into five types.

Rahim (1986a) and Rahim and Bonoma (1979) differentiated the styles of handling interpersonal conflict on two basic dimensions, concern for self and for others. The first dimension explains the degree (high or low) to which a person attempts to satisfy his own concern. The second dimension explains the degree

Figure 3.1
Integrative and Distributive Dimensions of Styles of Handling Interpersonal Conflict

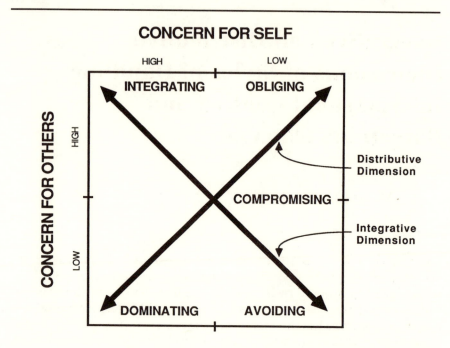

(high or low) to which a person wants to satisfy the concerns of others. It should be pointed out that these dimensions portray the motivational orientations of a given individual during conflict (Rubin & Brown, 1975). A study by Ruble and Thomas (1976) yielded general support for these dimensions. Combination of the two dimensions results in five specific styles of handling interpersonal conflict: integrating (high concern for self and others), obliging (low concern for self and high concern for others), dominating (high concern for self and low concern for others), avoiding (low concern for self and others), and compromising (intermediate concern for self and others).

Further insights into the styles of handling interpersonal conflict may be obtained by organizing them according to the integrative and distributive dimensions of labor-management bargaining suggested by Walton and McKersie (1965). Figure 3.1 shows the five styles of handling interpersonal conflict and their reclassifications into the integrative and distributive dimensions. The integrative dimension (integrating-avoiding) represents the degree (high or low) of satisfaction of concerns received by self and others. The distributive dimension (dominating-obliging) represents the proportion of the satisfaction of concerns received by self and others. In the integrative dimension, integrating attempts to

increase the satisfaction of the concerns of both parties by finding unique solutions to the problems acceptable to them. Avoiding leads to the reduction of
satisfaction of the concerns of both parties as a result of their failure to confront
and solve their problems. In the distributive dimension, whereas dominating
attempts to obtain high satisfaction of concerns for self (and provides low satisfaction of concerns for others), obliging attempts to obtain low satisfaction of
concerns for self (and provides high satisfaction of concerns for others). Compromising represents the point of intersection of the two dimensions, that is, a
middle ground position where each party receives an intermediate level of satisfaction of their concerns from the resolution of their conflicts.

Each individual has a particular preference for the selection and use of a
behavioral style in dealing with a conflict. In a conflict situation, if a person
insists on maintaining his original position, he will be using a dominating style
and if he relaxes his demands and attempts to satisfy his opponent, he exhibits an
obliging style. This dominating-obliging or distributive dimension is purported
to be appropriate for use in zero-sum conflicts or win-lose situations. The other
diagonal in Figure 3.1, which represents the integrating-avoiding or integrative
dimension, may apply to conflict situations involving potential positive-sum
conflicts or win-win situations. The objective of this study was to investigate the
relationships of the integrative and distributive dimensions of the styles of handling interpersonal conflict and bargaining outcome.

One of our major assumptions in this study was that an individual's preferences for the different styles of handling interpersonal conflict could be used to
predict a bargaining outcome. To investigate this relationship, three things had to
be obtained: a measure of the Ss' preferences for handling interpersonal conflict,
the generation of a dyadic conflict in an experimental situation, and a measure of
the Ss' gains and losses in this conflict situation.

METHOD

Subjects

The Ss of this study were 70 students in several MBA research methodology
classes at Youngstown State University. The Ss participated in an experiment
one of the requirements of the course. The average age and full time work
experience of the Ss were 25.75 (SD = 3.79) and 5.41 (SD = 3.56) years,
respectively. About 28 percent of the Ss were female.

Instrument

The Ss completed the Rahim Organizational Conflict Inventory–II (ROCI-II),
Form C, which measures the five styles of handling interpersonal conflict with
peers (Rahim, 1983a). The instrument measures the five styles of handling
interpersonal conflict, as conceptualized before, with 28 items, each cast on a

five-point Likert scale. Responses to items for each subscale are averaged to create five continuous scales. A higher score represents greater use of a conflict style.

As reported by Rahim (1983b,c), the internal consistency reliability of the subscales, as assessed by Cronbach alpha and Kristof's (1969) unbiased estimate of reliability, were greater than .70. The test-retest reliability of the subscales were greater than .75 except compromising scale which was .60. The reliabilities of the ROCI-II compare quite favorably with the existing instruments on modes of handling interpersonal conflict. The subscales were constructed on the basis of multiple factor analyses (principal-factor solution and varimax rotation). The intercorrelations of the subscales ranged between .03 and .33. The correlations of social desirability (Crowne & Marlowe, 1960) and lie (Eysenck & Eysenck, 1968) scales and the five subscales of conflict styles indicate that the five subscales were relatively free from social desirability or response distortion bias. Only the correlation between social desirability scale and integrating subscale ($r = .29$) was significant.

Procedure

The Ss were presented with the following situation. Forty percent of their final grade was to be based on a research paper to be prepared in groups of two. The paper's grade would be equally divided between quantitative (research design, statistics, computer work, etc.) and qualitative (literature review, hypotheses, write-up, and so on) aspects. Each S was asked to indicate ahead of time the proportion of each section on which his individual grade would be based. The only qualification was that each S would have to take responsibility for exactly 50 percent of the total paper. An S taking responsibility for 30 percent of the qualitative section would have to take responsibility for 70 percent of the quantitative section. Each section was to be graded independently and consequently an S's final grade would be based on his agreed distribution of responsibility. The Ss were then matched up in groups of two such that conflict would be present. The Ss requesting mostly quantitative responsibility (QR) were matched and vice versa. If an S requesting 10 percent QR was paired with one requesting 30 percent QR, the dyad would have to bargain such that 100 percent of the quantitative grade was accounted for between them. This was the assumed source of conflict. The Ss were then required to negotiate and arrive at a resolution.

Measurement of Cooperativeness

Three measures of cooperativeness were computed on each of the distributive and integrative dimensions. The first was the difference between the two opponents' dominating (DO) subscale scores, referred to here as the DD subscale. If the DD subscale was positive, it indicated less cooperativeness than the partner. Therefore, it would result in a resolution favorable to the uncooperative partner, as hypothesized. The second subscale was the DO subscale which was the difference between the two opponents' obliging (OB) subscale scores. A positive DO subscale score indicated greater cooperativeness than the partner. The third subscale, the DR subscale, was computed by subtracting each S's obliging score from dominating score and then subtracting from this the partner's corresponding difference.

For the integrative dimension three similar subscales were constructed using the integrating and avoiding scores. The II subscale was the difference between the two opponents' integrating (IN) subscale scores. The IV subscale was the difference between the two opponents' avoiding (AV) subscale scores. The IA subscale was computed by subtracting the each S's avoiding score from integrating score and then subtracting from this the partner's corresponding difference.

Measurement of Conflict

Before forming the groups each S was asked to identify his preferences for different levels of responsibility for the quantitative section. Different percentage levels of quantitative responsibility (QR) were identified on a questionnaire and the Ss were asked to rank them from one to ten, least to most preferred. The questionnaire was given out twice at an interval of one week, the results averaged and adjusted to a zero to one point scale. From this questionnaire it was possible to identify each partner's preferred alternative as well as the loss in preference points (PF) associated with any other alternative. A single participant's measure of conflict would then be the preference he would have to give up to move to his partner's optimal point.

The final loss of each S's preference (LP) that resulted from the bargaining game was calculated as 1.0 minus the S's preference level at the point of conflict resolution. Also calculated was the maximum potential loss in preference (LPmax), which was 1.0 minus the S's preference level at the partner's optimum. The preference bargained away was then defined as PBA = LP/LPmax. This represented the amount of individual movement in the bargaining process. Finally, relative preference bargained away, was defined as, RPBA = PBA − PBApartner. This was a measure of how much was given up in the bargaining process relative to the partner. An example for a sample group is given in Figure 3.2. The range on RPBA was −1 complete domination by self, to +1 indicating complete domination by partner.

Analysis

Six separate regression analyses were run with RPBA as the dependent variable and DD, DO, DR, II, IV, and IA as independent variables.

Figure 3.2
Measurement of Conflict

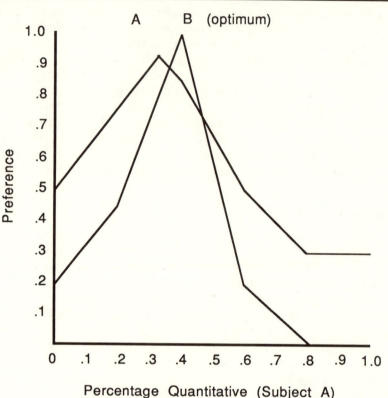

Percentage Quantitative (Subject A)
1 - Percentage Quantitative (Subject B)

Data Computations: Resolution at 30 % Quantitative A

Subject A data computations: Subject B data computations:

LPmax = 1 - .85 = .15   LPmax = 1 - .50 = .50
LP = 1 - .95 = .05   LP = 1 - .75 = .25
PBA = .05/.15 = .34   PBA = .25/.50 = .50
RPBA = .34 - .50 = -.16   RPBA = .16

Table 3.1
Regression Analysis ($N = 35$)

Dependent Variable	Independent Variable	b	a	R^2	F
RPBA	DR	-.345	-.042	.56	42.15[*]
RPBA	DD	-.425	-.032	.52	36.26[*]
RPBA	DO	.260	.101	.10	3.77
RPBA	II	.052	-.022	.01	0.19
RPBA	IV	.058	-.023	.01	0.29
RPBA	IA	-.040	-.005	.00	0.06

[*]$p < .0005$

RESULTS

The results are shown in Table 3.1. The separate effects of DR and DD subscales on RPBA were significant but the effects of DO subscale and the remaining subscales associated with the integrative dimension were all nonsignificant. The unstandardized regression coefficients of the three subscales constructed from the distributive dimensions had correct signs. The DR, DD, and DO subscales explained 56, 52, and 10 percent of the variance in RPBA, respectively. The II, IV, and IA subscales explained little or no variance in RPBA.

DISCUSSION

This study indicated that the styles of handling interpersonal conflict can be used to predict bargaining behaviors of the conflicting parties in a dyadic situation. Both the DR and DD subscales were significant predicators of conflict resolution. The greater the DR subscale, for instance, the more dominating was an indivudal in a conflict situation relative to his partner, and the more dominating a person was the less he was willing to give up to his partner during the bargaining process. RPBA, therefore, was expected to be inversely related to measures of dominating or uncooperative behavior. The DO subscale was not as good a predictor of bargaining behavior. Even though the regression coefficient was nonsignificant ($p < .07$) it had the correct sign indicating some further validity to the model.

The conflict situation was an example of a zero-sum game and the results of this study were consistent with this situation. Since there could be no mutual gains from negotiation, the integrative dimension would not be applicable. The nonsignificance of the subscales constructed from the integrative dimension supports this hypothesis.

At least two areas of future research present themselves. It appears that different styles of handling conflict may be used to deal with different conflict situations effectively. Categorizing situations and relating these to the styles used would be an area of interesting research. The second area would involve examination of the role of communication in conflict. The present study represented only an initial step in these directions. This study provided additional evidence of validity of the ROCI-II.

4

Interdependence Approach to Conflict Management in Organizations

Dean Tjosvold

Organizational behavior researchers have increasingly recognized the importance of conflict. As this and other edited volumes attest, they are investigating negotiations, bargaining, arbitration, and mediation (Bazerman & Lewicki, 1982, Tjosvold & Johnson, 1983). Theorists argue that political interests, diversity, heterogeneity, and subgrouping heighten conflict and affect organizational decision making (Pfeffer, 1981). Conflict occurs in performance appraisal, task teams, and strategic management. Industrial relations researchers have called for more attention to the variety of labor-management conflict and alternative ways to manage it (Kochan & Verma, 1983).

In addition to its significance and inevitability, researchers have argued that conflict can be constructive. However, *conflict itself is neither productive nor destructive*. Employees must have values, procedures, and skills to manage conflict to gain its benefits and reduce its costs. This review develops an approach that has the potential to be a powerful, elegant way to understand and manage conflict in organizations.

Researchers have recently emphasized that organizational members use cognitive schemas, social construction, and interaction to interpret their experiences (Bartunek, 1984; Burrell & Morgan, 1979; Gioia & Manz, 1985; Smircich & Stubbart, 1985; Weick, 1979). Shared interpretations and meanings are central to the organization's culture (Jelinek, Smircich, & Hirsch, 1983). Employees, it is argued here, use their expectations, values, perceptions, attributions, and standards of fairness to conclude they are in conflict and to decide how to manage it (Averill, 1982; Pondy, 1967).

The purpose of this chapter is to examine conflict from the perspective of how employees interpret the meaning that conflict has for their relationship and, in

The author thanks the Social Sciences and Humanities Research Council of Canada for its financial support.

particular, their dependence upon each other. Their experience of their interdependence is critical to understand their conflict behavior. Whether people conclude that their major aspirations and goals are cooperatively related or that their interests are competitive very much affects the course and consequences of conflict. This paper outlines the interdependence approach to conflict, and discusses how it complements other approaches to defining and managing organizational conflict.

CONFLICT IN COOPERATION AND COMPETITION

Deutsch's (1949, 1973, 1980) theory of cooperation and competition has proved very useful to examine interdependence and conflict. Considerable research document that goal interdependence consistently affects the dynamics and outcomes of interaction (Johnson, Maryuma, Johnson, Nelson, & Skon, 1981; Johnson, Johnson, & Maryuma, 1983; Tjosvold, 1984).

According to Deutsch, persons (or groups) are in cooperation when they believe their goals are compatible and positively related; one's goal attainment helps others reach their goals. They are in a win-win situation in which people can be successful together. In competition, persons conclude that their goals are incompatible and negatively linked; one person's progress interferes with others' reaching their goals. They are in a win-lose situation where success for one makes success for others more difficult. These are of course "pure" cases and relationships usually have both, but it is the predominant interdependence that has the greater impact.

People in most situations can focus on cooperative or competitive goals. Project team members may believe they have primarily cooperative goals in that they will be successful if the group completes the project, or that they have competitive ones in that they want to demonstrate that their ideas and efforts are superior to others. It is not the objective goal interdependence, but the conclusion participants make about how their goals are predominately related that affects their interaction.

Conflict exists in both cooperative and competitive situations. Surely when people are trying to win and outdo each other they will conflict. But a great deal of conflict, perhaps most conflict in organizations, occurs in cooperation. Project team members who are highly committed to the group goal may conflict over the best means to accomplish it and over the fair, effective method of sharing the benefits and burdens of their joint effort.

Defining Conflict as Incompatible Activities

It is common to consider conflict in terms of opposing interests, but as the interdependence approach highlights, this view confounds conflict with competition. This confusion is serious because, as is shown later, the dynamics and outcomes of conflict depend upon whether interdependence is considered cooperative or competitive. Conflict must be defined distinctly from goal interdependence.

Conflict is defined here in terms of incompatible behaviors and activities rather than interests and goals (Deutsch, 1973, 1980). At least one person's behavior is thought to be obstructing, interfering, blocking, or in some other way making another's behavior less effective. Incompatible activities can occur without any recognition, but it is only when persons conclude that the other's actions are incompatible with their own that they experience conflict and begin to react emotionally and behaviorally to it. It is the way the conflict is interpreted that affects conflict management.

DYNAMICS OF COOPERATIVE AND COMPETITIVE CONFLICT

Several comprehensive reviews of the research on interdependence and conflict are available (Deutsch, 1973, 1980; Pruitt & Syna, 1983; Tjosvold, 1985). This section describes major findings. The ideas of cooperation and competition are able to summ·rize considerable experimental and organizational research on conflict (see Figure 4.1).

Cooperative Conflict

People who are able to discuss conflict while they interpret and recognize that they are pursuing cooperative goals handle conflicts much differently than those with competitive links. People who emphasize their cooperative dependence consider the problem a mutual one, and seek agreements that are advantageous to all.

Confronted with a discussion of opposing ideas and interests, people in cooperation have been found to feel resisted and challenged. They are uncertain that their own ideas are adequate and their interests can be fully met. They are motivated to explore and understand opposing views and needs to satisfy their curiosity and resolve their uncertainty about whether their own position is adequate. After open-mindedly explaining their position and exploring opposing views and interests, they understand the shortcomings in their own perspective, appreciate the desires and requirements of others, and try to integrate other ideas and aspirations to develop a fresh viewpoint that responds to the reasoning, perspective, and needs of others. They work to reach mutually satisfactory decisions based on the ideas and interests of several people; their relationships are also strengthened and they are confident they can resolve conflicts in the future (Pruitt & Lewis, 1975; Tjosvold & Johnson, 1977, 1978; Tjosvold & Deemer, 1980; Tjosvold, 1982).

Figure 4.1
Approaches to Conflict

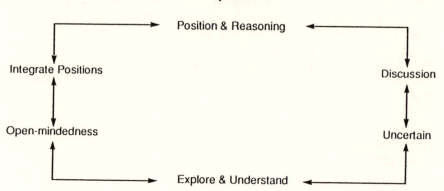

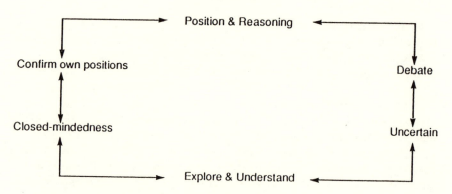

Competitive Conflict

Conflicts discussed with the intent to outdo and ''win'' have been found to proceed much differently. People in competitive conflict indicate they are pursuing their interests even at the expense of others, and that they are prepared to force their position on others if necessary. They want to win and are willing, even eager, to have the other lose.

As they debate their opposing views and interests, people in competition have been found to feel uncertain about the adequacy of their own positions and try to understand the other's arguments. However, they defend their own position vigorously and use their understanding of other positions to try to win over others. They become locked into position bargaining in which they try to assert their conclusions against others.

They try to understand the other in a closed-minded way. They want to find weaknesses in his arguments, not to modify their own conclusions. They want to counterattack, undercut other positions, and make their own views and interests dominate. They may conclude that they must use superior authority or other means to impose their own superior solutions. Competitive conflict often results in a failure to reach an agreement or a solution imposed by the more powerful. The protagonists also develop personal ill-will and have little confidence that future problems can be solved.

These findings suggest that the cooperative approach to conflict is more generally successful, but they are consistent with a contingency perspective. A competitive approach is a major alternative approach that is apt to be effective in some circumstances. Research has begun to document the conditions when competitive conflict is useful (Rahim, 1986a).

IMPLICATIONS FOR DEFINING ORGANIZATIONAL CONFLICT

The interdependence approach has the potential to be an elegant, powerful way to understand and influence conflict in organizations. This section examines the implications of this approach for the widely accepted definition of organizational conflict as opposing interests within a mixed-motive relationship.

Organizational researchers typically consider conflict in terms of bargaining and negotiation, and consider conflict to be based on opposing interests and preferences; conflict occurs in mixed-motive situations (Bacharach & Lawler, 1981; Bazerman & Neale, 1983; Walton & McKersie, 1965). The common interests of persons motivate them to continue to work together and reach an agreement, but their opposing interests require bargaining.

Defining conflict as mixed motive has been useful. Conflict is a relationship characteristic; indeed, conflict is seen as deriving from interdependence. This definition suggests positive functions for conflict. Persons need to reach agreement on their opposing interests in order for them to pursue their common ones. Collective bargaining is a well known conflict, but organizational members in many settings must also seek compromises and agreements on their differing interests and preferences.

However, from the standpoint of interdependence research, the mixed-motive perspective misleadingly implies that conflict occurs because individuals and groups, although they have some common goals, have competing interests. Persons with completely common interests should not then experience conflict.

But not only can people with the same interests conflict, they often do. Much of the conflict in and out of organizations has little to do with opposing interests and goals. Two co-workers with the same goal of developing a new market plan may not disagree at all about who should do what and how the credit should be shared. Despite this agreement on interests, they may dispute the best way to begin, how they can prepare, type of consultants needed, the theories they should use, and so on. Policymakers may want a successful strategy so that they prosper with the company, but disagree sharply over the actual risks and opportunities of the available options. Labor and management may disagree about how certain organizational decisions should be made even if they agree upon wages, grievance handling, and fringe benefits. Contrary to the mixed motive perspective, there are not competitive, opposing elements in all conflict. Persons with highly overlapping interests and goals will at times disagree and conflict.

As these examples illustrate, not all conflict is rooted in interests. Many conflicts have to do with opposing views, beliefs, and opinions with few if any incompatible goals. Debates and discussions are frequent within organizations. Workers, supervisors, and executives find many issues in which they have opposing perspectives and conflict as they try to reconcile them and make decisions.

The definition of mixed-motive and opposing interests also suggests a link between opposing interests and conflict that is so direct that it need not be investigated. But the dynamics between objective opposing interests and conflict are not automatic. One employee may be angry at a co-worker who insists on gossiping whereas another employee encourages the co-worker to tell more. A worker may be in conflict by blaming the union for a recent settlement; another holds management responsible. The extent to which persons experience conflict depends upon their perceptions. expectations, and evaluations of the situation (Averill, 1982; Pondy, 1967). Perceptions of other's behavior, attributions of these behaviors, standards of fairness, expectations, and evaluations all determine whether persons experience conflict as well as how they manage it.

APPROACHES TO MANAGING ORGANIZATIONAL CONFLICT

Organizational researchers have investigated strategies to manage conflict. What strategies, they ask, are useful and under what conditions? In contrast to this emphasis on strategies and their effects, the interdependence approach examines managing conflict on an experienced, psychological level. What is most critical is not the strategy taken but the conclusions people reach about how they are managing their conflict, especially whether they are cooperatively or competitively interdependent.

Researchers have argued that the traditional Prisoners' Dilemma Game (PDG) is inadequate to study conflict because employees have more than two options. They expanded the PDG to include two dimensions that yield five behavioral options (Blake & Mouton, 1964; Rahim, 1983b; Thomas, 1976). The two dimensions are assertiveness defined as behavior intended to satisfy one's interests and cooperativeness which is behavior intended to satisfy the concerns of others.

These dimensions yield five strategies: Obliging, avoiding, forcing (competing), compromising (bargaining), and confrontation (problem solving). Researchers attempt to describe these strategies, identify their impact, and, taking a contingency perspective, identify situations in which they are appropriate.

This approach to managing conflict has several important uses. It clearly communicates that managers have options and need not, indeed should not, handle conflict in the same way all the time. Managers can get a better understanding of what their alternatives are, and think about when they might use them. These strategies, although not specific action plans, suggest the steps managers might take and what strategies might be appropriate under different conditions (Rahim, 1986a).

To be highly useful, this and other approaches to conflict strategies must document reliably the effects of the different strategies. Research does indicate that people can distinguish these strategies, and that in many circumstances collaborative problem solving has a positive impact on conflict management (Burke 1970; Cosier & Ruble, 1981; Lawrence & Lorsch, 1967; Ruble & Thomas, 1976).

However, as research on threats in bargaining illustrates, documenting the reliable effects of strategies is difficult. Early experiments dramatically indicated that the availability and use of threats escalate conflict (Deutsch & Krauss, 1960, 1962). But later experiments, conducted under different conditions, found that people could react more positively to threats and that threats could facilitate mutually advantageous solutions (Kelley, 1965). In the early studies, it appears that people concluded that the threatener was trying to dominate and embarrass them, became competitive themselves, and retaliated; whereas in other experiments they took the threats as information that could help them reach a mutually useful solution (Tjosvold, 1974, 1983).

It is well recognized that the success of any strategy depends upon the conditions; however, much less recognized is that *how employees experience and react to any strategy depends on the situation*. Withdrawing from a conflict can be given various meanings and responded to much differently. It can be experienced as a kind, magnanimous gesture or as a trick to lull one into complacency. Employees react to the strategies of others in conflict based on how they interpret the conflict. Strategies such as threats and smoothing that people believe are competitive attempts to win have a much different impact on the course of the conflict than threats and smoothing over that target experience as cooperative gestures.

For example, a supervisor orders a worker to discontinue her present methods and use a new approach. They are in conflict for the worker's activities have been blocked; however, the worker may believe that her supervisor is handling the conflict cooperatively or competitively. Let's say that she believes the supervisor intends to improve the quality but reduce the quantity of her work. If she values higher quality, she does not experience the conflict as frustrating her goals. If she values quantity but not quality, she views the conflict as frustrating her goals. These cognitions determine whether the conflict is experienced as cooperative or as competitive and whether the worker is open-minded or hostile toward the supervisor.

INVESTIGATING THE EXPERIENCE OF MANAGING CONFLICT

The interdependence approach highlights the importance of the meaning given to conflict strategies, and, in particular, the conclusions people make about whether they are managing their conflict cooperatively or competitively. What does this mean for future research? How can knowledge about strategies and interdependence be integrated?

To make the research on interdependence and conflict more useful, much more work is needed to understand the schemas people use to conclude that the conflict is cooperative or competitive. People use rules to make these decisions. Some of these rules are particular to individuals and subgroups. But there are probably rules that are shared generally in a culture on what constitutes cooperative and competitive conflict modes.

Strategies certainly affect conclusions, for the other's concrete actions are used to give meaning and make conclusions. Coercive and forcing influence, sarcastic remarks, deceptions, and insults are often experienced as competitive (Tjosvold, 1977b, 1979; Tjosvold, Johnson, & Fabrey, 1981; Tjosvold, Johnson, & Lerner, 1980). People appear to conclude that these strategies make them look personally weak and incapable; they have lost face and must compete with the other to demonstrate their own strength (Tjosvold, 1983). These strategies are taken as evidence that the perpetrator is only concerned with his own interests and unconcerned about others' needs; he wants to win. They retaliate and try to win themselves, and the result is escalating and costly conflict.

On the other hand, taking the other's perspective, being open to influence, and conveying acceptance of the other are generally seen as cooperative (Johnson, 1971; Tjosvold & Deemer, 1980; Tjosvold, 1981). They convey that the person wants to listen, understand the other's interests and arguments, and is working for mutually useful solutions.

However, neither researchers nor managers can assume that people will inevitably conclude that strategies are competitive or cooperative, for the strategy is only one source of information. The prior relationship between the protagonists also affects conclusions. A command by a trusted friend may be considered a positive attempt to work cooperatively whereas a raised eyebrow by a foe is experienced as a competitive tactic that requires counterattack.

How participants frame the issues and their time perspective also affect their conclusions (Neale & Bazerman, 1985). Managers who are committed to being right and having their position dominate are apt to conclude that disagreement is competition. Managers who take a longer view and see their objective as their department developing the right decision—not that they are right—are apt to discuss opposing views openly and cooperatively.

Timing is also important. Sharing information at the beginning of discussing a conflict can be experienced as useful and cooperative. Near the end it may seem an obstruction and raise suspicions why the information was not shared earlier.

Especially important for organizations, role expectations affect people's conclusions about the conflict. Employees have different expectations for managers than for peers. A boss may be allowed to end a conflict decisively without developing competition; he is doing his job and promoting the interests of the whole department. On the other hand, a co-worker who uses a directive strategy may be thought focused only on his own interests and be considered highly competitive.

The importance of schemas suggests an important link between research on conflict and on organizational culture. The shared meanings within an organization are apt to affect how its members interpret and respond to conflict. Culture is likely to influence the kind of strategies used, expectations, and evaluation criteria that affect conclusions about conflict. It may be that people who have a shared vision and feel valued and trusted as persons tend to experience their conflicts as cooperative (Peters & Waterman, 1982).

Other Dimensions

In addition to interdependence, other conclusions reached about the nature of the conflict are important. How do they decide whether to handle the conflict in an open or in a covert manner? Conclusions about whether the conflict is handled openly or covertly and how active and dynamic the strategies are would seem to be particularly relevant and have important effects on conflict management (Cosier & Ruble, 1981; Ruble & Thomas, 1976). Another dimension is importance. When do people believe that the conflict is serious and deserves immediate attention or that it is a mere annoyance? The relationship of these dimensions to cooperation and competition should also be investigated.

Knowledge of cognitive schemas and rules in conflict is potentially very useful for managing conflict. This knowledge would help managers use strategies and procedures that would be experienced as they intend them to be. If they want a cooperative approach, they can choose actions that typically convey this intent. Of course, these rules will never perfectly predict how people experience conflict management; individuals have their own rules and use different kinds of information as they apply their rules to draw conclusions. This reasoning underscores the need for people to develop norms and procedures that allow them to discuss how they are managing conflict, what their intentions are, and check each other's conclusions about whether they are working cooperatively or competitively.

CONCLUDING COMMENTS

Whether people conclude they are cooperatively or competitively managing their conflict substantially affects their behavior and success. They do more than just perceive the other's strategies; they interpret and draw meaning from the conflict and the other's actions to decide whether they are pursuing joint goals or if they are pursuing their own interests at the other's expense. Research studies have demonstrated that such conclusions very much affect whether they are open- or closed-minded, whether or not they strengthen or weaken their relationship, and if they develop useful solutions to the underlying problem.

Research on cooperation and competition has important implications for considering organizational conflict. Definitions that conflict is based on opposing interests and involves a mixed-motive situation misleadingly confound conflict with competition. Much organizational conflict occurs when people have overlapping interests and compatible goals.

The interdependent approach emphasizes that cooperative and competitive approaches are very different ways to manage conflict. People must decide first whether a cooperative or competitive approach is desirable and then use their knowledge of the organization's cultures as well as the cognitive schemas and rules to develop concrete action plans that communicate and develop the desired mode. Of course, as intentions are often miscommunicated in conflict, people need to check whether in fact they are experiencing the conflict as intended.

Viewing conflict in terms of cooperation and competition is parsimonious and may help to incorporate conflict findings into areas of management. Leadership research, for example, tends to assume that managers and subordinates have cooperative goals; however, as the interdependent approach suggests, they may still often have conflict. Managers and subordinates should not assume that they will experience these conflicts as cooperative, but work to develop a cooperative context to help them use conflicts productively.

Research findings provide strong support that a cooperative approach has generally more productive dynamics and outcomes than a competitive means of handling conflict. Yet certainly there are times when a competitive approach to conflict management is called for and may be more useful. In keeping with contingency theory, research is needed to document the conditions and ways that competitive conflict contributes to organizations. The interdependence approach also embellishes the contingency perspective. The situation not only affects whether cooperative or competitive modes are more appropriate, but also the situation affects the concrete ways that these modes are implemented. Research is needed to illuminate the cognitive schemas and organizational values people use to decide whether they are conflicting cooperatively or competitively.

5

The Difference in the Meaning of Forcing in the Conflict Management of Actors and Observers

Evert van de Vliert
Hugo C. M. Prein

For decades after World War II, researchers used a one-dimensional approach to studying ways of conflict management.* In this one dimension, competition and cooperation formed as opposite poles (Deutsch, 1949). More recently, Blake and Mouton (1964, 1970) proposed a two-dimensional conflict grid. The independent dimensions were "concern for the production of results" and "concern for people." Other authors redefined these dimensions as assertiveness vs. cooperativeness (Thomas, 1976) and as "concern for self" vs. "concern for others" (Rahim, 1983b, 1986a). The dimensions interact to form five styles of conflict management. These styles are: *forcing* (assertive, uncooperative), *avoiding* (unassertive, uncooperative), *compromising* (moderately assertive, moderately cooperative), *problem solving* (assertive, cooperative) and *accommodating* (unassertive, cooperative).

Our study is a secondary analysis of the data from 32 survey studies. It investigates whether people think about conflict styles in terms of the classic competition-cooperation dichotomy or the five-part grid, and what conditions affect their decision to use the one-dimensional or the two-dimensional conceptualization. We propose that the cognitive representation of the four nonforcing types of conflict management have more in common with each other than with the cognitive representation of forcing. Our evidence also indicates that thinking in terms of forcing vs. nonforcing is stronger in observers than in actors.

*With thanks to Sipke E. Huismans for his methodological advice and to Martin C. Euwema, Aart Hazewinkel, Leendert Koppelaar, M. Afzalur Rahim and Dean Tjosvold for their critical commentary on earlier versions of this paper.

THEORETICAL FRAMEWORK

Assumptions Underlying the Conflict Grid

In the description of the "managerial conflict grid," Blake and Mouton (1964) were torn between two ideas—the conflict styles, and the assertiveness and cooperativeness dimensions. On the one hand, in their conceptualization and operationalizations, they assign the central importance to the five types of conflict management. On the other hand, they implicitly view the two dimensions as nine-point interval scales, which interact to produce the five conceptions of conflict management and their corresponding behaviors. Of the $9 \times 9 = 81$ positions in the grid, the following five are developed theoretically: forcing (9,1), avoiding (1,1), compromising (5,5), problem solving (9,9) and accommodating (1,9).

Scholars who emphasized the two explanatory dimensions saw, in each of the five types, a tendency to display specific conflict behavior, influenced by basic attitudes toward the interests of oneself and those of the opposite party (for example, Blake & Mouton, 1964, 1970; Brown, Yelsma & Keller, 1981; Kabanoff, 1985; Kilmann & Thomas, 1975; Pruitt & Rubin, 1986). The following four interrelated assumptions are characteristic for their outlook (with quotes from Blake & Mouton, 1970): (1) the dimensions form universal basic attitudes (p. 417: "Whenever a man meets a situation of conflict, he has at least two basic considerations in mind"); (2) each point of interaction of the two dimensions receives a certain personal emphasis in each individual (pp. 417–18: "It is the amount and kind of emphasis he places on various combinations of each of these elements"); (3) the personal pattern of varying emphasis on the points of interaction of the two dimensions determines which cognitive style and "back-up" style of conflict management one employs (p. 418: "that determine his thinking in dealing with conflict"); (4) the individual cognitive style of conflict management determines the likelihood of one's actual reaction to the conflict (p. 419: "When these basic styles are understood, one can predict for each how a man operating under that style is likely to handle conflict"). Taken together, these assumptions imply that individuals have a personalized cognitive map of subjective interrelations among the five types of conflict management, which may be operationalized in terms of the pattern of the desirability or the likelihood of each type of behavior. This supports the conflict grid as a verifiable theoretical model.

Validity of the Conflict Grid

The relationships among the types of conflict management specified in the conflict grid have been tested in several observer and actor studies. Ruble and Thomas (1976), and Cosier and Ruble (1981) have performed three validation studies, using the cognitive representation of conflict management in observing opponents as the criterion. In different studies, they showed that the hypothesized differences do indeed appear among the five types of conflict behavior on an ordinal level. On only one point did they detect a striking deviation from the model. It appeared that compromising by the opposite party was seen as at least as much of a cooperative style of conflict management as problem solving and accommodating.

Building on this empirical work, a few studies were conducted to see if the conflict grid holds true for the cognitive representation of own conflict behavior of actors (Prein, 1976; Van de Vliert & Hordijk, 1986). Using different research methods in these studies, we repeatedly came to the conclusion that the theoretical relationships among forcing, avoiding, problem solving and accommodating can be confirmed on an ordinal level. But like Ruble et al. we found that compromising usually has much more of a cooperative meaning than is indicated in the conflict grid. Kabanoff (1985) studied the relationships among the actor-reported styles of conflict management, not directly, but via the causal relationships between the two dimensions and the five types of own conflict behavior. Along that line too, it appeared that one-dimensional conceptualizations of styles of conflict management must be rejected in favor of the two-dimensional grid.

An Alternative Hypothesis

The secondary analysis discussed here, uses the cognitive representations of both one's own and others' conflict handling. Unlike the above-mentioned researchers, we do not try to confirm the theoretical relationships among the five types of conflict behavior, while simultaneously disconfirming the competition-cooperation dichotomy. For two reasons, we investigate whether the five-part grid tends toward a two-part competition-cooperation.

A first argument for the alternative conceptualization of the conflict grid is derived from the fact that the two basic dimensions of conflict management correspond with the two main dimensions from models of interpersonal behavior (Brown, Yelsma & Keller, 1981; Kiesler, 1983; Ruble & Thomas, 1976). It is evident that the dimensions in the conflict grid have been interpreted as unipolar scales and the dimensions in the models of interpersonal behavior as bipolar scales. If we lengthen the unipolar scales in the classical grid downwards and to the left, we have four quadrants based on the bipolar dimensions: assertiveness–self-denial and antagonism–cooperativeness. Using the common definitions and measurements found in the literature, we verified in which quadrant the five types of conflict behavior best fit. While the styles of avoiding, compromising, problem solving and accommodating seemed to belong in the quadrant on the upper-right, forcing convincingly tended toward the quandrant on the upper-left. Forcing is described and operationalized almost universally in terms of a win-lose contest in which pressure and the execution of power are common tactics.

Forcing is related to "moving against the other" (Thomas, 1979, p. 157) and therefore must be more closely associated with the presence of opposition rather than the absence of collaboration. The consequence of all this is that the four more cooperative types of conflict behavior will resemble each other more than the antagonistic style of forcing.

The assumption that forcing cognitively takes on an isolated position in relation to the other styles of conflict management, is furthermore based on the recently published (de-)escalation model (Van de Vliert, 1984, 1985). A central issue within this model is that avoiding, compromising, problem solving and accommodating all have a short-term de-escalating effect, in which the frustrations of the parties involved do not increase. Forcing, on the other hand, has a short-term escalating effect, in which the frustrations actually do increase.

On these grounds, our alternative hypothesis reads: *The cognitive representations of the four nonforcing types of conflict behavior will resemble each other more than the cognitive representation of forcing.*

Actor-Observer Hypothesis

Because the conflict grid makes no theoretical distinction between one's own and others' conflict management, the five-part typology and alternative hypothesis applies to actors as well as observers. Upon closer inspection, this is anything but self-evident. The circumstances under which the same conflict behavior is interpreted differ considerably. Actors have so much more information concerning the historical, contextual, intentional and other backgrounds of their behavior (Jones & Nisbett, 1971), that their cognitive representations of that behavior, in general, will be more realistic and more subtle than those of the observers. In accordance with this, Linville (1982), Linville and Jones (1980) and Wilder (1981) have empirically shown that one's cognitive map concerning "in-group" members is more complex and differentiated than his or her cognitive map concerning "out-group" members. Among other things it appears that one passes judgment on oneself or one's own group in less extreme, black-and-white terms than on another person or group.

Consequently, in terms of the competition-cooperation dichotomy and the conflict grid, the fairly differentiated five-part in the conflict grid will usually be more valid for actors than for observers. Conversely, the competition-cooperation dichotomy will give a more adequate conceptualization of conflict management in others than conflict management in oneself. In short: the classic two-part model and the subsequent five-part model are both valid, though under different circumstances. Formulated as the actor-observer hypothesis: *In the cognitive representation of conflict behavior, the tendency to contrast forcing with nonforcing will be stronger in observers than in actors.*

The study reported mainly concerns the difference between actors and observing opponents and not the difference between actors and neutral observers.

METHOD

Secondary Analysis

The hypotheses about the cognitive representations of forcing vs. nonforcing conflict management can be tested by means of earlier studies in which the cognitive similarities or differences among the five types of conflict behavior are reported. The studies from Table 5.1, which were taken in secondary analysis, satisfy three criteria: (1) an indication was present as to the cognitive similarities/differences among all five grid styles of conflict management (usefulness); (2) use was made of a questionnaire which, either by the researchers themselves or by others, was shown to be satisfactory in terms of cluster homogeneity, stability, or interjudge agreement (reliability); (3) the respondents were not the same as in one of the other reanalyzed studies (independence). On the basis of the last criterion, the studies discarded were: parallel studies of the same group (Kabanoff, 1987; Kilmann & Thomas, 1977; Kravitz, 1987; Prein, 1984) and retest studies, after a lapse of time (Brown, Yelina, & Keller, 1981; Van de Vliert & Hordijk, 1986).

Table 5.1 shows that the 32 reanalyzed studies use a variety of measuring instruments and respondents. Twenty-seven survey studies dealt with the own style of conflict management, in general or in conflicts with certain other individuals. These are actor studies. In the three experiments performed by Ruble, the subjects were questioned about the style of conflict management in the opponent. The two observer studies by Kabanoff contained evaluations of conflict behavior of fellow group members, regardless of whether the person was an observing opposite party or an outsider.

Arithmetical Operations

A preliminary question here is concerned with which criterion one must use to test the hypothesis that forcing cognitively takes on an isolated position with respect to the nonforcing styles of conflict management. What is "not isolated"? The answer to this question is implied in the theoretical relationship between the average cognitive distance of forcing with, respectively, avoiding, compromising, problem solving and accommodating (M_1), on one side, and on the other, the average cognitive distance of the nonforcing styles of conflict management relative to each other (M_2). Since the conflict grid is presented by Blake and Mouton (1964, 1970) as a square, of which the sides have a length of 8, the ten theoretical distances among the five types of conflict behavior are known. According to the computations of these anticipated distances indicated in Table 5.2, one can use $M_1 : M_2$, that is, $8.24 : 7.38 = 1.12$, as testing criterion. Therefore, there is only mention of a cognitively isolated position of forcing if it is empirically shown that $M_1 : M_2 > 1.12$.

Table 5.1
Overview of the Reanalyzed Studies, with Their Respective Measuring Instruments, Respondents, and Conflict Situations

Study	Measuring instrument	Respondents	Conflict situation
Actor studies			
Prein (1976), study I	Prein (1976)	282 educational managers/others	functionary vs. colleague
Idem, study II	Idem	43 professional helpers	functionary vs. colleague
Kilmann & Thomas (1977)	Thomas & Kilmann (1974)	86 students	general
Baxter & Shepherd (1978)	Hall (1969) and Thomas & Kilmann (1974)	57 students	varied sex and affective relationship
O'Reilly & Weitz (1980)	Thomas & Kilmann (1974)	140 managers	general
Brown, Yelsma & Keller (1981)	Thomas & Kilmann (1974)	51 students	general
Drake, Zammuto & Parasuraman (1981)	Thomas & Kilmann (1974)	241 students	general
Putnam & Wilson (1982)	Putnam & Wilson (1982)	360 organization members/students	supervisor
Rahim (1983), study I	Rahim (1983)	1219 managers	superior/ colleague/ subordinate
Idem, study II	Idem	297 students	Idem
Prein (1984)	Rahim (1983)	42 students	general
Mills, Robey & Smith (1985)	Thomas & Kilmann (1974)	199 project managers	general
Kabanoff (1986)	Thomas & Kilmann (1974)	505 students	general
Kozan (1986)	Rahim (1983)	134 managers	superior/ colleague/ subordinate
Morley & Shock-ley-Zalabak (1986)	Thomas & Kilmann (1974)	118 organization members	general
Van de Vliert & Hordijk (1986)	Hordijk & Van de Vliert (1983)	175 building-employees	diverse, low intensity
Idem	Idem	164 building-employees	diverse, high intensity
Boozer (1987)	Rahim (1983)	150 students	team members

Table 5.1
(Continued)

Hammock, Richard-son, Pilkington & Utley (1987), study I	Rahim (1983)	420 students	general
Idem, study II	Idem	185 students	friend/sibling
Idem, study III	Idem	153 students	professor/ parent/friend
Kravitz (1987)	Thomas & Kilmann (1974)	96 managers	normal
Weider-Hatfield & Hatfield (1987), study I	Rahim (1983)	125 managers	superior/ colleague/ subordinate
Idem, study II	Idem	100 managers	superior
Hammock (unpublished)	Rahim (1983)	148 students	friend/partner
Rahim (unpubl-ished), study I	Rahim (1983)	600 public administrators	functionary vs. superior
Idem, study II	Idem	290 executives	Idem
Observer studies			
Ruble & Thomas (1976), study I	single questions and semantic dif-ferential scales	150 students	manager vs. colleague
Idem, study II	semantic differ-ential scales	65 students	manager vs. colleague
Cosier & Ruble (1981)	semantic differ-ential scales	100 students	general
Kabanoff (1987)	behavioral rating scale	78 students	general
Kabanoff (unpublished)	behavioral rating scale	71 students	general

The theoretical model of the conflict grid specifies the relationships among the five types of conflict behavior in the form of geometrical distances. The sum of the ten distances amounts to $4(8.0) + 2(11.31) + 4(5.66) = 77.26$. On the other hand, the measurements for the interrelated cognitive similarities, which were either published or sent to us, had the form of intercorrelations among the five reported types of conflict behavior in 29 of the 32 studies. In order to make the empirical measurements comparable to the theoretical measurements, the cor-relation coefficients in each study were first converted into geometrical measure-ments by means of the multidimensional scaling program MINISSA (Lingoes &

Table 5.2
Theoretical and Empirical Cognitive Distances among Styles of Conflict Management, Expressed in Geometrical Measurements of Distances

Combination of styles of conflict management*	9,1 1,1	9,1 5,5	9,1 9,9	9,1 1,9	M_1	1,1 5,5	1,1 9,9	1,1 1,9	5,5 9,9	5,5 1,9	9,9 1,9	M_2	$M_1:M_2$
Theoretical distance	8.0	5.66	8.0	11.31	8.24	5.66	11.31	8.0	5.66	5.66	8.0	7.38	1.12
Actor studies													
Prein (1976), study I	11.13	7.45	9.51	10.41	9.63	8.74	11.52	10.37	3.09	3.09	1.94	6.46	1.49
Idem, study II	8.17	10.39	5.23	10.38	8.54	4.98	10.38	6.64	10.02	2.12	8.95	7.18	1.19
Kilmann & Thomas (1977)	9.13	6.76	5.68	10.70	8.07	8.18	11.25	4.01	4.01	6.84	10.70	7.50	1.08
Baxter & Shepherd(1978)	10.35	10.93	9.96	10.77	10.50	7.65	10.38	5.35	3.65	2.42	5.80	5.88	1.79
O'Reilly & Weitz (1980)	10.83	10.00	1.29	10.80	8.23	7.15	9.98	.64	9.99	6.56	10.02	7.39	1.11
Brown et al. (1981)	4.53	9.83	8.25	9.77	8.09	8.24	9.79	6.28	6.23	4.48	9.84	7.48	1.08
Drake et al. (1981)	11.01	10.83	5.17	10.98	9.50	5.40	10.75	2.38	8.05	3.07	9.61	6.54	1.45
Putnam & Wilson (1982)	10.85	12.02	11.11	11.48	11.37	9.12	9.59	7.47	1.38	1.67	2.55	5.30	2.15
Rahim (1983), study I	11.17	10.52	12.16	9.69	10.89	5.62	9.87	2.17	4.25	3.79	8.01	5.62	1.94
Idem, study II	11.16	8.33	5.71	8.40	8.40	11.16	11.16	3.84	2.76	7.36	7.36	7.27	1.16
Prein (1984)	11.82	10.99	10.45	11.83	11.27	4.63	9.12	.01	4.63	4.63	9.12	5.36	2.10
Mills et al. (1985)	8.54	8.66	6.26	10.40	8.47	8.66	10.40	4.25	4.24	6.27	9.56	7.23	1.17
Kabanoff (1986)	11.88	8.04	4.15	9.13	8.30	8.04	9.13	4.15	8.58	8.58	5.57	7.34	1.13
Kozan (1986)	10.38	10.81	12.05	8.98	10.56	6.36	10.81	4.57	4.57	2.39	6.36	5.84	1.81
Morley & Shockley-Zalabak (1986)	10.07	8.59	4.25	10.70	8.40	8.66	10.37	2.89	5.19	6.74	9.80	7.27	1.15

Van de Vliert &													
Hordijk (1986)	8.96	10.54	9.66	10.52	9.92	5.97	9.80	1.89	5.12	5.13	9.68	6.26	1.58
Idem	6.28	10.51	10.40	8.88	9.02	8.72	10.51	3.61	3.19	6.28	8.88	6.86	1.31
Boozer (1987)	11.17	9.05	10.47	11.22	10.48	9.49	9.25	5.24	1.60	5.30	4.47	5.89	1.78
Hammock et al. (1987),													
study I	12.60	9.10	10.26	11.26	10.80	9.10	10.27	8.41	1.54	2.36	2.36	5.67	1.90
Idem, study II	13.10	10.21	11.16	11.36	11.46	9.22	9.85	8.63	1.06	1.37	1.30	5.24	2.19
Idem, study III	9.44	10.06	10.41	10.43	10.08	7.72	10.47	3.86	3.03	4.41	7.42	6.15	1.64
Kravitz (1987)	11.58	11.57	5.18	8.17	9.13	5.99	10.06	3.43	7.56	6.35	7.35	6.79	1.34
Weider-Hatfield & Hat-													
field (1987), study I	10.15	10.79	10.15	10.31	10.35	7.93	10.20	3.89	2.97	4.14	6.73	5.98	1.73
Idem, study II	10.15	4.64	6.74	12.83	8.59	6.26	9.44	6.48	4.30	8.21	8.20	7.15	1.20
Hammock (unpublished)	8.86	11.19	11.18	8.68	9.98	9.08	11.18	8.69	2.80	2.79	2.80	6.22	1.60
Rahim (unpublished),													
study I	11.83	7.32	10.15	10.49	9.95	7.85	10.57	3.71	3.76	4.67	6.90	6.24	1.59
Idem, study II	10.90	7.00	6.09	10.87	8.71	9.90	10.97	4.47	1.60	7.00	8.45	7.07	1.23

Observer studies

Ruble & Thomas (1976),													
study I	6.73	10.90	9.06	11.39	9.52	8.45	7.35	9.43	1.71	5.51	6.73	6.53	1.46
Idem, study II	8.43	11.0	9.39	12.72	10.39	8.25	8.85	7.90	2.56	2.82	5.33	5.95	1.75
Cosier & Ruble (1981)	8.81	11.65	10.25	10.69	10.35	7.63	10.47	7.52	5.01	1.14	4.06	5.97	1.73
Kabanoff (1987)	11.85	11.88	7.82	14.28	11.46	4.67	4.48	7.37	4.47	3.06	7.38	5.24	2.19
Kabanoff (unpublished)	11.77	11.02	10.02	11.90	11.18	9.15	4.92	.15	4.26	9.14	4.93	5.43	2.06

* 9,1 = forcing; 1,1 = avoiding; 5,5 = compromising; 9,9 = problem solving; 1,9 = accommodating.

Roskam, 1973). In all cases, a two-dimensional representation of the five styles was shown to suffice, as the solution fits well with the data (stress $< .001$). Secondly, in each study, the scale of the ten geometric distances, thus obtained, was increased until the sum of these empirical distances reached 77.26, and thereby was equal to the sum of the theoretical distances. Thirdly, the average cognitive distance was calculated between forcing and nonforcing (M_1) and also among the nonforcing styles relative to each other (M_2).

In three studies no intercorrelations were reported (Cosier & Ruble, 1981; Ruble & Thomas, 1976, studies I and II), but the behavior types were put into relationship to two underlying orthogonal dimensions. In these cases, the ten geometric distances among one another were calculated by means of the Pythagorean theorem. Afterwards, the distances were again enlarged until their sum amounted to 77.26. The final scores and averages are shown in Table 5.2.

RESULTS

The last column in Table 5.2 indicates that all the studies demonstrate that the four cognitive distances between forcing and nonforcing are, on the average, larger than the six cognitive distances among avoiding, compromising, problem solving and accommodating ($M_1 : M_2 > 1$). In 29 of the 32 studies, this difference is larger than the criterion of 1.12 (binomial test, $p < .001$). Moreover, in the 29 studies for which $M_1 : M_2 > 1.12$ applies, the deviation from the criterion of 1.12 is significantly larger than in the three studies in which $M_1 : M_2 \leq 1.12$ (Mann-Whitney, $U = 3.5, p < .01$). Both results support the alternative hypothesis that the cognitive representations of the four nonforcing types of conflict behavior have more in common with each other than with the cognitive representation of forcing. The five-part typology does indeed tend towards a two-part typology, competition-cooperation. Upon further consideration, it appears that the alternative hypothesis is supported by the actor studies as well as the observer studies.

What the actor-observer hypothesis comes down to is that the tendency to think in a dichotomy of forcing vs. nonforcing will be weaker in the reporting of one's own behavior than of other's behavior. In operational terms this hypothesis implies that the predominance of M_1 over M_2 in the last column of Table 5.2 will be smaller in the 27 actor studies than in the five observer studies. The results confirm this (Mann-Whitney, $U = 34, p < .02$). The cognitive representations of one's own forcing vs. nonforcing conflict management shows less difference than those of other's forcing vs. nonforcing conflict management. If it concerns one's own behavior, one apparently thinks more in terms of the five-part of the conflict grid, if it concerns the behavior of the opponent then it is more likely that one thinks in less subtle terms, such as competition-cooperation.

DISCUSSION

Earlier research has shown that the classic conceptualization of forms of conflict management as a competition-cooperation dichotomy is inadequate and should be replaced by the two-dimensional conflict grid (see, in particular, Kabanoff, 1985; Prein, 1976; Ruble & Thomas, 1976). Our basic conclusion is that in rejecting the one-dimensional model one throws out the baby with the bathwater.

Our analysis has persuaded us that the five-part typology tends to contrast between forcing and nonforcing conflict management. This tendency seems to be moderated by the position taken by one who perceives the conflict behavior. Actors generally think of their own conflict management with relative subtlety, more or less in terms of the conflict grid. Observers in the role of opponent or outsider seem to present cognitively a more distinct division between others' forcing and nonforcing reactions to the conflict. The theoretical and practical implications of these results deserve ample attention.

This analysis has several limitations. The different measuring instruments, respondents and conflict situation make parallel comparisons difficult. For example, several studies had low reliability in their subscales, the generalizability of data from students may be questionable, and the results may not apply to strongly escalated conflicts.

Theoretical Significance

In the description of the theoretical framework, six studies were discussed in which the conflict grid of Blake and Mouton (1964, 1970) was validated through the use of the cognitive representations of respondents' own and others' conflict management. None of the authors recognized that one may have been able to obtain other results if one had studied observers instead of actors, or conversely, actors instead of observers. Our study highlights the importance of actor-observer differences. For actors, the original conflict grid forms a reasonably suitable model, provided that one places compromising between problem solving and accommodating (cf. Van de Vliert & Hordijk, 1986). For observers, our results suggest an alternative model, in which the meaning of forcing takes on a very isolated position in relation to avoiding, problem solving, compromising, and accommodating. Observers think of the behavior of others as if it were multidimensional on the one-dimensional foundation of forcing vs. nonforcing. Whether this is equally strong and similarly valid for opponents and outsiders, calls for further research.

The fact that the actor-observer difference is found across different studies also confirms that the conflict grid is more than a framework for the description and operationalization of behavioral types. Evidently, it is possible to make generalizations about a system of meaningful cognitive relationships among the five styles of conflict management, of which the actor-observer difference forms a part. We have attempted to capture that system in the metaphor of different cognitive maps, that indicate the interrelations among the types of conflict management. The pattern of interrelationships is shown on the cognitive map in terms of the desirability or the likelihood of each behavioral type.

The fact that forcing has a different, possibly more antagonistic meaning for observers than for actors, has several implications. The same people use different cognitive maps in the evaluation of conflict behavior. There is a predisposition to gauge one's own and others' forcing behavior with two different approaches. Secondly, on the cognitive map of observers, forcing forms a more deviant and therefore, more salient behavioral alternative than on the cognitive map of actors. Thirdly, the smaller cognitive distance between forcing and nonforcing conflict management in actors implies that actors, in that regard, make use of a more differentiated cognitive map than observers do (compare Linville, 1982; Linville & Jones, 1980; Wilder, 1981). Possible causes of this are unfamiliarity with others' reasons and being unaware of one's own way of behaving (Jones & Nisbett, 1971; Thomas & Pondy, 1977). Fourthly, communication about forcing and nonforcing is likely to be difficult between the actor and opponent or outsider, while opponent and outsider in that respect will understand each other much better. The divergent assessment of forcing could easily develop into a new conflict issue between the actor and observing opponent. Finally, it is likely that with the forcing behavior of the actor, the opposite party, on the basis of its interpretation of that behavior, will become all the more frustrated and will switch over to forcing as well.

Thomas and Pondy (1977) argued that the parties in conflict attribute to themselves, as actors, more problem solving and compromising behavior, and the opponents observed by the actors, more forcing behavior. Our study indicates that actors and observers use different cognitive frameworks to interpret conflict behaviors. Our finding on actor-observer difference in the cognitive map offers an explanation for Thomas and Pondy's argument. As the opponent experiences more contrast between forcing and nonforcing conflict management in the actor than the actor experiences, the opponent will interpret forcing in the actor as less integrating and more hostile than the actor will do.

Implications for Interventions

That forcing as conflict management has a less aggressive meaning for actors than observers, seems important not only for the parties themselves if they want to deescalate the conflict, but also for those outsiders who either study or want to influence conflict behavior. The parties in conflict could take advantage of exchanging thoughts about how they experience each other's forcing behavior (compare Thomas & Pondy, 1977). The message for actors is that they can manage conflict more constructively by telling the opposite party, for which reasons, and with which intentions they use forcing. On the other hand, the advice to constructively oriented opponents is to discuss with the actor why and how he or she uses forcing and what one experiences with that as an observing opponent.

Researchers and interventionists, while posing questions and interpreting answers and observations, need to take into account that the intentions to use forcing or actual forcing behaviors are interpreted by the actor as less agocentric and more cooperative than when interpreted by opponents and outsiders. This difference in the experiencing of forcing can also play a role during the jointly diagnosing of a conflict. A diagnosis based on the cognitive map of an outsider runs the danger of being discarded by the actor because of the deviation from one's own standpoint, based on a different cognitive map.

The actor-observer difference in the cognitive representation of forcing is of interest to interventionists because it offers a pretext for strategic change in the conflict situation. In the terminology of Van de Vliert (1985), the different cognitive maps of conflict management form antecedent conditions of conflict issues, which are of use in escalating or deescalating the conflict. Conflict stimulation is possible by ignoring any exploration of the dual differences in the cognitive map involving actor A and opponent B and actor B and opponent A. It is also possible to bring up the differences as a potential extra conflict issue. Furthermore, one can strengthen A and B in their one-sided negative vision of the forcing behavior of the opponent. In fact, one then forms alternating coalitions with A against B and with B against A.

In this context, deescalating interventions have in common that they make the actor and observer aware of their difference in cognitive map, for example through the use of role shifting, or by exchanging images of forcing. A simple intervention, which makes use of the fact that each party is an actor as well as an observer, is to have the client describe, respectively, the subjective meaning of respondent's own forcing behavior, the subjective meaning of other's forcing behavior and which similarities and differences exist between them. This technique is intended to call up the cognitive dissonance between the actor image and the observer image, and thus, break through the observer's thinking in the unnecessary contrast of forcing vs. nonforcing (compare Eiseman, 1978).

PART II

Communication and Conflict

Introduction

Linda L. Putnam

One of the basic elements included in most definitions of *conflict* is social interaction. In fact, some researchers define conflict as "the *interaction* of interdependent people who perceive incompatible goals and interference from each other in achieving those goals" (Folger & Poole, 1984, p. 4). The study of interaction, in turn, centers on the role of communication in the antecedent, process, and consequence stages of conflict.

As an antecedent, communication is frequently treated as semantic misunderstandings or breakdowns that stem from and are fed into conflict situations (Thomas, 1976). Communication also effects the formation of opposing positions. Specifically, contradictions between message and action, verbal digs at the other party, and differences of opinion between disputants isolate issues for dispute and shape the meanings and the emotional reactions to conflict. Finally, communication functions as preformulated strategies or "planned interactions," as exemplified in conflict style research (see Putnam & Poole, in press, for a reivew of this literature).

But communication is much more than an antecedent variable. It defines the enactment or manifest stage of conflict. Thus, researchers manipulate the amount and modality (written, face-to-face, telephone) of interaction, examine the influence patterns of participants, study message sequences that lead to cooperation and competition, and assess communicator competencies in managing disputes. Since early research on communication and conflict dispelled the myth that more communication leads to cooperation (Hawes & Smith, 1973), subsequent studies have centered on the uses and sequences of messages strategies and tactics, the management of information exchange, and the transformation of issues during conflict interaction (Putnam & Poole, in press).

Communication is also a consequence of conflict situations in that past controversies shape future interactions. The research in this area examines how conflict increases or decreases communication between groups; how it redefines networks and coalitions (Benson, 1975); how it changes organizational structures; and how it alters the flow, amount, and formal channels of communication (Hage, 1974). Links between the aftermath and the antecedent conditions of conflict suggests that communication facilitates the cyclical nature of conflict; the end of one interaction sets the stage for future encounters (Pondy, 1967). Indeed, communication and conflict are intertwined in a symbiotic relationship:

both are developmental, ongoing processes interdependent on each other. Since communication permeates every stage and level of conflict, it is more than a variable: it constitutes the essence of conflict. That is, it underlies the formation, perceptions, enactments, outcomes, and aftermath of disputes.

The five contributions in this section of the book further our understanding of the symbiotic link between communication and conflict. The chapter by Donohue and the one by Bies center on the antecedent-process relationships between communication and conflict while those by Jones; Roloff, Tutzauer, and Dailey; and Putnam and Wilson focus on the process dimensions. Although the chapters vary from superior-subordinate conflicts to negotiation and mediation, they share a common interest in the content and function of messages in disputes. This overview summarizes each contribution and highlights the role of communication in each chapter.

Chapter 6, "Criteria for Developing Communication Theory in Mediation," by William Donohue lays out the practical, epistemological, and metatheoretical criteria for a communication-based theory of mediation. Employing action science as a model, Donohue suggests ways that knowledge claims can achieve external validity by working with practitioners. He offers a mid-range approach between deductive, causal models and inductive, descriptive accounts, one that meets the criteria of generalizability and contextual sensitivity. His chapter concludes by describing a research program that adheres to a mid-range view of theory development for the study of communication and mediation.

Donohue's chapter centers on the way communication shapes antecedents of conflict through structure, function, and process. In particular, he suggests that the assumptions, goals, and perceived realities that each party brings to the dispute shape contextual constraints. These realities are enacted in and have an effect on interaction coherence, patterns of communication over time, and relational control of participants. Thus Donohue's model addresses the way that interaction between participants intertwines conflict antecedents and processes.

In Chapter 7, "Managing Conflict Before It Happens: The Role of Accounts," Robert Bies concentrates on the latent stage of conflict development (Pondy, 1967). In particular, his chapter examines the giving of accounts prior to decision making to reduce or to shape perceptions of potential conflicts. Accounts, then, are messages that managers give subordinates to channel controversies and to mitigate against the undesirable effects of nonrealistic conflicts. Through reviewing relevant literature on conflict, justice, and bargaining, Bies presents three types of accounts—causal, ideological, and referential—and discusses how the timing, adequacy, and sincerity of accounts might influence the way conflicts are channeled.

In Bies' chapter, message sending is treated as an antecedent of conflict, one that functions to reduce communication breakdowns between superiors and subordinates. Communication frames the way each person envisions conflict situations—their emotional states and attributions of intent. Accounts aim to center perceived conflicts on the issues of justifications, shared values, and negative consequences of decisions. Although Bies admittedly treats communication as one-way, his chapter makes a strong statement for the role of message sending in the formative stages of a conflict.

The remaining three chapters focus on the role of message strategies in mediation and negotiations. Since they each treat communication in a similar way, their contributions will be examined collectively. In "Lag Sequential Analyses of Mediator-Spouse and Husband-Wife Interaction in Successful and Unsuccessful Divorce Mediation," Tricia Jones employs the mediation process analysis to compare the interaction patterns of mediators, husbands, and wives in 18 successful and 18 unsuccessful divorce mediations. Jones coded each message of the participants and tested for the contiguous patterns of mediator-spouse and husband-wife interaction. Results reveal that successful mediators guide the disputants to talk about themselves, to use summaries, to employ reciprocal problem-solving messages, and to break up conflict cycles between husbands and wives. Husband-wife interaction in successful mediations are characterized by reciprocity in information exchange, expressions of feelings, and agreements. In general, however, mediators carry the primary burden for facilitating problem-solving interaction in divorce mediations.

The last two chapters focus on the role of argumentation in facilitating integrative and distributive settlements in bargaining. Ironically, they uncover opposite findings for the integrative outcomes. In "The Role of Argumentation in Distributive and Integrative Bargaining Contexts: Seeking Relative Advantage but at What Cost?" by Michael Roloff, Frank Tutzauer, and William Dailey, the authors employ undergraduate students in two bargaining simulations—one on civil suit damages (the distributive task) and the other on price negotiations between a buyer and a seller (the integrative task). The researchers track the outcomes of each session and code talk turns for each bargainer into such categories as offers, types of arguments, concessions, agreements, rejections, and information seeking. They report that arguing about responsibility and workability leads to deadlocks for the distributive task. For the integrative negotiations, use of persuasive arguments correlates positively and significantly with deadlocks and negatively with agreeability and number of offers. Communicating agreeability, in contrast, is positively associated with achieving integrative outcomes.

Using naturalistic data from teachers' negotiations, Linda Putnam and Steve Wilson examine "Argumentation and Bargaining Strategies as Discriminators of Integrative Outcomes." They isolate the talk on 16 agenda items, code the statements of each negotiator and team member into two category systems: one on argumentation and one on bargaining strategies. Then they track the effect of argument type and bargaining strategy on four hierarchical categories of integrativeness for each of the 16 issues. Their findings suggest that workability arguments, exploratory problem-solving statements, and promise-asks concession-demand comments are linked to highly integrative settlements, particularly to bridging and sharpening, while reaffirmation of position through opinion giving distinguishes trade-off and win-lose outcomes.

The Roloff, et al., and Putnam and Wilson chapters differ in their findings on the role of persuasive arguments in bargaining. Roloff et al. suggest that agreeability and offers rather than persuasive appeals promotes joint benefits while the Putnam and Wilson study contends that arguments on the workability of proposals in conjunction with exploratory problem solving, asks concessions, and demands aids in achieving creative solutions. Although some of these differences may stem from employing divergent category systems, the two studies are similar in their analyses. They differ, however, in operational definitions of persuasive arguments and workability. Also, the simulated tasks in the Roloff, et al., research differ in form and content from a multi-issue contract negotiation in the Putnam and Wilson investigation. In the Putnam and Wilson chapter argument shapes the definition of issues but in the Roloff, et al., research it functions primarily to advance claims and achieve relative advantage in the simulations. Other differences that may account for opposite findings between the studies include use of students versus use of expert negotiators, zero-history bargaining versus negotiations framed by normative behaviors, uncertainty in motivation to settle versus strong incentive to reach an agreement, bargaining by individuals rather than teams, and absence of time-outs versus use of caucus sessions. The contrast of the two studies makes a strong appeal for future research on argumentation and negotiation.

These three empirical papers represent efforts to understand how communication influences the outcomes of a dispute. Since two of the studies are drawn from naturalistic settings and one from a carefully controlled experimental design, they illustrate the versatility of coding interaction into message functions and tracking the content and sequences of bargaining talk. Through studying message exchanges between negotiators, researchers can decipher how proposals develop, what leads to escalation and deescalation at different points in the conflict, and how messages shape the nature of agreements or the conditions of an impasse. Communication and conflict are indeed intertwined. To understand how individuals do and should handle conflict effectively, it is imperative that we expand our research on the cyclical role that communication plays in defining, enacting, and shaping the outcomes of conflicts.

6

Criteria for Developing Communication Theory in Mediation

William A. Donohue

In his book *Social Interaction as Drama*, Hare (1985) uses a dramaturgical model to account for episodes in conflict resolution. He begins detailing this model by describing the four types of plays typically identified in histories of drama: tragedy and comedy, in which the characters control the plot; and melodrama and farce, in which the plot controls the characters. Tragedy and melodrama develop serious human concerns with an unhappy ending while comedy and farce demonstrate a lightness of style with a happy ending. So, for example, if the playwright seeks to explore a serious subject an initial decision must be made: Should the characters control the plot or the plot control the characters, that is, should the play evolve as tragedy or melodrama?

In developing communication theory to account for mediation phenomena researchers face this same question, but in a different form. Namely, should the theory control the phenomena we observe, or should the phenomena control the kind of theory we develop? Or, can we identify some form of inquiry in which both theory and phenomena actively inform one another to learn more about mediation? This chapter centers around these key epistemological questions. As I attend more conferences and consume more articles related to conflict and mediation I discover increased eagerness among communication scholars to build theories or perspectives that apply specifically to the mediation context. Should we build theories or perspectives of mediation using the same criteria we might use for building ideas about other communication phenomena, or should we consider some different criteria tailored to the needs of mediation and mediators?

My argument, here, moves in the latter direction. I feel that criteria for developing communication theory in mediation need articulating for several reasons. First, criteria for building theory might facilitate moving between the various types of mediation contexts since the data generated from these theories intended to explain phenomena from these contexts would be created from one value system. For example, if we adopt the value that theory ought to grow from, and aim toward, solving practitioner problems, then researchers would be able to evaluate the external validity of research products. Second, mediators see communication processes as very central to their job performance (Folberg & Taylor, 1984). If researchers adhere even loosely to a set of criteria for building theory, some consistency in research products might emerge that would, in turn, facilitate communication between practitioners and researchers.

I intend to argue in this chapter that communication theorists ought to struggle with three key theory construction issues. First, I probe the functional issue and contend that our theories or perspectives ought to be useful for both practitioners and researchers. Second, I explore the epistemological issue of theoretical stance and argue that relying on one epistemological framework for building theory may not reasonably accomplish this functional objective. Third, I conclude these issue discussions by focusing on some key metatheoretical concerns and argue that our substantive accounts of mediator communication ought to examine various structural, functional and process features of communicative phenomena. The final section outlines our communication research program according to the extent to which it conforms to the criteria outlined here.

THE FUNCTIONAL ISSUES

The first question that should be raised in building theory about any phenomena relates to function; what work does the theory need to perform to make it valuable? To answer this question I shall turn to the perspective defined recently by Argyris, Putnam, and Smith (1985) termed Action Science. Action Science was created as an attempt to merge theory and practice to improve both the theory construction and the practical problem-solving process. Argyris et al. (1985) develop this perspective around three criteria. First, knowledge ought to be created in the service of solving practical problems. Adhering to this value helps the users of research products gain access to an important resource while researchers benefit from practitioner insight and enthusiasm about the subject of inquiry. This position does not argue that practitioners ought to be responsible for generating explanations for their practices. Rather, it argues that researchers and practitioners should contribute their respective expertise to create a product greater than each is capable of creating independently.

Second, "knowledge should include empirically disconfirmable propositions that can be organized into theory and falsified by practitioners in real-life contexts" (Argyris et al., 1985, p. 232). Theories adhere to the canons of scientific rigor, but gain added external validity by seeking falsification in real-life contexts. This second criterion separates Action Science from evaluation research because the emphasis remains on theory construction, and not just learning whether or not programs have met their objectives. Also, this position does not deny the value of laboratory efforts if those efforts move ultimately to serve practitioner needs.

Third, the Action Science perspective adheres to the principle that "knowledge should speak to the forming of purposes, not just the means by which to achieve them'' (Argyris, et al., 1985, p. 234). This principle frames Action Science as a kind of critical theory consumed with taking stands about the values inherent in the research process. As a result, empirical claims are subject to rational criticism based in normative values in addition to scientific criticism based in values for objective truth.

I intend to argue that theories of mediation should adhere to an Action Science perspective. Because mediation practitioners face very significant communication problems, they need access to communication explanations to help solve these problems. For example, in divorce mediation, couples often launch into extraordinarily bitter disputes in which they present several different issues in very short statements. Mediators must make split-second decisions about when to intervene, and then how to pull apart those issues to provide insight to the disputants. Understanding how such timing processes work, and explaining why some interventions function better than others to improve problem solving would be very valuable information to mediators. Mediators single out communication as one of their most significant problems (Moore, 1986), and one that remains as the least well explained.

In addition to helping mediators, an Action Science orientation helps researchers learn more about communication processes. Since mediation begins in response to a need for rational discourse, the communication during initial phases of mediation can become quite emotional. Studying communication placed under such stressful limits quickly reveals its capacities. Thus, building theories to understand and explain communication phenomena in such contexts appears quite capable of revealing important insights.

An example of a research program in communication developed from Action Science values is the often-cited work on relational control by Watzlawick, Beavin, and Jackson (1967). While most recognize this work for its contribution to understanding the relationship between language and relational control, the real goal of this research focused on helping practitioners explain behavior disorders. This research stimulated tremendous interdisciplinary interest in studying relational control while also contributing significantly to our theoretical understanding of how language is used to negotiate relational parameters. Founding their program on practitioner needs assisted the authors theoretically as well as pragmatically by infusing tremendous energy into their research program.

Having forwarded the case that practitioner input is essential for communication theory construction in mediation, I must proceed by identifying an epistemological stance and a metatheoretical position most able to serve both practitioner and researcher interests. Accordingly below I mean to focus on the epistemological issues associated with creating communication theory in mediation.

EPISTEMOLOGICAL ISSUES

The communication discipline, like other social sciences, routinely struggles with the problem of determining what counts as knowledge. How should we account for social phenomena to avoid both compromising the integrity of the phenomena and trivializing the generalizability of our claims? Most attempts to identify "the best" epistemological stance (for example, Miller & Berger, 1978; Pearce, 1978) address the problem on internal philosophical grounds by arguing for or against a stance in the absence of significant external constraints. This chapter has already committed itself to the position that theory must evolve from the external anchor of practitioner needs. As a result, we must work to assess major epistemological positions according to the extent to which those positions are capable of yielding explanations or conceptual frameworks that adapt readily to practitioner problems.

Based on this constraint two epistemological criteria seem relevant: First, the conceptual apparatus ought to lend at least some level of generalizability to the research products so that practitioners can translate the research into practical recommendations. Even if the research simply suggests that some communication patterns appear more closely associated with some outcomes than others, then that research has given the practitioner general guidance that may not have existed previously. Second, the conceptual apparatus must also demonstrate some sensitivity to the manner in which contexts develop during mediation. The volatile nature of mediation can yield dramatic alterations in interaction patterns such that using an epistemological stance that glosses over the evolution of such patterns might not serve the mediator very well.

The struggle to manage both generalizability and contextual sensitivity mirrors the apparently ageless dispute over using an inductive, social constructionist perspective (for example, Berger & Luckmann, 1967), or a deductive, positivistic, covering-law approach (e.g., Berger, 1977). The constructionist position in communication research (e.g., Pearce & Cronen, 1980) conceptualizes communication phenomena as evolving continuously into different, changing social orders. As a result, the perspective remains ultimately sensitive to contextual evolution since constructionists really explore how communication builds social contexts. The final research product is an inductively derived, descriptive account of the way in which certain phenomena, for example, metaphors or language cues, evolved through the course of the event.

The covering-law approach, on the other hand, begins with a deductively formulated theory of the causal interrelationships between structural properties of communicative phenomena. The interest in generating laws that transcend contextual evolution necessitates conceptualizing phenomena at higher levels of abstraction that gloss over the moment to moment changes so revered by the constructionists. On the other hand, the generalizability afforded by the covering laws permits the researchers to claim that when a certain set of initial conditions prevail, X behavior causes Y response. Such causal claims helps research users develop strategies to implement X behaviors to create Y responses.

The dilemma created by my position that mediation theories in communication ought to achieve both contextual sensitivity and generalizability appears insurmountable given the radically contrasting epistemological positions of constructionism and positivism. That dilemma can be displayed more clearly by focusing on the manner in which each epistemology seeks to resolve the issue of control. For the positivist, control works as a centrally organizing principle for creating causal claims. Control over experimental procedures and theoretical principles lies exclusively with the experimenter as a means of isolating causal effects. If subjects gain any measure of control in manipulating initial conditions precision is compromised and the experimenter cannot argue for the integrity of the causal claims. As a result of this rigid control requirement, the experimenter must work with the phenomena at levels abstracted well beyond how the phenomena functions "in reality." The goal of this process is a complete, precise accounting of the forces causing the phenomena's functioning.

In the constructionist position, control is the exclusive province of the subjects. Conceptually, the researcher hopes to focus on those phenomena that appear to emerge as significant to subjects. Methodologically, more researcher intrusion into the process creates less naturalistic observations and compromises the integrity of the process. As a result of preserving subject control, the researcher works with the phenomena at very low levels of abstraction so the phenomena reveals its essential qualities as it functions "in reality." The goal of this research process is to provide a necessarily incomplete accounting of those phenomena in only those contexts that appeared most significant to the subjects.

I suggest that achieving functional levels of both generalizability and contextual sensitivity requires searching for a third alternative might work to integrate inductive and deductive epistemological positions to achieve these two objectives. This alternative approach is guided by the principle that researchers and subjects ought to share control over the course of the theory construction process. Again, Action Science assists us in searching for this alternative approach because it seeks to interrelate positivistic, empirical claims and constructionist, interpretative claims about mediation processes by beginning the research process descriptively and then using this understanding to build explanations of mediation phenomena. I shall now identify four developmental criteria that begin with interpretive accounts of mediation and move toward more explanatory accounts.

To begin understanding how mediation contexts are constructed communicatively, the inquiry process might profitably begin with researcher involvement in experienced mediator networks, and in consuming tapes and transcripts of actual mediation sessions. Mediators are very sensitive to communication patterns and how they evolve over time. Moving to the transcripts helps the researcher get a feel for these patterns in action. For example, in a recent article, a practitioner (McIsaac, 1986) identified several different family types in divorce mediation and some communication patterns associated with those family types. I have witnessed several of these same patterns in my examination of actual divorce mediation transcripts. Understanding mediators' perceptions of communicative processes and learning their values about mediation helps set the stage for building a descriptive base to remain sensitive to contextual changes in mediation.

After becoming integrated into the mediation process, the researcher can begin undertaking a program of systematic descriptive work capable of accounting for features of the mediation context. Since many types of descriptive perspectives are available for understanding communication phenomena in mediation, the researcher probably ought to select a perspective capable of accomplishing the functional goals outlined above. I find that mediators value language-based conceptual frameworks because ultimately they must translate the researcher's products into some verbal intervention. In addition, these frameworks generally deal with observable phenomena that generate considerable intuitive appeal. For example, focusing on social markers in speech (Scherer & Giles, 1982) might help identify disputant use of various interaction features that communicate more or less collaborative intentions. Such information might assist mediators in creating interventions to increase disputant use of such markers.

However, it is not enough simply to identify an interesting feature or two of interaction. The acquired framework should identify a sufficient range of features and their interrelationships to capture potential contextual changes in the mediation phenomena. For example, the social markers perspective (Scherer & Giles, 1982) might be expanded into a theoretical framework that integrates various types of markers to monitor changes in relational definitions, topics and issues, and strategic moves. By focusing on the interrelationships among markers we might learn that certain markers tend to covary with more or less cooperative interaction patterns.

As patterns of interrelationships evolve certain explanations of the mediation phenomena might begin to emerge. At this third step we begin to create the explanatory perspective advocated by the Action Science perspective. For example, why would we expect to see the observed interrelationships between the various social markers disputants were using in interaction? Many well developed theories of communication are available to draw upon to develop propositions about disputant-mediator interaction patterns. For example, Speech Accommodation Theory (Giles, Mulac, Bradac & Johnson, 1987) offers a well developed theoretical perspective for explaining interaction patterns. The process of convergence and divergence, conceptualizing the extent to which interactants reciprocate one another's interaction forms, might be used to explain conflict escalation and deescalation patterns. Selecting a theoretical framework allows the researcher to develop testable, falsifiable propositions, as advocated by the Action Science perspective. Such propositions seek to create generalizable knowledge that mediators can use to create more collaborative interaction among disputants.

The final criterion for developing this alternative approach relates to judging the "truth value" of the explanations. In the positivistic, covering-law approach, truth value is only a product of the empirical, theory-testing enterprise. Once the conceptual definitions are formulated, the research can only be challenged by questioning the operational definitions. This alternative, theory-in-use approach seeks to access researcher and practitioner values in assessing the phenomena, the conceptual framework, and the research methods used in the study. As suggested above, vigorous researcher-practitioner interaction lies at the heart of creating mediation questions of interest in this mid-range approach. As a result, the "truth value" of the claims lies in the intersubjective agreement between researchers and practitioners as they attempt to continuously examine and implement the research products.

These four criteria serve as the basis for achieving the two goals specified above for developing communication theory in mediation: context sensitivity and generalizability. Since practitioners and researchers work closely in the theory construction process, the propositions resulting from this process remain sensitive to contextual evolutions in the mediation interaction, while creating generalizable products easily translatable into intervention recommendations. The research process begins at very low levels of abstraction as a means of incorporating the integrity of the phenomena into the conceptual framework further enhancing its ability to pick up critical shifts in disputant-mediation interaction. ihus, an alternative, theory-in-use approach seems preferable to relying exclusively on a constructionist or a positivist perspective.

METATHEORETICAL ISSUES

Having created a framework of functional and epistemological parameters for developing communication theory in mediation, I shall now specify some of the substantive features that researchers might consider when building their theories of communication in a mediation context. I derived these features primarily from my communication research perspective, but in keeping with the functional criteria established previously, I have discussed these features with professional mediators who seem to find them most valuable. Nevertheless, the true value of these features lies in their scientific application in actual mediation settings.

In identifying the substantive features any communication theory of mediation ought to contain, I seek to explore the structural, functional, and process dimensions of communication as they relate to the mediation context. Structurally, the theory ought to account for the manner in which interactants create and develop the meaning or significance of their acts. As conflict intensity increases, the implications and assumptions disputants and mediators attach to one another's comments can be confusing. Coordinating meaning (Pearce & Cronen, 1980) is necessary to develop a resource interactants can use for decision making. Mediators and disputants displaying insensitivity to meaning differences stand to exacerbate conflict intensity.

The two levels of meaning that appear most relevant for coordinating perspectives include deep structure and surface structure. Littlejohn and Shailor (1986) tap deep structure issues when working to define the realities and assumptions underlying mediator and disputant interventions and strategies. Their model focuses on three forms of social reality: moral reality including assumptions about proper human life, conflict reality including meanings for conflict itself, and justice reality relating to ideals about equity in outcome. The research products consist of descriptions of each participant's discourse on each of the three forms of reality and their subdivisions. The authors then compared these realities and the disputant's apparent willingness or ability to understand one another's realities. The authors concluded that the mediators failed to prescribe a norm of justice that might have facilitated coordination of perspectives and ultimately greater cooperation and agreement. Thus, tapping the deep structure of meaning gives researchers access to factors influencing dispute outcomes.

In addition to monitoring deep structure, communication theories ought to provide some account of surface structure features of the interaction. These features tap the pragmatic ways in which interactants use communication to negotiate their social order. For example, rules theories of communication (see Donohue, Cushman & Nofsinger, 1980) account for the organization of talk and can be used to detect the manner in which interactants negotiate relational parameters or use conflict rituals to obscure their intentions. Since this is the level at which mediators spend most of their time trying to interpret the significance of disputant interaction forms, theories of communication in mediation ought to pay particular attention to these structural problems.

In addition to these structural issues, the theory development process ought to provide a functional account of communication. As suggested above, communication serves many functions in mediation. Among its most significant functions communication serves to coordinate expectations about goals (Craig, 1986). In mediation, disputants enter the process with formally stated, explicit goal differences, for example, child custody and visitation order creation or adjustment. They manage their communication as a means of achieving their agenda. In concert with these needs the mediator also faces the need to achieve specific goals. Organizations supporting mediators rely quite heavily on the mediator's ability to keep disputants from using more formal and expensive dispute resolutions options such as courts and social service personnel. Since disputants and mediators organize so much of their communication around goal achievement it seems reasonable to argue that any theory of communication in mediation ought to provide some conceptual apparatus to account for the strategic use of communication. Literature in compliance gaining, negotiation, and persuasion offers rich conceptual tools for understanding how interactants use communication to manage goal orientations.

As a result of these overt goal differences, interaction in mediation evokes significant displays of emotion. When people fight they weave a complex web of personal, relational issues into the substantive features of their disputes (see Hocker & Wilmot, 1984). This emotional intensity often functions as a vehicle to direct the course of the substantive issues in dispute (Thoennes & Pearson, 1985). For example, in one of the divorce mediation transcripts I used for my research, the disputants spent most of their time rehashing dirty laundry as a means of persuading the mediator that the other could not be trusted to adhere to any agreements. This intense, emotional negotiation served as the framework for creating the unusually specific parameters of the visitation agreement. This evidence supports the compelling conclusion that communication used in the service of relational/emotional goals ought to occupy an important place in any account of communication in mediation.

Process issues must also be considered when building communication theory of mediation from two perspectives. First, the theory ought to account for change over time as a means of remaining sensitive to contextual influences. How did the interaction move sequentially to create a sense of cooperativeness or competitiveness among disputants, for example. In many forms of mediation disputants move rapidly from issue to issue with the mediator trying to provide some direction to the chaos. Tracking this movement helps the researchers and mediator evaluate intervention decisions. Failing to account for this movement glosses over a process that moves very rapidly toward its conclusion.

The second dimension of process that appears relevant to understanding mediation relates to interaction coherence, or making connections between communication acts (Craig & Tracy, 1983). When responding strategically to any given context individuals use communication to conceal some intentions by revealing other goals that can obscure true intentions. In addition, as the conflict intensity and emotional nature of the interaction context expands, the intrusion of these relational messages into the process further complicates the research effort. For example, disputants negotiate relational control in many different forms including the use of politeness and deference patterns, the use of directive forms, attempts to structure the other's prior utterance, and so on. This multiple-action problem dictates that researchers provide some conceptual apparatus to capture coherence because this problem ties directly to the first process priority: charting change over time. Charting such change by focusing only on a few features of the interaction can provide misleading information to mediators who must use the research products to enhance cooperative interaction.

These metatheoretical parameters provide general guidelines for focusing on the substantive communication problems in mediation that may ultimately yield interesting insights about communication and may also help mediators work more effectively with disputants. To illustrate the manner in which these functional, epistemological and metatheoretical issues can contribute to communication theory construction in mediation, I will outline our communication research program in mediation. Hopefully, this discussion will assist in revealing how communication theory can contribute significantly to mediators wishing to gain access to the "magic that happens once I close the door and begin the process."

AN ALTERNATIVE RESEARCH PERSPECTIVE

Our mediation research program (Donohue, Diez & Weider-Hatfield, 1984; Donohue, Allen & Burrell, 1985; Donohue, in press) focused on divorce mediation since we felt that this form of mediation was gaining considerable attention around the country, and because children were the beneficiaries of increased disputant cooperation. We began our efforts by getting involved in divorce mediation organizations and by acquiring a set of audio recordings of divorce mediations from Jessica Pearson's National Science Foundation research project (see Pearson & Thoennes, 1984). After extensive discussions with mediators and examination of the tapes we discovered that they were very interested in learning which mediator strategies, in response to which disputant negotiation strategies, help create a more cooperative dispute resolution context.

To address this problem we selected theory in communicative competence (see Bostrom, 1984) arguing that competent mediators demonstrate two important skills: accurate interpretation of disputant communication patterns as a means of timing interventions, and maintaining a broad range of performance, or intervention skills capable of increasing disputant cooperative interaction. Interventions that sought to establish functional levels of relational distance, increase interaction coherence to clarify issues and establish a productive structure for decision making were judged as the most critical intervention skills.

To begin our program we transcribed 21 of these actual divorce mediation tapes, selecting ten that ended in agreement, and 11 that ended in no agreement. After coding both disputant negotiation strategies and mediation intervention strategies we learned that the coherence strategies discriminated most between the agreement conditions. Mediators concentrating on pulling out issues in the face of intense disputant attacks seemed most capable of creating more integrative interaction. In addition, mediators using a full range of coherence tactics appeared more able to control the conflict and move the disputants forward more productively.

We designed this program from its inception to adhere to the criteria listed above for building theories of mediation. Functionally, our involvement in mediation circles gave us a set of glasses through which we gained a strong sense of which disputant and which mediator phenomena were important concerns to mediators. We decided that extensive mediator/researcher interaction would have the greatest potential for building stronger insights about communication as well as demonstrating the greater capacity to aid the mediation practice. For example, we have been able to isolate specific intervention and timing tactics that function quite effectively for mediators in redirecting dysfunctional disputant interaction patterns. At the same time we have learned a great deal about language structures that characterize cooperative and competitive, aggressive discourse.

Mediators find this kind of information very useful because, epistemologically, we made the decision to create products that were sufficiently generalizable so mediators could establish some reasonable priorities about selecting and timing their interventions. This was accomplished by comparing mediation tactics across the agreement–no agreement conditions and by searching for those interventions discriminating most between those two contexts. This study design did not permit us to claim causal relationships for the language variables we used for discrimination; rather, we chose to view these results as preliminary to a more well controlled, field experiment in a manner consistent with McGillicuddy,

Welton and Pruitt's (1987) study of different models of mediation. Future research will involve developing a set or propositions from the communicative
competence theory and testing them in a field experiment setting. Nevertheless,
we came away from the research with a picture of how agreement and no
agreement mediators and disputants differ communicatively from one another.
To track contextual change we performed time-series analyses of the data to
further complete our understanding of agreement condition differences. That
information became very useful for mediators in creating intervention policy
decisions.

The major metatheoretical weakness of our research centers around the lack of
information about deep structures of meaning. By focusing on surface level
language variables we integrated disputant and mediator goals into the theory and
sought to take account in multiple ways of their relational development, as well.
However, this approach focuses on the trees and forsakes the forest. We never
accessed a more global understanding of the assumptions and values mediators
and disputants used to found their tactics and strategies. Relying on Littlejohn's
work to accomplish this goal might prove valuable in future research.

CONCLUSIONS

Clearly, the most significant value proposed by this paper centers around a need
to involve practitioners in the theory construction process. The remaining epistemological and metatheoretical issues proposed in this paper reflect my academic values regarding the most productive way of creating theory and research
useful to practitioners. And, I know better than to believe that my values regarding these two issues will disseminate rapidly because academics cling religiously
to their epistemological and metatheoretical stances. However, I believe that
academics are probably more open to redirecting their research functionally to
make it useful to audiences that really need it. Mediators need a well developed
research foundation in communication. The perspective used to satisfy this need
probably makes less difference than acknowledging that the need exists and must
be addressed. I made the decision early on to begin working to satisfy this need,
and this paper reflects the epistemological and metatheoretical positions that
seem to have clicked with both my theoretical interests and mediators' practical
needs.

Having made this apology it must be noted that I remain quite surprised about
how much our theory has developed as a result of practitioner input. For example, our understanding of how language is used to negotiate interpersonal relationships as well as issues in disputes could only have emerged as a result of
extensive practitioner input. Unfortunately, most scholars in communication
receive training that places little value on practitioner input to the research
process. Evidence for this claim pervades our journals since most of the articles
contain precious little that translates directly into knowledge useful to practitioners. Application and theory development seem to be viewed as opposite ends

on the "serious academic enterprise" continuum, despite Kurt Lewin's claim that there is nothing more practical than a good theory. I now believe that "good theory," at least in mediation, cannot be developed unless mediators and related practitioners are involved in the process. I hope our research makes one small step in that direction.

7

Managing Conflict before It Happens: The Role of Accounts

Robert J. Bies

For most managers, allocating resources to subordinates is a central activity (Pfeffer, 1981). For example, on an annual basis, managers make budget and salary decisions, and they regularly make decisions on specific subordinate requests for additional money or time. In many situations, however, the manager may be unable or unwilling to "satisfy" the subordinate's resource demands. As a result, the subordinate may be disappointed, if not frustrated and angry, and such feelings create a situation of potential conflict (Thomas, 1976).

Even though the manager decides not to satisfy a subordinate's resource demands, there is no necessary relationship between the "objective" characteristics of that decision and the subordinate's conflict behavior (Deutsch, 1969). Rather, whether the situation evolves into a conflict episode depends on the subordinate's conceptualization of the situation (Thomas, 1976). Of particular importance in the conceptualization process is the subordinate's assessment of the manager's motives and intentions (Thomas & Pondy, 1977). For example, assuming the decision is detrimental to the subordinate's interests, the subordinate is more likely to get angry at the manager when the decision is perceived as intentionally detrimental rather than unintentional, and perpetrated for socially unacceptable rather than socially acceptable reasons (Averill, 1982). Moreover, such feelings of anger are more likely to elicit an aggressive response on the part of the subordinate (Ferguson & Rule, 1983), which may induce or escalate conflict between the manager and subordinate.

To mitigate any conflict-inducing responses on the part of the subordinate, a manager often provides an *account* (Bies, 1987a), which is an explanation with a justification for the decision (Bies, 1987b). For example, the manager might provide an excuse to mitigate his or her responsibility for the decision; or, the manager might appeal to a shared value or goal, such as "efficiency," to justify

My thanks to the following people for their valuable assistance in the evolution of this paper: Max Bazerman, Robert Baron, Linda Putnam, Deborah Weider-Hatfield, Afzalur Rahim, Susan Smith, and the two anonymous conference reviewers.

the decision; or, the manager could claim that the subordinate's initial expectations were "unrealistic," suggesting the outcome is better than the subordinate had initially thought.

Although managers typically provide an account subsequent to the decision making process (Bies, 1987a), the manager may provide it *prior to* the decision as well (Bies, 1987b), or what is commonly referred to as a disclaimer (Hewitt & Stokes, 1975). For example, in anticipation of a possible unfavorable outcome, a manager may claim that he or she *might* be "unable to satisfy the subordinate's demands because of possible budget cutbacks by top management." Whether the account is provided anticipatorily or concurrently with the decision, the manager has provided the subordinate with a more favorable schema to interpret the decision and its consequences. By providing a more favorable interpretation of the situation, the manager may actually resolve the conflict before it happens.

In this chapter I argue that an account is a strategy of conflict management in that it can mitigate any negative responses on the part of the subordinate which may induce or escalate conflict. While a similar argument was proposed by conflict researchers over a decade ago, (Horai, 1977; Thomas & Pondy, 1977), surprisingly little theorizing has been done on the role of accounts in conflict management. Thus, my purpose here is to provide the initial step in filling this gap in models of conflict management, and, as a result, broaden the domain of theory and research on communication and conflict in organizations.

The chapter is divided into two sections. The first presents a topology of accounts. Drawing on research from a variety of domains (for example, justice, negotiation, anger, aggression), the empirical evidence is reviewed and situational factors which influence the effectiveness of accounts are identified. The second section will focus on implications for theory and research on communication and conflict in the manager-subordinate relationship.

A TOPOLOGY OF ACCOUNTS AND A REVIEW OF THE EMPIRICAL EVIDENCE

In making an unfavorable resource allocation, a manager may become the target of subordinate anger and retaliation—reactions which are likely to induce or escalate conflict. Bies (1987b) suggests that the severity of such reactions are primarily influenced by three factors: (a) the manager's *apparent responsibility* for the unfavorable allocation; (b) the manager's *motives* for making the decision; and (c) the *undesirability* of the decision. If a manager could influence the subordinate's perceptions of any or all of these three factors with the use of an account, then there should be a mitigation of those subordinate responses which may induce or escalate conflict (for example, anger, feelings of injustice, retaliation). Bies (1987a) proposed three categories of accounts which parallel the factors outlined above. In this section, the empirical evidence for each type of account is reviewed, and situational factors which influence the effectiveness of accounts are identified.

Lessening Apparent Responsibility: Causal Account

A *causal account* is an explanation containing a reason to mitigate the manager's responsibility for an unfavorable outcome, or as it is more commonly known: an excuse (Scott & Lyman, 1968). For example, a manager could claim that it was "a decline in the economy which forced budget cutbacks or salary freezes" rather than a deliberate action on his or her part. The purpose of a causal account is to suggest that the situation left the manager no other choice in making the decision. Since the manager had no other alternatives to the chosen action, a causal account claiming mitigating circumstances should reduce the amount of blame attributed to the manager by the subordinate (Shaver, 1985). As a result, there should be less disapproval of the manager, and less anger directed toward the manager.

The empirical evidence supports this line of reasoning. In a series of laboratory experiments, Bies and Shapiro (1987; in press) examined the effects of a causal account claiming mitigating circumstances on people's reactions to a variety of unfavorable outcomes (for example, budget cutback, no job offer). In each of these studies, it was found that the presence of a causal account for an unfavorable allocation decision reduced people's feelings of unfairness and disapproval of the decision maker relative to the absence of a causal account in a similar situation. These findings from the laboratory have been replicated by Bies and his colleagues in a series of field studies of subordinates' reactions to news of a rejected resource proposal (Bies & Shapiro; in press; Bies, Shapiro, & Cummings, 1987), and job candidate reactions to receiving no job offer (Bies & Moag, 1986).

Research on anger and aggression provides corroborating evidence in support of this line of reasoning. For example, in a series of studies that pertained to excuses given for a social transgression, Weiner, Amirkhan, Folkes, and Verette (1987) found that giving a "good" excuse—that is, one which claimed mitigating circumstances—lessened the anger of the wronged party than when a "bad" excuse (no mitigating circumstances) or no excuse was provided (cf. Averill, 1982). In addition, the good excuse subjects had a less unfavorable evaluation of the harmdoer than did subjects in the other two conditions, a finding which is corroborated by other studies (e.g., Rule, Dyck, & Nesdale, 1978; Zillman, Cantor, & Day, 1976).

Providing a causal account also acts to mitigate the behavioral responses that can escalate conflict. For example, providing a causal account has been found to mitigate potential conflict-inducing responses such as complaints (Zillman et al., 1976; Folger & Martin, in press) and retaliation (Mallick & McCandless, 1966). In addition to mitigating conflict-inducing responses, a causal account may also influence the wrong party to act in a more conciliatory way toward the harmdoer (Weiner et al., 1987).

Framing Motives: Ideological Account

An *ideological account* is an explanation containing an appeal to basic belief systems based on important shared values and goals (Bies, 1987b). For example, in imposing a budget cut or a salary freeze, a manager might claim that such action was taken to maintain "competitive superiority" or "organizational survival." The purpose of an ideological account is to place the decision in a broader normative framework that will exonerate the manager—that is, make the decision appear more legitimate (Snyder et al., 1983). Although an ideological account suggests that the manager had more discretion in the decision that in a causal account, such discretion was guided by higher-order motives. By focusing on the propriety of his or her motives, a manager may be able to lessen the subordinate's feelings of disapproval, which may reduce the possibility of conflict (Thomas & Pondy, 1977).

One study provides support for this line of reasoning. In a study on aggression, Nesdale, Rule, and McAra (1975) examined the effects of information which suggests an aggressive action was due to a good motive or a bad motive. After witnessing the action, the subjects were informed that the harmdoer had either a good or bad motive for his actions. Nesdale et al. (1975) found that subjects were more likely to approve of the harmful action when an explanation of the harmdoer's actions suggested a good motive for the action.

In addition to focusing on the propriety of the manager's motives, an ideological account may make salient the shared goals of the manager and subordinate. For example, by appealing to a shared goal of "competitive superiority" as the reason for budget cutbacks, a manager is attempting to focus the subordinate's attention on their common purpose—that is, "defeating" the external "enemy." Such an external focusing of attention may act to unite the manager and subordinate (Coser, 1956), and thus minimize the expression of conflict behavior between themselves (compare Sherif, Harvey, White, Hood, & Sherif, 1961).

Framing Consequences: Referential Account

A *referential account* is an explanation that attempts to minimize the undesirability of the negative consequences by providing a more favorable referent standard to evaluate an outcome (Bies, 1987b). There are three basic types of referential accounts: social, temporal, and aspirational. First, using social comparison information (compare Festinger, 1954), a manager could point to other people who received worse outcomes. For example, a manager could point out that "your 10% budget cut is a lot less than the company wide average cut of 20%." Second, a manager could provide temporal comparison information to suggest better future outcomes (compare Albert, 1977). For example, in context of budget cuts, the manager could suggest that "maybe next year's budget will be better." A variation of the temporal reference is the hypothetical "what if" simulation scenarios like "the budget cut *could* have been worse" (compare Kahneman & Tversky, 1982). Finally, in an attempt to recalibrate a person's aspirations, a manager could suggest that the subordinate's initial expectations were "unrealistic." As such, the outcome was "*really* much better" than the subordinate had initially thought.

Only a few studies have examined the effects of referential accounts. In a laboratory simulation study, Bies (1982) had one group of subjects receive information in which the decision maker suggested that the recipient might receive better "sales contract" or "budget allocation" in the future. Another group of subjects did not receive such information. As predicted, those subjects who received a referential account with information about future outcomes expressed less feelings of injustice and characterized the news less negatively than those subjects who did not receive such information.

A series of studies by Folger and his colleagues have examined the effects of providing possible "what if" scenarios to what actually happened as an alternative temporal comparison point (Folger & Martin, in press; Folger, Rosenfield, Rheume & Martin, 1983; Folger, Rosenfield & Robinson, 1983). In each of these studies, subjects were provided an alternative scenario in which imaginable outcomes were either (a) as bad or worse than those produced by existing arrangements (low referent), or (b) more desirable (high referent). As predicted by Folger and his colleagues, they found the amount of anger and resentment was less in the "low referent" case than in the "high referent" case. Extrapolating from these findings, a manager may be able to mitigate conflict-inducing responses by suggesting that an unfavorable allocation "could have been worse."

Factors Which Influence the Effectiveness of Accounts

The effectiveness of accounts is influenced by three key situational factors. These three factors are (1) the timing of the account, (2) the perceived adequacy of the account, and (3) the perceived sincerity of the account giver.

Timing of the Account

The first factor that can influence the effectiveness of an account is its timing. Timing refers to whether account is provided before or after the allocation decision. For example, prior to any decision, a manager could suggest to a subordinate that "top management is considering budget cutbacks, so the resources may be unavailable." Or, after the decision, the manager could provide a similar account that "top management disallowed your request due to budget cutbacks."

Three studies have focused on the influence of the timing of an account. In a study on aggression, Zillman, Cantor, & Day (1976) had subjects provoked by a rude experimenter and informed of mitigating circumstances for such behavior

(a) before provocation, (b) after provocation, or (c) not at all. Physiological data revealed that prior knowledge of mitigation reduced excitatory responses the most, followed by those subjects who received that information after the provocation and not at all, respectively. Retaliatory behavior in the form of complaints about the experimenter were significantly lower in the prior mitigation condition relative to the other two conditions. In the conditions in which mitigating information was supplied after the provocation or not at all, there was no significant difference in the amount of retaliatory behavior.

A similar influence of timing has been found in other studies. For example, Johnson and Rule (1986) found that angered participants evaluated their provoker more favorably and retaliated less when they were informed of mitigating circumstances before rather than after being insulted. Kremer and Stephens (1983) compared the effects of providing mitigating information immediately after or several minutes after the provocation on retaliation behavior. They found that the delay of mitigation information eliminated the conflict-reducing aspect of an account.

Taken together, these results suggest that providing an account prior to the unfavorable outcome is likely to be more effective in reducing conflict than providing it after the decision. Moreover, the results suggest that the longer the delay of an account, the more diluted its effects on mitigating responses which contribute to inducing or escalating conflict.

Perceived Adequacy of the Account

The effectiveness of an account can also be influenced by the perceived adequacy of the account (Bies, 1987b), that is, the perceived sufficiency and credibility of the reasons given by the manager. For example, in two studies—a laboratory experiment and a field study—Bies and Shapiro (in press) found that although a causal account reduced feelings of anger and injustice, such effects were mediated by the perceived adequacy of the account. These findings are consistent with research by Folger and his colleagues (Folger, Rosenfield, & Robinson, 1983; Folger & Martin, in press), which shows that providing adequate, not inadequate, justification for changes in allocation procedures mitigates feelings of discontent toward the decision maker.

Perceived Sincerity of the Account Giver

Apart from judgments of adequacy, the manager's apparent sincerity in communicating the account is another important factor (Bies, 1987b). For example, in a study on dyadic negotiation, Rubin, Brockner, Eckenrode, Enright, & Johnson-George (1981) unexpectedly found that a negotiator's causal account claiming mitigating circumstances resulted in higher negative ratings and more blocking from the other negotiator. The researchers concluded that a causal account did not have the predicted effects because the one negotiator may have appeared insincere. In other words, the appearance of insincerity may undermine the manager-subordinate bargaining relationship (compare Gruder, 1971), and, as a result, become a contributing factor to organizational conflict (Baron, 1985; in press [a]).

Summary

A review of empirical studies provided converging evidence that an account can mitigate responses which may induce or escalate conflict. In both laboratory and field settings, a causal account reduced feelings of anger and disapproval, and retaliatory behavior. Although less research attention has focused on the ideological and referential accounts, the pattern of results was similar to that of a causal account.

The review suggests, however, that the effectiveness of accounts is influenced by three key situational factors. The three factors are (1) the timing of the account, (2) the perceived adequacy of the account, and (3) the apparent sincerity of the account giver. The next section will focus on the implications of this review of empirical evidence on accounts and factors which influence their effectiveness.

IMPLICATIONS FOR THEORY AND RESEARCH ON COMMUNICATION AND CONFLICT

The use of accounts as a strategy of conflict management was first suggested by conflict researchers over a decade ago (see, for example, Horai, 1977; Thomas & Pondy, 1977). However, the strategic implications of accounts have largely been ignored in current models of conflict management. This omission is somewhat surprising since managers frequently give accounts with the intent to reduce, if not eliminate, the potential for conflict when they deliver news of an unfavorable outcome (Bies, 1987a). Furthermore, since managers spend up to 20 percent of their time managing conflict (Thomas & Schmidt, 1976), and also place an emphasis on efficiency in conflict management (Lissak & Sheppard, 1983), it is likely they rely heavily on the use of accounts because they are easily provided.

A review of empirical research on accounts provides additional evidence that such an omission is not warranted. Research findings from a variety of domains suggest that if a manager provides an account along with news of an unfavorable outcome, then he or she may reduce subordinates' feelings of anger and retaliatory behavior. This assumes, of course, that the account is timely, adequate, and given in a sincere manner. As such, the present analysis provides strong support for the argument that an account should be viewed as a strategy of conflict management, particularly at the early stages of a conflict episode.

The major premise underlying this argument is that an unfavorable resource allocation will *not* necessarily escalate into a manager-subordinate conflict. That is, in some cases, an account may actually resolve conflict before it happens. For example, after the unfavorable outcome has been allocated by the manager, the subordinate may not have conceptualized the situation in terms of conflict. If a manager provides an account at that time, and it is perceived as adequate and sincere, then the subordinate may find the situation acceptable and no basis for conflict. However if a manager fails to provide an account, or the account is perceived as untimely or inadequate or insincere, then there is an increased likelihood of conflict between the manager and subordinate.

This is not to suggest that an account can or will always resolve conflict before it happens. For example, in a situation where the resource is very important to the subordinate, or the manager-subordinate relationship is not based on trust, an unfavorable outcome is very likely to result in conflict. In such situations, an account may only lessen, but not eliminate, conflict between the manager and subordinate. Alternatively, as suggested by the research findings of Rubin et al. (1981), an account may escalate conflict in some situations. Thus, as a general case, it is argued that an account acts to shape the nature and direction of a conflict episode; however, in some cases, the use of an account may eliminate the conflict altogether.

Given a manager's account can mitigate conflict-inducing responses by the subordinate, further research needs to examine which aspects of the account are more important in influencing these responses. For example, are accounts processed in an almost "mindless" fashion (cf. Langer, 1978)? That is, is it the "form" of the account (for example, sincerity) which is important rather than the "substance" of the account (for example, the specific type of account)? Or, are the form and substance of the account inextricably linked together? For example, acting like "intuitive jurists" (Hamilton, 1980), do people first analyze the reasons given in the account, and then incorporate informational cues such as the account giver's sincerity to confirm or disconfirm the validity of the reasons provided in the account? Answers to such questions are necessary to more fully understand the influence of accounts as a conflict management strategy.

The use of accounts as a conflict management strategy must also take into consideration the potential tradeoffs confronting the manager. On the one hand, an account may prevent the escalation of conflict, which can be important for the stability of the manager-subordinate relationship. In addition, subordinates may feel they have a "right" to an account for an unfavorable outcome as part of a "social contract" governing the manager-subordinate relationship (compare Bies & Moag, 1986; Rousseau, 1987). As a result, the manager may be "required" to give an account to maintain the subordinate's support (Bies et al., 1987), which suggests another functional aspect of accounts.

On the other hand, a manager's account may also act to lessen the subordinate's motivation to search for alternative solutions to the rejected proposal (compare Goffman, 1952). As a result, an account may have demotivating implications and undermine some of the constructive aspects of conflicts such as creative problem solving (Deutsch, 1973; Thomas, 1976). In addition, if a subordinate believes that he or she has been deceived by the manager's account, then the resultant feelings of betrayal and distrust of the manager may lead to retaliation and the escalation of conflict. The possible tradeoffs in the use of accounts represents another direction for future research on communication and conflict.

Finally, the analysis presented in this chapter focused on the use of accounts as part of a one-way communication process between the manager and subordinate. That is, a manager communicates an account to the subordinate. While many organizational communications during conflict fit this pattern (Putnam & Poole, in press), in some cases the communication of accounts involves a two-way process. For example, in response to the manager's account of an unfavorable resource allocation, a subordinate may counter with an alternative account to relegitimate his or her initial position, or to attempt to delegitimate the manager's position (compare Martin, Scully, & Levitt, 1986). Following this line of reasoning, whether a manager's account will mitigate conflict-inducing responses may depend, in part, on the nature or presence of the subordinate's account. Thus, as an extension of the argument presented in this paper, the interplay between manager and subordinate accounts represents another direction for future research.

CONCLUSION

This chapter has argued that an account is a strategy of conflict management. While accounts can be used to deceive people (see Bies, 1987b, for an analysis of the moral implications raised by the use of accounts), I am not advocating or endorsing the use of accounts for such purposes. Rather, I am arguing that managers *do* use accounts when they communicate news of an unfavorable outcome (Bies, 1987a), and such explanations play a role in the management of conflict in a manager-subordinate relationship. Indeed, in some cases, the use of an account may actually resolve conflict before it happens.

8

Lag Sequential Analyses of Mediator-Spouse and Husband-Wife Interaction in Successful and Unsuccessful Divorce Mediation

Tricia S. Jones

The process of mediation involves persuasion and information exchange for the development of perceptual congruence leading to the formation of agreement between disputants who are usually at impasse. As such, mediation is inherently a communication process that should be studied in terms of significant communication strategies and tactics related to success.

This study examines patterns of interaction between mediators and spouses and husbands and wives involved in successful and unsuccessful child custody divorce mediation. The potential utility of this research includes: (1) providing empirical evidence of disputants' responses to mediator behaviors in successful and unsuccessful mediation, (2) indicating patterns of interaction between disputants that may require mediator intervention, and (3) developing practical suggestions for training and application in divorce mediation.

EFFECTIVE MEDIATOR COMMUNICATION IN DIVORCE MEDIATION

The mediator's purpose is to facilitate communication between the parties and to guide the parties into cooperative, problem-solving orientations to resolving substantive issues in dispute (Jones, 1985). Divorce mediation presents a true test of a mediator's effectiveness. Unlike traditional labor-management mediation, divorce mediation involves parties who are often ignorant of mediation (Pearson, Thoennes, & Vanderkooi, 1982), are embroiled in a painful process of

The author would like to thank Dr. Jessica Pearson, Director of the Research Unit of the Association of Family & Conciliation Courts, Denver, Co., and the Divorce Mediation Research Project (1981–1984) for providing the original audiotapes used in this study.

relational termination (Haynes, 1981; Irving, 1981), are defensive due to loss of face incurred in the dissolution of the relationship (Bohannon, 1970; Kressel, Jaffee, Tuchman, Watson, & Deutsch, 1980), and are prone to adopt distributive orientations (Haynes, 1982; Milne, 1978). Conflict issues in divorce exacerbate the difficulty of the mediation. The issues often combine relational and substantive concerns (McKenry, Herrman, & Weber, 1979), affect other people (usually children) involved in the divorce (Coogler, Weber, & McKenry, 1979), and concern the future as well as the present relationship between the parties (Meyer & Schlissel, 1982).

Based on observations of divorce mediation, Pearson (1981) presents a summary of effective mediator behaviors in this context: (1) developing a habit of agreement early in mediation by having disputants agree on procedural and structural matters, (2) reinforcing agreement making by verbally rewarding all interim agreements, (3) instilling a sense of commitment to mediation by noting the benefits of compromise and the disadvantages of the adversarial process, (4) breaking impasse by suggesting solutions, (5) allowing for the controlled venting of anger, and (6) utilizing caucuses to discuss motives and positions.

The mediator's role in facilitating accurate information exchange has proven to be a critical determinant of success in divorce mediation (Donohue, Allen, & Burrell, 1985; Slaiku, Culler, Pearson, & Thoennes, 1985). Donohue, Allen, and Burrell (1986) hypothesized that successful mediators achieve more integration following evaluation (complementing, enforcing interaction rules, commenting on disputants' commitment to the mediation process) and framing (giving information, restatement, offering suggestions, providing reflection, rephrasing) interventions than unsuccessful mediators, and tested this hypothesis using lag sequential analysis. Their results indicated that successful mediators solicited cooperative responses following their requesting, framing, and evaluation interventions when issues were discussed, and when proposal developments were suggested. These results provide support for the argument that disputants' responses to mediator interventions differ in successful versus unsuccessful sessions. However, the general nature of the categories used in this analysis prohibits the indication of patterns of disputants' responses to mediator behaviors that comprise the general categories.

While the previously reported research indicates expectations for general patterns of interaction between mediators and disputants for effective, or successful, mediation, two problems remain. First, this research does not fully examine patterns of interaction in unsuccessful mediation. It cannot be taken for granted that patterns of interaction in unsuccessful mediation are merely the reverse of patterns in successful mediation. Identification of mediator-disputant patterns of interaction in unsuccessful mediation may additionally be illustrative of adequate and inadequate mediator interventions. Second, this research does not investigate disputant-mediator interaction, or the behaviors disputants use that result in certain mediator responses. Again, a comparison of such patterns in successful and unsuccessful mediation may further the understanding of effective and ineffective mediator interventions to counteract, deemphasize, encourage, or eradicate specific disputant behaviors. Thus, the following research questions are presented:

RQ #1: In successful divorce mediation, what are the dominant patterns of mediator-spouse interaction?

RQ #2: In unsuccessful divorce mediation, what are the dominant patterns of mediator-spouse interaction?

RQ #3: What are the similarities and differences between dominant patterns of mediator-spouse interaction in successful and unsuccessful divorce mediation?

RQ #4: In successful divorce mediation, what are the dominant patterns of spouse-mediator interaction?

RQ #5: In unsuccessful divorce mediation, what are the dominant patterns of spouse-mediator interaction?

RQ #6: What are the similarities and differences between dominant patterns of spouse-mediator interaction in successful and unsuccessful divorce mediation?

DISPUTANT COMMUNICATION IN DIVORCE MEDIATION

Disputant orientations in negotiation and mediation are usually discussed as being cooperative or competitive. Authors have labelled these orientations in the following ways: pro-social versus antisocial (Roloff, 1976), expressive versus instrumental (Fitzpatrick & Indvik, 1982), and integrative versus distributive (Walton & McKersie, 1965), with the latter being the most common. An integrative orientation is cooperative with an emphasis on the voluntary exchange of open and accurate information and the active adoption of a problem-solving stance. A distributive orientation is competitive with an emphasis on avoiding accurate information exchange and adopting a win-lose stance to maximize individual gains. However, it should be noted that these orientations are not truly dichotomous or mutually exclusive. Disputants may act in a more-or-less integrative or distributive manner and disputants may interchange integrative and distributive behaviors throughout an interaction.

Integrative behaviors are conducive to effective conflict management while distributive behaviors are not. Integrative behaviors are perceived more positively by the receiver (Ruble & Thomas, 1976), are more likely to promote open and honest communication (Deutsch, 1969; 1973), are more likely to facilitate attitude change (Walton, 1965), and are more likely to increase the potential for conflict management (Lewis & Fry, 1977; Theye & Seiler, 1979) than distributive behaviors. Conversely, distributive behaviors lead to an escalation of destructive conflict interaction (Deutsch, 1960) and lower joint outcomes (Fisher, 1972), as well as encourage negative attribution behaviors from the other (Sillars, 1980).

Integrative behaviors consist of supportive communication, integrative information exchange, and problem solving. Supportive communication involves expressions of support, empathy, agreement, common interests, and acceptance of responsibility. Most marital conflict research reveals that reciprocity of supportive communication is the most critical factor in distinguishing between distressed and nondistressed relationships (Birchler, Weiss, & Vincent, 1975; Gottman, 1979; Mettetal & Gottman, 1980). Integrative information-exchange behaviors—description, disclosure, requests for information, and summarization—indicate good faith (Fahs, 1981), decrease defensiveness (Johnson & Dustin, 1970), and increase understanding (Danet, 1980). Problem-solving behaviors, presentation and evaluation of solutions, communicate a willingness to act cooperatively (Donohue, Diez, & Weider-Hatfield, 1984) and may induce reciprocal behavior (Gulliver, 1979).

Distributive behaviors may be either direct or indirect (Sillars, Pike, Jones, & Redmon, 1983). Direct distributive behaviors—faulting, rejection, prescription, and disagreement—are blatant attacks designed to persuade or coerce the opponent into submission. Because of their explicitness, they escalate the conflict into an intense, interpersonal battle (Gouran & Baird, 1972). Indirect distributive tactics—hostile questioning or joking, presumptive attribution, and avoidance of responsibility—are designed to indicate displeasure with the process or the opponent. Attribution statements, the most commonly researched indirect tactic, are usually reciprocated (Gottman, 1979).

Three patterns of interaction between disputants in divorce mediation are of interest: (1) reciprocity of integrative behaviors, (2) reciprocity of distributive behaviors, and (3) complementarity of behaviors, or a pattern involving the consistent use of one type of behavior (integrative or distributive) following the other (integrative or distributive) that may indicate dominance of one disputant over the other (Emery & Ellis, 1980; Fisher, 1983). To discover which patterns characterize successful versus unsuccessful divorce mediation, the following research questions are presented:

RQ #7: In successful divorce mediation, what are the dominant patterns of husband-wife interaction?

RQ #8: In unsuccessful divorce mediation, what are the dominant patterns of husband-wife interaction?

RQ #9: What are the similarities and differences between dominant patterns of husband-wife interaction in successful and unsuccessful divorce mediation?

RQ #10: In successful divorce mediation, what are the dominant patterns of wife-husband interaction?

RQ #11: In unsuccessful divorce mediation, what are the dominant patterns of wife-husband interaction?

RQ #12: What are the similarities and differences between dominant patterns of wife-husband interaction for successful and unsuccessful divorce mediation?

METHOD

Measurement

Audiotaped interaction of 36 (18 successful and 18 unsuccessful) divorce mediation sessions were coded using a revised version of the Mediation Process Analysis (Slaiku, Luckett, & Costin-Meyers, 1983). Lag sequential analyses were performed on the mediator-spouse, spouse-mediator, husband-wife, and wife-husband interactions for successful and unsuccessful sessions. Success was operationalized as achievement of a formal agreement signed by the parties.

Audiotapes of the 36 mediation sessions used for data in this study were gathered from divorce mediation programs in Los Angeles, Hartford, and Minneapolis. A total of 83 sessions had been recorded. The 36 sessions used for analysis were selected according to the following decision rules: (1) Only single-session mediations were used in order to eliminate confounding effects from occurrences between mediation sessions. (2) Since the average length of the sessions was approximately one and one half hours, only tapes ranging from 30 minutes to two hours were used. (3) Sessions involving substantial dialogue by attorneys or other parties involved in, but not central to, the dispute were not used. (4) Only sessions conducted in English were used. (5) Only sessions of adequate audibility were used.

Three coders were trained in unitizing and content coding. The unit of analysis in this study was the thought unit, defined as the minimum meaningful utterance having a beginning and ending. The thought unit is typically a simple sentence or independent clause in which the subject and/or predicate are expressed or implied. The thought unit was selected for use in this research because it is more congruent with the conceptual nature of naturally occurring interaction and has proven superior to other forms of unitizing for such data.

The revised Mediation Process Analysis (MPA) was used for content coding. The MPA consists of seven general categories: process, information, summarize-other, self-disclosure, attribution, solutions, and agreements. Twenty-seven subcategories comprise the general categories. For a more thorough description of the MPA, see Jones (1985).

The coders were trained in unitizing and content coding in a three-stage process. First, coders were given copies of the MPA and a list of unitizing decision rules and examples. Second, coders practiced unitizing and content coding on transcripts of mediation interaction. Third, coders practiced unitizing and content coding on audiotapes of mediation interaction.

At the end of this training process, which took approximately 12 weeks, reliability on unitizing and content coding was tested using Scott's (1955) *pi*. Unitizing reliability was .97. Interrater reliability for each general category was: process, .95; information, .93; summarize-other, .87; self-disclosure, .90; attribution, .90; solutions, .89; and agreements, .91. Overall content reliability was .91. Since unitizing and content reliability exceeded previously established levels of acceptability (.85), the coding of actual data began. Subsequent reliability checks on unitizing and content coding were conducted throughout the coding process to insure against slippage. All subsequent reliability checks proved satisfactory.

Analysis

Lag sequential analyses were performed on the mediator-spouse, spouse-mediator, husband-wife, and wife-husband interaction for the successful sessions and for the unsuccessful sessions. In lag sequential analysis, a criterion behavior is selected and the transitional probabilities of occurrence of all other behaviors are calculated with respect to the criterion behavior at LAG 1 to MAXLAG (Sackett, 1974). The transitional probabilities are computed as z scores. At p $\leq .05$, z scores indicating statistical significance are $\geq \pm 1.96$.

Calculations of z scores were computed using Morley's (1984) correction of Sackett's (1974) original formula. All analyses were performed only for LAG 1 relationships. Higher order analyses (LAG 2 through MAXLAG) were not performed due to the lack of control over intervening speakers between the criterion and response behaviors. To avoid Type I error, possible with extremely large samples (N = 42,285 units), three criteria in addition to the ± 1.96 z score were used: (1) the frequency of each criterion behavior category had to be ≥ 1 percent of the entire data set, (2) conditional probabilities (observed) had to be approximately twice as large as the unconditional probabilities (expected values by chance), and (3) the response behavior with respect to the criterion must have occurred 30 or more times (Ting-Toomey, 1983). These additional criteria are more stringent than those used in previous lag sequential analyses (Putnam & Jones, 1982a; Sackett, 1974; Ting-Toomey, 1983).

However, even with the attempt to employ stringent criteria that decrease the potential for spurious results, this data analysis should be viewed as exploratory and descriptive due to the current debate concerning the adequacy of the lag sequential statistic (Dindia, 1986; Hewes, 1985; Morley, 1987). Hewes argues that lag sequential analysis is suspect due to its failure to test for homogeneity and stationarity between and within subjects. In addition, lag sequential analysis suffers from a "perfect measurement presupposition," or the presumption that all acts are perfectly coded. While the high levels of interrater reliability on unitizing and content coding in this research may belie the second major objection to some extent, it is not sufficient evidence for an unqualified acceptance of lag sequential analysis.

RESULTS

In lag sequential results, significant positive scores indicate that the response behavior followed the criterion more than expected by chance alone, and significant negative scores indicate the reverse. Since the lag sequential analyses in this study were performed only at LAG 1, all reported results refer to contiguous acts. Further, all significant lag sequential results reported here are significant at the p ≤ .05 level.

Research questions #1 through #6 concerned differences in mediator-spouse and spouse-mediator interaction patterns in successful versus unsuccessful mediation. The results for research question #1, dominant patterns of mediator-spouse interaction in successful divorce mediation, indicate the following.

When mediators made statements about mediation, spouses responded with requests for information ($z = 6.95$) but did not provide information about themselves ($z = -3.29$). When mediators made agenda statements, spouses reciprocated agenda statements ($z = 6.78$), requested information ($z = 3.39$), and expressed their feelings ($z = 2.00$). Spouses responded to agenda statements with disclosive agreement less than expected ($z = -2.11$).

When mediators requested information, spouses in successful sessions provided information about themselves ($z = 7.60$) but did not request information ($z = -3.23$) or indicate problems with solutions ($z = -3.39$). Similarly, when mediators requested clarification, spouses provided information about themselves ($z = 4.43$) and others ($z = 4.84$) not central to the dispute, but did not request information ($z = -3.27$), agree with the mediator ($z = -2.01$), or indicate problems with solutions ($z = -2.31$).

Spouses in successful sessions typically responded to a mediator's summarization statements with disclosive agreements ($z = 4.35$) and disagreements ($z = 2.95$). Following mediators' summarizations, spouses did not request clarification ($z = -2.35$) or offer solutions to the dispute ($z = -2.23$).

When mediators in successful sessions expressed their own feelings, spouses responded with self-disclosure agreements ($z = 2.74$) and nonspecific solution talk ($z = 2.33$). No response behaviors by spouses were found to occur less than expected by chance following the mediators' expression of feelings.

When mediators offered solutions, spouses in successful sessions reciprocated those offers ($z = 6.17$) and indicated problems with the solutions ($z = 9.07$). However, spouses did not respond by providing information about themselves ($z = -2.78$), information about others ($z = -2.20$), or expressing their feelings ($z = -3.10$). Mediators' nonspecific solution talk resulted in spouses offering solutions ($z = 4.46$), reciprocating nonspecific solution talk ($z = 9.05$), indicating problems with solutions ($z = 4.66$), and discussing agreements made before mediation ($z = 2.47$). However, spouses did not respond with information about their spouses ($z = -2.50$), about themselves ($z = -4.04$), or about others ($z = -2.55$).

Research question #2 concerned dominant patterns of mediator-spouse interaction in unsuccessful sessions. Results of the lag sequential analyses indicate the following.

When mediators made statements about mediation, spouses requested information ($z = 11.09$) and indicated problems with solutions ($z = 2.56$), but did not respond with information about their children ($z = -2.23$), their spouses ($z =$

-2.04), or themselves ($z = -2.75$). When mediators made agenda statements, spouses in unsuccessful sessions did not make statements of self-disclosure agreement ($z = -2.35$).

In unsuccessful sessions, when mediators requested information, spouses provided information about themselves ($z = 5.56$) but did not request information ($z = -5.14$) or indicate problems with solutions ($z = -2.70$). Mediators' requests for clarification resulted in spouses providing information about their spouses ($z = 3.71$), themselves ($z = 2.85$), and others ($z = 5.03$); but did not result in spouses requesting information ($z = -2.68$), expressing feelings ($z = -2.28$), or indicating problems with solutions ($z = -2.04$).

Mediators' summarization statements were responded to by spouses in unsuccessful sessions with disclosive agreements ($z = 7.18$), but did not prompt spouses to provide information about themselves ($z = -2.36$). Finally, mediators' disclosures of their feelings were reciprocated by spouses in unsuccessful sessions ($z = 4.57$).

In response to research question #3, the mediator-spouse results suggest that minor differences occur in disputants' responses to mediators' process, information, summarization, and self-disclosure behaviors in successful versus unsuccessful sessions. However, major differences are apparent between successful and unsuccessful mediation in disputants' responses to mediators' solutions behaviors.

The similarities and differences between mediator-spouse interaction for successful and unsuccessful divorce mediation are apparent in the following five areas. *First,* mediators' use of procedural behaviors stimulated disputants' questions but inhibited their provision of information. Disputants in successful sessions became involved in discussion of agenda issues by making agenda statements, requesting information, and disclosing feelings, while disputants in unsuccessful sessions did not. *Second,* mediators' requests for information and clarification stimulated disputants to present information about themselves and others outside of the immediate relationship. However, disputants in unsuccessful sessions also provided information about their spouses, while disputants in successful sessions did not. *Third,* mediators' summarization behaviors elicited agreement from disputants. However, disputants in successful sessions also were willing to disagree with the mediators' summarization while disputants in unsuccessful sessions were less willing to provide information about themselves following a mediator's summarization. *Fourth,* when mediators expressed their feelings, disputants in successful sessions agreed and proceeded to discuss alternatives for resolution. Disputants in unsuccessful sessions reciprocated the mediators' expressions. *Fifth,* only the disputants in successful sessions responded positively to mediators' solution-oriented behavior. When mediators offered solutions the disputants reciprocated or presented problems with the solutions. Mediators' use of nonspecific solution talk encouraged a broader range of problem-solving behaviors from disputants, including offering solutions, engaging in nonspecific solution talk, presenting problems with solutions, and referring to agreements achieved before mediation.

Research question #4 concerned the dominant patterns of spouse-mediator interaction for successful sessions. The lag sequential results indicate the following:

When spouses provided information about their spouses, mediators in successful sessions requested information ($z = 3.21$) but did not make statements about mediation ($z = -6.23$), the agenda ($z = -2.09$), and did not engage in nonspecific solution talk ($z = -4.20$). However, when spouses provided information about themselves, mediators requested clarification ($z = 3.89$) and summarized the spouses' statements ($z = 3.08$). In response to spouses' information about themselves, mediators did not make suggestions for negotiation behavior ($z = -7.71$), engage in nonspecific solution talk ($z = -4.82$), or discuss agreements, either tentative ($z = -2.59$) or final ($z = -4.31$). When spouses provided information about another party not involved in the dispute, mediators typically responded by requesting clarification ($z = 2.51$) and summarizing the spouse's statement ($z = 2.05$). Mediators typically did not respond by correcting negotiation behavior ($z = -2.28$), disclosing agreement ($z = -5.96$), offering solutions ($z = -3.89$), or engaging in nonspecific solution talk ($z = -2.87$).

Requests for information by spouses in successful sessions elicited statements of disclosive agreement ($z = 1.97$) and statements about mediation ($z = 2.79$) from mediators. Mediators did not request information ($z = -7.33$) or clarification ($z = -11.69$) following requests for information from spouses.

When spouses made self-disclosure agreement statements, mediators responded with statements about mediation ($z = 3.69$) and indicated problems with solutions ($z = 2.16$). Mediators did not request information ($z = -3.94$) or make self-disclosure agreements ($z = -3.59$) or disagreements ($z = -5.16$). When spouses in successful sessions expressed their feelings, mediators typically did not respond by offering solutions ($z = -5.55$) or indicating problems with solutions ($z = -5.26$).

When spouses made attribution statements about their spouse, mediators made attribution statements about others ($z = 2.06$). Mediators did not respond by making statements about mediation ($z = -2.20$), indicating agreement ($z = -5.08$), or engaging in nonspecific solution talk ($z = -5.19$).

In successful sessions, spouses' offers of solutions were reciprocated by mediators ($z = 2.61$). Mediators also responded by engaging in nospecific solution talk ($z = 2.73$), indicating problems with solutions ($z = 2.04$), and making statements of the final agreement ($z = 3.12$). Mediators did not respond typically by making agenda statements ($z = -4.95$), providing information about others ($z = -3.61$), requesting clarification ($z = -3.80$), disclosing agreement ($z = -2.00$), or disclosing their feelings ($z = -2.94$).

Research question #5 concerned the dominant patterns of spouse-mediator interaction in unsuccessful sessions. When spouses in unsuccessful sessions provided information about their spouses, mediators responded with requests for clarification ($z = 2.42$) but did not respond with self-disclosure agreement ($z = -3.03$) or nonspecific solution talk ($z = -3.03$). However, when spouses provided information about themselves, mediators requested information ($z = 4.04$)

and did not typically respond with disclosive agreements ($z = -7.50$) or disagreements ($z = -3.61$), offers of solutions ($z = -3.04$), or nonspecific solution talk ($z = -10.35$). Similarly, information about others provided by spouses elicited requests for information ($z = 3.23$) and clarification ($z = 2.61$) from mediators. However, these same spouse behaviors were not followed by mediators' suggestions for negotiation behavior ($z = -2.50$), empathic statements ($z = -2.35$), offers of solutions ($z = -2.20$), or nonspecific solution talk ($z = -3.67$).

When spouses in unsuccessful sessions requested information, mediators provided information about mediation ($z = 4.43$) and disclosed agreement ($z = 2.10$). Mediators responded to these requests for information less often than expected with requests for information ($z = -6.96$), requests for clarification ($z = -2.55$), and nonspecific solution talk ($z = -2.61$).

When spouses disclosed agreement, mediators in unsuccessful sessions engaged in nonspecific solution talk ($z = 2.73$) but did not make empathic statements ($z = -3.60$) or attributional statements about others ($z = -2.00$). Mediators reciprocated spouses' self-disclosure disagreement ($z = 5.12$) and did not request information ($z = -3.42$) following spouses' disagreement statements. When spouses expressed their feelings, mediators in unsuccessful sessions responded with empathic statements ($z = 2.87$). Finally, when spouses made attribution statements about their spouses, mediators typically did not respond with statements about mediation ($z = -5.97$) or offers of solutions ($z = -2.75$).

In response to research question #6, the results of the spouse-mediator lag sequential analyses generally indicate that successful and unsuccessful mediators respond differently to disputants' information, self-disclosure, and solutions behaviors. The most notable difference is in responses to solutions offered by disputants.

Five general patterns of behavior are evident in the results. *First,* presentation of information about spouses was discouraged by successful mediators through the use of requests for new information and was encouraged by unsuccessful mediators through requests for clarification of that information. This pattern was reversed when disputants presented information about themselves or about other people, and successful mediators further encouraged disputants by summarizing the disputants' comments. *Second,* provision of all types of information discouraged both successful and unsuccessful mediators from engaging in solution-oriented behaviors. *Third,* disputants' requests for information provoked mediators to provide information about the process of mediation and to disclose agreement. These requests discouraged mediators from requesting information or clarification. *Fourth,* successful and unsuccessful mediators responded differently to disputants' disclosive agreements and disagreements. When disputants disclosed agreement, mediators in successful sessions did not agree, disagree, or request information, instead they provided information about mediation or presented problems with solutions. Unsuccessful mediators responded to disputants' agreements by engaging in nonspecific solution talk. While successful mediators did not respond significantly to disputants' disagreements, unsuccessful mediators reciprocated those behaviors. *Fifth,* only mediators in successful sessions responded to disputants' offers of solutions. The mediators' responses reciprocated offers, engaged in nonspecific solution talk, presented problems with solutions, and presented statements of final agreement.

Research questions #7 through #12 pertain to dominant patterns of husband-wife and wife-husband interaction in successful and unsuccessful divorce mediation. Question #7 asked, "In successful divorce mediation, what are the dominant husband-wife patterns of interaction?" The following significant lag sequential results were found in response to this question.

When husbands provided information about their children, wives responded by disagreeing ($z = 2.47$) providing their own information about the children ($z = 4.22$). When husbands provided information about their spouses, again, wives disagreed ($z = 4.83$) and reciprocated that information ($z = 2.50$). In addition, wives responded less than expected to this behavior by expressing their feelings ($z - -2.17$). Finally, in terms of information provision, when husbands gave information about themselves, wives reciprocated ($z = 2.03$) and provided information about their spouses ($z = 3.55$), but did not express their feelings ($z = -2.22$).

Requests for information from husbands in successful sessions elicited attribution statements about their spouses ($z = 3.49$) from wives. Wives typically responded to husbands' disclosive agreements with nonspecific solution talk ($z = 2.33$). They typically did not respond to husbands' disclosive agreements with disagreements ($z = -2.79$). Wives reciprocated husbands' disclosive disagreement statements ($z = 2.15$) in successful sessions. In addition, when husbands disagreed, wives made attribution statements about their spouses ($z = 3.37$) but did not make self-disclosure agreement statements ($z = -2.05$). Wives also reciprocated husbands' expressions of feelings ($z = 2.69$), but did not respond to these expressions of feelings by indicating problems with solutions ($z = -2.04$). When husbands made attribution statements about their spouses, wives responded more than expected with self-disclosure disagreements ($z = 2.91$) and expressions of feelings ($z = 2.47$).

Research question #8 concerned dominant patterns of husband-wife interaction for unsuccessful divorce mediation. When husbands in unsuccessful sessions provided information about themselves, wives typically did not respond with disclosive agreement ($z = -2.35$). When husbands requested information, wives provided information about others not central to the dispute ($z = 2.47$), did not request information ($z = -2.14$), and did not disagree ($z = -3.80$). Wives reciprocated husbands' self-disclosure disagreements ($z = 5.26$). In addition, when husbands disagreed, wives responded less than expected with information about themselves ($z = -1.97$) and self-disclosure agreements ($z = -2.03$). Wives also reciprocated husbands' expressions of feelings in unsuccessful sessions ($z = 3.35$), but in response to these behaviors, wives did not provide information about others ($z = -2.90$). Finally, when husbands made attribution statements about their spouses, wives responded with disagreement ($z = 4.92$).

Research question #9 concerned the similarities and differences between the dominant husband-wife interaction patterns for successful and unsuccessful divorce mediation. The results indicate significant differences in wives' reciprocation of information. However, in both successful and unsuccessful sessions, wives reciprocated self-disclosure statements.

More specifically, the similarities and differences can be summarized in terms of five patterns. *First,* wives in successful sessions reciprocated husbands' provisions of information about the children, about spouses, and about themselves, while wives in unsuccessful sessions did not. In addition, wives in successful sessions disagreed when husbands presented information about the children or their spouses, did not react to these behaviors by expressing their feelings, and responded to husbands' information about themselves by providing information about their husband. *Second,* both wives in successful and unsuccessful sessions appeared to evade husbands' requests for information. Wives in successful sessions responded to these requests by making attribution statements about their husbands while wives in unsuccessful sessions countered these requests by providing information about others not central to the dispute and curtailing statements of disagreement and requests for information. *Third,* wives in successful and unsuccessful sessions reciprocated husbands' disagreements. In addition, husbands' disagreements reduced the likelihood of wives' agreement statements. The only difference in these patterns was that wives in successful mediation also responded to husbands' disagreements with attribution statements about their husbands while wives in unsuccessful mediation provided less information about themselves. *Fourth,* both wives in successful and unsuccessful mediation reciprocated husbands' expressions of feelings. *Fifth,* wives in successful and unsuccessful sessions responded to husbands' attribution statements about their wives with statements of disagreement. However, wives in successful sessions also responded with expressions of their feelings.

Research question #10 concerned dominant patterns of wife-husband interaction in successful divorce mediation. The statistically significant lag sequential results for this question indicate the following:

Husbands reciprocated wives' information about the children ($z = 6.20$), and in response to this information, also provided information about their spouses ($z = 2.19$). When wives gave information about their spouses, husbands responded by giving information about themselves ($z = 4.02$), but did not express their feelings ($z = -2.42$). Husbands also reciprocated wives' statements of information about themselves ($z = 2.56$). Further, when wives gave information about themselves, husbands also responded more than expected with information about their spouses ($z = 3.62$) and with requests for information ($z = 1.96$) but responded less than expected with expressions of feelings ($z = -2.58$).

When wives requested information, husbands provided information about others not central to the dispute ($z = 4.36$). Husbands reciprocated wives' disclosive agreements ($z = 4.65$) in successful sessions, and were less likely than expected to respond to wives' disclosive agreements with disclosive disagreements ($z = -2.16$). When wives disclosed disagreement, husbands typically did not respond by expressing their feelings ($z = -2.63$). However, when wives expressed their feelings, husbands reciprocated this behavior ($z = 3.54$).

When wives in successful mediation sessions made attribution statements about their spouses, husbands disagreed ($z = 5.82$). And when wives offered solutions, husbands presented problems with the solutions ($z = 5.67$).

The results of the lag sequential analysis for wife-husband interaction in unsuccessful divorce mediation indicate the following answers for research question #11.

Husbands in unsuccessful sessions reciprocated wives' provision of information about the children ($z = 8.17$). When wives' gave information about their spouses, husbands responded with information about themselves ($z = 3.20$) but did not disclose their feelings ($z = -2.39$).

When wives requested information in unsuccessful sessions, husbands responded with expressions of feelings ($z = 3.30$). Husbands responded to wives' disagreements by making attribution statements about their spouses ($z = 2.54$) and by not requesting information ($z = -2.29$). However, when wives in unsuccessful sessions made attribution statements about their spouses, husbands typically responded with disclosive disagreements ($z = 3.54$).

In response to research question #12, concerning the similarities and differences between patterns of wife-husband interaction in successful and unsuccessful divorce mediation, the results indicate patterns of reciprocity of information, but not reciprocity of self-disclosive statements.

More specifically, five areas of similarity and difference are evident. *First*, husbands in both successful and unsuccessful sessions reciprocated wives' provision of information about the children. Husbands in successful sessions also reciprocated wives' information about themselves, but husbands in unsuccessful sessions did not. When wives gave information about their husbands, both husband groups responded with information about themselves. There was also a tendency for husbands to avoid expressing their feelings when wives presented information about the husbands or about themselves. *Second*, wives' requests for information provoked husbands in successful sessions to provide information about others and provoked husbands in unsuccessful sessions to express their feelings. *Third*, husbands in successful sessions reciprocated wives' disclosive agreements and expressions of feelings. When wives disagreed, husbands in successful sessions were less likely to express their feelings while husbands in unsuccessful sessions made attribution statements about their wives. *Fourth*, when wives made attribution statements about their spouses, husbands in both successful and unsuccessful mediation responded with statements of disagreement. *Fifth*, wives' offers of solutions provoked husbands in successful sessions to present problems with the solutions.

DISCUSSION

In response to the research questions, definite differences in mediator-spouse and husband-wife interaction patterns occurred in successful versus unsuccessful mediation. In deciphering the general utility of these results, two general topics can be addressed: (1) conclusions about effective mediation gleaned from a review of mediator-spouse interactions in successful and unsuccessful mediation, and (2) patterns of positive and negative reciprocity and complementarity between disputants indicative of potential needs for mediator intervention.

According to these results, four practical suggestions for effective mediator communication can be offered. *First,* effective mediation involves specific information-gaining behaviors. Successful and unsuccessful mediators elicited information by simply requesting information or clarification. However, successful mediators controlled the provision of information by guiding the disputants to talk about themselves rather than to talk for their spouse. These results support the findings of Donohue et al. (1985) and Slaiku et al. (1985) which indicate that the mediator's role in facilitating accurate information exchange is a critical determinant of success. More important than the exchange of any information is the exchange of appropriate information. By guiding disputants only to talk for themselves, successful mediators facilitated truly integrative information exchange (Sillars, Pike, Jones, & Redmon, 1983) and may have decreased the defensiveness of the disputants (Johnson & Dustin, 1970). *Second,* effective mediation involves the use of summarization behaviors. These behaviors stimulate patterns of supportive communication among disputants by provoking agreement and allowing for the enhancement of integration (Donohue, Allen, & Burrell, 1986). *Third,* effective mediation avoids reciprocity of disputants' distributive behaviors. The results indicate that only unsuccessful mediators became involved in reciprocal disagreement cycles with disputants. As previous research indicates, the avoidance of distributive reciprocity reduces the potential for conflict escalation (Gouran & Baird, 1972). Mediators who engage in distributive reciprocity with disputants not only encourage further escalation, they also damage disputants' perceptions of their impartiality, a critical factor in maintaining the disputants' trust and cooperation (Jones, 1985). *Fourth,* and probably most important, effective mediation stimulates reciprocal problem-solving behaviors. Only successful mediators encouraged reciprocity of solution offers and solution evaluation. As Simkin (1971) argues, facilitating the discussion and analysis of potential solutions is the heart's blood of the successful mediation process.

Results of the husband-wife and wife-husband interactions are most illuminating when considered in terms of reciprocal-integrative, reciprocal-distributive, and complementary patterns. These patterns are presented and discussed in terms of potentially effective mediator interventions.

Reciprocity of integrative behaviors involved both integrative information exchange and supportive communication. Disputants reciprocated information about themselves, expressions of feelings, and agreements. While they also reciprocated other types of information, specifically information about children and spouses, these exchanges also encouraged complementary patterns of information followed by disagreement or abstinence from further information provision. These results emphasize the significance of the first conclusion on effective mediation; guide disputants in sharing information and disclosures about themselves, but not about others. Interestingly, there was no reciprocity of integrative problem-solving behaviors. Coupled with the strong reciprocity patterns evident in the mediator-spouse interactions, it is apparent that mediators bear the responsibility for initiating and continuing problem-solving behaviors, as Moore (1986) has suggested.

As reported in previous literature (Gottman, 1979; Sillars et al., 1983) there were strong patterns of reciprocity of distributive behaviors involving disagreements and attributions. Mediators who allow these patterns to continue, or participate by reciprocating these behaviors, are reinforcing destructive conflict cycles that impede effective resolution.

Complementary patterns were not as common as reciprocal patterns, although two did emerge from this analysis. Disputants requesting information (integrative) were often met with avoidance, or worse, attribution statements made against them (distributive). It appears that disputants respond positively to information-gaining tactics performed by a mediator, but respond negatively to those same tactics performed by another disputant. Hence, mediators may intervene to control information-gaining processes to make them as effective as possible. Finally, while disputants reciprocate offers of solutions from a mediator, they argue against these solutions when presented by another disputant. For maximum facilitation of the problem-solving discussion, mediators should emphasize their role in presenting offers for solutions.

Future research should address the following areas. First, an examination of differences in mediator-wife and mediator-husband interaction, rather than mediator-spouse interaction in general, would indicate adjustments that mediators should make when utilizing the suggested interventions with the different disputants. Second, an analysis of patterns of interaction within phases of mediation could illustrate differences in the impact of these patterns depending upon when they occur in the mediation process. As Moore (1986) argues, this information also could be significant in formulating more sophisticated comprehension of appropriate mediator intervention. Third, it is critical for researchers to examine how the participants in mediation perceive these patterns in terms of their recognition and interpretation of patterns as key elements in their satisfaction with the mediation process.

9

The Role of Argumentation in Distributive and Integrative Bargaining Contexts: Seeking Relative Advantage but at What Cost?

Michael E. Roloff
Frank E. Tutzauer
William O. Dailey

. . . the purpose of any debate is to arrive at the best possible solution to the problem that motivated it . . . so in debate the principal test is to see which of two competing claims will stand up better in the face of informed criticism. . . .

Ehninger and Brockriede (1978: p. 15)

Argument, as usually managed, is the worst sort of conversation, as in books it is generally the worst sort of reading.

Jonathan Swift (1667–1745)

The first duty of a wise advocate is to convince his opponents that he understands their arguments and sympathizes with their just feelings.

Samuel Taylor Coleridge (1772–1834)

Negotiation is a communication process composed partially of arguments advanced with the aim of creating an exchange agreement and/or management of a conflict. Given this perspective, the first quotation implies that negotiators try to reach such accords by promoting positions consistent with their own interests and criticizing those of their counterparts from the same self-interested perspective. Presumably, the emerging settlement will be of high quality since it is the one that survived the intense scrutiny of opposing self-interested, critical, and rational advocates.

Consistent with Swift's assessment, we will review evidence that all too frequently negotiators confront situations or choose courses of action that transform argumentation from a "tool," which builds solid and fair agreements to a "battle-axe" with which to pummel the opposition into submission, or a "shield" to stave off their attacks. Contrary to Coleridge's advice, the advocates become motivated to disparage each other's arguments and interests (regardless of their perceived legitimacy) in order to gain debating advantage. These gladiatorial contexts subvert the positive potential of argumentation.

Because it is neither desirable nor practical to negotiate without some degree of argumentation, it is essential that researchers identify those factors that make argumentation ineffective or even dysfunctional. This chapter is an attempt to highlight those variables. Our treatise will be divided into three sections: argumentation and negotiation; argumentation in distributive bargaining contexts; and argumentation in integrative bargaining contexts.

ARGUMENTATION AND NEGOTIATION

Rieke and Sillars (1984, pp. 7–8) define *argumentation* as "the whole process of advancing, rejecting, and modifying claims while *argument* refers to a single claim, an assertion without support, or a claim with support." In essence, argumentation occurs as debaters attempt to build a strong case to bolster their views relative to those of their counterparts. Negotiators engage in argumentation as they justify, explain, rationalize, and legitimatize their own offers and question those they receive (Bacharach & Lawler, 1981). Hence, argumentation is a process leading to and resulting from the modification of proposals (Putnam & Geist, 1985).

Several implications arise from this general definition of argumentation. First, argumentation should be observable within the discourse occurring during negotiation. Three sets of cues should reflect the degree of argumentation: issue domains, forms of argument, and patterns of interaction.

Issue domains are those topics, events, or items sufficiently important to at least one of the bargainers that a significant degree of argumentation is focused upon them. They are, in essence, what are being argued about. Ehninger and Brockriede (1978) suggest that issues in debate are those questions of sufficient importance, such that if one advocate is unconvincing with regard to them, his or her case is placed in significant jeopardy. In some instances, the issue domains are contained in briefs prepared prior to the negotiation (Lewicki & Litterer, 1985; Rieke & Sillars, 1984) and merely enacted during it. In others, unanticipated topics may emerge only after negotiation begins but are critical to the outcomes (Donohue, Diez, Stahle, 1983).

Forms of argument are the claims and reasoning processes utilized while negotiators analyze the issue domains. For example, Putnam and Geist (1985) examined six types of claims (declarative, evaluative, policy, factual, definitive, and classificatory) and eight reasoning processes (analogy, causal, sign, authority, generalization, classification, opposites, and hypothetical example) occurring during collective bargaining. These tactics are the means by which advocates attempt to prevail in a given issue domain.

Interaction patterns represent the argumentative stimulus-response configurations apparent within the negotiation (see, for example, Putnam & Jones, 1982a). One can focus on the number or proportion of speaking turns spent disagreeing about a given issue domain or the number of *consecutive* speaking turns in which the bargainers disagree with one another within a given domain. Such patterns may highlight areas in which the bargainers are unable to persuade one another and may be a predictor of subsequent deadlocks.

Our second implication suggests that argumentation is governed by social conventions. In formal debate, two such conventions are burden of proof and the burden to go forward with the debate (Ehninger & Brockriede, 1984). Traditionally, burden of proof refers to the responsibility of an advocate for change to prove that the current state of affairs is unjust or harmful and that some alternative state is more desirable. If unable to provide such evidence, the status quo is maintained. The burden to move forward rests with both sides of a debate. Advocates must respond to challenges to their positions or lose relative advantage. Minimally, negotiators are required to repeat their claims in the face of criticism and, more persuasively, refute the challenges.

Similarly, Donohue (1981a, 1981b), has developed a rule-governed framework for viewing distributive bargaining which focuses upon the necessity of responsiveness for achieving larger individual benefits. In his view, if across a series of speaking turns a bargainer is unresponsive to the opposing negotiator's attacks and unable to advance his or her own, that bargainer is at a relative disadvantage and will be unable to acquire a larger share of the outcomes.

The final implication posits that while the primary function of argumentation is to persuade one's counterpart, other functions may be served. For example, we have assumed that arguments are presented as support for the negotiator's case. Therefore, they should be logically and explicitly related to the overall position. It is possible however, that some arguments are presented that are unrelated to the overall case or are not expected to be persuasive to the opponent. Negotiators may advance arguments simply as a delay mechanism (Walcott, Hopmann, & King, 1977), as a means of convincing interested third parties to pressure the opponent (Rieke & Sillars, 1984), or to prove their capability and fidelity to the constituency to which they are accountable (Walton & McKersie, 1965). These alternative goals may complicate negotiation outcomes since the arguments are not intended to be accepted by the opposition nor are they directed toward them.

Thus, argumentation is an important tactic for achieving a variety of bargaining goals and should be pervasive within the discourse of negotiation. However, we believe that its effectiveness is influenced by the negotiation context in which it occurs and we will therefore focus upon it's role in distributive and integrative situations.

Argumentation in Distributive Bargaining Contexts

Distributive bargaining contexts are those in which parties perceive that they can only acquire needed resources at each other's expense. These perceptions may emerge from situations containing salient stimuli such as fixed and scarce resources (Lewicki & Litterer, 1985), and frequently occur in negotiations over single issues (Pruitt, 1981). Distributive bargaining may also arise from a general outlook negotiators bring with them called the "mythical fixed pie" (Bazerman, 1983; Bazerman & Neale, 1983). In essence, bargainers believe that all negotiations are of a win-lose nature, whereas in reality most have the potential for mutually beneficial settlements (Pruitt, 1981). Adopting such an outlook renders argumentation an important weapon in a negotiator's arsenal. Our exploration of its potency will focus on two outcomes: relative advantage and deadlocks.

Argumentation as a Determinant of Relative Advantage

Donohue (1981a, 1981b) has developed a framework for analyzing argumentation in distributive bargaining contexts. His perspective is based on three assumptions: (1) the competitive nature of distributive bargaining stimulates the expectation that each utterance is a tactic designed to gain advantage; (2) in such contexts, negotiators are motivated to discover each other's expected outcomes in order to assess strength; and (3) an advocate's overall position in the negotiation is equal to the sum of each utterance compared to subsequent utterances over the course of the interaction. Within these assumptions, Donohue argues that negotiators maneuver to establish control or relative advantage over the course of their interaction. A number of specific rules are posited which predict how control will vary and suggest that successful bargainers should blunt attacks while continuing to advance their own.

Research is generally supportive of this position. Successful negotiators compared to their unsuccessful partners are perceived to be more enthusiastic throughout the interaction, more punitive, and less sympathetic (Donohue, 1978). Moreover, interaction analysis indicates that winning negotiators relative to losers make more offers but fewer concessions, are more likely to reject their counterpart's concessions, and are more likely to respond to challenges with direct denials rather than partial agreements (Donohue, 1981b). Finally, a measure of relative advantage garnered from the interaction codes is positively correlated with bargaining success (Donohue, 1981a).

Certainly, this perspective and supporting research suggests that argumentation can be a great advantage to an advocate and is critical to a researcher trying to understand and predict bargaining outcomes. However, certain conditions may limit the generalizability of these advantages.

First, not all arguments are advanced with a sincere intent to persuade the opponent (Walcott, Hopmann, & King, 1977). In fact, two negotiators may be in collusion (implicit or explicit) to advance and retreat from arguments in a predetermined fashion as a means of exerting influence on their own constituencies (Walton & McKersie, 1965). In such cases, patterns of relative advantage may be an illusion simply reflecting some other underlying process. In fact, the quality of argumentative response may be less important than the timing of concessions so that the tacit agreement is not threatened.

Second, the perspective ignores nonargumentative determinants of relative advantage. Relative advantage may flow from preinteraction factors such as power. For example, the negotiated outcomes from interactions between superiors and subordinates may be a function of their relative authority in the organization in addition to (or rather than) relative advantage arising from their argumentation (Bacharach & Lawler, 1980). If superiors have the right to make a final decision with regard to an issue, subordinates may maintain relative advantage throughout the negotiation and still achieve less compliance than deserved. Similarly, negotiators who have more attractive alternatives to reaching a negotiated agreement than those of their partners may enter negotiations with relative advantage and can maintain it despite being relatively unresponsive to their counterpart's arguments (Bacharach & Lawler, 1981). Unfortunately, the veracity of this analysis has not been tested since bargainers in Donohue's simulation appear to have been of equal power.

Third, the predictive power of argumentation may depend upon the ability and willingness of the negotiators to agree to demands that they find persuasive. If, for some reason, negotiators are reluctant to make concessions (even if they believe them to be warranted), argumentation may be ineffective and even dysfunctional. Extending upon Donohue's analysis, bargainers unwilling to make concessions should be motivated to attack the position of the opposition as a means of gaining relative advantage. If the opposition is equally reluctant to concede, their best recourse is to reciprocate the argumentation as a means of maintaining or regaining their edge. It should be obvious that this cycle can spiral toward a deadlock since neither side can give in and, unlike other forms of debate, no neutral third party is present to decide the winner. Indeed, Donohue (1981a) reported that in deadlocked negotiations, 52 percent of the opponents' reactions to a strong attack were at the same level of strength as the attack, while only 36 percent of the responses in nondeadlocking groups were reciprocated.

We wish to pursue this third limitation since it indicates the crux of the problem of argumentation in distributive bargaining. While argumentation may lead to relative advantage and individual bargaining success, it may also prompt reciprocal patterns of disagreement and deadlocks.

Argumentation as a Prelude to Deadlocks

In some cases, negotiators' ability and willingness to reach agreement is constrained by their lack of authority to commit to a settlement without the approval of a constituency. The negotiators are hypothesized to be subject to forces which keep them true to their constituency (McGrath, 1966). Indeed, when mechanisms exist that make bargaining representatives accountable (for example, low authority, elections, monitoring), they become more contentious (Carnevale, Pruitt, & Britton, 1979; Pruitt, et al., 1978), stay closer to their constituents' preferred positions (Frey & Adams, 1972; Gruder, 1971; Gruder & Rosen, 1971; Organ, 1971; Pilisuk, Kiritz, & Clampitt, 1971; Roloff & Campion, 1987; Tjosvold, 1977a), and are more likely to deadlock (Friedman & Jacka, 1969; Gruder & Rosen, 1971; Klimoski & Ash, 1974; Roloff & Campion, 1987).

Concern for their image in the eyes of the constituency may motivate low authority bargainers to be more argumentative. If both bargainers have low authority, they may reciprocate each other's level of argumentation as a means of gaining relative advantage and as a result, deadlock. Even if one or both find the arguments persuasive, their inability to commit to an agreement could prevent them from settling (Walton & McKersie, 1965). Indeed, low authority bargainers should vocalize the potential unacceptability of an agreement to the constituency as a reason for rejection. On the other hand, high authority bargainers may be more independent of constituency pressure and, as a result, willing to make concessions when persuaded they are necessary. This implies their level of argumentation may be lower and the ability to settle higher.

We conducted a study in which we tested our reasoning. Briefly, undergraduates participated in a bargaining simulation in which they adopted the roles of lawyers attempting to negotiate an out-of-court settlement in a civil demages suit (Williams, 1970). Each participant was randomly assigned the role of attorney for the plaintiff or defendant. Within the scenario, the parents of a six-year-old child were suing a chemical company for damages suffered when the child crawled under a 12-foot fence and, upon swimming in a retaining pool for toxic waste, suffered burns over 80 percent of his body. Authority was manipulated by randomly assigning each pair of opposing lawyers to a condition in which they could settle the case independently of their clients (high authority) or one in which they had to acquire their respective clients' approval of any agreement (low authority). Confederates played the role of clients.

Our statistical analyses of the argumentation contained within transcripts of the negotiation yielded some support for our perspective. First, low authority bargainers were somewhat more likely than those with high authority to advance workability arguments (that is, statements indicating the client must approve the settlement, the client would find the settlement undesirable, or the client is firmly committed to his or her position). This implies low authority bargainers used their lack of power as an argument to force their counterparts to make concessions. Second, low authority bargainers were significantly less likely than those with high authority to seek information about their opponent's reaction to proposals or about their opponent's client in general. This pattern suggests a relatively high degree of relational distance existed between low authority bargainers.

In terms of bargaining outcomes, we discovered that low authority negotiators were significantly more likely than those with high authority to deadlock. While our analysis indicated this relationship was *partly* mediated by low levels of information seeking conducted by low authority bargainers, neither information seeking nor any of our argumentation measures could completely account for the association between authority and deadlocks.

Although unanticipated, we did find one type of argumentation was significantly related to deadlocking. Regardless of level of authority, the more bargainers argued about who was responsible for the accident, the more likely they reached an impasse. This issue domain is crucial in the scenario and if dwelled upon is counterproductive. After all, the scenario clearly indicated the child was harmed but it was unclear who was responsible for the tragedy. Moreover, accepting responsibility for a harm puts one at relative disadvantage (Donohue, 1981b) and obligated to make concessions. Hence, regardless of authority level, bargainers may have been motivated to attack and defend on this issue in the hope of winning but instead, deadlocked.

Whether this issue domain proves equally difficult in other distributive bargaining situations is of interest. It may be a form of attributional conflict (Horai, 1977; Kelley, 1979) in which individuals can reach agreement about the occurrence of a problem but disagree vehemently about its cause or responsibility for its cause. Given some scholars have speculated that such conflicts are nearly impossible to resolve (Orvis, Kelley, & Butler, 1976), focus on this issue domain may be dysfunctional regardless of context, and negotiators are advised not to dwell upon it.

While the negative impact of argumentation evidenced in our research is somewhat different than hypothesized, it is clear that groups who are unable to reach agreement are argumentative in at least one domain and we found no evidence that argumentation facilitates reaching agreement. Next, we will consider whether a similar effect occurs in integrative contexts.

Argumentation in Integrative Bargaining Contexts

As noted earlier, scholars believe most bargaining contexts have integrative potential (Fisher & Ury, 1981; Pruitt, 1981). This is especially true of those situations involving multiple issues of different priority to the negotiators. In such cases, bargainers may be able trade-off concessions on low priority items for gains on high priority issues (Pruitt, 1981). Even when such issues are not readily apparent, bargainers may be able to manufacture new ones which increase the integrative potential of the situation.

Given our analysis to this point, argumentation would seem inconsistent with this process. Instead of creating mutually beneficial offers, bargainers try to persuade one another to lower their priorities and accept a lesser offer. As a result, they overlook each other's concerns, "dig in," and at best, only a compromise can be expected (Fisher & Ury, 1981; Pruitt, 1981). Indeed, Pruitt (1983b) conceptually and operationally categorizes persuasive arguments as part of contentious behavior.

When persuasive arguments are combined with coercive behaviors (for example, positional commitments, threats, and status putdowns), the resulting index is negatively related to measures of integrative agreements such as joint benefits. Although differing in label, variables containing persuasive arguments such as patter (Fry, Firestone, & Williams, 1983; Lewis & Fry, 1977; Pruitt & Lewis, 1975, Study 2; Schulz & Pruitt, 1978), distributive behavior (Kimmel, et al., 1980), and pressure tactics (Carnevale, Pruitt, & Seilheimer, 1981; Pruitt & Lewis, 1975, Study 1) have been negatively correlated with joint profits. Overall, Pruitt (1981) reports that across ten studies, the mean correlation between various measures of contentiousness and joint benefits is −.35. Moreover, across a number of studies, the conditions that yield high joint profits also evidence low contentiousness (Ben-Yoav & Pruitt, 1984a; 1984b; Carnevale & Isen, 1986; Carnevale, Pruitt, & Britton, 1979; Carnevale, et al., 1981; Pruitt & Lewis, 1975, Study 1; Pruitt, et al., 1978).

Given this consistently damning evidence, it is somewhat surprising that Pruitt (1981; 1983a; 1983b) suggests that competitive behavior may facilitate reaching integrative agreements. Contentiousness may force a reluctant opponent to face the conflict and may signal areas of priority and firmness. In particular, persuasive arguments are hypothesized to provide information about the interests that underlie one's position (Pruitt, 1981). Consequently, one's partner becomes motivated to resolve the conflict and can use information garnered from arguments to construct an integrative offer.

Thus, persuasive arguments can have both facilitative and debilitating effects on the discovery of integrative agreements. If true, statistically controlling for the negative impact of persuasive arguments should uncover a positive relationship between persuasive arguments and joint benefits. Our earlier analysis indicates persuasive arguments lead to deadlocks. Hence, controlling for deadlocks should yield a positive correlation between arguments and joint profit.

While a positive influence may be uncovered, an alternative and more important form of argumentation may be identified. If as Bazerman and Neale (1983) suggest, negotiators have a "fixed pie" bias, then the discovery of integrative agreements will be inhibited until the negotiation is reframed into a "dual concern" perspective (Pruitt, 1983b). Argumentation is a means of recasting perspective. But the form of argumentation is different from the way in which it has been traditionally measured in integrative bargaining research.

Generally, persuasive arguments have been defined as statements "aimed at changing the other's attitudes on the issue" (Pruitt, 1981: 181). In essence, these arguments are self-oriented and, in the typical buyer/seller simulation used in integrative bargaining research, are focused upon the quality of product and market pressure. Alternatively, one might advance arguments about the nature of the bargaining situation with the aim of establishing redefinition of the context.

This reorientation might take place in two issue domains. The first focuses on overt appeals to work together to achieve high joint benefits. Pruitt (1983b) has hypothesized that expressions of concern for the other's needs and opinions will facilitate integrative bargaining. Presumably, this might take place through behaviors such as seeking information (question asking) and expressions indicating the desirability of working together. Requesting the partner's reaction to a proposal appears positively correlated with joint profit (Fry, Firestone, & Williams, 1983; Lewis & Fry, 1977; Pruitt, et al., 1978; Pruitt & Lewis, 1975, Study 2). However, appeals to work together are not correlated with joint benefits (Pruitt & Lewis, 1975, Study 1).

The second issue domain concerns plan argumentation. Pruitt (1983b) hypothesized that integrative agreements are more likely when bargainers signal flexibility with regard to their own proposals and those of their counterparts. This implies a willingness to make frequent adjustments in own offers and consideration of those offers from the partner. The first may be reflected in the number of different offers generated, which has been positively correlated with joint benefits (Pruitt & Lewis, 1975, Study 1). The latter may be reflected in the responses to offers. To generate perceptions of flexibility, one should avoid outright rejections or even placebic justifications (for example, "that isn't good for me") in favor of signs of consideration (for example, "that might work," "maybe"). The latter cues communicate a willingness to work together without necessarily committing to the offer.

In order to evaluate this speculation, we conducted a study which measured the various communication codes discussed earlier and related to them deadlocks and integrative outcomes. Undergraduates negotiated in a simulation used widely in integrative bargaining studies (Pruitt, 1981). One member of the dyad was randomly assigned to be the buyer for a department store and the remaining member was the seller for a wholesaler. The two attempted to negotiate the prices of three appliances: vacuum cleaners, TV sets, and typewriters. In order to create variation in the communication codes, deadlocks, and integrative outcomes, we replicated part of the design used by Pruitt and Lewis (1975, Study 1).

Our results provided partial support for our thesis. First, the more bargaining dyads engaged in persuasive argumentation, the more likely they deadlocked. In fact, persuasive argumentation was the strongest predictor of deadlocking of any communication variable measured in this study. Second, the degree of persuasive argumentation was negatively related to attaining integrative outcomes. Importantly, this relationship dissipated when controlling for deadlocks. Thus, increasing levels of persuasive argumentation were positively associated with deadlocking which in turn resulted in less integrative agreements. Among dyads not deadlocking, there was no relationship between persuasive argumentation and reaching an integrative agreement.

Of the aforementioned measures of reframing, only one appeared to facilitate reaching integrative agreements. The more bargainers communicated signs of agreeability (that is, statements indicating at least tentative acceptance or consideration of the opponent's offers), the greater the integrativeness of their settlement. This relationship remained even when controlling for deadlocking. Surprisingly, appeals to work together to reach an agreement were uncorrelated with the integrativeness of the settlement and negatively correlated with communicating signs of agreeability. Also, seeking information from the opposing negotiator was *negatively* correlated with integrativeness and communicated agreeability.

Thus, these data suggest that communicating flexibility through reactions to offers is an important factor in discovering integrative agreements. Appeals to work together, advancing persuasive arguments, and seeking information do not appear to successfully reframe the negotiations and in the case of the latter two variables, actually appear dysfunctional. Setting and keeping a positive tone appears critical. Perhaps, Fisher and Ury (1981) are correct when they urge bargainers to understand and acknowledge their opponents' interests and when confronting pressure, "don't push back."

CONCLUSIONS

Before summarizing, it is important that we consider potential limitations of the data we used to evaluate our perspective. First, we have built our case upon the words of college students. It might be argued they are not representative of "real" arguers and such may be the case. Yet research conducted among non-college populations suggest similar debilitating roles for argumentation. For example, Koren, Carlton, and Shaw (1980) focused on the relationships between solution proposals (number of new or modified proposals), criticism (attacks upon the other's position or character), and responsiveness (acknowledgements, agreements, or acceptances of others' claims and proposals) on the ability of marital dyads to resolve a conflict and their satisfaction with the resolution. For both dependent variables, criticism had a negative impact while responsiveness and issue proposal were positively related. Moreover, Gottman (1979) found that unhappily married couples engaged in more cross-complaining than did happily married couples whereas the latter engaged in more validation loops in which arguments are acknowledged rather than reciprocated. Furthermore, happily marrieds were better able to enter into contracting loops in which proposals for solutions are accepted (deadlocks avoided). While coding systems are different, they imply that an overemphasis on argumentation is harmful to reaching marital accord just as it was in our simulations.

Second, our use of role playing may also have prompted less argumentation than occurs in actual negotiations and the results are understated. Donohue, et al. (1984) compared the communication patterns occurring in actual and simulated negotiations and found that in general, actual negotiations contained more attacking and less integrative behavior than simulations. Hence, the problem may be worse than our data indicate.

Third, our simulations only allowed us to focus on part of the argumentation domain. For example, the scenarios provided key definitions and explicit outcomes associated with offers. The role of argumentation in shaping the definition of issues (Bacharach & Lawler, 1981) is entirely absent and should be explored.

Fourth, the arguments generated by our respondents seemed reasonable for the bargaining contexts but were often extended beyond the information provided in the scenario. Whether their contrived nature prompted resistance is unclear. In some cases, real negotiators may also experience the same uncertainty as to the veracity of the opponents' arguments. Without independent verification, actual negotiators may be equally uncertain and resistant.

Within these obvious limitations, we believe our research indicates that argumentation, as usually managed, makes for the worst form of negotiation. Persuasive argumentation is related to deadlocks and agreements of low integrativeness. Indeed, one could speculate that being argumentative by nature (Infante, 1981; Infante & Rancer, 1982) may be a hindrance rather than asset for a negotiator. Hence, the desire to gain debating advantage is a dangerous motivation. One must assess the probability that continued argumentation will achieve relative advantage and compare it to a clear risk of deadlocking. A better alternative may be to send tentative signs of agreeability and avoid dwelling upon dangerous issue domains such as fault finding. In that manner, the integrative potential of the situation may be realized to a greater extent than through continued persuasive argumentation.

10

Argumentation and Bargaining Strategies as Discriminators of Integrative Outcomes

Linda L. Putnam
Steve R. Wilson

Bargaining is typically defined as a "process whereby two or more parties attempt to settle what each shall give and take or perform and receive, in a transaction between them" (Rubin & Brown, 1975, p. 2). It is this process of giving and taking and of exchanging proposals and counterproposals that makes bargaining a unique activity. Process also represents a particular perspective or a theoretical frame for understanding negotiations. That is, by calling bargaining a "process of social interaction," theorists are suggesting that the actions of participants evolve over time and shape the types of settlements that negotiators reach (Rubin & Brown, 1975; Walton & McKersie, 1965).

This research adopts a process perspective to test the relationship between types of interaction and negotiated outcomes. First, it assumes that bargaining messages are multifunctional; that is, each action can be linked to a variety of purposes. The belief that bargaining messages serve multiple goals necessitates the use of several category systems to analyze interaction. A second assumption is that strategic and substantive aspects of interaction are intertwined; that is, the activities of initiating issues, exchanging proposals, and attacking and defending positions function as both strategic maneuvers and substantive problem solving. This study operationalizes this assumption by examining the content of bargaining arguments and the function of bargaining strategies. A third assumption is that negotiated settlements evolve from the way bargaining issues and processes shape outcomes.

In effect, this chapter adopts a process perspective to examine the types of bargaining strategies and the substance of arguments that lead to integrative outcomes. Employing a naturalistic, descriptive study, the researchers develop transcripts from interactions at the table and in caucus meetings. After isolating the talk on 16 agenda issues, the researchers code each statement in the bargaining and classify each agenda item into a category system of integrativeness to test for the links between bargaining interaction and negotiated agreements.

INTEGRATIVE AND DISTRIBUTIVE OUTCOMES

One way of classifying outcomes in bargaining emanates from Follett's (1941) distinction between creative problem solving and compromise. Compromise represents settlements based on splitting the difference between two opposite positions while creative problem solving evolves from generating novel or new solutions. Follett's (1940) work is the precursor of Walton and McKersie's (1965) distinction between integrative and distributive bargaining. Distributive outcomes refer to fixed-sum negotiations characterized by one person winning and the other party losing. Distributive outcomes are typically linked to hard bargaining and intense competitiveness. Integrative outcomes, in contrast, are agreements that reconcile the interests of both parties and yield high joint benefits (Pruitt, 1986).

Although Walton and McKersie (1965) cast integrative and distributive bargaining as subprocesses of negotiation, researchers typically treat the two approaches as different models of bargaining (Bartos, 1970; Pruitt, 1981, 1983a; Lewicki, Weiss, & Lewin, 1987). Distributive models typically focus on ways of maximizing individual gains through the distribution of limited resources while integrative bargaining centers on approaches to joint problem solving. By treating the two approaches as discrete, researchers could categorize bargaining outcomes as distributive or integrative based on the win-lose score of each party or on the amount of joint gain in a settlement (Donohue, 1981a, 1981b, Pruitt & Lewis, 1975).

Recent research, however, suggests that integrative and distributive bargaining may be components of the same overall model (Lax & Sebenius, 1986; Putnam, in press; Lewicki, Weiss, & Lewin, 1987). Hence, the interaction of participants, their perceptions, and their expectations may influence outcomes more strongly than do resource constraints or zero-sum motives. When researchers treat negotiations as containing components of both integrative and distributive solutions, outcomes cannot be easily classified into *two* distinct categories. Rather each settlement represents degrees of integrativeness. In this model each issue settled in the bargaining contains some degree of integrativeness (joint gain) and some amount of distributiveness (win-lose). In this chapter degrees of integrativeness are represented by a hierarchical model of outcomes developed from a modification of Pruitt's (1983a) categories.[1] The following hierarchy contains four levels that range from most to least integrative:

1. *Bridging*—the creation of a new proposal. The addition of information claims, or interpretations to the proposal that shift the focus and transform the initial issues; expanding the pie or increasing available resources and options for reformulating problems.

2. *Sharpening*—meeting the demands of one party while reducing the costs and burdens of the other party. Using redefinition or language clarification to reduce opposition to the initial proposal and to reduce the opponent's costs; highlighting, clarifying, or redefining the original proposal to make it acceptable to the opponent.

3. *Trade-offs*—merging concessions to create a package that would be acceptable to both sides; exchanging low priority items for high priority gains; logrolling; splitting the difference; finding a middle ground.

4. *Win-lose*—adopting an issue as initially proposed or dropping an item from the settlement. Minor alternations could be made on the issue, but the settlement represents win-lose through acceptance or through rejection of the issue.

In this study, each item in the negotiation is classified into one of the four levels or degrees of integrativeness. This coding process incorporates the packaging or combining of agenda items. In effect, packaging could not occur without a discussion of the merits, priorities, and interrelatedness of each issue.

BARGAINING STRATEGIES AND TACTICS

Bargaining strategies encompass the tactics that operationalize orientations, intentions, and practices. Strategies usually refer to the program or series of bargaining tactics (for example, tough versus soft strategies, problem solving versus competitive approaches) while tactics are the communicative behaviors that operationalize the strategies (for example, threats, information exchange). Bargaining tactics such as offers, counterproposals, and concessions carry out the process of bargaining while simultaneously conveying a particular strategy through the firmness, flexibility, affect, or neutrality embedded in the message.

Only a modicum of studies directly address the links between particular bargaining tactics and negotiated settlements. Consistent findings suggest that integrative outcomes are linked to frequency in offering proposals and counterproposals (Lewis & Fry, 1977; Pruitt & Lewis, 1975); use of positive affect statements (Theye & Seiler, 1979); eliciting reactions to opponent's proposals (Pruitt & Lewis, 1975); use of initiations, agreements, and exploratory problem solving (Hopmann, 1974); fewer references to party identity (Morley & Stephenson, 1977); and frequent use of other-supporting statements, acceptances, procedural suggestions, and conciliations (Donohue, 1981b; Donohue, Diez, & Hamilton, 1984; Putnam & Jones, 1982a, 1982b). Integrative bargaining is tentative and exploratory, seeking to expand rather than control alternative solutions.

Even though traditional research suggests that the giving of concessions promotes cooperative settlements (Esser & Komorita, 1974), frequent and substantial yielding can lead to low joint outcomes (Ben-Yoav & Pruitt, 1984b). Concession making is primarily integrative when it is systematic and in small increments. Bargainers who seek integrative outcomes typically explore a number of options at the same profit level before conceding to another level (Kelly & Schenitzki, 1972). In like manner information giving may not be a precursor to integrative outcomes. In situations of high aspiration and low trust, bargainers obtained higher joint gains through tacit messages that conveyed preferences for and against offers indirectly rather than through open and honest information exchange (Kimmel, et al., 1980).

Bargaining tactics that are typically linked to distributive outcomes include threats (Leusch, 1976); putdowns, irrelevant arguments, and negative affect statements (Lewis & Fry, 1977); positional commitments (Walton & McKersie, 1965; Lewicki & Litterer, 1985); repetition of arguments, and persuasive attacks (Pruitt & Lewis, 1975); and faulting, rejecting, and disagreeing (Sillars, et al., 1983). Use of these tactics, however, can serve both integrative and distributive functions. Threats and commitments force the opponent to pay attention while they convey boundaries for acceptable settlements (Pruitt & Gleason, 1978). Commitments, demands, and repetition of positions not only convey firmness but they communicate priorities, signal important items, and dislodge bargainers from a rigid stance (Pruitt, 1986). However, these contentious behaviors can lead to distributive outcomes through escalation of issues and last minute compromises (Pruitt, 1983b).

This literature review then suggests the following tentative links between bargaining tactics and negotiated outcomes:

H_1: Bridging and sharpening outcomes will demonstrate a higher proportion of statements in the categories of exploratory problem solving, initiations, ask concessions, and information giving than will trade-off and win-lose outcomes; thus, these tactics will correlate positively and significantly with the integrativeness of a settlement.

H_2: Trade-off and win-lose issues will employ a higher proportion of charge faults, threats and commitment statements than will agenda items resolved through bridging and sharpening; thus, these tactics will correlate negatively and significantly with the integrativeness of a settlement.

ARGUMENTATION CATEGORIES

The effective use of bargaining strategies, especially contentious behaviors, however, depends on a bargainer's adeptness in arguing and substantiating proposals, on the opponent's skill in debate, and on the way the opponent defends his case (Pruitt, 1983b). Since bargaining is characterized by proposal exchange, one key function of communication in bargaining is its role in proposal development, defense, and debate. (Bacharach & Lawler, 1981; Keough, in press; Putnam & Geist, 1985; Putnam, et al., 1986; Walker, 1985; Wilson & Putnam, 1986).

Previous studies on argument and bargaining have used different criteria to classify arguments, including the type of resources that form the basis for arguments (Bacharach & Lawler, 1981) and the relationship of arguments to the opponent's position (Walcott & Hopmann, 1975). Given our interest in the relationship between argumentation and proposal development, we employ a classification scheme tied to the attack and defense of proposals. This scheme originates in the systems of *stasis* developed by classic rhetorical theorists (Golden, Berquist, & Brown, 1983). Although no exact list of *stases* is accepted by every author, four to five types are widely recognized (e.g., Nobles, 1978;

Patterson & Zarefsky, 1983; Ziegelmueller & Dause, 1975). This study focuses on the following five types of bargaining arguments:

1. *Harm arguments:* arguments that present or refute problems with the present system; ones that justify the need for or advantages of modifying the current policies; arguments about the severity, significance, or widespread prevalence of a problem. For example:

[The] board must realize that the teachers are being eaten alive with these [insurance] rates.

The board does not feel that the salary difference is the result of sex discrimination. The issues are the position they hold and the duties involved.

2. *Inherency arguments:* arguments that demonstrate that a harm was or was not caused by the current system and will or will not dissipate on its own if the current system continues. Inherency arguments sometimes cite structural (e.g., contract language) or attitudinal reasons that harms will continue. For example:

We're forced to be low and stay low [on salaries] due to the levy limitation in the district and the freeze in the state.

Class size should be less of a problem in the future, as enrollments drop over the next few years (example created by authors).

3. *Implementation arguments:* arguments that claim the proposal is acceptable or unacceptable to one or both bargainers or their constituents; statements about the acceptability of absolute ranges. For example:

Nobody else in this corporation is going to object to a policy that would cost less.

This window period of July 1 to September 15 for withdrawal of names is not going to get by the board . . . The board will not agree to this window period.

4. *Workability arguments:* arguments that assert or refute the claim that a proposal would or would not function efficiently or effectively; arguments that a proposal would not work because of monetary resources, expertise, or manpower. For example:

[The superintendent] can afford this [salary] package . . . last year . . . he made up the difference in not replacing resignations.

[The teachers] are going to want us to . . . look at other insurance agents. We've done this so many times . . . their representative on the insurance committee [last time] . . . didn't understand half of what the agent was telling us . . . it isn't worth it again.

5. *Disadvantage arguments:* arguments that claim a proposal will or will not create new problems; arguments that claim the proposal will lead to new harmful consequences. For example:

If we meet his request for an 8.3% [salary] increase then we will have to lay off teachers.

What difference is there between the [proposed] computer list . . . and the formal signature of authorization each year? People either want to be a [union] member or they don't.

These five types of arguments represent points of contention that frequently materialize in debating a proposed course of action (Nobles, 1978, p. 162). This study suggests that a relationship exists between argument type and the integrativeness of the settlement for each agenda item. If integrative bargaining stems from identifying and defining essential problems, generating potential solutions, and keeping decisions tentative until alternative proposals are presented (Lewicki & Litterer, 1985; Pruitt, 1986; Walton & McKersie, 1965), harm and inherency arguments should center on the nature and scope of problems that justify proposals. Workability arguments should focus on the feasibility of proposals, potentially leading to the modification of an initial offer. In contrast, implementation arguments should convey inflexibility toward alternative proposals. Consequently, we hypothesize that:

H_3: Bridging outcomes will contain a significantly higher proportion of harm, inherency, and workability arguments than will win-lose outcomes; thus, these argument types will correlate positively and significantly with the integrativeness of outcomes.

H_4: Trade-off and win-lose outcomes will contain a significantly higher proportion of implementation arguments than will bridging and sharpening issues; thus, this argument type will correlate negatively and significantly with the integrativeness of outcomes.

In addition to defending current proposals, arguments in bargaining also lead to new proposals (Putnam & Geist, 1985; Putnam et al., 1986). Proposal development refers to the conditions of an offer. It addresses the nature and composition of a proposal rather than the need for, workability of, and utility of the offer. Most coding schemes fail to differentiate between messages that defend existing proposals and those that develop new ones (see, for example, Donohue, Diez, & Stahle, 1983; Walcott, Hopmann, & King, 1977); other schemes recognize this distinction but report only the overall frequency of proposal offers (Pruitt & Lewis, 1975). This study employs a four-category scheme developed from a content analysis of approximately 30 percent of the proposal statements made in the bargaining. The four categories are:

P_1: *Consideration of candidate proposals*—statements about what the proposal should be; comments about what the other side would think of our proposal.

P_2: *Consideration of resource availability*—statements about resources that are available to support any proposal; questions about the existence of resources; criteria for determining resource availability. P_2 statements might imply workability, but no direct link is made to the affordability inference.

P_3: *Comparison to previous or external proposals*—statements that compare or contrast proposals to previous proposals or ones outside the district; comparisons of proposals on the table with guidelines set in caucus sessions.

P_4: *Discussion of opponent's proposals*—comments that anticipate what the other side is likely to offer; discussion of the other side's motives, opinions, or reasons for making proposals.

Given the exploratory nature of this research, we posit the following broadly defined hypotheses:

H_5: The four outcome types will differ in their use of proposal development categories.

H_6: The proposal development categories will correlate significantly with the integrativeness of outcomes.

METHOD

Participants

This research employed a case study, ethnographic method to analyze bargaining strategies and argumentation in the negotiations of a small midwestern school district. The school district was comprised of 155 teachers, six schools, and 3,300 students and had engaged in collective bargaining for seven years, since the passage of the public employees bargaining law. The teachers' team consisted of 11 members who represented the high school, the middle school, and the elementary schools and their professional negotiator—the Uniserv director from the state teachers' association. The board's team consisted of five elected school board members, the superintendent, two principals, and their hired professional negotiator. The board had employed this professional negotiator throughout the district's bargaining history.

The two sides engaged in full contract negotiations over a 25-page contract and settled in ten hours. The negotiation consisted of two prebargaining meetings for each side, two eight-minute sessions at the table, four two-hour caucus meetings interspersed with three 30-minute "private" meetings between the two professional negotiators. This practice of allowing the two bargainers to meet in "private side-bar" sessions began two years before this study and appeared to expedite the process of reaching a settlement. A questionnaire completed by 73 percent of the teachers revealed that 76 percent of them were satisfied with the settlement, with only 2 percent indicating general dissatisfaction.

Data Collection

A team of three researchers observed and took field notes of prebargaining sessions, actual negotiations, caucus meetings, side-bar sessions, and the ratification meeting. One researcher observed the school board's caucuses, one

Table 10.1
Operational Definitions of Bargaining Strategies and Tactics

TACTICAL MANEUVERS

1. THREATS--withholding of potential rewards and sanctions if the other person does not comply; providing negative consequences.

2. PROMISE--offering rewards or sanctions if the other person complies in a stated manner; providing positive consequences.

3. DISAGREEMENT--disagreeing with the previous statement, rejecting a previous statement or part of a proposal; an explicit statement of disagreement.

4. AGREEMENT--giving agreement, assistance, acceptance, or approval of another person's arguments; retracting a position in the face of resistance.

5. CHARGE FAULTS--attributing lack of good faith, incompetence, or negligence to another person; making derogatory remarks.

6. DEMANDS--calling on the other person to make accommodations; demanding the other person to demonstrate willingness to negotiate; demanding a concession from the other person.

PROPOSAL STRATEGIES

1. INITIATION--provides an initial offer, proposal, or counterproposal; initiates candidate proposals on the floor for consideration. Candidate proposals must be specific policy suggestions and must not have been previously discussed as a proposal.

2. COMMITMENT--takes a firm position; indicates that a position is final; demonstrates firmness in holding to a position, with specific and explicit consequences.

3. EXPLORATORY PROBLEM SOLVING--searches for a mutually beneficial proposal; provides flexibility in responses to proposals; promotes the exploration of alternatives; indicates potential consideration of a proposal.

4. GIVES CONCESSIONS--makes an explicit concession; accepts the other person's proposal or position; approves of the other person's offer.

5. ASKS CONCESSIONS--asks or implies that the other person should concede (weaker in tone than demanding a concession).

INFORMATION AND CLIMATE MANAGEMENT MESSAGES

1. INFORMATION GIVING--providing information, evidence or substantiation in support of the speaker's position; giving evidence, examples, past occurrences to support a point; reporting back to teams on the other side's proposals.

2. OPINION GIVING--asserting a claim or judgment; making evaluations or giving opinions about an issue under discussion; speculating or guessing what will happen in the bargaining; assessing or evaluating issues and bargaining activities. Statements that contain both opinion giving and information giving should be coded into the category that reflects the essence of the message. Opinions about information are coded as opinion giving.

3. SEEKING INPUT--asking for additional information; requesting data; asking for opinions or reactions; seeking clarification.

4. HUMOR--offering humorous statements; making light of topics under discussion; releasing tension with humor or jokes.

5. PROCEDURE--requesting or making statements about the procedures of the bargaining process; questions or statements about the agenda; who does what at what time; where participants should be; how the bargaining should be conducted; and changes in the bargaining routine.

CODING RULE: Statements should be coded into the tactical maneuver or proposal strategies before consideration of information and climate management categories. Statements that appear to fit more than one category should either be subdivided or should be coded into the category that best expresses the meaning of the statement.

the teachers' caucus, and one the side-bar sessions between the two bargainers. The researchers were trained in taking shorthand field notes, recording near-verbatim dialogue of interactions, and the general atmosphere of the bargaining event. Field notes were transcribed and expanded into fully typed notes shortly after the observations. Ninety pages of field notes were transcribed in sequential order with appropriate labels for speaker, bargaining sessions, sequential number of caucus and side-bar meetings. The researchers also collected written proposals exchanged between the sides, past contracts, memorandum of agreements, and the signed final contract to aid in tracking the development of bargaining issues.

Coding Schemes

Bargaining strategies and tactics were coded through the use of an adapted version of Walcott and Hopmann's (1975) Bargaining Process Analysis II (BPA II, see Table 10.1). Previous use of the BPA II indicated that it was a reasonably valid and reliable system (Putnam & Jones, 1982b).

An argumentation category system was developed for this study. This system originated from the five stases: harm, inherency, workability, implementation, and disadvantage; and four proposal development categories presented in the argumentation section of this paper. The unit of analysis in this study was a sentence or a complete statement, unless subsequent sentences in the same contribution merely extended the previous sentence. An extension, however, could be no longer than four sentences. Each statement was coded twice, once into the bargaining strategy system and once into the argumentation category system. Categories within the two coding schemes were mutually exclusive and exhaustive.

In addition to coding communicative acts, the researchers classified each agenda item into one of the four outcome categories, based on the evolution of the topic over time. An agenda item was a topic in the proposed contract usually delineated by article and section of the contract. Some items were divided into subissues based on a splintering of the main issue during bargaining interaction or in the making of counterproposals.

Data Analysis

In the first stage of this analysis, we listed the agenda items and blocked off sections of the talk that dealt with each item (see Table 10.2 for a list of the 16 agenda items in the bargaining). After labeling each statement in the bargaining as addressing an agenda item, the researchers typed up new transcripts listing sequential comments for each topic. For each statement researchers recorded bargaining session number, caucus versus bargaining session, teacher versus board, speaker, type of outcome, bargaining tactics, and argumentation category.

The researchers prepared flow charts of issue development for the 16 agenda

Table 10.2
Bargaining Issues: Frequencies and Reliabilities

Issue	Number of Statements	Relative Frequency	Average Reliability	Overall Reliability	Outcome Category
Salary	249	30.7%	.70	.80	Trade-Off
Sick Leave-Severance Pay	62	7.6%	.75	.80	Trade-Off
RIF	47	5.8%	.65	.77	Sharpening
Grievance	61	7.5%	.69	.75	Trade-Off
ECA-Coaching	39	4.8%	.69	.76	Sharpening
Dues Deduction	55	6.7%	.63	.78	Sharpening
Retirement	13	1.6%	.71**	.83	Bridging
Personal Leave	25	3.1%	.71**	.83	Win-Lose
Single versus Family Insurance Rates	19	2.3%	.82	.89	Win-Lose
2-year Contract	24	3.0%	.71**	.83	Sharpening
Insurance Premiums	145	17.9%	.72	.79	Bridging
ECA-Coordinators	42	5.2%	.69	.75	Win-Lose
Mileage	9	1.1%	.71**	.83	Trade-Off
Teacher Evaluation	6	.7%	.71**	.83	Win-Lose
Academic Freedom	6	.7%	.71**	.83	Win-Lose
Just Cause Standards	5	.6%	.71**	.83	Win-Lose
TOTAL	809 *	100.0			

* Total number of statements excludes 33 procedural messages which were omitted from the analysis.

** These issues were coded collectively. Hence, summaries of reliability coefficients cross all six issues were identical.

items. They began with the original proposal and noted at each point when it was altered, modified, or transformed. Comparison of the changes within a proposal, especially differences between the original and the final outcome, guided researchers in categorizing the 16 agenda items. To determine reliability of coding, two independent coders studied the data assembled on each issue and classified each agenda item into an outcome category, yielding an overall agreement of 93 percent.

In the next stage of analysis, the researchers computed the frequencies and proportions of talk for each bargaining tactic and each argumentation category. Proportions were derived from dividing raw frequencies in a given category by the total number of statements for that agenda item. For example, discussion of the salary issue led to a total of 249 statements; 20 of these were commitment tactics. Hence, the proportion of commitment statements on salary was $20/249 = .08$. Proportional data normalizes frequency distributions across categories and across issues. In this analysis, the 16 bargaining items comprised the subjects for statistical testing.[2]

Next, correlations and Smallest Space Analyses were run on the proportional data to collapse the categories that were conceptually and empirically similar.[3] Finally, hypotheses were tested with one-way ANOVAs across the four bargaining outcomes for each category and with Pearson correlations between proportions and degrees of integrativeness. Univariate tests were employed because of the limited number of issues in the bargaining ($N = 16$) and because the correlational analyses revealed low to negative relationships among the categories. To determine which outcomes were accounting for differences, a Student-Newman Keuls post hoc comparison was employed.

The one-way ANOVAs were examined for homogeneity of variance. For categories with questionable homogeneity, a logarithmic transformation $\log_{10}$-(data + 1) was used to normalize these proportions prior to accepting or rejecting the hypotheses. Proportional frequencies for each category were correlated with the degree of integrativeness of each outcome across the 16 issues. Hence, outcome types were treated as ordinal data arranged hierarchically from the most to least integrative and correlated with the proportion of statements in a given category for a specific issue.

RESULTS

Reliabilities and Category Frequencies

Four trained coders classified 842 statements into the 16 bargaining tactics and into the nine argumentation categories. Due to the complexity of the category systems, the four coders employed consensus coding. They agreed on the division of statements into units (unitizing) and then independently coded each statement. The coders met and pooled their responses, discussed differences in classification, and reached consensus for each statement in question. Approximately 60 hours of coding were devoted to this consensus method. The coders found the method particularly valuable for analyzing naturalistic interaction, because the complexity of the substance and syntax of each statement allowed for multiple interpretations. Since one of the coders observed the bargaining sessions, she was able to place each statement into a larger framework to aid in making appropriate interpretations. Reliabilities were calculated from the independent judgments of the four coders. Table 12.2 reports the average agreements across the categories for each issue and the overall agreement determined by the total number of statements for a given issue.

Low frequency counts for some categories necessitated combining conceptually and empirically related tactics. Specifically, the category of procedure (N = 33) was dropped from further analysis because it could not be coded sensibly for argumentation categories. Promises and demands received less than ten frequencies. Correlations among the categories revealed that ask concessions and demands were interrelated ($r = .47$) and that promises had the highest positive correlation with demands ($r = .21$) and ask concessions ($r = .19$). Also, they emerged in the same quadrant of a nonmetric multidimensional Smallest Space Analysis (Norton, 1980). Hence, the three categories, hereafter labelled PAD, were combined which reduced the number of bargaining strategies to 13.

Hypothesis Testing

Three of the 13 bargaining tactics and one of the nine argumentation categories emerged as statistically significant in tests of one-way ANOVAs across the four outcomes. Also, five of the correlations between proportional frequencies and integrativeness of outcomes were significant. H_1 speculated that bridging and sharpening outcomes will differ from trade-off and win-lose issues in their proportional use of exploratory problem solving, initiations, information giving, and ask concessions. This hypothesis was supported for exploratory problem solving and asks concessions, but not for initiations and information giving. Specifically, exploratory problem solving messages were used in greater proportion for *bridging* than for the other three outcome types ($F (3,15) = 3.065, p < .05$). As Table 10.3 suggests, the mean proportion for bridging was considerably higher than for the other three outcome types (Bridging, $M = .19$, Sharpening, $M = .06$; Trade-offs, $M = .04$; Win-lose, $M = .03$).

The combined category of PAD characterized the *sharpening* outcome more than it did the other three types ($F (3,15) = 6.95, p < .006$, Sharpening, $M = .07$; Bridging, $M = .02$; Trade-offs, $M = .02$; Win-lose, $M = .01$). Correlations with outcomes reaffirmed H_1 with categories of exploratory problem solving ($r = .56, p < .01$) and PAD ($r = .45, p < .03$) demonstrating the highest relationships with integrativeness (see Table 10.4). Initiations and information giving, unlike predicted in H_1 were negatively linked to integrativeness (Initiations, $r = -.39$, p $< .05$; Information giving, $r = -.15$, ns). Table 10.3 suggests that initiations typify trade-off, win-lose, and bridging outcomes more

Table 10.3
Bargaining Strategies—Means and F Ratios

Strategy		Overall Statistics		1	By Outcome[a] 2	3	4
Threats	N	14	Freq.	2	2	9	1
	%	1.7	Mean	.01	.01	.01	.002
	$\underline{F}$	.46	SD	.01	.03	.02	.01
Disagree	N	53	Freq.	9	12	26	6
	%	6.6	Mean	.07	.07	.08	.03
	$\underline{F}$	.80	SD	.02	.02	.08	.06
Agreement	N	26	Freq.	8	2	13	3
	%	3.2	Mean	.06	.01	.04	.03
	$\underline{F}$	.41	SD	.02	.01	.05	.07
Charge Faults	N	31	Freq.	17	1	11	2
	%	3.8	Mean	.06	.01	.02	.01
	$\underline{F}$	1.68	SD	.08	.01	.02	.02
PAD	N	27	Freq.	6	12	6	3
	%	3.3	Mean	.02	.07 **	.02	.01
	$\underline{F}$	6.95 **	SD	.03	.02	.02	.02
Initiation	N	50	Freq.	12	7	19	12
	%	6.2	Mean	.11	.06	.13	.12
	$\underline{F}$	.59	SD	.06	.07	.09	.09

134

		Total	1	2	3	4
Commitment	N / Freq.	41	1	9	20	11
	% / Mean	5.1	.01	.05	.03	.05
	F̲ / SD	.66	.01	.03	.05	.06
Exploratory Problem Solving	N / Freq.	59	15	10	26	8
	% / Mean	7.3	.19	.06	.04	.04
	F̲ / SD	3.01 *	.16 *	.05	.05	.05
Gives Concessions	N / Freq.	25	4	9	9	3
	% / Mean	3.1	.01	.05	.10	.04
	F̲ / SD	.64	.02	.04	.11	.07
Information Giving	N / Freq.	228	49	45	88	46
	% / Mean	28.3	.27	.26	.33	.27
	F̲ / SD	.46	.06	.06	.10	.07
Opinion Giving	N / Freq.	166	23	41	54	48
	% / Mean	20.6	.11	.25	.10	.26
	F̲ / SD	3.36 *	.05	.01 *	.09	.11 *
Seeking Input	N / Freq.	70	10	13	32	15
	% / Mean	8.7	.07	.09	.10	.10
	F̲ / SD	.28	.01	.05	.01	.06
Humor	N / Freq.	17	2	2	7	6
	% / Mean	2.1	.01	.01	.01	.03
	F̲ / SD	.71	.01	.01	.01	.03
Total			158	165	320	164
%			.19	.21	.40	.20

* P<.05
** P<.01

aOutcomes: 1 = Bridging, 2 = Sharpening, 3 = Trade-Offs, 4 = Win-Lose

135

than they do sharpening issues. Information giving did not characterize any of the four outcomes (Bridging, $M = .27$; Sharpening, $M = .26$; Trade-offs, $M = .33$; Win-lose, $M = .27$), suggesting that information giving can serve many functions in the negotiation (see Putnam & Jones, 1982b).

Hypothesis$_2$ was disconfirmed. Neither charge fault nor commitment statements were aligned with trade-off nor win-lose outcomes (see Table 10.3). However, 31 of the 41 positional commitment statements were made during discussion of items that resulted in trade-offs or win-lose settlements, thus, a trend exists in favor of the hypothesis, but one which was not substantiated by the proportional frequencies.

One particularly unexpected finding was the link between *opinion giving* and two bargaining outcomes ($F(3,15) = 3.36$, p $< .05$, see Table 10.3). Specifically, win-lose outcomes ($M = .26$) and sharpening outcomes ($M = .25$) demonstrated a higher proportion of opinion giving statements than did bridging ($M = .11$) and trade-off settlements ($M = .10$). Also, a surprising finding for H$_2$ was that threats were positively rather than negatively associated with integrativeness ($r = .42$, p $< .05$, see Table 10.4). However, since there were only 14 threats used in the negotiation, the correlation between threats and integrativeness should be interpreted with caution. In like manner, positional commitment statements did not correlate significantly nor negatively with the integrativeness of the outcome ($r = .01$, $p < .50$), even though the absolute frequency of commitment statements was higher for trade-off and win-lose outcomes than for bridging and sharpening settlements (see Table 10.4).

Hypothesis$_3$ posited that harm, inherency, and workability arguments would be linked to bridging outcomes. This hypothesis was confirmed for *workability* arguments. *Bridging* solutions employed more workability arguments than did the other three outcomes ($F(3,15) = 5.96$, $p < .01$; Bridging, $M = .15$, Sharpening, $M = .03$; Trade-offs, $M = .06$; and Win-lose, $M = .03$, see Table 10.5). Correlation coefficients also indicated that workability ($r = .43$, $p < .03$) arguments were linked to the integrativeness of an outcome. These findings, however were too exploratory to draw firm conclusions from this data.

Hypothesis$_4$ specified that implementation arguments would be proportionally greater for issues resolved through trade-offs and win-lose than for those resolved through bridging. This hypothesis was disconfirmed. Even though win-lose outcomes demonstrated a higher proportion of implementation statements than did the other three outcomes (Win-lose; $M = .13$; Bridging, $M = .04$, Sharpening, $M = .07$, Trade-offs, $M = .06$), tests of differences among the four outcomes were not significant ($F = 1.29$, *ns*). The correlation between integrativeness and implementation leaned in the distributive direction, but it was nonsignificant ($r = -.15$, *ns*).

Finally, in response to H$_5$ and H$_6$, the four outcomes did not differ significantly in their use of *proposal development* categories. However, two of these categories exhibited trends for potential differences. P$_2$—Consideration of Resources Available for proposals correlated $r = .34$, $p < .10$ with the inte-

Table 10.4

Correlations with Integrativeness of Outcomes

BARGAINING STRATEGY	CORRELATION[a] COEFFICIENTS	p
Threat	.42	.05 *
Disagree	.26	.16
Agree	-.08	.37
Charge Fault	.26	.16
Initiation	-.39	.05 *
Commitment	.01	.50
Gives Concession	-.16	.27
Exploratory Problem Solving	.45	.03 *
Information Giving	-.15	.29
PAD	.56	.01 **
Opinion Giving	-.08	.38
Humor	-.27	.16
Seeking Input	-.20	.23
ARGUMENTATION CATEGORY		
Harm	.34	.10
Inherency	.35	.09
Implementation	-.15	.29
Workability	.47	.03 *
Disadvantage	-.04	.45
P1	-.21	.22
P2	.34	.10
P3	-.20	.22
P4	-.30	.13

* p<.05   df = 16
** p<.01

[a] The positive and negative signs for the correlation coefficients were reversed. In the actual data a negative sign indicated a high positive correlation with integrative outcomes (Bridging and sharpening were coded 1 and 2, respectively).

Table 10.5
Argumentation Categories—Means and F Ratios

Strategy	Overall Statistics		By Outcome[a]			
			1	2	3	4
Harm	N 99	Freq.	24	32	24	19
	% 12.3	Mean	.15	.19	.05	.11
	F 1.07	SD	.01	.16	.05	.09
Inherency	N 21	Freq.	9	4	5	3
	% 2.6	Mean	.03	.02	.01	.01
	F .62	SD	.04	.02	.01	.02
Implementation	N 87	Freq.	12	13	44	18
	% 10.8	Mean	.04	.07	.06	.13
	F 1.29	SD	.06	.05	.10	.07
Workability	N 69	Freq.	24 **	7	31	7
	% 8.6	Mean	.15	.04	.06	.03
	F 5.96 **	SD	.002	.05	.05	.03
Disadvantage	N 63	Freq.	5	14	30	14
	% 7.8	Mean	.02	.08	.08	.06
	F .45	SD	.02	.06	.08	.07
P_1	N 365	Freq.	71	87	128	79
	% 45.2	Mean	.56	.55	.55	.55
	F .01	SD	.19	.14	.19	.11
P_2	N 19	Freq.	0	1	17	1
	% 2.4	Mean	0	.01	.02	.003
	F .78	SD	0	.02	.04	.009
P_3	N 42	Freq.	9	3	21	9
	% 5.2	Mean	.03	.01	.14	.02
	F 2.12	SD	.04	.02	.17	.04
P_4	N 42	Freq.	4	4	20	14
	% 5.2	Mean	.01	.02	.03	.09
	F 1.33	SD	.02	.03	.05	.08
		Total	158	165	320	164
		%	.19	.21	.40	.20

** $P < .01$

[a]Outcomes: 1 = Bridging, 2 = Sharpening, 3 = Trade-Offs, 4 = Win-Lose

grativeness of an outcome and P_3—Comparison with previous and external proposals differentiated, to some extent, among trade-off and the other three outcomes (F (3,15) = 2.12, $p < .15$, Trade-offs, $M = .14$; Bridging, $M = .03$; Sharpening, $M = .01$; Win-lose, $M = .02$). These trends indicated that discussing resource availability was part of building novel alternatives while comparing proposals with past settlements or with other districts facilitated logrolling and compromise settlements.

DISCUSSION

This study of bargaining interaction tested for the relationship between bargaining strategies, argumentation, and negotiated settlements. The researchers coded settlement types for 16 agenda items in a ten-hour teachers' negotiation. The coding scheme consisted of four outcomes arranged hierarchically from the most to the least integrative. Deliberations on each bargaining item in caucus and negotiation sessions were broken into statement units and coded in one of 16 bargaining strategies (13 strategies after combining three of them) and one of nine argumentation categories. Results supported two of the hypotheses and disconfirmed two of them.

Bridging solutions emerged from a high proportional use of exploratory problem solving statements and workability arguments. These findings suggested that bargainers reformulated problems and expanded alternatives by challenging the feasibility of each side's proposals. These findings were consistent with previous research in that exploring options and indicating flexibility characterized integrative settlements (Hopmann, 1974; Walton & McKersie, 1965). Exploratory problem solving statements conveyed that bargainers were willing to consider movement, to suggest possible agreements, and to question reasoning or evidence in support of their position. Statements varied from ambiguous references to concessions (e.g., "I think we can resolve the window period for dues deduction." "I'm not willing to go equal bucks for ECA, but I'm willing to move on this one.") to conditional offers and suggestions of restraints (e.g., "If you take the computer list, we can get around the authorized forms." We're lower than we want to go, but in perspective it's not too low."). Workability arguments focused on the affordability, efficiency, and feasibility of each side's proposals. Of particular importance in understanding how bridging solutions developed were the pro and con arguments nested within each of these categories. Bridging solutions emerged when the parties confronted their differences directly and explored the consequences of each solution through tacit messages embedded in arguments rather than through open exchange of information about each other's positions (Kimmel, et al., 1980).

Sharpening outcomes were distinguished by the use of PAD and opinion-giving statements. These settlements met the needs of one party and reduced the burdens of the opponent typically by isolating sections of the original proposal, reducing objections to it through redefinition or clarification, and then reducing the burdens of the opponent. For example, dues deduction emerged from isolating the computer list portion of the issue, redefining the authorization cards, compromising on the window period, and reducing administrative costs. Asking for concessions and making demands seemed to correspond with eliciting specific reactions from opponents, a strategy previously linked to trial and error forms of integrative outcomes (Lewis & Fry, 1977; Pruitt & Lewis, 1975). Perhaps eliciting concessions and reactions from the opponent targeted aspects of a proposal that were open to agreement, and promises functioned to reduce the opponent's burdens.

The results of opinion giving were surprising in that this strategy distinguished both sharpening and win-lose outcomes. These statements suggested that opinion-giving messages helped team members establish boundaries for positions through voicing likes and dislikes about the bargaining process, the opponent, or the opponent's proposals; formulating interpretations of the opponent's behavior; and anticipating future moves of the opponent. Opinion-giving statements then appeared to facilitate sharpening outcomes by highlighting priorities and discovering ways of meeting one side's demands by reducing the costs of the opponent. Opinion-giving statements also facilitated win-lose outcomes by reaffirming a team's position, making positions seem rigid. and closing off continued deliberations on certain topics.

An additional category merits brief attention. Contrary to previous research, threats did not emerge as descriptors of win-lose outcomes. In fact, threats correlated positively with the integrativeness of a settlement. Content analysis of threats revealed that both deterrent and compellant threats were used with compellant ones in the majority (65 percent). Most of the threats asked the opponent to behave in a particular way to avoid delaying the negotiation process or to avoid demands for agenda items that the other side strongly opposed. Threats appeared to establish a formula for differentiating between language and money items in the contract and for reinforcing the district's norm of setting the contract without fact finding or mediation.

This study is limited by one bargaining group, a small number of agenda items, and low frequencies for some of the bargaining strategies and argumentation categories. The fact that the overall settlement for this bargaining event was integrative and received high marks of satisfaction from participants may explain some of the findings of this study. Results might differ for a bargaining session that ended in impasse or third party intervention. Also, these findings are limited by ethnographic data and reliance on single acts rather than sequences of strategy use. Past studies have shown that contentious behaviors (such as threats) matched by resistance or by one-upmanship attacks lead to impasse (Pruitt, 1983b; Putnam & Jones, 1982a). Hence the presence or absence of sequential patterns might affect the links between strategies and outcomes.

Despite limitations of this study, our results suggest that both the strategy and the content of interaction impact on negotiated settlements. Moreover, our research suggests that interaction is multifunctional and that both strategy use and argumentation yield insights into the integrativeness of a settlement. This study also makes a case for employing a hierarchical coding system for analyzing integrative outcomes.[4] More research on negotiation process needs to track the evolution and outcome of bargaining issues. Only when we understand how process and substance fuse, can we fully explain how creative solutions develop from opposing positions.

NOTES

1. For a more complete discussion of bridging, expanding the pie, cost cutting, non-specific compensation, and alteration, see Pruitt (1983a). Froman and Cohen (1970) present empirical and conceptual comparisons of logrolling and compromise.

2. Campbell (1975) argues that degrees of freedom in data comparison result from multiple data points. "The process of a kind of pattern matching . . . in which there are many aspects of the pattern . . . that are available for observation" (p. 182). In this study the 16 agenda items serve as degrees of freedom for examining patterns of behavior.

3. The four bargaining outcomes were analyzed with a CROSSTABS procedure to determine the number of zero cells for the 16 bargaining strategies and the nine argumentation categories. Although cell sizes were low for threats, humor, and P_2, they were sufficient for data analysis. Some of the bargaining issues, for example, mileage, teachers evaluation, and so on, were low in overall number of statements, but when collapsed with other issues in their outcome category, these low frequencies did not result in zero cells across the four outcomes.

4. The researchers ran *t* tests and correlations for outcomes coded into integrative (bridging and sharpening) and distributive categories (trade-off and win-lose) and found only two statistically significant categories; exploratory problem solving and workability. Hence, breaking outcomes into four hierarchically arranged categories proved to be a more precise test of links between bargaining interaction and type of settlement than traditional bipolar categories.

PART III

Negotiation

Introduction

Margaret A. Neale

Over the years the study of negotiation has undergone many transitions. One might even suggest that negotiation research has closely mirrored, though lagging behind, the changes that have occurred in the study of organizational behavior. Organizational behavior was initially a "scientific" study of human behavior, using the analogy of "worker as machine" (Taylor, 1916). One of negotiation's earliest incarnations was as economic and game theory, using economic assumptions and paradigms to explain bargainer behavior (Nash, 1950; Rapoport & Chammah, 1965; von Neumann & Morgenstern, 1947; Zeuthan, 1950). In both instances, the behaviors being explained were the result of rational individuals interacting with one another.

In the 1930s and 1940s, the work of Elton Mayo (1945) and his contemporaries forced a new perspective in organizational behavior—that of the worker as a complex, social being. While much later chronologically, the next serious transition for negotiation researchers was to move beyond the tenets of economic theory. Although Follett (1924) first described the positive aspects of integrative conflict management, behavioral theories of negotiation did not receive much attention until the publication of Walton & McKersie's (1965) book *A Behavioral Theory of Labor Negotiations*.

Until the early and mid-1970s, the major research investigating bargaining and negotiation typically occurred among two very disparate groups—the institutional economists and the social psychologists. The social psychologists focused on such issues as negotiator personality and demographics, initial offers, power disparities, and concession behavior among other topics (compare Rubin & Brown, 1975). The institutional economists paid attention to strike activity and contract negotiations, attempting to discern what situational factors were responsible (Cross, 1969). These two groups, however, worked in isolation. There seemed to be little of interest to psychologists in the work of the economists and little to interest the economists in the individual and dyadic negotiation research conducted by the psychologists.

In the last ten years, however, negotiation research has made another of its transitions—viewing negotiation from a decision-making perspective. This research has facilitated the repair of the economist/psychologist split. That is, variables of interest to both groups find application in this cognitive approach to understanding negotiation (Lax & Sebenius, 1986; Raiffa, 1982).

Of the four chapters that are in this section, all of them explicitly address the cognitive or decision theoretic view of negotiation. In Chapter 11, *Cognitive Aspects of Negotiation: New Perspectives on Dyadic Decision Making* which reviews recent cognitive negotiation research, Neale, Northcraft, and Bazerman identify four new areas of interest. While the specifics of each of these new directions is described in detail in the manuscript, it should be noted that each of these contexts has moved considerably beyond the view that negotiation is a phenomenon limited to industrial relations practitioners or used car salespeople. Rather, negotiation and the actors involved with this process are found in all areas of organizational life. As suggested by Fisher and Ury (1981),

Negotiation is a fact of life. You discuss a raise with your boss. You try to agree with a stranger on a price for his house. . . . Everyone negotiates something every day. People negotiate even when they don't think of themselves as doing so. A person negotiates with his spouse about where to go for dinner and with his child about when the lights go out. . . . Negotiation is the basic means of getting what you want from others. It is back-and-forth communication designed to reach an agreement when you and the other side have some interests that are shared and others that are opposed. (p. 2)

Based upon the work of Thompson and Hastie (in press), the development of accuracy in a negotiator's assessment of the other party—of his or her utilities across issues; future negotiating moves; and his or her own aspiration levels, reservation price, strategy and behavior—are examined. The second area of research examines negotiating expertise. Neale and Northcraft (in press) suggest that experts are those who are able to produce great outcomes. Identifying three ways in which great outcomes can occur, they suggest that, for true negotiating expertise, an individual must develop a strategic conceptualization (or cognitive map) of the negotiating process.

The other two research areas focus on examining some of the basic assumptions of negotiation. Previous research into the process and outcome of negotiation has always taken for granted (1) the choice to negotiate rather than implement some other form of exchange process and (2) the choice of an opponent.

The Chapter 12, *Goal Setting, Interdependence, and Conflict Management*, Earley and Northcraft illustrate the costs and benefits of goal setting in an interdependent task and the impact of both public and private knowledge of goals in task negotiation and coordination. They examine two different forms of task interdependence (serial and reciprocal) and suggest that goal setting can facilitate performance in such tasks if the goals set are made public. Setting goals has proved beneficial in improving individual performance because it anchors expectations, stimulates strategy search, and encourages effort. With interdependent tasks (and at least two parties), the setting of joint goals (a form of negotiation) is expected to manage the conflict inherent in such tasks. Unlike the other chapters in this section, this approach is highly theoretical and speculative. It does, in contast to the other empirical studies, have the potential of stimulating an entirely new direction of research.

Starke and Notz, in chapter 13, *Impact of Managerial Arbitration and Subunit Power on Bargainer Behavior and Commitment,* bring a slightly different focus to this section. Their work centers on the impact of strategy selection by a manager and relative power (vis-à-vis the negotiating opponent) of his or her subordinates on preintervention (that is, negotiating) behavior. This particular piece highlights two novel concerns. First, there is an implicit assumption that the intervention of a manager may have an effect on subordinate negotiation that is qualitatively and quantitatively different than that consistent with the intervention of a traditional third party. The manager's intervention differs from more traditional third parties in his or her long-term involvement with the parties and the dispute and the ability to switch intervention roles (thus, having the potential to control both outcome and process of the dispute if desired).

Further, this chapter and its focus on commitment begins to highlight another gap in the negotiation research—the relationship between strategy selection and emotion. The process of commitment to an organization, an agreement, or a relationship is not solely based upon cognition. The emotional component of this process represents an area in negotiation that has generally been overlooked.

The last chapter in the section continues the perspective of decision making in negotiation, while specifically extending the emphasis and importance of affect. With few exceptions (see Carnevale & Isen, in press), negotiation research has been notorious in ignoring the impact of affect on decision making. While such concerns have only recently been addressed in the organizational behavior literature (Kelley, 1984), the literature in negotiation is characteristically lagging. Investigating the impact of affect on negotiator cognitions and judgment provides yet another piece to the puzzle. Rajesh Kumar, in his *Affect, Cognition, and Decision Making in Negotiation: An Integration* (Chapter 14), examines the bargaining behavior between Japanese and American business people. He suggests that differing cognitions, expectations and cultural mores lead to the different negotiating styles of the Americans and Japanese. Given that negotiation is an interdependent process, these disparate styles result in unpredictable patterns of responses between these two groups. The spiral of negative affect and the implications of such emotions on subsequent cognitions and strategy decisions is explored.

In sum, the four chapters comprising this section provide a realistic perspective of the cognitive emphasis of current research in bargaining and negotiation. One can clearly see the influence of both economics and psychology in the lineage of negotiation research. The pendulum that once favored economics has now almost completely shifted toward a psychological orientation with the increasing emphasis on affect and its influence on judgment and cognition. As in the field of organizational behavior, the direction and emphasis of research changes over the years. What we have presented in this section is the current and near-future emphasis of negotiation research. Where these streams will lead future researchers remains to be seen.

11

Cognitive Aspects of Negotiation: New Perspectives on Dyadic Decision Making

Margaret A. Neale
Gregory B. Northcraft
Max H. Bazerman

Pruitt (1983a) defines negotiation as a process by which two or more interdependent parties who do not have identical preferences across decision alternatives make joint decisions. The distinctive aspect of this definition is its focus on negotiation *as a decision-making process*. We find this focus particularly useful, since decisions are the aspects of negotiation over which the negotiator has the most control. Examining negotiation from a decision-making perspective is a recent innovation. While the empirical literature on negotiation has a long tradition, typically, it has examined situational (contextual features) and dispositional (negotiator personality traits) influences on negotiator performance (Rubin & Brown, 1975; Lewicki & Litterer, 1985). Examples of contextual features would include the existence or lack of a ''zone of agreement'' and the type of dispute resolution procedure to be invoked in the event of impasse. Examples of negotiator personality traits would include risk propensity and perspective taking ability. Interestingly, contextual features and participant personalities tend to be relatively fixed within a negotiation exchange.

Alternatively, negotiator information-processing strategies—the ways negotiators select information and integrate negotiation information and make decisions—are an aspect of the negotiation exchange over which participants have a great deal of control. Raiffa's (1982) excellent book outlines the study of how to prescribe the best decision for a negotiator, given the best assessment of the opponent's decision-making process. A complementary stream of research has focused on the judgmental deficiencies of negotiators (compare Neale & Bazerman, 1985a; Bazerman & Carroll, 1987). This research describes how nego-

The third author's contribution to this paper was supported by the Dispute Resolution Research Center at Northwestern University.

tiators deviate from rationality. The advantages of this descriptive approach for improving negotiation effectiveness is that it allows negotiators (1) to identify deficient cognitive patterns that need to be corrected in their decision processes and (2) to make better assessments of the likely behavior of opponent negotiators.

The descriptive study of negotiator cognitions has been limited to identifying a wide range of judgmental deficiencies that affect negotiators. For example, this research has shown that individuals (1) ignore the decision-making processes of the other negotiator (Samuelson & Bazerman, 1985; Bazerman & Carroll, 1987), (2) assume a mythical fixed-pie (Thompson & Hastie, in press; Bazerman, Magliozzi, & Neale, 1985), (3) nonrationally escalate their commitment to a previous course of action (Bazerman & Neale, 1983), (4) are overconfident (Bazerman & Neale, 1982a; Thompson & Hastie, in press), (5) are affected by the frame in which information is presented (Neale & Bazerman, 1985b), and (6) are irrationally affected by the saliance of information (Neale, 1984). The overall picture that emerges from this research is that negotiators are systematically affected by a large number of cognitive biases.

This paper outlines current developments that are extending this perspective in the study of negotiations. Four current trends in the study of negotiator cognition are discussed: (1) the impact of cognitive biases on the accuracy of negotiator judgment, (2) the decisions that negotiators make concerning whether or not to engage in a negotiation, (3) the rationality of matching processes by which negotiators end up negotiating with a particular opponent out of a pool of possible opponents, and (4) the role of experience and expertise on negotiator judgment and effectiveness. Taken together, we see this paper outlining some of the developing directions in the study of negotiator cognition.

ACCURACY IN NEGOTIATION

The research on negotiator cognitions reviewed above has taken an approach of examining the impact of biases on the outcomes of negotiations, infering deficiencies in accuracy. Thompson and Hastie (1988) have outlined a program of research which focuses on how cognitive biases affect the accuracy of many important judgments that are required to negotiate effectively. In addition to examining whether or not negotiators who are more accurate achieve more successful agreements, this research outlines the cognitive demands facing the negotiator.

Many negotiation researchers note that the task of negotiation requires many accurate assessments (Lax & Sebenius, 1986; Raiffa, 1982). Thompson and Hastie (in press) provide a taxonomy of these demands. They argue that the negotiation task requires that the negotiator must accurately make judgments in at least the following domains:

Judgments of the other party. These judgments include perceptions of the other negotiator's personality, strategy, and behaviors.

Judgments of self. These judgments include perceptions of one's own aspiration level, reservation price, behavior and personality.

Judgment of utilities across issues. These judgments are concerned with the focal negotiator's ability to assess their own utility across issues, and the parallel utilities of their opponent. These assessments are critical for finding mutually beneficial trade-offs across issues.

Judgments of offer–counteroffer moves. These judgments deal with the ability to assess future negotiating moves contingent on more immediate moves.

Thompson and Hastie (in press) have found that individuals are likely to be very inaccurate before the beginning of the negotiation. Before you meet the opponent, you are likely to have severe limitations on making these assessments. However, most of the accuracy improvement that negotiators will develop occurs in the very early portion of a negotiation. This suggests that we should be concerned not only with the preparation that a negotiator does before entering into a negotiation, but also with the negotiator's ability to learn during the negotiation, especially during the very early stages. This suggests that making assumptions and being closed-minded are particularly dangerous limiting cognitions in negotiation.

The study of accuracy is a natural extension of the previous literature on negotiator cognition. It moves us from inferring the process by which biases affect us to directly assessing the impact of biases on negotiator accuracy. This line of research provides a process criterion to aim for in improving negotiator decision making.

CHOOSING WHETHER OR NOT TO NEGOTIATE

Virtually all of the negotiation literature focuses on situations in which it is expected that two (or more) parties will engage in a negotiation. However, many situations are ambiguous in terms of the social demands to negotiate or not negotiate. When do people choose to negotiate? For some, negotiation is a common activity. For others, it is unusual and uncomfortable. Neale and Northcraft have recently begun research to help understand the decision of whether or not to negotiate, and common mistakes that negotiators make in this choice.

When the term "negotiation" is used generally, it is likely in reference to a particular set of behaviors centering around the exchanging of (usually expensive) goods or services for money, the formal exchange between management and labor in the institutionalized setting of collective bargaining, or to international exchanges which attempt to allocate resources or make "deals on a global level" (Lewicki & Litterer, 1985). Other forms of exchange seem to be classified as transactions—those interactions for which there is no opportunity for the participants to alter the nature (that is, price or terms) of the exchange. However, the opportunities for negotiation are considerably more widespread than these limited categories suggest. Thus, an area of investigation which has largely remained untouched is (1) examining the ubiquitious nature of negotiation and

(2) identifying factors which lead individuals to perceive a situation as a "negotiation" rather than a "transaction."

Negotiation is often broadly defined as "the process whereby two or more parties attempt to settle what each will give and take, or perform and receive, in transaction between them" (Rubin & Brown, 1975). While this is an admittedly generic definition of an exchange process, bargaining and negotiation is often described with greater specificity by identifying certain unique characteristics. Lewicki and Litterer (1985) suggest that negotiation occurs when:

1. Conflict of interest exists between two or more parties.
2. No fixed or established rules exist for resolving the conflict.
3. The parties prefer to search for agreement rather than to fight openly, capitulate, break off interaction, or take their dispute to a higher authority to resolve. (p. 5)

Rubin and Brown (1975) identified five characteristics of negotiation, of which two are common to the Lewicki and Litterer (1985) definition. These five characteristics are:

1. Two or more parties involved.
2. Conflict exists between the parties.
3. Parties are joined in a form of voluntary relationship.
4. Division and exchange of tangible and intangible resources.
5. Sequential evaluation of alternatives.

There seems to be nothing in either of these attempts to define or specify the negotiation process which would lead individuals to limit so severely the types of exchanges classified as negotiations. In fact, both of these characteristic sets seem to suggest that negotiations can occur in almost any social exchange setting.

In determining the factors which might influence an individual's decision making in this domain, the literature on negotiation offers several candidates. Factors such as issue importance (Pruitt, 1983a; Neale & Bazerman, 1985a), relative power of the exchange participants, and resource dependence (Fisher & Ury, 1981) have been shown to influence negotiator success (that is, the attainment of those resource allocation advantages associated with a negotiated outcome). The perceived probability of attaining a successfully negotiated outcome may mediate the choice of exchange process (transaction or negotiation), such that those factors which influence negotiator success might indirectly determine the particular process choice. A fourth factor which may influence exchange process choice is an individual difference variable—the propensity to negotiate.

Traditionally, research in negotiation has been divided into two camps: individual differences and situational influences. The first proposes an individual difference perspective and suggests that negotiated outcomes are the result of intrinsic traits, characteristics, or orientations of the negotiator. The second model—the structural influences model—suggests that negotiated outcomes and processes are determined primarily by contextual variables, bargaining strategies, and characteristics of the disputed issues (Lewicki & Litterer, 1985).

The second or structural model has found more support in the recent literature as individual differences measures have routinely accounted for very little variance in behavior. However, the research upon which these conclusions are based investigates the impact of situation and disposition after the individual finds him/herself in a negotiating situation. The choice scenario which is the focus of this research occurs prior to the exchange interaction and may be qualitatively and quantitatively very different. That is, the import of structural and dispositional variables may have a very different relationship when influencing the choice of transacting or negotiating.

Beyond the differences in temporal orientation between this and previous research in negotiation, a second reason for considering dispositional variables is based upon a recent review of the literature on dispositional influences on job attitudes (Staw, Bell, & Clausen, 1986). They suggest that research from a dispositional or individual difference perspective is regaining popularity. Weiss and Adler (1984) suggest that the poor predictive power of dispositional variables may be the result of their use in an atheoretical manner to explain additional variance in situational studies. Thus, they suggest that the theoretical rigor of the research was directed towards understanding situational influences of behaviors; dispositional variables were, at best, an afterthought.

The influence of the dispositional variable (propensity to negotiate) and the three structural variables (issue importance, relative power, and resource dependence) can be summarized in a model presented in Figure 11.1. The proposed model is a hybrid, incorporating both social cognition and rational choice components in a two stage process. In the first stage, the propensity to negotiate drives the perception of whether negotiation is a viable exchange alternative. If negotiation is perceived as an option, an evaluation is made in the second stage of the probability that negotiation can or will succeed in improving the exchange outcome. The estimated probability that the negotiation will improve the exchange outcome is a function of the structural variables; probability of outcome improvement acts as a mediating variable and propensity to negotiate moderates the relationship between estimated probability of improvement and the exchange process choice. Since no research to date has addressed the question of exchange process choice, the model presented in Figure 11.1 should be considered speculative and as a mechanism to guide future research.

MATCHING AND NEGOTIATION

The last section noted that the existing negotiation literature has been limited to examining situations in which an individual has chosen to begin a negotiation. In addition, the existing literature assumes that a negotiator has already identified

Figure 11.1
Factors Affecting Exchange Process

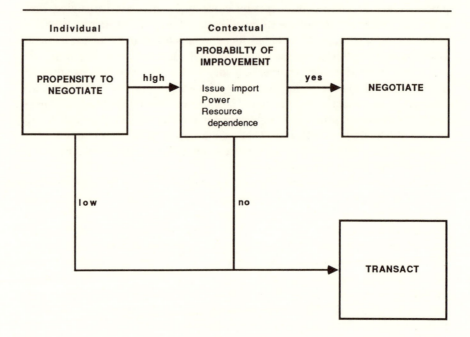

his/her negotiation opponent. That is, the negotiation literature has assumed that two (or more) individuals have already decided to negotiate with each other. In contrast, most of our more important life negotiations involve simultaneous matching and negotiation processes. For example, when you last purchased a house, the process consisted of matching with the correct house *and* negotiating the price of that house. The wrong house at the right price *or* the right house at the wrong price would be a mistake. Thus, understanding the simultaneous matching and negotiation process is critical to a complete view of negotiator cognition.

Another example of this matching occurs in job markets. For example, consider the job markets for newly minted MBAs. Every year, sixty thousand enter the U.S. job market. How do these individuals obtain the best match with an employer and negotiate favorable terms of employment? Behavior in these markets is highly influenced by the institutional nature of these markets. The matches in the MBA job market occur with minimal intervention from business schools. However, in other labor markets, the match is almost entirely determined by an institutionalized system. The job market for residents and hospitals is governed this way. Prior to having an institutionalized structure, very poor matches occurred, hospitals were going without doctors, agreements were reached too early (in the second year of medical school in some cases), and the system was unstable—parties on both sides had an incentive to change agreements.

In 1951, hospitals and medical schools adopted a centralized matching clearinghouse, known as the National Resident Matching Program (NRMP). The NRMP receives information from each hospital on how many positions it has available, as well as a ranked preference ordering of the graduating medical students who have applied for one of its positions. From the students, NRMP receives a ranked preference ordering of the hospitals to which he or she has applied. The clearinghouse then employs an algorithm that matches the preference of the hospitals and those of the students. This match is rational in the sense that no two participants from opposite sides of the market prefer each other to the parties to whom they have been matched. In addition, if you aggregate the utility of students and hospitals and put them on opposing axes, the NRMP solution is pareto optimal.

The solutions generated in the MBA market appear not to be pareto optimal (Sondak & Bazerman, 1987). Yet, parties in this market would have no interest in a computer algorithm. Why? In this competitive market, participants want control and believe that they can outperform the algorithm—even if they do believe that the algorithm would create better matches in general. Why don't natural markets generate rational outcomes? These markets are important to both parties and a great deal of satisficing occurs. When faced with the choice of taking a good offer or risking it for a great offer, most students are fairly risk averse and lock in the opportunity available. With offers occuring at different times, it is hard for a rational solution to emerge.

Rationality is limited as a result of the social dilemma facing the participants in such markets. If one firm (or hospital) wants to obtain a competitive advantage, it may be able to improve its competitive position by placing pressure on a potential employee by making an offer very early in the process with a short fuse (deadline). The employee may then choose to take a sure thing rather than the risk of turning down the offer and returning to the market. However, if all (or many) firms respond in this manner, everyone will be recruiting earlier and earlier, with less and less information about the other side of the market. This is precisely what happened in the hospital market. Unfortunately, what is in the competitive interests of any particular firm may not be in the interest of the collectivity of firms or the collectivity of potential employees.

This analysis suggests that we may need to define an optimal set of behaviors differently at different levels of analysis. We can examine the rational behavior for the firm given a particular set of institutional circumstances. We can identify the solution that would maximize the sum of the utility of all actors in the market. Or we can define rationality in terms of an institutional structure that encourages actors to behave in ways that will lead to the collective good. The interconnection of these various decisions is critical to minimizing irrational behavior in matching problem.

How rational are the decisions made in Sondak and Bazerman's experimental markets that attempt to simulate naturally occurring conditions? Not particularly rational. Offers are not managed well, and tough choices often need to be made. The quality of the set of matches that emerge are far from the matches that would occur using a rational algorithm. In addition, there is substantial evidence that the simultaneous demands of the matching problem reduce the effectiveness of the negotiation process.

EXPERTS AND EXPERIENCE

Research which focuses on negotiation as an interdependent decision-making process has emphasized the impact of cognitive biases on negotiator judgment and subsequent outcome. Recently, however, the results of both basic and applied research on cognitive biases has been called into question. The majority of the negotiation research as well as virtually all of the initial research identifying and specifying cognitive heuristics has been conducted in laboratory settings. These studies typically use student subjects negotiating or making decisions in areas in which they have little task-specific knowledge (Neale & Northcraft, in press). Further, Hogarth (1981) suggests that researchers have tended to focus on the discrete processes of choice and prediction within the stimulus impoverished walls of the laboratory rather than the complex, changing, feedback-rich natural environment in which decision makers can develop task-domain knowledge. Thus, feedback and expertise would ameliorate or eliminate the influence of these decisional biases on expert decision makers in real world settings.

Important to this discussion is the notion of expertise. A number of researchers have tried to specify the nature of expertise (Boulding, 1958; Einhorn, 1974; Fiske, 1961; Johnson, Duran, Hassebrock, Moller, Prietula, Feltovick, & Swanson, 1981). While these definitions range in complexity, one practical operationalization of an expert is an individual whose decisions produce great outcomes. Great outcomes, however, can be generated by three distinctly different processes. First, great outcomes can occur because of random factors. One is simply lucky. Second, great outcomes can occur because of task-specific experience. For example, an individual may be trained to respond in a certain manner to particular situational cues. Expertise, however, is more than simply task-specific learning. Experts are expected to be able to produce great outcomes under a variety of conditions—their expertise is transferable (Fiske, 1961). The third mechanism for producing great outcomes is the expert's development of a cognitive map of the domain over which he/she is an expert.

Recent research using expert subjects in both novel and routine situations (in the real world as well as in the laboratory) has examined the importance of expertise in innoculating decision makers from cognitive bias. Neale and Northcraft (1986) report that expert negotiators generally outperformed amateur (student) negotiators in a novel competitive market negotiation. However, the experts were as influenced as the amateurs to the framing and anchoring-and-adjustment bias. In the study of expertise and *routine* tasks, Northcraft and Neale (1987) report that expert residential real estate negotiators and amateurs were significantly influenced by the anchor of the listing price. In neither research setting did expertise or experience with the task, or real world setting (that is, opportunity for feedback) reduce the impact of cognitive biases on the negotiated outcome.

The results of these two studies suggest that expertise and real world scenarios may not be the panacea for decision makers. From these studies, two research questions arise:

1. Why is it that experts do not learn from experience to avoid the systematic biasing of cognitive heuristics?
2. Why is it that training does not ameliorate the influence of cognitive biases in experts' decision making?

One model which may facilitate an understanding of the missing pieces of the puzzle is provided in Figure 11.2. One can imagine the process of making a decision as being composed of a plan, an action, and an outcome. However, there are two additional components which are necessary for the production of a great outcome. The outcome must produce *feedback* and the decision maker must have a *strategic conceptualization* of the process in order to identify to which

Figure 11.2
Factors in the Development of Expertise

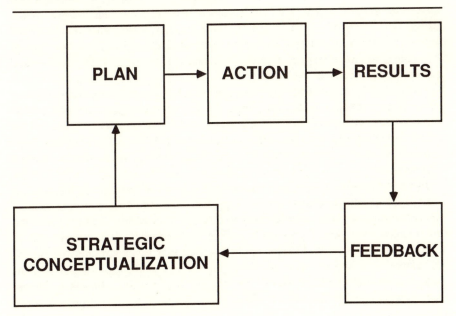

aspect of the feedback to attend and how to incorporate that feedback into the strategic conceptualization.

Feedback is a critical component in the development of expertise. Without feedback as to performance, the decision maker has little opportunity or reason to alter his/her behavior to improve performance (Landy & Farr, 1982). If feedback is ambiguous, nondiagnostic, or misleading, it cannot be corrective and may even reinforce inappropriate responses (Einhorn & Hogarth, 1978). Factors which reduce a decision maker's ability to learn from feedback fall into two broad categories: psychological and practical barriers.

Psychological barriers include (1) lack of search for and use of disconfirming feedback (Hastorf & Cantril, 1954; Rosen & Tesser, 1970; Staw, 1976), (2) incorrect interpretation of the causes of the outcome (Kelley, 1972; Nisbett & Ross, 1980), and (3) the use of unaided memory for coding, storing and retrieving outcome information (Einhorn, 1980; Einhorn & Hogarth, 1978). Practical constraints on the use of corrective feedback include (1) determining to what type of feedback to attend (Einhorn & Hogarth, 1978) and (2) the unobservability of outcomes which were not chosen (Bazerman & Neale, 1982a).

Thus, the feedback provided by experience may be problematic in both its gathering and its interpretation. However, suppose that high quality diagnostic feedback is available, is that a sufficient condition to insure "great outcomes." As suggested by Figure 11.2, another important factor in expertise is the development of a strategic conceptualization of the domain.

The significance of strategic conceptualization to expertise is considerable. Dawes and Corrigan (1974) suggest that expertise means knowing what environmental cues need to be monitored and which can be ignored. It defines which environmental parameters are critical and which are irrelevant in light of the causal schema by which the task is framed. Further, during the trial-and-error strategy acquisition phase, a strategic conceptualization limits the universe of hypotheses to test, allowing the decision maker the mechanism for selecting and incorporating feedback. As Johnson et al. (1981) suggest, experts make decisions by classifying situations as tasks with which they are familiar and applying previously successful solutions. Thus, the correct strategic conceptualization provides the appropriate perceptual set by which environmental cues can be monitored and evaluated. The right perceptual set is what makes feedback diagnostic and what makes an expert, expert. The wrong perceptual set simply interferes.

From a decision theoretic perspective, the notions of strategic conceptualization coupled with diagnostic feedback provide new guidance to researchers in understanding expertise—particularly in a negotiation setting. The results of the empirical work reported previously (Neale & Northcraft, 1986; Northcraft & Neale, 1987) suggest that avoidance of decision bias by experts may be tied to the extent to which the strategic conceptualization of the negotiation task includes procedures that specifically address the potential decision biases. Thus, the strategic conceptualization is likely to deal *primarily* with the prevention of decision bias.

It is unlikely that the development of negotiation specific expertise would revolve around the prevention of decision bias. Additionally, attempts to "debias" decision makers has been met with only limited success (Fischhoff, 1982). Researchers, then, need to consider other avenues of inquiry for mechanisms to alleviate the influence of decision bias on negotiator performance.

If cognitive bias in negotiation is not under conscious control, amelioration of bias may depend upon the identification of noncognitive aids to decision making. For example, worksheets have been used successfully to overcome the availability bias in decision makers (Northcraft & Neale, 1986). The development of computerized decision aids as a means of compensating for decision bias seems particularly promising in this vein. The most sophisticated approach to the avoidance of decision bias via decision aids is the use of expert systems (Gorry & Krumland, 1983). The a priori specification of the decision process by the expert system prevents transitory cognitive processes from having an impact. Further, such specification allows for public scrutiny. Faulty assumptions and incorrect computation strategies in the expert systems are more likely to be exposed and corrected. The expert system, then, can provide a comparison for decisions made by human decisions makers.

Whether expert systems (or decision aids of other sorts) hold real promise for de-biasing negotiators remains an issue to be settled by future researchers. However, perhaps the important issue addressed here is in restructuring the definition of experts and expertise. Perhaps experts need not make decisions with "great outcomes" all the time, they just need to make decisions with better outcomes.

CONCLUSION

Traditionally, research on negotiation has been concerned with normative models and the descriptive study of situational and dispositional determinants of negotiation effectiveness. Part of this focus likely results from the economic and institutional roots of negotiation research. The negotiators that researchers thought about in the past (for example, labor-management negotiators) always knew when a negotiation situation existed and with whom they would be negotiating. However, as the organizational literature recognized negotiation as a more ubiquitous organizational activity, it also became necessary to focus on the decisions being made by organizational actors in competitive situations. Managers want to know how to make more intelligent decisions in competitive situations, and it is a decision perspective that is most likely to provide this guidance.

Recently researchers have come to see negotiation as a decision-making process. A literature has developed which shows that a great deal of the suboptimality that can be observed in negotiation results from deficiencies in the information processing strategies of negotiators. This paper has attempted to build upon that developing literature to show that a decision theory perspective is critical to realizing a more complete and robust understanding of the negotiation process and the outcomes of negotiation. The development of negotiator accuracy, the choice to negotiate, the selection and matching of negotiation opponents, and the development of negotiator expertise are all research issues whose resolution will augment this new understanding. Each of these research topics represents a new direction in negotiator cognition research. When combined with earlier research on situations and dispositional determinants of negotiator performance, a decision theory perspective on negotiation offers a powerful new way for helping to make individual, organizational, and international negotiations more understandable and eventually more effective.

12

Goal Setting, Resource Interdependence, and Conflict Management

P. Christopher Earley
Gregory B. Northcraft

INTRODUCTION

Conflict is an element basic to human endeavors. As individuals interact and engage in inconsistent activities or compete for scarce resources conflict will occur (Rahim, 1986a). Conflict management refers to individual and organizational interventions designed to optimize levels of conflict such that individual and organizational goals are accomplished (Katz & Kahn, 1978; Rahim, 1986). Recent research in conflict management has followed two paths. On the one hand, conflict management research has focused on *contextual* features and the impact of these features on the ability of disputants to reach agreement. Included in the list of contextual considerations are: the economic realities of a dispute, such as payoff contingencies (Rappoport & Chammah, 1965), the existence (or lack) of a "zone of agreement" (see, for example, Raiffa, 1982) which dictates whether solutions acceptable to both parties are attainable; structural arrangements, such as the impasse procedures put in place to resolve formal conflicts in the event of impasse (for example, Neale, 1984) which substantially influence disputants' willingness to work toward a mutually agreeable solution; and behavioral strategies and tactics, such as the development of integrative approaches to conflict management (Pruitt, 1983a). All of these contextual concerns share a primary focus on aspects of the conflict *external* to the disputants.

In contrast to this external focus is a complementary *internal* focus proposed in the work of Walton and McKersie (1965). Walton and McKersie suggest that the realities of contextual characteristics are not nearly so important to the under-

The authors would like to thank E. Locke and E. Mannix for their helpful comments on an earlier draft of this chapter. Support for this chapter was provided, in part, by a grant from the University of Arizona's Center for Microcontamination Control.

standing of conflict management as the disputants' cognitions about those context characteristics. This concern has led some researchers (for example, Hartnett et al., 1968; Sherman, 1967) to focus on personality characteristics (such as risk-taking propensity) to understand dispute resolution behavior. In its most recent incarnation, the cognitive approach to understanding conflict management has led researchers to examine the implications of viewing conflict management as a process of judgment (Neale & Bazerman, 1985a). This infusion of conflict management research with models of human judgment, and its biases and shortcomings (see Nisbett & Ross, 1980), seems particularly appropriate in view of the recent dominance of these models in research on individual decision behavior (see, Kahneman, Slovic, & Tversky, 1982).

Goal setting is a management tool which fits both of these emphases in conflict management research. Goal setting often exists as a contextual feature of the work environment—for instance, when goal setting or goal assignment is a mandated organizational activity. Goal setting also activates cognitive processes which can dramatically influence performance. Unfortunately, little work has attempted to bring together the goal-setting and conflict-management literatures, despite indications that goal setting has a positive contribution to make in the field of conflict management (for example, Huber & Neale, 1986a). This chapter focuses on the importance of goal setting as a technique of conflict management. Specifically, goal setting may be helpful to the management of conflict arising in situations of high interdependence. Interdependence refers to situations in which an individual's work activities are dependent on some other individual's actions. Under conditions of high interdependence there is potential for conflict. This chapter will begin by summarizing the nature of interdependence and its potential for generating conflict. Next a short review of goal setting will be presented. The role of goals in the performance of interdependent tasks then will be discussed. Finally, a discussion of a goal-setting approach to manage conflict resulting from task interdependence will be presented.

TASK INTERDEPENDENCE

Task interdependence refers to the interconnections between tasks such that the performance of one task depends on the successful performance of other tasks (Kiggundu, 1981, 1983). Interdependence also reflects the degree to which an individual is dependent on and directly supports others in task accomplishment (Thompson, 1967). Interdependence occurs when work flows from one individual to another individual such that successful performance by the latter individual (the receiver) depends on the performance of the former individual (the initiator). Several researchers (Galbraith, 1978; Susman, 1976; Slocum & Sims, 1980; Thompson, 1967) have suggested that as task interdependence increases, there must be a corresponding increase in co-worker coordination, communication, and mutual adjustment to maintain performance. The need for mutual adjustment and extensive communication arises from the uncertainty inherent in highly interdependent task situations which require information to be gathered and processed during task execution.

From the perspective of the conflict management literature, the focus of past interdependence research on the initiated/received dichotomy is somewhat misleading because it extracts interdependence from the larger organizational context. An important source of conflict in work settings is attributable to resource dependencies within interdependent relationships. More important than whether interdependencies are initiated or received is whether these initiated and received interdependencies map into symmetrical or asymmetrical resource dependencies. This symmetry concern gives rise to a second critical dichotomy: serial (asymmetrical) interdependence versus reciprocal (symmetrical) interdependence. Serial (asymmetric) interdependence exists if the outputs or outcomes of one individual are dependent on resources received from another individual but not vice versa. Reciprocal (symmetric) interdependence exists if the outputs or outcomes of two individuals are mutually dependent such that the outputs or outcomes of each individual necessarily influence the outputs or outcomes of the other person. For instance, the relationship between a welder and a forklift truck operator is serial: the welder can only work as long as the forklift operator supplies the welder with needed materials. A reciprocal interdependent setting is exemplified by the exchange between colleagues working together on a research project. In this circumstance, project success is tied to the joint actions of both colleagues. Note that in the serial (asymmetric) condition the outcomes of the welder may be hindered by the actions of the forklift operator while the forklift operator's outcomes will not be affected by the welder's actions. On the other hand, the reciprocal (symmetric) interdependent colleagues *necessarily* influence one another's outcomes (e.g., project success) by their individual actions.

The nature of the interdependence implies that the outcomes of one individual are influenced by the actions of another individual. It is this dependence that acts as the catalyst of conflict; conflict will arise in an interdependent setting if the actions of one individual interferes with the outcome attainment of another individual (Katz & Kahn, 1978; Rahim, 1986a; Strauss, 1962). This is not to imply, however, that interdependencies lead to irreversible conflict (Rahim, 1977). Rather, the potential for conflict in an interdependency increases as resources become scarce and exchanges become potentially exploitive (Baldwin, 1978; Walton, Dutton, & Cafferty, 1969).

While interdependencies in work setting certainly map onto power relationships, conflict arising from the use of power is *not* the focus of this chapter. The study of power generally focuses on the intentional use of resource dependencies by one individual to influence or change the actions of another (see, for example, Hirschmann, 1970). Interdependencies in work setting do provide power to individuals (through resource dependencies), and the use of this power can produce conflict if, for instance, one individual intentionally exploits resource dependencies in a way which frustrates the efforts of an interdependent other. However, this chapter looks at conflict which arises in interdependent work settings when each individual is pursuing his or her own agenda and thereby *unintentionally* frustrates the efforts of an interdependent other. Thus, interdependent work arrangements may give rise to conflict in two different ways: unintentional and intentional (power) resource control. This paper focuses on the management of conflict arising from unintentional resource control in interdependent work arrangements.

GOAL SETTING

The basic process of goal setting includes five stages (Locke, 1968; Locke, Shaw, Saari, & Latham, 1981). The first stage is the general work environment in which a worker operates. The typical focus of this environment is the worker's supervisor who acts as the source of a goal. A worker who receives a goal from his or her supervisor next must cognitively process it. After interpreting the externally provided goal, an individual evaluates the utility of the goal. Several studies have demonstrated that the most critical aspects of this evaluation concern factors external and internal to and interactive with the individual such as obedience to authority, rewards, participation, competition, and expectancy of success concerning goal achievement (Locke, Latham, & Erez, in press). Based on this evaluation, the externally provided goal may or may not be internalized (adopted) by the individual. Assuming that the goal is internalized, it them becomes the individual's own personal goal. This personal goal is the focus of the individual's action. It is the aim or object of the individual (Locke et al., 1981). Finally, although not explicitly represented in the goal-setting model (Locke, 1968), the individual uses a particular task strategy to translate the goal into actual performance.

The specific mechanisms through which goals influence performance can be placed into two categories (Locke et al., 1981): those having a *direct* effect (effort, persistence, and directed attention) on an individual, and those having an *indirect* effect (strategy development). An important distinction between these two types of effects is that the direct influence is primarily motivational—an allocation of the individual's energy-related resources to task performance. The indirect effect is primarily cognitive—the way in which a plan or strategy is developed to utilize the mobilized, energy-related resources. The indirect effect of a goal refers to the strategy development, or planning, engaged in by the individual (Earley, Wojnaroski, & Prest, 1987).

CONFLICT MANAGEMENT BY GOAL SETTING FOR INTERDEPENDENT WORK

Serial Interdependence. In situations of serial work interdependence, the effects of goal setting will depend on whether goals are set by the initiating worker (A) or receiving worker (B) in the interdependent relationship. Goal setting *by the initiator* (A) in serial interdependence should be beneficial. In this case, A's goal will provide A with a structure to work within while providng B important information about A's intended (or probable) production levels. A's goal stimulates task strategy development with which *both* individuals can coordinate activity and thereby decreases the potential for conflict due to resource dependence. This assumes that B receives, accepts, and trusts A's goal.

The ability of goals to energize action and stimulate strategy search may be frustrated if the *receiver* in a serial interdependent relationship has goals. The interdependent receiver (B) will develop a work strategy after being assigned (or setting) a goal. However, a work strategy alone will not necessarily increase input prediction or coordination—the outputs that B receives from A—and can lead to frustration. In the example presented earlier, a welder who receives materials from a forklift operator may wish to perform at a higher rate than is possible given the intention or actions of the forklift operator. If the welder is given a challenging goal and develops an effective strategy, his or her performance may still suffer since it hinges on the supplies delivered by the forklift operator. Likewise, the energizing effect of goals on effort is likely to create conflict between the welder and the forklift operator. As additional energy is channeled toward task performance but is blocked due to factors outside of the welder's control, frustration is likely to build and conflict occur. Unlike a block due to a situational constraint such as broken machinery, the locus of the frustration is with another individual whose actions may be misinterpreted as being malicious.

As suggested above, a side-effect of goal setting by the receiver in serial interdependence concerns the inferences the receiver may make about the initiator. If individual B fails to receive from A needed inputs, individual B may attribute this to malicious activity on the part of individual A. As goals become increasingly covert, the likelihood that individual B will misattribute the actions of individual A also increases. Thus, goal setting by the receiver under circumstances of serial interdependence may exacerbate conflict between individuals. However, it may be possible to reduce this conflict if the interdependent initiator (B) is aware of and accepts the receiver's goal and either adjusts his or her own goal accordingly or convinces the receiver to change his or her goal.

Reciprocal Interdependence. In situations of reciprocal interdependence (such as a negotiation) goal setting functions as both a contextual and cognitive variable. At the contextual level, the goal acts as a stimulus to motivate individual performance. At the cognitive level, the goal serves to define each worker's appropriate performance level through a process of "anchoring-and-adjustment." The psychological literature on "anchoring-and-adjustment" has shown that (a) a reference point (even if arbitrarily chosen) will significantly influence judgments, and (b) subsequent judgments will not be adjusted away from the reference point to reflect accurately new information (Slovic & Lichtenstein, 1971). The reference point cognitively "anchors" each worker's judgments. In an adversarial negotiation, for instance, a predetermined bargaining goal (such as desired hourly wage or final selling price), regardless of how reasonably chosen, can act to anchor a disputant's views of the reasonableness of subsequent offers by the other side. This suggests that goal setting may insulate interdependent workers from persuasion attempts during negotiations by motivationally and cognitively "chilling" each side's willingness to bargain.

The contextual and cognitive effects of goal setting in situations of reciprocal interdependence may facilitate *individual* outcomes perhaps at the expense of *joint* outcomes. If a negotiator has a settlement goal which he or she is motivated to attain and which anchors judgments of what constitutes a fair settlement, myopic attention to the goal might decrease integrative problem solving (in favor of goal attainment) by the party with the goal. This would decrease the probability of reaching an integrative joint agreement. If both parties cognitively are chilled, neither may be willing to negotiate and the probability of settlement should be reduced accordingly. Goal setting also may decrease the probability of settlement if both parties have goals that are mutually exclusive (Huber & Neale, 1986b). As with serial interdependence, goals that are not shared may also lead negotiators to misattribute others' actions as malicious or adversarial. This also would be expected to decrease the probability of an integrative agreement being found.

On the other hand, goal setting may enhance joint outcomes and reduce conflict in a reciprocal interdependence if the interdependent individuals have goals that are mutually compatible and consistent with an integrative agreement. For instance, Huber and Neale (1986b) found that the highest joint outcomes for negotiating dyads occurred if both negotiators had moderate goals or if one individual had a high goal and one individual had a moderate goal. In their study, the moderate and difficult goals were to achieve individual profits of $4600 and $5400, respectively, and an integrative agreement yielded individual profits of $5200. The combinations of goals yielding the highest joint profits were both achievable given the constraints of the task. Thus, goal setting may be a technique for dealing with conflict functionally and thereby maximizing joint outcomes in a reciprocal setting providing that the goals possessed by individuals direct them toward an integrative agreement.

As interdependence increases, resource dependencies become more likely sources of conflict. As noted earlier, if conflict is to be minimized as interdependence increases, there must be a corresponding increase in worker coordination, communication, and mutual adjustment (see, for example, Slocum & Sims, 1980). The contribution of goal setting as a technique to manage resource dependency conflict lies in its capacity to increase co-worker coordination and mutual adjustment by acting as a communication medium and a basis for joint negotiation of activities.

The previous discussion of goal setting has highlighted its power to improve *individual* performance both contextually as a source of motivation that directs effort and cognitively by anchoring expectations and driving strategy search and development. At best, improved individual performance through goal setting may help interdependent performances, for example, when the initiator in a serial interdependent work relationship has goals. At worst, goal setting may lead to conflict in an interdependent relationship if one individual's outcome attainment is frustrated due to the goal-directed actions of another individual. If interdependence is reciprocal, integrative individual outcomes may be attained only at the expense of improved (or even acceptable) joint outcomes.

The assumption that goal setting by the initiator in a serial interdependent work relationship can be useful in optimizing levels of conflict is dependent on the degree to which the goal is *public, communicated,* and *accepted* by the interdependent parties. Although it is not within the scope of this chapter to review the process through which goals are communicated (for a review, see Locke et al., 1981), it is nevertheless important to assume that goals made public are communicated accurately. If B knows what goals A has set, those goals become a critical input to B in the interdependent relationship. Knowing A's goals should help B better predict A's performances and coordinate his or her own performance. While not eliminating resource dependency conflict entirely, the increased prediction and coordination afforded B through goals should substantially decrease the potential for conflict. In addition, the symbolic act of sharing the goal (showing mutual respect and consideration) will increase the likelihood that it will be accepted by the interdependent other and provide the opportunity for the parties to discuss the goal (Katz & Kahn, 1978). Of course, these benefits do not accrue if A's goal remains private unless B infers A's goal from his or her actions.

Goal publicness also promises important reductions in potential resource dependency conflicts when goals are set by the receiver in a serial interdependent relationship. Goal setting by the receiver (B) in situations of serial interdependence leads to frustration if A's behavior frustrates B's goal pursuits. However, if B shares his or her goal with A, A may be able to adjust his or her behavior to accommodate B's goal pursuits, or at least warn B that B's goals are unrealistic and need to be revised. This increased communication also should decrease the likelihood that B will perceive A's behaviors (if goal frustrating) as malicious or adversarial. In either case, if B shares his or her goals with A, the potential for conflict from the resource dependency will be decreased.

Further, the additional coordination obtained by B through goal publicness should decrease B's need for contingency planning for subsequent serial resource dependencies. Thus, public goal setting by the receiver in situations of serial interdependence should have substantial ''trickle down'' benefits of conflict minimization elsewhere in the organization.

Even further conflict minimization can be achieved in serial interdependence if the sharing of B's goal with A results in a *negotiation* of both A's performance and B's goals. Not surprisingly, this possibility of *joint goal negotiation* holds the best promise for conflict management when interdependence is reciprocal. Reciprocal resource dependence suggests that simple goal setting may not minimize conflict since goal attainment by one party may still be at the expense of the other person. Jointly negotiated goals instead may yield resource distributions of higher benefit to *both* parties.

Interestingly, research suggests that the achievement of high joint benefit in situations of reciprocal interdependence is dependent on both parties having moderate to high aspirations and a problem-solving orientation (see, for example, Huber & Neale, 1986b; Pruitt, 1983a). By motivating high levels of performance and stimulating strategy search and development, goal setting provides a useful antecedent condition for the achievement of integrative (high joint benefit) resolutions to reciprocal resource dependencies.

This assumes, of course, that the integrative potential in a resource conflict comes with the possibility of mutual goal attainment for both parties. In circumstances where integrative potential is low, *joint bilateral* goal setting should increase the probability of mutual goal attainment and thereby increase the probability of a settlement. Thus, in situations of reciprocal interdependence it seems important for goals to be either publicly shared or set jointly to prevent private commitment to the pursuit of mutually exclusive outcomes. Goal setting is not as likely to have a detrimental effect on conflict management in interdependent conflict if initial joint goal setting or goal sharing ensures the existence of a ''zone of agreement''—or highlights the need to discover one jointly.

In summary, joint negotiation and disclosure of goals should be critical to effective performance in situations of interdependence. Joint disclosure of goals across an interdependent relationship ensures, at the least, increased coordination via knowledge of expected levels of effort and performance, and resources made available by the participants as well as an understanding concerning the purposeful nature of the interdependent other's actions. Joint goal disclosure may lead even to joint negotiation of goals and outcomes beneficial for both participants. In either event, the information shared (i.e. goals) via joint negotiation and disclosure of goals should serve to coordinate the activities of individuals in a resource dependency thereby optimizing the attainment of individual and organizational goals (Rahim, 1986a).

Implications—Theoretical

The contribution of goal setting as a conflict management technique lies in its emphasis on the importance of communicating goals publicly to optimize levels of resource dependence conflict for individual and organizational goal accomplishment. This contribution can be broken into two components: the relevance for the conflict management and goal-setting literatures.

The role of goal setting in managing conflict in interdependent settings depends, in part, on the publicness of individuals' goals. Given the salience of a performance goal relative to the subtleties of an interdependent setting, it is clear why goal setting might lead to a disregard for non-goal information—such as the desires and aspirations of interdependent others. What this suggests is that private goals within an interdependent setting may create forces to achieve a goal regardless of the considerations of others. An unfortunate outcome of this process might be a tendency to focus on short-term outcomes rather than long-term integrative solutions to problems. Joint negotiation and disclosure of goal setting, in contrast, create forces that highlight considerations of others.

When interdependence is serial, joint negotiation and disclosure of goals can assist in coordinating and predicting behavior. When interdependence is reciprocal, goal setting may have a ''chilling'' effect on negotiations if both sides have goals that were not jointly negotiated and are mutually incompatible. Goal setting in situations of reciprocal interdependence in which disputants' views of appropriate settlements are private may decrease their willingness to make concessions, and may narrow disputants' focus on goal attainment rather than conflict resolution. In contrast, bilateral goal setting in situations of reciprocal interdependence ensures high aspirations and a problem-solving orientation, thereby laying the foundation for resource dependency resolutions of high joint benefit.

The conflict management technique described highlights the rather consistent, intra-individual effects of goal setting. First, joint negotiation or disclosure of goal setting can enhance goal commitment and cooperation by increasing an individual's control over the task situation and increasing his or her's perceived fairness of it. Further, goals provide individuals a basis by which subsequent performance is judged, thereby enhancing the self-reactive motives of an individual. The goal acts as a basis for estimating how much effort must be spent during task performance. The goal also stimulates strategy development which is beneficial to performance to the extent that an individual can successfully enact the strategy. The strategy provides an individual with a specific template for action including estimations concerning the behavior of interdependent others. Such a perspective supports a schema-based model of goal setting (Campbell, in press; Earley & Perry, 1987; Lord & Kernan, 1987). From a schema approach, the goal serves as a driving force for search processes through which a strategy is developed. This chapter suggests that this goal-setting and strategizing process might be differentially influenced by the cues derived from the interdependent situation. In other words, the greater the salience of the interdependence (as in the reciprocal condition), the greater the tendency for the strategy to include contingencies based on the actions of others. If strategies reflect the nature of the interdependent situation, this would lead us to place greater faith in a schema-based model of performance.

Implications—Practical

With regard to conflict management, the beneficial effects attributable to goal setting may be limited to those settings in which individuals share their goals so as to direct and regulate their actions. As goals are shared, the likelihood that individuals will be in conflict with one another over resources decreases due to increased coordination of activities. This is not to imply that goal sharing inevitably will reduce conflict, but it may be helpful for those individuals who are highly dependent on others. By publicly sharing goal aspirations, interdependent workers may negotiate jointly their activities to avoid unnecessary conflicts. In addition, this form of goal exchange will help avoid the misattributions that may occur if goals remain secret and covert.

Goal setting can be detrimental in interdependent work settings if goals are neither made public nor provide a communication medium across the interdependence (that is, both interdependent parties participate in mutual goal setting). Goal myopia may lead a negotiator to overlook reasonable counteroffers and alternative problem solutions. Thus, goal setting may lead to enhanced success in gaining immediate rewards in a negotiation at the expense of more integrative, long-term solutions. Again, this seems extremely unlikely if goal setting is done publicly and jointly by both parties locked in a reciprocal resource dependence setting.

Finally, the impact of goal setting as a technique for conflict management depends on the acceptability of the goals to both interdependent parties. Public goals provide the antecedent condition needed to ensure that goals are mutually agreeable. Further, the task strategy effects of goals can help ensure that a worker's actions coordinate with those of dependent others. The use of goal setting under these circumstances is likely to be successful in reducing or eliminating conflicts due to resource dependencies.

13

The Impact of Managerial Arbitration and Subunit Power on Bargainer Behavior and Commitment

Frederick A. Starke
W. W. Notz

Since the recession of 1981–82, many organizations have experienced a decline in the resources available to them. As resource availability has declined, the potential for conflict over the allocation of scarce resources has increased. This conflict often manifests itself during the budgeting process, when decisions are explicitly made to allocate resources to certain areas and activities, and to deny them to others. There are few mechanisms in organizations that allow subunits to negotiate formally with each other in an attempt to resolve conflicts that may exist between them. Instead, someone in the hierarchy—usually a common superior—is called upon to resolve conflicts between subunits.

Consider how this process worked not long ago in the federal government when David Stockman, then director of the Office of Management and Budget, and Caspar Weinberger, secretary of Defense, presented their arguments to President Reagan regarding cuts in defense spending. Stockman argued that spending should be cut by $30 billion, while Weinberger argued for a cut of only $7 or $8 billion. After listening to each man's arguments, President Reagan ordered them to compromise, and they finally agreed on a figure of $11 billion.

The Stockman-Weinberger episode raises several important issues for organizational researchers. The first issue concerns interdepartmental conflict. In the example above, resource scarcity clearly played a role in causing interdepartmental conflict to develop. The parties involved in the conflict made a formal presentation to top management (the president), who listened to the arguments made by each side. In this case, the president was acting in the role of arbitrator.

Second, management of interdepartmental conflict is important, but there is much uncertainty about how it is best accomplished. In the budget example cited above, top management exhorted the disputing parties to compromise and eventually imposed a compromise upon them. This decision structure is commonly used, but its efficacy is rarely questioned. Given the widespread occurrence of interdepartmental conflict, it would seem prudent to examine alternative conflict resolution structures.

Third, the Stockman-Weinberger conflict demonstrates the great potential the budget-setting process offers for the sudy of conflict management and the use of power. Several authors (Cyert & March, 1963; Pfeffer & Salancik, 1974; Pfeffer & Leong, 1977; Hills & Mahoney, 1978; Pfeffer & Moore, 1980; Wildavsky, 1968, 1979; Pfeffer, 1981; Provan, Beyer, & Kruytbosch, 1980) have argued that budgets emerge only after much political maneuvering and tacit bargaining between various elements. In disputes of this nature, the power of the participants is often a significant determinant of success.

CONFLICT AND THE BUDGETING PROCESS

Some of the conflict that is evident in budget setting is caused by individuals pursuing their own self-interest, but conflict may also be caused by the *procedure* normally used to set budgets. Typically, each unit in an organization submits a proposed budget for the next fiscal year. Each unit may ask for more than it really needs because it assumes that other departments are doing likewise, and that top management will probably cut back each request by some amount. Conflicting demands among departments (as manifested by excessive requests) are then resolved by top management, essentially through an imposed compromise.

When managers impose solutions on disputing subordinates, they are acting in the role of arbitrator. While this role has been recognized by some scholars (Mintzberg, 1973; George, 1972), little is known about the impact of management's conflict resolution procedures on the expectations, behavior, and commitment of the parties who are competing for resources.

The existence of competing demands and an arbitrator to resolve them suggests that the budget-setting process in organizations is similar in important respects to labor-management negotiations where arbitration is used. Research in that area has shown that the mode of third party intervention influences the behavior and commitment of the disputing parties (DeNisi & Dworkin, 1979; Magenau, 1980; Notz & Starke, 1978; Subbarao, 1978). This research has also demonstrated that bargainers anticipating a conventional arbitration intervention behaved in a more intransigent fashion than bargainers anticipating either no intervention or other types of interventions.

It seems likely that parties in a budget dispute, like their counterparts in labor-management negotiations, will also assume that a compromise decision rule will be used by the manager/arbitrator. If so, then the intransigent behaviors and attitudes observed in other conflict arenas could also be expected here.

The negative effects of conventional arbitration (CA) in labor relations conflicts have led to the development of final offer arbitration (FOA) as an alternative (Stevens, 1966; Feuille, 1975). When FOA is used, the disputing parties are told prior to negotiations that if they cannot reach an agreement on their own, they will be required to submit their "final offer" to an arbitrator who will pick *one* of the offers in its entirety. FOA is assumed to act as a deterrent since each party risks a severe cost if they fail to bargain seriously. The FOA structure has been implemented in labor-management disputes, and the empirical evidence generally supports the prediction that FOA induces serious bargaining and narrows the difference between the disputing parties (Bellman & Graham, 1974; Feuille, 1975; Holden, 1977; Notz & Starke, 1978; DeNisi & Dworkin, 1979; Subbarao, 1978).

The FOA structure may have merit as a conflict management technique in budget setting. Accordingly, one goal of the research reported here was to explore the use of FOA in a setting other than the traditional two-person conflict found in labor/management disputes. In this study, three-person groups—anticipating either FOA or CA, and composed of members with either equal or unequal power—attempted to reach an agreement on how to divide up a given amount of budget money. A second goal of the research was to test the comparative effects of CA and FOA on bargainer aspirations, behavior, and commitment. Specifically, we hypothesized that, compared to CA triads, FOA triads would have lower aspiration levels prior to bargaining, behave in a more conciliatory fashion during bargaining, and be more committed to the budget allocation (whether negotiated or imposed) after bargaining ended.

Budgets, Coalitions, and Power

A major difference between labor-management conflicts and resource allocation conflicts within organizations is that the latter generally involve more than two parties. When more than two parties are involved, the possibility exists that coalitions will form. Generally speaking, individuals form coalitions to achieve goals that they could not achieve through individual action (for example, coalition political parties). The social psychology literature contains numerous studies of coalition behavior in laboratory settings (see Gamson, 1961, 1964; Miller & Wong, 1986; Murnighan, 1985; Riker, 1962; Vinacke & Arkoff, 1957), but conflicting findings are much in evidence. Additionally, in these studies the parties were required to reach an agreement on their own since there was no third party to impose a settlement on them.

The availability of an arbitrator and variation in the arbitrator's decision rule may have a significant impact on coalition formation. The compromise decision rule normally applied in CA motivates the disputing parties to take extreme positions as they attempt to offset the affects of the expected compromise. However, when individuals take extreme positions, they are less likely to form a coalition. An FOA decision rule, on the other hand, discourages the parties from adopting extreme positions and may facilitate a search for agreement, partial or complete. Partial agreements, that is, coalitions, might increase the uncertainty of the remaining party(s) and might thereby induce total agreement. It was therefore hypothesized that coalition formation would be more likely in an FOA structure than in a CA structure.

It is also important to consider the effects of CA and FOA when the disputing parties have differing amounts of power. Power influences the allocation of scarce resources (Cyert & March, 1963; Thompson, 1967; Pfeffer & Salancik, 1974; Weick, 1969; Pfeffer, 1981). In the absence of arbitration, high power individuals in a group would normally be expected to get more resources than would low power individuals. Arbitration, however, is usually assumed to dampen the power differences of the disputing parties. Thus, in unequal power groups, when high power persons attempt to get their way, low power persons might use the arbitrator to protect themselves. In equal power groups, an arbitrator may have less impact since the participants would not feel the need to be protected. Three hypotheses were developed around the power variable. First, equal power triads should be able to reach a negotiated settlement more easily than unequal power triads, regardless of the intervention mode that is used. Second, compared to unequal power triads, equal power triads should have lower aspiration levels prior to bargaining, behave in a more conciliatory fashion during bargaining, and exhibit greater commitment to the settlement (negotiated or imposed) after bargaining has ended. Third, the positions of the two low power members of unequal power triads should be closer to each other than they are to the position of the high power person.

In terms of the differential effects of CA and FOA, FOA triads should be less dominated by powerful individuals than CA triads, because a high power individual would probably not risk making an extreme offer and having it rejected by the arbitrator. Under CA, however, each person in the triad has an incentive to demand extreme amounts of resources.

METHOD

Subjects and Experimental Task

The subjects were 93 male undergraduates enrolled in an Introduction to Business course. They received bonus points toward their course grade for participating in the experiment. Subjects were randomly assigned the role of dean of a (fictitious) university college. Their task was to negotiate (with two other subjects also playing dean roles) next year's budget allocation for the three professional colleges in the university. If they could not reach an agreement themselves, an arbitration decision was imposed upon them.

Variables and Design

The first independent variable in a 2 × 2 design was the mode of third party intervention (FOA or CA). The other independent variable was the nature of the power relationships in the triads (equal or unequal).

The first dependent variable—the aspiration level of subjects—was measured by asking subjects to indicate, immediately prior to negotiations, what they honestly felt would be a reasonable allocation of the professional budget among the three professional colleges (in percent). The second dependent variable was the outcome of the bargaining session, measured by the total of the percentage point difference separating the three deans. The third dependent variable was the subjects' level of commitment (both attitudinal and behavioral) to the settlement they reached themselves or had imposed on them.

Attitudinal commitment was measured by asking subjects questions such as (1) how responsible they felt for the outcome of the negotiations, (2) how willing they were to use the same intervention procedure again, (3) how reasonable they felt the arbitrator's decision was (if relevant), and (4) how committed they were to the settlement they reached themselves or had imposed on them. *Behavioral* commitment was measured first by observing whether subjects appealed the arbitrator's decision (low commitment) or did not appeal it (high commitment). This appeal procedure permitted a more sensitive test of commitment since it allowed subjects to risk all or a portion of the bonus points they had earned up to that time.

Experimental Procedure

Three subjects were seated in the same room and briefly told about the procedures that would be used. They were then given background information which included (1) enrollment figures for the Colleges of Engineering, Law and Agriculture for the last four years, (2) a history of how the total professional budget had been allocated during the last four years, (3) estimated enrollments in the three faculties for the next year, and (4) task instructions indicating that each individual would play the role of one of the deans and that the three deans were to attempt to come to an agreement on how the professional budget should be allocated for the coming year.

Power Conditions

Subjects in the equal power condition received background information indicating that the three faculties were roughly equal in power (that is, their enrollments had not fluctuated greatly during the last four years nor were they dramatically different), and the three faculties had received roughly equal shares of the budget during the last four years. Subjects assigned to the unequal power condition received background information indicating that the three faculties were not equal in power (that is, their enrollments had fluctuated rather dramatically during the last four years and were also quite different), and the three faculties had received unequal shares of the budget during the last four years. In both these conditions the background information indicated that student enrollment was the primary (but not the only) criterion that the president had used to allocate the budget during the last four years. The way power was operationalized here is closest to the concept of "legitimate" power (French & Raven, 1968).

Once this background material had been digested by the subjects, the experimenter randomly assigned the three roles. He then separated the subjects and gave them further instructions which described the college they headed, the strong and weak points about their own and the other colleges, and their payoff schedule. Payoff schedules were asymmetrical, that is, as one subject's share of the total budget increased, the points the subject received increased while the points the two other subjects received decreased. An agreement could be reached if each subject was willing to accept two points out of a possible ten (subjects were not aware of this intersection). Subjects were told not to share their payoff schedule with the other subjects. After subjects had read this material, the experimenter returned to their separate rooms and gave each subject further written instructions dealing with the mode of intervention that would be used if the subjects would not reach an agreement on their own.

Conventional Arbitration Conditions

The prenegotiation instructions indicated that triads would be allowed to bargain up to 45 minutes in an attempt to reach an agreement on the allocation of the professional budget. If they could not reach an agreement in that time, they would be required to submit their offers to the president of the university. The offer of each subject contained his offer for his own faculty and his offer for the other two faculties (totalling 100 percent). Subjects were told that the president (acting as an arbitrator) would impose an equitable compromise that would be binding on all three deans. The prenegotiation instructions contained a detailed explanation of how this process had worked in the previous year.

Final Offer Arbitration Conditions

The prenegotiation instructions were identical here, *except* that subjects were told that the president would consider the three offers and would *not* compromise, but would pick the *one* package that he felt was in the best interest of the university as a whole. After subjects completed a prenegotiation questionnaire, they were brought together in the bargaining room and began bargaining.

After 35 minutes the experimenter returned and gave a ten-minute warning. After ten additional minutes the experimenter returned and asked the subjects if they had reached agreement. If they had, they signed an agreement form indicating the percentage of the total budget each college would receive. Subjects were then separated and filled out a postnegotiation questionnaire which asked how responsible they felt for the agreement they had reached, and how accurately they recalled some of the data in the background information they had been given previously. Once this had been completed, subjects who reached an agreement were given a postsettlement questionnaire which was designed to assess how committed they were to the agreement and how willing they were to bargain again under the intervention procedure they had used. Subjects were then debriefed.

Triads that had not reached agreement were separated and asked to fill out the

"Offer to Arbitrator" form. Several minutes later the experimenter returned to pick up this form from each subject. The subjects were told that an experienced administrator from the faculty of Administrative Studies, acting in the role of university president, would make the arbitration decision and that the subjects' offers would be given to this person for an immediate decision. Subjects were asked to fill out the postnegotiation questionnaire (noted above) while they were waiting for the arbitrator's decision.

The experimenter then left the room, ostensibly to take the three offers to the arbitrator (there actually was no arbitrator). While the subjects were filling out the postnegotiation questionnaire, the experimenter made the arbitration decision. In the CA conditions, the decision was made by first constructing a 3 × 3 matrix with the rows made up of "offers from" and the columns made up of "offers for." The offers for each faculty were then added up and divided by three. This compromise settlement was noted on the three "Offer to Arbitrator" forms and then returned to each member of the triad along with the postsettlement questionnaire noted above.

In the FOA conditions, the experimenter constructed an identical matrix and then picked the offer which was closest to a predetermined ideal based on the facts in the background material that all subjects had been given. This offer was noted on the three "Offer to Arbitrator" forms and then returned to the members of the triad along with the postsettlement questionnaire.

In both the CA and FOA conditions, the experimenter returned to the subjects' separate rooms approximately ten minutes later and picked up the postsettlement questionnaire. Subjects were then debriefed.

RESULTS

The results are presented in four major areas: (1) manipulation checks, (2) preintervention attitudes (aspiration levels), (3) bargaining behavior, and (4) postintervention attitudes (commitment) and behavior (appeals of the arbitrator's decision).

Manipulation Checks

It is important that subjects understand the intervention procedure (DeNisi & Dworkin, 1979). Accordingly, they were asked to indicate the extent to which they thought the president/arbitrator could compromise when making the budget allocation decision. The scale ranged from 1 (no compromise possible) to 7 (complete freedom to compromise). The mean for FOA subjects was significantly lower than that for CA subjects (2.50 vs. 4.42), $F(1,88) = 39.97$, $p < .001$ (all tests are one-tailed unless otherwise noted). This indicates that subjects understood the intervention procedure.

In order to check the power manipulation, subjects were asked to indicate the extent to which they felt their rightful share of the budget should be increased or decreased relative to the other faculties. In each triad there were three possible comparisons: Engineering-Law; Engineering-Agriculture; and Agriculture-Law. The absolute difference in the responses for these three pairs within the triad was significantly greater in the unequal power conditions, $F(1,27) = 9.46, p < .05$, which supports the power manipulation.

Prenegotiation Aspiration Levels

It was hypothesized that FOA triads would have lower aspiration levels than CA triads. Each subject was asked to indicate, in percentage terms, what he felt would be the most reasonable settlement for himself and for the other two people in the triad. Since each subject's response totalled 100 percent, it was possible to calculate the difference between what each individual felt was a reasonable settlement for himself versus what the other members of the triad felt was a reasonable settlement for him. The mean difference for FOA triads was significantly less than the mean difference for CA triads (47.67 vs. 72.33), $F(1,26) = 4.24, p < .05$. The mean difference for triads in the equal power condition was significantly smaller than that for triads in the unequal power condition, $F(1,26) = 3.61, p < .05$; this also indicates that the power manipulation was successful.

As a further check of aspiration levels, each subject was asked to indicate the extent to which the share of the budget of the other two triad members should be increased or decreased. Subject opinions about each of the other two members of their triad were then totalled. FOA subjects felt that other members of their triad should have their share of the budget increased significantly more than did CA subjects $F(1,89) = 4.08, p < .05$. Thus, the aspiration levels of FOA subjects were lower than that of CA subjects.

Subjects were also asked to indicate their opening offer on the prenegotiation questionnaire. Each subject's offer for his own faculty was then compared to the opening offers of the two other subjects for his faculty and a total difference score was calculated. CA triads had a significantly higher mean difference in opening offers than FOA triads (145.81 vs. 109.14), $F(1,26) = 3.45, p < .05$. The mean difference score for triads in the unequal power condition was significantly higher than the corresponding mean for triads in the equal power condition (178.13 vs. 123.86), $F(1,26) = 5.30, p < .01$.

Another measure of aspiration levels involved comparing the opening offer of each party with the "optimum" allocation of the total budget for the three faculties. This "optimum" was a proportional allocation of funds based on a moving average of the enrollment trends over the last four years for each of the faculties. The difference between each individual's opening offer for himself and the "optimum" answer was then summed for each triad to get a total difference score. This analysis revealed that the mean for the FOA triads was significantly lower than the mean for the CA triads (36.43 vs. 51.63), $F(1,28) = 4.64, p < .05$. The unequal power triads had significantly higher means than the equal power triads (50.81 vs. 37.36), $F(1,28) = 3.51, p < .05$. These two findings indicate that FOA subjects had significantly lower aspirations than CA subjects, and equal power groups had significantly lower aspirations than unequal power groups.

The final measure of aspiration levels involved comparing subject perceptions of what they felt constituted a reasonable settlement with the "optimum" allocation using the same procedure noted above. Again, the mean for the FOA triads was significantly smaller than the mean for the CA triads (16.60 vs. 24.13), $F(1,28) = 3.20, p < .05$.

In summary, the analyses of aspiration levels were very consistent across different conceptual measures and indicated that (a) members of FOA triads had lower aspirations than members of CA triads, and (b) members of equal power triads had lower aspirations than members of unequal power triads. There were no significant interactions in any of these analyses.

Bargaining Behavior

It was hypothesized that FOA triads would be closer to agreement at the end of bargaining than CA triads. To test this, the total percentage point difference separating the three deans' final positions was analyzed using the same procedure as that used for opening offers. For all triads, the mean percentage point difference in the final positions of CA triads was significantly higher than the comparable mean for FOA triads (74.88 vs. 21.33), $F(1,27) = 6.44, p < .01$. There were eight FOA triads and five CA triads that reached agreement through negotiation (differences not significant). When these triads were excluded from the analysis, the mean for CA triads was still significantly higher than the mean for FOA triads, $F(1,14) = 7.06, p < .01$. Thus, FOA triads were closer to agreement than CA triads at the end of bargaining.

Another measure of bargaining behavior involves assessing how far each of the parties moved from their opening position by the end of the bargaining session. Considering only those triads that were unable to agree, there was significantly more movement in FOA triads than in CA triads. Movement was defined as the difference in opening offers minus the difference in offers to the arbitrator. The mean movement for CA triads was 79.0 and for FOA triads 133.0, $F(1,28) = 7.6, p < .01$. CA triads started bargaining an average of 168.2 points apart, moved an average of 79 points during bargaining, and ended bargaining an average of 89.2 points apart. FOA triads started an average of 174.0 points apart, moved an average of 133.0 points, and ended an average of 41.0 points apart. Thus, compared to CA triads, FOA triads started further apart prior to bargaining and ended up closer together at the conclusion of bargaining.

With respect to the power variable and its impact on bargaining behavior, subjects were asked how close they were to reaching agreement with both of the other members of their triad. Subjects in the equal power condition (mean = 3.19) were significantly closer to reaching agreement than subjects in the unequal power condition (mean = 2.03), $F(1,50) = 11.77, p < .001$.

Coalition Formation During Bargaining

To test whether coalitions developed during bargaining, subjects were asked to indicate on the postnegotiation questionnaire how close they were to reaching agreement individually with either of the other subjects in the triad. For example, the Engineering dean was asked to indicate how close he was to reaching an agreement individually with the Law dean and the Law dean was asked to indicate how close he was to reaching agreement individually with the Engineering dean. An analysis of these reciprocal relations in the three possible pairs within the triad revealed no main effects of intervention mode or power, but did show a significant two-way interaction between these two variables, $F(1,26) = 4.98, p < .05$. In the unequal power–CA condition, the two low power subjects (Law and Agriculture) were much closer to agreement with each other than they were individually with the high-power subject (Engineering).

Coalitions in Offers to the Arbitrator

In triads where agreement was not reached, a calculation was made of how close each of the three possible pairs of subjects were in their offers to the arbitrator. This closeness measure was developed by taking the absolute value of the difference between each pair of subjects' offers to the arbitrator. For example, assume the dean of Engineering had made an offer to the arbitrator of 45, 25, and 30 percent, respectively for Engineering, Law and Agriculture and that the dean of Law's offer was 40, 35, and 25 percent for Engineering, Law, and Agriculture, respectively. The closeness measure for the Engineering-Law pair would then be: $/45-40/ + /25-35/ + 30-25/ = 20$ percentage points. The two closeness measures (Engineering-Law and Engineering-Agriculture) were averaged and compared to the closeness measure for the low-power pair (Agriculture-Law). Based on this calculation, it was found that in the unequal power condition, the two low-power deans (Law and Agriculture) were significantly closer to each other than either one of them was to Engineering, $F(1,14) = 4.62, p < .05$.

Postnegotiation Commitment

Both attitudinal and behavioral measures of postbargaining commitment were used to assess bargainer commitment to the settlement they reached themselves or had imposed on them.

Attitudinal Measures

It was hypothesized that FOA triads would have greater feelings of commitment to, and responsibility for, outcomes than CA triads. Subjects were asked the following questions: (1) How fair was the imposed (or negotiated) settlement? (2) How committed are you to the outcome? (3) How willing are you to use the same intervention procedure in the future? (4) How reasonable was the imposed (or negotiated) settlement? (5) How responsible did you feel for the outcome of negotiations?

At an individual level of analysis, the means for FOA subjects were significantly higher on all five questions than the means for CA subjects. If only those individuals who had settlements imposed on them were considered, the same general pattern was evident, but the significance levels were lower. Since the five commitment variables were highly intercorrelated (all p's $< .001$), they were combined into an overall commitment index. Based on this index, FOA subjects (mean = 4.63) were significantly more committed to the settlement than CA subjects (mean = 3.90), $F(1,87) = 8.06$, $p < .005$.

Practically speaking, managers are concerned with the commitment of groups as well as individuals. Accordingly, the preceding analysis was repeated on a triadic basis. This analysis also revealed that FOA triads were significantly more committed than CA triads. If only those triads that had a settlement imposed on them were considered, the same general pattern was evident as in the individual case. Since the five commitment variables when considered on a triadic basis were also fairly highly intercorrelated (all p's $< .05$), they were combined into a triadic commitment index. Based on this index, FOA triads (mean = 13.89) were significantly more committed to the settlement than CA triads (mean = 11.76), $F(1,25) = 8.61$, $p < .005$.

Neither the individual nor the triadic analyses of commitment showed any significant main effects of power, nor were there any interaction effects between power and mode of intervention.

The Win-Lose Effect

Some critics have argued that FOA losers (those whose offer has been rejected by the arbitrator) will be significantly less committed to the imposed settlement than FOA winners and those bargaining under CA. In this experiment there were five categories of subjects: FOA winners, FOA losers, FOA agreers, CA agreers, and CA nonagreers. Using the commitment index noted above, the commitment levels of subjects in these five groups were analyzed. There were, in fact, significant differences between them $F(4,87) = 14.27$, $p < .0001$. At $p < .05$ (Sheffé test), the following pairs were significantly different (means in parentheses): FOA winners (6.22) and losers (3.60); FOA agreers (4.77) and FOA losers (3.60); CA nonagreers (3.54) and FOA agreers (4.77); CA nonagreers (3.54) and FOA winners (6.22); CA agreers (4.64) and FOA winners (6.22); and FOA agreers (4.77) and FOA winners (6.22). These data indicate some evidence for a win-lose effect in FOA. However, the more striking finding is that FOA losers were not significantly less committed than any CA subjects; this means that there is really a "win" effect in FOA and a "lose" effect in CA.

A final commitment-related issue is the extent to which budget-setting procedures encourage the disputing parties to adopt an organization-wide perspective on the most effective allocation of available resources. In this study, subjects were asked to indicate, on a seven-point scale, the extent to which they felt the settlement (negotiated or imposed) was in the best interest of the university as a whole. The mean for FOA subjects was significantly higher than the mean for CA subjects (4.89 vs. 4.04), $F(4,87) = 8.27$, $p < .0001$. There were also significant differences in the five categories of subjects noted above. At $p < .05$ (Sheffé test), the following pairs were significantly different (means in parentheses): FOA winners (6.57) and FOA losers (3.92); FOA winners (6.57) and FOA agreers (4.96); FOA winners (6.57) and CA agreers (5.07); and FOA winners (6.57) and CA nonagreers (3.56); CA agreers (5.07) and CA nonagreers (3.56); and FOA agreers (4.96) and CA nonagreers (3.56). These findings support the argument that the budget setting process influences commitment levels.

Behavioral Measures

In addition to the attitudinal measures of commitment, two behavioral measures were developed. These involved subject decisions about (1) whether or not to appeal the arbitrator's decision, and (2) the magnitude of the appeal.

With respect to (1), a chi-square analysis showed that CA subjects appealed the arbitrator's decision significantly more often than FOA subjects, $X^2(1) = 3.8$, $p < .05$. There were no power effects. With respect to (2), there were no significant differences between FOA subjects and CA subjects in terms of the amount of points they appealed for.

DISCUSSION

Compared to CA subjects, FOA subjects had lower aspirations prior to bargaining, behaved in a more concessionary way during bargaining, and were both attitudinally and behaviorally more committed to the imposed or negotiated budget at the end of bargaining. There was some evidence of a win-lose effect in FOA (Starke & Notz, 1981), but even FOA losers were not significantly less committed than any CA subjects. Subjects in unequal power groups had greater aspirations and larger opening offers than subjects in equal power triads. In the unequal power groups the offers to the arbitrator of the two low power members were significantly closer to each other than they were to the high power member.

Overall, these results suggest that a procedure like final offer arbitration may be useful beyond the traditional labor relations context. The finding that FOA yielded positive attitudinal and behavioral results in a pervasive organizational activity like budget setting is encouraging, but implementation of FOA as part of a budget-setting procedure would require some substantial departures from current practice. Instead of units submitting their requests to management, they would negotiate with each other about the optimum budget allocation for the organization as a whole. In these negotiations various ideas to use the available resources more effectively might well emerge. In addition, the various subunits might find more common ground than they originally anticipated. If the negotiations did not lead to an agreement, then the FOA intervention could be applied by top management.

This type of process should affect each subunit's "view of the world." Organizational theorists continually stress the importance of subunit identification with the overall goals of the organization. This requires individuals in the various parts of the organization to see things from multiple perspectives and to be able to assess correctly what specific allocation of resources is in the best interest of the organization as a whole. In this study, FOA subjects felt that the budget allocation (whether negotiated or imposed) was significantly better for the overall organization than CA subjects did. Apparently, the nature of CA and FOA caused differential aspiration levels and behavior; these, in turn, resulted in a more positive view—in the FOA condition—of how the budget allocation would affect the functioning of the total organization.

There are several threats to external validity in this study, some of which can be identified because of earlier research. For example, bargaining behavior and the distribution of outcomes have been found to be quite different when the bargainers' resources are earned—as they usually are in real-world settings—as compared to when they are unearned—as in the present study (Miller & Wong, 1986). Similarly, face-to-face bargaining, like that of the current study, has been found to produce more contentious behavior than non-face-to-face bargaining, as in the tacit bargaining that is evident in many real-world settings (Carnevale & Isen, 1986). There are, of course, other variables—such as the experience of the bargainers, the multiple roles (third party and other) of managers (Kolb & Sheppard, 1985), the history and anticipated future of the bargainers in the organization and with each other, and the complex relationship between monetary and other interrelated issues—whose threat value to the external validity of these results is largely unknown, but may be important. In short, the generalizability of these findings beyond the narrow confines of this particular experimental context is problematic.

One way of remedying these deficiencies is to conduct full-blown field experiments. However, field experiments are expensive and it is usually very difficult to persuade practitioners of their utility. We believe that a more practical alternative is to use traditional laboratory experimentation and rich-context simulation (Greenhalgh, Neslin, & Gilkey, 1985) to improve external validity incrementally. This strategy requires that the variables incorporated into the design of the experiments be selected not only because of their presence in real-world organizations, but also because of their *theoretical* importance. The importance of the latter requirement must not be underestimated; mere differences between laboratory settings and real-world organizations are not necessarily plausible threats to external validity. Only when those differences can be shown to produce interaction effects should they be considered plausible threats.

Notwithstanding the obvious necessity of well-controlled research on these issues, casual observation suggests that managers are frequently called upon to resolve resource allocation conflicts, and that when they do so they are acting, either implicitly or explicitly, as arbitrators. The decision structures that managers employ in this role, or that subordinates expect managers to employ, will have a substantial effect on subordinate negotiating behavior and subsequent commitment.

14

Affect, Cognition, and Decision Making in Negotiation: A Conceptual Integration

Rajesh Kumar

Negotiation has typically been conceptualized as a form of decision making that occurs under conditions of mutual interdependence (for example, Kochan & Verma, 1983; Pruitt, 1981). Within this framework of interdependence, the respective parties attempt to reach a mutually satisfactory agreement through the pursuit of various micro-level strategies. The micro-level strategies pursued by participants entail among them the use of concessions, promises, and threats. Pruitt (1981), for example, develops a strategic choice model which attempts to delineate the various micro-level strategies that the negotiators can pursue—namely unilateral concessions, competitive behavior, coordinative behavior. These strategies represent alternative ways by which negotiators can hope to come to some agreement. Implicit in the strategic choice model is the notion of negotiation as problem solving. The notion of problem solving is well exemplified in Walton and McKersie's (1965) distinction between distributive and integrative bargaining. By developing novel solutions, integrative bargaining can help reconcile the parties' interests at a level that may yield high mutual benefits to either party.

This conception of negotiation as problem solving would seem to entail following a certain sequence of behaviors (for example, exchange of task-related information, concession making, agreement) in a script-like manner (Abelson, 1976). A script consists of a sequence of events that occur in a temporally ordered way in a given situation. Thus, in a negotiation situation, the exchange of information would appear to be a prerequisite for subsequent negotiation behaviors. More generally, Graham and Sano (1984) have identified a series of four stages through which negotiation proceeds in all societies. The stages identi-

Funding for this work has been provided by a grant 86-028 from the National Institute of Dispute Resolution. I would like to thank the anonymous reviewers for helpful comments on an earlier draft of this paper.

fied by them are: (a) non-task sounding, (b) task-related exchange of information, (c) persuasion, (d) concessions and agreements. Although the identification of these stages would seem to suggest or impart a universality to the process of negotiation, it must be borne in mind that the relative importance of these stages certainly varies across societies (Graham & Sano, 1984). In some cases, these differences may be so great as to almost constitute a qualitative difference. What the above suggests then, is that there may be no universal model of a negotiation process.

This chapter will identify some of the possible antecedents of differences in negotiation models, but perhaps even more importantly will try to spell out the affective consequences of differences in cognitive representation of negotiations associated with different models. It will delineate the different types of negative emotions that are likely to arise in either party and will show the relationship between negative emotions and subsequent negotiation behavior.

COGNITIVE-AFFECTIVE INTERACTION IN NEGOTIATIONS

As a decision-making process entailing interaction between members of different groups, negotiation belongs to a class of social situations entailing interdependence. To the extent that this is the case, a similar set of principles is likely to be operative in the negotiation setting as in any form of interpersonal encounter. One characteristic feature of social relationships is that they are replete with affect (see Berscheid, 1983; Kelly, 1984).

Affect, in turn, provides a strong directive force or the motivation for subsequent behavior (Kelley, 1984). Although there is some work in the negotiation literature that lays emphasis on the affective dimension in negotiations (see, for example, Carnevale & Isen, 1986; Ikle, 1964), little systematic attention has been given in trying to study the relationship between individuals' preexisting cognitions and the subsequent affective consequences. This is surprising in view of the fact that most contemporary models of social cognition (see Higgins, 1987; Higgins, Strauman & Klein, 1986) locate the antecedents of affect in prior cognitions. A characteristic feature of these models is that individuals are known to enter social encounters with certain preestablished cognitive structures. Commonly called *schemata* (see Bartlett, 1932; Fiske, 1982; Taylor & Crocker, 1981), these cognitive structures provide a frame of reference for an actor entering a social situation.

To the extent that there is a mismatch or a discrepancy between what is out there and what is expected or should happen, an individual or individuals concerned are likely to experience a negative affective reaction (see, for example, Higgins, 1987; Katz, 1978). The magnitude of the affective reaction is dependent on the perceived discrepancy, in other words, the greater the discrepancy, the greater the magnitude of the negative affect that is generated in the party.

The affect that is generated in the course of interaction may influence negotiation behaviors in a variety of ways. On the one hand, a negative affective state leads to cognitive simplification processes (see Easterbrook, 1959; Janis & Mann, 1977; Staw et al., 1981) with such simplification processes affecting the abilities of participants to think in an integrative fashion (Pruitt & Rubin, 1986). It may also affect the motivation of participants to make concessions to each other (Gladwin & Kumar, 1986). In addition, the negative actions and attitudes of one party are likely to elicit a similar response in the other (Gottman, 1979).

What the above suggests then is a close interlinkage between cognitions, affect, and behavior. Although several writers have stressed the importance of cognitive content, it has been studied under a variety of different labels—namely, *schemas* (Fiske & Linville, 1980; Taylor & Crocker, 1981), *prototypes* (Hayes-Roth, Hayes-Roth, 1977; Posner & Keele, 1968, 1970; Reed, 1972), and *scripts* (Abelson, 1981; Schank & Abelson, 1977). The most generic of these concepts is the notion of the schema, which may be defined as a "cognitive structure which contains knowledge about the attributes of a concept and the relationships among these attributes" (Fiske & Taylor, 1984, p. 149). Although the concept of a schema has become much more popular in the psychological and the social sciences literature (see, for example, Fiske & Taylor, 1984; Lau & Sears, 1986), it necessitates making a set of "structural assumptions" concerning how the various attributes are interlinked in memory. The necessity of making such assumptions may be avoided if we view cognitive content from the perspective of constructs that are available and/or accessible to individuals (Higgins, King, & Mavin, 1982).

By construct availability we mean whether or not a given construct is present in memory, whereas by construct accessibility we mean the ease with which a given construct is used in information processing (Higgins, King, & Mavin, 1982; Tulving & Pearlstone, 1966). From this perspective, differences in cognitive content imply differences in availability and/or accessibility of constructs across individuals. To the extent that such differences exist, individuals may interpret the same stimulus event differently (see Cantor & Mischel, 1977; Higgins, King, & Mavin, 1982) and may be prone to different negative emotional reactions.

A conceptual scheme that systematically organizes these constructs for the purposes of interpersonal evaluation has recently been proposed by Higgins (1987). The model suggests that interpersonal evaluations are dependent on a set of standards that individuals bring to bear on the situation. Different standards are associated with different constructs so that differences in cognitive content are no more than differences in standards that people use for processing information. There is a fair amount of evidence that has clearly implicated the role of personal constructs in evaluating oneself and others (see, for example, Higgins, King, & Mavin, 1982; Kelley, 1955; Kuiper & Derry, 1981; Markus, Smith & Moreland, 1985; Markus & Smith, 1981; Shrauger & Patterson, 1974). More recently, Markus, Smith, & Moreland (1985) have pointed out that, to the extent the stimuli are ambiguous, a fast response is required and one is involved and/or has a lot of knowledge about the issue concerned, the self is definitely going to be implicated in the perceptual process. Interestingly enough, many of these conditions specified by Markus and her colleagues are a fairly characteristic feature of negotiation situations. The ambiguity of stimuli is greater across than within cultures (Bauer, 1961); and given the task-oriented nature of the activity, the bargainers wish to end the negotiations as soon as possible (Pruitt, 1981). All this highlights the importance of self-relevant constructs in forming judgments about others in the course of a negotiation situation.

STANDARDS UTILIZATION AND THE DYNAMICS OF INTERPERSONAL NEGOTIATION

The Notion of a Standard

A standard may be viewed as a frame of reference that serves as a basis for evaluating one's and/or other individuals' performance and/or attributes. Lewin (1951), for example, noted that these judgments are dependent on the frame of reference that is used for evaluation. The frame of reference may either be the dominant norms and values of one's culture, one's aspirations/past performance, or others' achievements. Drawing upon this earlier line of work, Higgins, Strauman, and Klein (1986) have distinguished among three major types of standards—factual points of reference, acquired guides and imagined possibilities.

In interaction between representatives of different societies/cultures, acquired guides are likely to be especially salient since they are closely associated with the dominant norms and values prevalent in a given culture. These guides define what is acceptable and what is unacceptable behavior. For example, a hard sell presentation on the part of the seller in the context of a buyer-seller negotiation may be legitimate in the U.S. culture but not in the Japanese one.

A fundamental distinction that is proposed between cultures that have a strong "ideal" orientation, in other words, they are cultures that emphasize the importance of one's personal goal, hopes, and aspirations vis-à-vis cultures that have a strong "ought" orientation, that is, cultures that emphasize fulfillment of duties and obligations. One can, of course, find a mix of both in each culture, notwithstanding the fact that one set of standards is likely to be more prevalent in one culture than in another. Another important dimension of standards relates to the perspective from which goals and obligations are viewed. Researchers have drawn a fundamental distinction between an individuals *own* personal standpoint and that of some *significant other* (see, for example, Higgins, Strauman, and Klein 1986; Turner, 1956). This distinction is of importance because differential perspectives may not only generate different negative emotional reactions (Higgins, 1987) but also because there may be systematic differences in the use of these perspectives across societies/cultures.

Combining these two perspectives yields four different types of standards—

ideal/own, ideal/other, ought/own, ought/other. Individuals across cultures are likely to differ in terms of which of these standards are the most accessible for them. To the extent that this is the case, individuals are likely to exhibit a different emotional reaction to the same event, since different sets of standards are associated with different sets of emotions (Higgins, 1987). The use of an ideal standard is said to generate dejection- and frustration-related emotions, while the use of an ought standard is typically associated with agitation-related emotions (Higgins, 1987). In turn, these different sets of emotions are associated with different behaviors—researchers have found, for example, frustration typically leads individuals to exert greater effort for achieving their goals while agitation-related emotions characterized by anxiety and threat, leads to passive withdrawal forms of behavior (Glass, 1955; Menninger, 1954).

Given the interlinkage between different standards and different emotional reactions, we will now focus on how these standards differ across societies/cultures.

Differences in Utilization of Standards

In what way then do the U.S. and Japanese cultures differ in terms of utilization of such standards? A number of writers have noted that a consistent theme in U.S. culture has been that of individualism and associated with it an emphasis on achieving one's goals/fulfilling aspirations. Consistent with this, the individual is seen as being primarily causally responsible for the outcomes that he obtains. In terms of the standards typology devised by Higgins, the U.S. culture could be said to be reflective of an ''ideal/own'' standard, since the orientation is always toward obtaining the most preferred outcome for oneself, regardless of its implications for others.

The Japanese culture stands in marked contrast to that of the United States. A universal theme in the Japanese culture is that of maintaining harmony (*wa*) (see, for example, Benedict, 1946; Christopher, 1982; Moore, 1967; Morbasch, 1980; Nakamura, 1964; Tung, 1981; Wagatsuma, 1984; Zimmerman, 1985). The commitment to maintaining a social order (harmony) carries with it the resultant emphasis on duties and obligations (*on* and *giri*). This emphasis is, for example, noted by Zimmerman, who writes ''the strong pull of duties and loyalties plays a large role in the emotions and psychological attitudes that operate just beneath the surface for most average Japanese'' (p. 73). The Japanese expectation would thus be that every individual should try to fulfill his obligation and should not in any way give offense, which may disrupt the harmony of the group otherwise. In view of the Japanese cultural assumption, ''that human nature is essentially good and that when free from all the external adversary influences, a person wants to live, and is capable of living in accordance with social norms'' (Wagatsuma, 1984, p. 372), it seems that it would not appear unrealistic to them to expect the other party to fulfill its obligations.

The Japanese emphasis on a long-term relationship Tung (1981), combined with their "situational sense of ethics" (Nakamura, 1964), increases, if anything in their eyes, the importance of duties and obligations. Instead of viewing nego- tiations as a "one-shot deal" (which is probably how Americans view it) they are more concerned with establishing an ongoing relationship between the two parties. Since over a long-term period the situation can change, which may adversely affect their interests, they are interested in dealing with an individual, who would be empathetic to their needs (even if contractually not necessary) by, perhaps, sacrificing his current profits for the sake of an overall harmony. That the Japanese are willing to make a similar concession if the situation changes unfavorably for the other party is documented in a case reported by Christopher (1982).

One can now perhaps get a better understanding of the role of trust, which, while perhaps important in all cultures, has a unique connotation in the Japanese culture. Richardson and Ueda (1981) describe the implications of the develop- ment of trust succinctly.

Once that trust is established, both parties put great emphasis on maintaining the rela- tionship over the long-term. That attitude often means foregoing short-term profits that could be gained by shifting to another buyer or supplier and being willing to be flexible about the terms of the contract when the other party is under pressure or short-term difficulties. (p. 152)

Although Richardson and Ueda describe the implications of development of trust, one could perhaps argue that some of the implications put forward by them may perhaps be necessary for the development of trust. The Japanese, it would thus appear, are oriented to use the "ought/other" standard as a criterion for evaluation.

Affect Induction in Japanese and U.S. Cultures

According to Figure 14.1, different emotional states are likely to be activated by the use of different standards. Higgins (1987), on a basis of extensive review, has distinguished between three different kinds of emotions—dejection-related (dissatisfaction, hopelessness, and so on), agitation-related (fear, anxiety, and so on), and frustration (anger and resentment). The emotional response generated in an individual is deemed to be a function of the degree of discrepancy between a specific attribute or performance and the specific standard which served as the basis of evaluation, as also the accessibility of such standards. The more accessi- ble a given standard, the more frequently the person will experience a particular kind of emotion and the greater the discrepancy, the greater will be the magni- tude of the emotional response thus generated. Recent work by Higgins (1987) has confirmed the above propositions derived from the model.

From the perspective of this study, the question is what kinds of emotions are likely to be generated in the negotiation process and subsequent to that the impact

Figure 14.1
The Cross-Cultural Dimension of Negotiations: A U.S. and Japanese Interaction

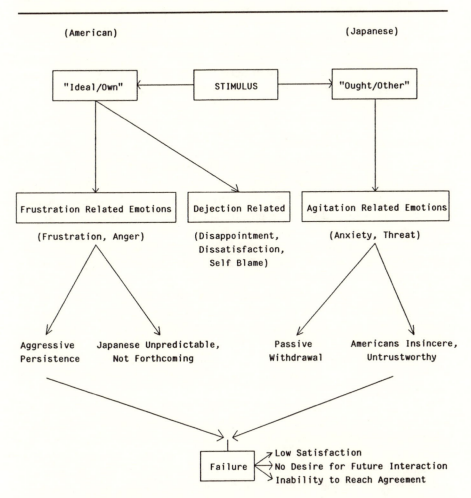

they have on negotiation outcomes. Given that Americans are "ideal/own" in their orientation, they are likely to be prone to frustration-related emotions, as also to dejection-related ones. Frustration-related emotions are a direct reflection of nonattainment of one's goals coupled, perhaps, with Roseman's (1984) notion that "frustration is associated with the perception of strength in the context of a negative event" (p. 27). The presence of frustration in U.S. business has, for example, been noted by Zimmerman (1985), who suggests that the frustrated executive tries harder and harder to achieve his goal, not realizing that such aggressive behavior will, if anything, further ruin the chances of obtaining a productive outcome.

The Japanese on their part are likely to be susceptible to agitation-related emotions, especially anxiety and threat, as well as resentment. This follows from the fact that actual/ought discrepancies are associated with the presence of agitation-related emotions. As has been emphasized earlier, the Japanese are very much concerned about maintaining harmony and when an attribute or performance of an individual is inconsistent with it—especially when it is face threatening (*kao*)—it is not only bound to cause anxiety but also may generate resentment, since the emphasis on maintaining harmony carries with it an associated moral imperative.

Implications of Affect Induction

One would expect a negative affective state to lower the level of trust between the respective parties. Various studies have shown (see Gouaux, 1971; Griffit, 1970; Veitch & Griffit, 1976) that a negative affective state leads to an increase in negativeness toward other people. In addition, various social cognition researchers have shown that a person's existing affective state (positive or negative) affects his categorization (judgment) of the stimulus object in question (see, for example, Bower, 1981; Clark & Isen, 1982; Hoffman, 1986; Isen et al., 1978).

These negative judgments are likely to affect each party's perception of the other's predictability, and dependability, and faith. According to Rempel, Holmes, and Zanna (1985), these three elements capture the essential dimensions inherent in a notion of trust. As a relationship evolves over time, the relative importance of each of these three components is likely to change, with faith substituting almost entirely for the components of predictability and dependability.

However, to the extent that a negative affective state is likely to undermine one's perceptions of others' predictability and dependability, it is unlikely that a relationship will ever approach a faith-like quality. Investigators (Rempel et al., 1985) have noted that faith is perhaps the most important element in a close relationship and it is one that progressively evolves. As these investigators note, faith reflects "the belief that one's partner will act in loving and caring ways whatever the future holds" (p. 109). The emphasis on faith is of particular importance in the Japanese society. The importance given to faith in such a society reflects the overriding importance of interpersonal considerations in such a society as compared with the U.S. one (see Nakane, 1970; Nakamura, 1964). One implication of this stress on the interpersonal element is the emphasis given to long-term relationships even in the context of a negotiating situation. Insofar as the Japanese view a negotiation in the context of a long-term relationship, they would undoubtedly be concerned in dealing with someone whom they believe possesses sincerity of intention. As suggested earlier, a negative affective state is likely to foster negative judgments and to that extent will hinder the development of a productive relationship.

Apart from influencing negotiation behavior via the cognitive mediation of trust, affect may more generally directly instigate behavior. Kelley (1984), notes for example, that the work of Abelson (1983) and Roseman (1984) is united by the theme that affect provides a general "orientation" or a "direction" for subsequent behavior. Different affective states are thus going to be linked up with the motivation to perform different behaviors. What kind of behaviors can we expect from the Americans and the Japanese? Given that Americans are likely to be prone to frustration-related emotions, one would expect them to display aggressive behavior. This tendency, on the part of U.S. executives, is perhaps strengthened by the fact that in the U.S. culture there is a tendency to fulfill one's goal in as short a time as possible as also by the cultural assumption, stated earlier, that "if one works hard and is competent," success will be attained.

The Japanese, who are likely to be prone to agitation-related emotions, that anxiety and threat, are likely to exhibit withdrawal. Withdrawal is a characteristic response among individuals who experience agitation-related emotions (see Glass, 1955; Menninger, 1954). The noncomplementary nature of the behavioral responses enacted by the two parties—the Americans continuing to persist, while the Japanese seek to withdraw—are likely to prevent either party from satisfactorily concluding a negotiation agreement.

CONCLUSION

This paper has attempted to highlight the interaction of cognitive and affective factors in influencing negotiation processes and outcomes; in addition, it also suggests that affect may play an important mediating role when individuals negotiate—using different negotiation models. These models are implicit in the standards that individuals use for enacting routinized behavioral sequences and forming interpersonal judgments. Individuals' preexisting cognitions in the nature of standards define their expectations for the interpersonal encounter and it is the violation of these expectations that accounts for affect generation in either party.

Different standards give rise to different types of negative emotions; these emotions, in turn, directly affect negotiation behavior as well as having indirect behavioral consequences via their impact on interpersonal judgments.

It must be borne in mind that the evaluation that individuals form of each other during the course of an interaction is not only likely to color that interaction but is likely to affect other interactions with members of that particular culture. It is well known that schemas once formed can be highly resistant to change— particularly those that have a high degree of affect associated with them. In view of the fact that interpersonal evaluations play an important role in negotiation processes and outcomes (see Pruitt, 1981; Rubin and Brown, 1975), it is somewhat surprising to note that *inferential* processes underlying these judgments have rarely been studied.

This chapter proposes a conceptual model in which an attempt is made to specify the *antecedents* of interpersonal evaluations, and also the importance of *affective factors* which crucially mediate the process. Much of this inferential activity takes place outside of an individual's conscious awareness (see Bargh, 1984) and this imparts an automaticity to the judgments and the affective responses of the individuals. Effective interaction in an intercultural negotiation context may, therefore, require the development of role-taking and empathetic skills. Many researchers view these skills as being essential to effective interaction (see, for example, Flavell et al., 1968; Hart & Burke, 1972). While necessary, it may not be easy to foster the development of such skills in view of differences in availability and accessibility of constructs across cultures. Nevertheless, such a modification would certainly represent an important first step in facilitating communicative competence of members in a negotiation setting.

PART IV

Mediation

Introduction

Gabriel F. Buntzman

A mediator is a facilitator. His or her role is to help two or more parties with real or apparent differences manage their conflict constructively as they search for a mutually acceptable settlement. Mediators, unlike arbitrators, may not impose "solutions" on the parties. Therefore, any definition of a successful mediation must incorporate the principle that an agreement is voluntarily reached.

Mediation probably is most closely associated with labor-management conflict. The role of mediation in non-labor-management dispute resolution may not be as widely recognized. However, the growing popularity of mediation as an alternative dispute resolution technique (ADR) outside the labor arena is remarkable. Maggiolo (1985) cites the growth of mediation in consumer, residential, prison, familial, and environmental conflicts. Mediation also can play an important role in managing conflict between nations (Levy, 1985) and in complex multi-party commercial disputes in international contexts (Henne, Levine, Usery & Fishgold, 1986).

The range of the works which comprise this section is not quite so broad, however. Included are papers dealing with mediation in several different contexts including labor-management conflict and interpersonal conflict. The topics and research methodologies employed in the chapters reflect the varied academic backgrounds of their authors—psychology, communication, and education—offering further evidence that applications of mediation extend well beyond labor-management issues.

In this section, Pruitt, Welton, Fry, McGillicuddy, Castrianno, Zubek, and Ippolito report the results of two studies based on field experiments in "Process of Mediation: Caucusing, Control and Problem Solving" (Chapter 15). First, they examined the effects of different levels of mediator power on the mediator's effectiveness. Three conditions of the experimental variable were established. In straight mediation, the condition in which the mediator's power was least, the case would simply be dropped if mediation failed. In the second condition, in which the mediator was considered to have an intermediate level of power, an unsuccessful mediation would be followed by arbitration by a different party. In the third condition, an unsuccessful mediation would be followed by arbitration in which the mediator would become the arbitrator. Here, the mediator would presumably have the most power. Pruitt et al. report that there are advantages and disadvantages to each condition.

The second study reported by Pruitt et al. focused on the effectiveness of several categories of mediator behavior in obtaining quality outcomes. These categories include posing substantive problems, proposing an agenda, and requesting reactions to ideas. A positive correlation between these behaviors and quality of outcomes was reported. In addition, the authors found that caucusing is a valuable technique when used appropriately. The authors then suggested some specific behaviors the mediator might use during caucuses to improve results, and their efforts provide a thoroughly readable examination of the effects of mediator power and behaviors on the quality of mediated outcomes.

Ross's "Beliefs of Mediators and Arbitrators Regarding the Effects of Motivational and Content Control Techniques in Disputes" (Chapter 16) is based on data collected in a survey of professional mediators and arbitrators. The main purpose of the study was to subject the Sheppard (1984) classification scheme of third party techniques to a more rigorous examination than was afforded by earlier researchers. The reader will recall that the Sheppard framework distinguishes three types of control: process control, content control, and motivational control. Ross concluded that his own data supports Sheppard's taxonomy. However, Ross also found that mediators, arbitrators, and arbitrator-mediators exhibited some potentially important differences. For example, mediators indicated some reluctance compared to arbitrators or arbitrator-mediators to propose a solution to disputants. In addition, arbitrator-mediators indicated that they are more likely to resort to caucus-like behavior (privately asking one side for a specific concession on an issue).

Some synthesis of the Pruitt et al. chapter and the Ross chapter seems possible. Ross's results indicate that more caucus-like behavior will be employed by arbitrator-mediators. Pruitt et al. found that caucusing behaviors resulted in higher quality outcomes. Together these suggest that mediations should be assigned to individuals versed in both mediation and arbitration rather than to individuals with expertise in only one of the two forms. However, additional research is warranted before strong prescriptions are made.

The next two chapters which have much in common, are to be distinguished from the first two in that they are conceptual works, whereas the former two are empirically based. First is Jones's work, "A taxonomy of Effective Mediator Strategies and Tactics for Non-labor-management Mediation" (Chapter 17). Many academics in addition to Jones—for example Lentz (1986), Moore (1986), and Weingarten (1986)—take the position that mediation outside the labor-management context is different from labor mediation. Jones argues further that improvements in our understanding and use of mediation in contexts other than labor-management disputes call for a reconceptualization of mediation for those situations.

According to Jones, a taxonomy for non-labor-management mediation should focus on five major areas: (1) mediator functions such as facilitating communication; (2) instructing the parties; (3) supportive tactics; (4) pressuring and power balancing; and (5) agenda-related behaviors such as caucusing. Jones does not argue that the five preceding categories of activities are unique to non-labor-management conflicts. However, she does argue that there is a difference in the degree to which they must be employed in non-labor-management mediations and that this difference necessitates a distinct taxonomy of appropriate mediator strategies and tactics.

The taxonomy proposed by Jones includes three strategies, Communication-Facilitation, Substantive-Directive, and Procedural. A study which compares the fit of empirical data to Shepard's taxonomy and Jones' taxonomy would now seem to be in order. This chapter is especially valued for the comprehensive enumeration of mediation strategies and behaviors the author provides.

The last few years have seen tremendous growth in the use of mediation in the management of familial disputes (Devlin & Ryan, 1986; Ingleby, 1986; Hamburg, 1985). In the last chapter presented in this section, "Incorporating Idiosyncratic Family System Characteristics in the Development of Agreements: Toward an Expanded Understanding of 'Success' in Child Custody Disputes" (Chapter 18), Hunt, Koopman, Coltri, and Favretto argue that success in mediation ought not to be measured by a simple computation of short-term gains and losses to the disputants. It is argued that, when disputants are forced by circumstances to coexist in a long-term relationship, as in child custody situations, success must be gauged over an extended time period. Furthermore, as situations are likely to change over time, a successful agreement according to Hunt et al. would be one into which sufficient flexibility has been built so that the evolving needs of the disputants can be accommodated. Hunt et al. argue that, because the disputants must interact over a long period of time, the goal orientation of mediators in child custody cases must change from conflict resolution to conflict management.

Taken together, the chapters of this section on mediation and dispute resolution are representative of contemporary thought on mediation as a conflict-management tool. It is earnestly hoped that they will serve as valued references and springboards for future research in this very important area of conflict management.

15

The Process of Mediation: Caucusing, Control, and Problem Solving

Dean G. Pruitt
William Rick Fry
Lynn Castrianno
Josephine Zubek

Gary L. Welton
Neil B. McGillicuddy
Carol Ippolito

Mediation is the process by which an outside party helps two or more disputants reach an agreement about a conflict they are having. The role of mediation has grown extremely rapidly in our society. Ten years ago, this phenomenon was largely confined to labor management and international settings, while today it is found in most realms of social interaction. Disputes about child custody, neighborhood noise, rental agreements, defective automobiles, contractual obligations between firms, where to locate dams, and many other issues are increasingly being mediated (Pruitt & Kressel, 1985).

We have done two studies concerning the conditions that influence the behavior of mediators and disputants and the impact of this behavior on the outcome of mediation. These studies focus in part on three controversies about mediator procedures that are found in the mediation movement today: the value of mediation/arbitration (med/arb), the extent to which the mediator should be directive, and the usefulness of caucusing.

A TYPICAL HEARING

Our data have been collected in community-based mediation centers in New York State. Hence, this chapter begins with a vignette of a typical hearing at one of these centers.

Originally presented as the keynote address to the first bi-annual conference of the International Association for Conflict Management, Fairfax, VA, June 22–25, 1987. The research on which this report is based was supported by two grants from the National Science Foundation: BNS83-09167 and SES85-20084.[1]

Two couples sat on either side of the table, glaring hostilely at each other. At the head of the table, a schoolteacher in her thirties was explaining the service. "First you, Mr. and Mrs. A, will have a chance to tell your side of the story and Mr. and Mrs. Z will listen quietly. Then you, Mr. and Mrs. Z, will have the same opportunity. After that we will discuss the situation and try to find a way to resolve it. The result will be a signed contract between you, which is enforceable in court. I want to assure you of complete confidentiality. Nothing you say will leave this room."

The couples were feuding neighbors whose controversy had reached a flash point propelling it into court. The judge, feeling that he could not handle the intricacies of the relationship between these disputants, had referred them to a dispute settlement center. The schoolteacher was a volunteer mediator provided by this center. It was not clear that the disputants understood everything she was saying, but it was clear that the proceedings were of considerable importance to them.

The As now told their story. There is a common driveway between the two families' houses. On two occasions, Mr. A had been trapped in his garage because of a car parked there by Mrs. Z's sister. Both times, he had gone to the Z house to complain and received a chilly reception. Then the Z children had run into his yard to retrieve a ball and broken some of his flowers. He had asked them to leave, whereupon Mr. Z had come over angrily and started yelling at him. After that, the Z children had called his teenagers names and ridden their bicycles on his lawn. Finally, one of his teenagers had been falsely accused of setting the Z family's car on fire and had been hauled into court.

The Z family story bore some similarity to that told by the As, but differed in several critical details. Mrs. Z's sister had parked only once in the common driveway, and the Z family had apologized and promised never to allow it again. The second car belonged to an unknown motorist. Mr. Z had gone over to complain because Mr. A had sworn at his children when they came into his lawn to get their ball. The Z children had not called anyone names or ridden their bicycles on any lawns, but the A teenagers had often made obscene gestures and ridden their *cars* on the Z lawn. Most recently, an A teenager had thrown a firecracker under the Z family car, causing it to catch fire. Two members of the Z family had seen him do it and had called the police.

While each side was telling its story, there were outbursts from the other of "that's not true" or "wait a minute," which the mediator strove to contain. After the stories had been told, a joint discussion ensued; but this was simply a rehash of the same accusations. To move things along, the mediator held private "caucus" sessions with each family. In these sessions, she urged them to think about the future rather than the past. She sharpened up the key issues and wrote them down, forming an agenda. The subsequent joint session was considerably more productive than the prior one, with the mediator and both disputants suggesting ways of resolving the issues.

At the end of the hearing, a contract was drawn up by the mediator and signed by all four disputants. It stipulated that the driveway would be kept open at all times; the younger generation would be polite and stay in their own yards except when carefully retrieving balls; and most importantly, future problems would be handled quietly in discussions between the adults. The Z family agreed to withdraw its legal complaint against the A teenager. Fortunately, their insurance company was willing to replace their car.

MEDIATION/ARBITRATION

Our first study (McGillicuddy, Welton, & Pruitt, 1987) examined a procedure called mediation/arbitration or, more commonly, med/arb. In this procedure, if agreement is not reached in mediation, the case goes to arbitration and a binding decision is made. We distinguished two forms of med/arb: med/arb(same), in which the mediator becomes an arbitrator if mediation fails, and med/arb(diff), in which another neutral party becomes the arbitrator if mediation fails. These procedures were compared with straight mediation, in which the case is dropped if mediation fails.

There is a controversy concerning these procedures. Proponents of med/arb-(same) argue that (a) this procedure encourages disputants to reach agreement during mediation because they fear loss of control in arbitration, and (b) the power to arbitrate gives mediators prestige, making it easier for them to encourage disputants to take the process seriously and to engage in problem solving.

Proponents of med/arb(diff) agree that the threat of arbitration encourages efforts to reach agreement. But they question giving a mediator the power to arbitrate because of the fear that he or she will become too forceful during the mediation phase and try to dictate a solution. They also regard mediation as bad preparation for arbitration, in that the mediator may become biased in favor of one side. Their solution is to put mediation and arbitration into different people's hands.

Proponents of straight mediation reject arbitration altogether. They argue that disputants should make their own decisions because they know the issues better than the mediator and also are more likely to comply with the final agreement if they have devised it themselves. They would rather have no decision, with the hope that the disputants will work it out later, than an imposed decision.

Our study involved a true field experiment, with random assignment of 12 cases to each of these three procedures. The cases came from the Buffalo City Court to the Dispute Settlement Center of Western New York. Disputants were told five times about the procedure to which they had been assigned, and mediators were told three times. Observers sat in the room during the hearings, content analyzing what was said, using an electronic event recorder. They also rated disputant motivation on three scales.

Our results support med/arb(same) over the other two procedures. In this condition, disputants were less angry and hostile toward each other. They also engaged in more problem solving, as indicated by the fact that they suggested more novel ideas for resolving the issues. Furthermore, they seemed more anxious to reach agreement and to please the mediator, which may explain why they engaged in more problem solving. In addition, they reached more agreements, though this result was not statistically significant.

Med/arb(diff) was a distant second. There was less problem solving from the disputants than in med/arb(same), and the mediators were less interested and involved in the hearings than in either of the other two conditions. Perhaps they felt like a fifth wheel, lacking ultimate responsibility for the case at hand.

Straight mediation produced the worst results of all. The disputants were especially hostile toward each other, swearing, asking biting questions, complaining endlessly about one another's behavior and character, while vaunting their own special qualities. In addition, they were especially noncreative in this condition, throwing out few new ideas. It is hard to believe that many of them would have gone on to solve their own problem.

The results for med/arb(same) suggest that a little *mediator power* is quite valuable in dispute resolution. It encourages greater seriousness of purpose and harder work by the disputants, discouraging unproductive exchanges and enhancing the likelihood of problem solving. This challenges the traditional view in U.S. mediation that a proper mediator should—in Roger Fisher's (1981) colorful terminology—be a "eunuch from Mars," totally powerless (and totally neutral).

Powerful mediators are quite common in many settings—the family, all types of organizations, international relations. They also tend to be powerful in many non-Western societies (Gulliver, 1979; Merry, in press). Furthermore, there is evidence from the international arena, supportive of our results, that more powerful mediators are more popular and more successful (Bercovitch, in press; Frei, 1976).

Nevertheless, as mentioned earlier, there are potential problems in giving mediators power. Power may tempt the mediator to try to dictate terms, producing an agreement that is neither very good nor very acceptable to the disputants. We believe that this problem is not severe in the dispute settlement center where our first study was conducted. The mediators from that center are trained in a democratic ideology that stresses the importance of consensual agreements. Furthermore, our data show that the disputants in med/arb(same) felt *less* pushed around by the mediator than in other conditions. We have, however, seen this problem in other centers where the democratic tradition is not so strong and there is greater time pressure enhancing the routinization of mediation.

Another possible problem with med/arb(same) arises if agreement is not reached during the mediation phase and the procedure moves on to arbitration. If caucus sessions have been held during the mediation phase, the mediator/arbitrator may have become *biased* and hence unable to make a dispassionate award. Caucus sessions are private meetings between the mediator and one of the disputants. We have found (in a result to be reported below) that disputants often make irresponsible charges against their opponents during such sessions. These charges, which cannot be refuted because the opponent is out of the room, may sway the mediator.

In short, there are arguments for and against med/arb(same). In its favor is the finding that it encourages disputants to make a serious effort to solve their own problems. In its disfavor is the possibility that it will encourage the third party to be too heavy-handed during the mediation phase, or produce bias that will mar the arbitration phase. As we see it, the advantages of med/arb(same)—when it can be used—outweigh the potential problems with this procedure. To combat the problems, mediator/arbitrators should (a) be trained to encourage and treasure disputant efforts to find their own solutions, (b) be allowed to take whatever time is needed to foster these disputant efforts, and (c) be trained to treat any accusations heard in caucus only as information about the speaker's views unless and until the person accused has had a chance to refute them.

MEDIATOR DIRECTIVENESS

Our second study provided evidence about the impact of mediator behavior on the outcome of mediation. We were particularly interested in the issue of how directive a mediator should be.

We continued gathering data at the Dispute Settlement Center in Buffalo and added to our sample the Neighborhood Justice Project in Elmira, New York. Seventy-three cases were collected in all. Two observers made verbatim transcripts of what was said in each hearing, carefully avoiding any information that could be used to identify the disputants or the mediator. The disputants and the mediator were then interviewed.

Transcripts and interview protocols were subsequently content analyzed. Many kinds of mediator intervention were coded, ranging in directiveness from challenging disputants to develop ideas to urging them to accept specific solutions. A special feature of this study was construction of an index of the quality of agreement, which reflects the extent to which the two disputants achieved what they were seeking in the final agreement.

We found three related types of mediator intervention that were predictive of high quality outcomes: posing substantive problems for the disputants to solve ($r = .27$), proposing an agenda ($r = .41$), and requesting reactions to ideas suggested by the mediator or the other disputant ($r = .23$). Mediators who made such interventions achieved agreements that better served the collective needs of the disputants than those who did not. What these interventions have in common is that they specify the issues and try to focus disputant attention onto them, while not endorsing any particular solution. It is this intermediate level of directiveness that appears to pay off most handsomely.

CAUCUSING

Results from both studies (see Welton, Pruitt, & McGillicuddy, in press) are relevant to the antecedents and impact of caucusing, another controversial mediator technique. As mentioned earlier, caucusing involves meeting separately with each party. Proponents of caucusing argue that this procedure helps to move difficult sessions toward agreement (Moore, 1987). Opponents fear that caucusing produces four problems (Markowitz & Engram, 1983; Pruitt, 1981):

1. Mediator bias, a topic discussed earlier.

2. Disputant perception of mediator bias, making the mediator less effective than he or she otherwise would be.

3. Undue mediator influence, making it easier to push unwise settlements onto the disputants.

4. Reduced opportunity for disputants to learn how to deal effectively with future conflict. Such skills are presumably best learned in joint sessions.

Not all cases go to caucus. To assess the conditions leading a mediator to call a caucus, we compared disputant behavior during joint sessions in the first third of the hearing for cases going, as opposed to not going, to caucus. While differing somewhat, our two studies revealed much the same picture about the antecedents of caucusing. In our first study, we found that disputants produced more persuasive arguments and fewer possible solutions in the cases that went to caucus. The latter finding appeared in the Buffalo but not the Elmira sample of our second study. In addition, we found for both samples that disputants were more hostile toward each other in cases that went to caucus. There was also evidence that they had been more hostile in the time leading up to the hearing. What all of this seems to say is that mediators ordinarily call caucus sessions in response to tension between the disputants and lack of movement toward agreement.

Five of our findings concern differences in the type of mediator behavior that occurs in caucus vs. joint sessions. With a single exception (to be noted), these findings were achieved either in both studies or in only one because the relevant measure was only made in that study. Overall, our findings suggest the value of caucusing in difficult cases.

The first finding is that mediators are more likely to resonate with a disputant, by verbalizing his or her viewpoint, in caucus than in joint sessions. Such behavior is presumably designed to build rapport, which can be useful in difficult cases. In Moore's words, it is aimed at "join(ing) psychologically with the party (by) identifying with (that) party's situation or emotions" (Moore, 1987, p. 93). This is harder to do in a joint session because it involves a form of intimacy that could make the other party suspicious.

The second finding is that caucus sessions allow mediators to talk positively about the other party and explain that party's position or needs. The aim of such remarks is presumably to encourage disputant problem solving by improving attitudes toward the other and fostering understanding of the other's viewpoint. Such remarks are probably harder to make with the other party in the room, because it might seem as if the mediator is trying to curry favor with the other.

The third finding is that mediators in caucus tend to challenge individual disputants to generate new ideas. Such efforts are probably less effective in a joint session, because it is too easy for the disputant to deflect responsibility for finding a solution onto the other party.

The fourth finding is that mediators are more likely to criticize disputant positions on the issues, in other words to provide reality testing to the disputants, in caucus than in joint sessions. Such behavior can facilitate problem solving. It is more appropriate in caucus sessions, as it could embarrass a disputant if done in front of opponent.

The fifth finding is that mediator ideas for solution are more likely to emerge from caucus than from joint sessions. Such ideas apparently emerge from problem-solving discussions between mediator and disputant. Again, it makes sense for such ideas to be presented in caucus, because the mediator is more likely to get a positive and honest reaction to a suggestion for compromise if the adversary is out of the room.

Other findings concern the behavior of disputants in caucus sessions, and also indicate that caucusing can be valuable in difficult cases. Swearing and angry displays were less frequent in caucus than in joint sessions. In our second study, 5 percent of all statements in joint session had such a character, but only 2½ percent of all statements in caucus. This suggests that tensions are down when the other party is out of the room, which should make disputants more creative and flexible.

In addition, information about underlying feelings, values, and goals was more often revealed in caucus than in joint sessions. Such information can be useful for building a win-win solution. One suspects that such information is more readily available in caucus, because disputants fear that they will be vulnerable if the adversary learns about why they want a particular solution. Mediators are often trained to ask for such information in caucus, which may also explain its increased incidence in that setting.

In our first study, we found that disputants were more likely to come up with new ideas in caucus than in joint sessions. This also makes sense, because tensions are lower and the other party is not there to hear the disputant make a tentative concession that he or she may later regret. This finding was replicated in the Buffalo part of the second study but not the Elmira part, which showed the opposite trend. The discrepancy between these centers may be due either to differences in philosophy about caucusing or to as yet unidentified differences in the type of case encountered.

The findings about mediator and disputant behavior just summarized make a positive case for caucusing. However some of our results also cast doubt on this procedure. Disputants were especially likely to put their adversary down while building themselves up in caucus sessions. They made heavy complaints about the other's behavior and often assassinated the other's character. They also bragged more in caucus than in joint sessions. This behavior is presumably due to the fact that the other was not present to refute what was said.

Some of these disputant statements were undoubtedly less than truthful. Hence, these results support one of the criticisms of caucusing—that mediators may be misled and become biased because the other party is not there to set them right. However, we do not view this as a fatal flaw. What is necessary, as mentioned earlier, is that mediators be taught not to believe the charges they hear in caucus unless the other party has had a chance to refute them.

In short, we find support for both sides of the controversy about caucusing. Much of the problem solving in our cases went on in caucus sessions, and one can understand why this was the case. Yet it seems likely that some disputants embroidered the truth during caucus sessions. In our view, the advantages of caucusing far outweigh the costs. But mediators should be careful not to believe all they hear in caucus, as they may otherwise become biased toward the party with less respect for the truth.

CONCLUSIONS

In summary, our studies shed light on three mediator procedures. First, they suggest that med/arb in which the same person plays the role of mediator and arbitrator has distinct advantages. A broader interpretation of this result is that a modicum of mediator power may be beneficial. Second, they suggest that better agreements will be reached if mediators try to specify the issues and focus disputant attention onto them. Third, they suggest that caucusing has many benefits and a few costs.

In evaluating these results, we should keep in mind that they are derived from research in a single arena of mediation, the community-based center. Hence, they need to be replicated before we can confidently generalize them to mediation in other arenas.

NOTE

1. Data for this chapter were gathered at two locations: (1) the Dispute Settlement Center of the Better Business Bureau Foundation of Western New York, where we were helped by Barbara Bittner, Mary Beth Cerrone, Mary Beth Goris, Ann Horanburg, James Meloon, Judith Peter (director), David Polino (associate director), Brenda Ransom, and Charles Underhill (president of the Foundation); (2) the Neighborhood Justice Project in Elmira, New York, where we were helped by Jill Dorfeld, Eldon K. Hutchinson, Joyce Kowalewski (former executive director), David Rynders (executive director), and Beverly Stearns. We are also indebted to Thomas Christian, Thomas Nochajski, and Helena Syna for their crucial input at the beginning of the second study; to Timothy Franz, Bret Grube, and Margaret K. Harwood, who conscientiously coded much of the data for this study; to Lisa Allen and Drew LaStella, for their expert help with data analysis; and to Michael Van Slyck, for help with planning both studies.

16

Beliefs of Mediators and Arbitrators Regarding the Effects of Motivational and Content Control Techniques in Disputes

William H. Ross, Jr.

Third-party dispute resolution procedures are becoming widely used in Western society. In addition to the traditional arena of labor-management relations, third-party procedures are being used to resolve environmental, child custody, and landlord-tenant disputes. Alternative Dispute Resolution (ADR) procedures such as mediation and arbitration offer attractive alternatives to court procedures for those seeking to resolve civil disputes. Businesses are experimenting with mediation, arbitration, and ombudsman programs as they seek to resolve commercial disputes in a cost-effective and timely fashion (Dubois, 1982).

Often the third parties involved in resolving these disputes have considerable latitude in their choice of dispute resolution techniques. Unfortunately, our understanding of third-party procedures and intervention techniques is in its infancy. One goal of the present study is to contribute to the development of a meaningful theory of third-party behavior. Sheppard (1983; 1984) offers a taxonomy for classifying third-party techniques. The present study tests whether this taxonomy provides a reasonable classification scheme for diverse intervention techniques.

A second, related, goal is to address the following question: Does Sheppard's theory apply equally to both mediators and arbitrators? A mediator can regulate the bargaining process, but, unlike an arbitrator, cannot render a binding decision. Even so, similarities between the procedures exist (Cooley, 1986; Crohn, 1985; Thibaut & Walker, 1978). Sheppard suggests that his taxonomy is a general classification scheme useful for understanding third-party strategies within a variety of procedures. Thus, the present study seeks to determine whether mediators and arbitrators, as separate groups, classify strategies in ways similar to Sheppard's classification.

THE SHEPPARD TAXONOMY

Sheppard (1983) observes that both mediators and some arbitrators typically use a number of techniques designed to promote settlement as the problem is discussed. He further suggests that each technique employs one or more types of underlying control:

1. *Process control* (PC). The intervening party attempts to direct how the disputants and other parties interact during resolution, but does not suggest the topics or other substantive aspects of interaction.
2. *Content control* (CC). The intervening party attempts to determine *what* is to be discussed but *not how* it should be considered.
3. *Motivational control* (MC). The intervening party attempts to motivate the parties to perform some desired action (for example, by making promises or threats).

The Sheppard taxonomy allows investigators to classify and better understand third-party techniques. Several writers have discussed PC techniques such as suggesting basic negotiation procedures (Young, 1975) or separating negotiators (Stevens, 1963; Pruitt, 1971).

McGrath and Julian (1963) observed laboratory negotiation groups and found that in both successful and unsuccessful groups, the ''chairmen'' (whose functions were similar to those of mediators) structured the discussion early in the session. Many of these activities would be classified as PC by Sheppard while others would be considered CC. McGrath and Julian found that PC had little effect on the likelihood of an agreement but CC increased the probability of an agreement.

CC techniques have also been advocated by other writers. CC techniques include: not discussing controversial topics (Stein, 1985; Jackson, 1952) and identifying what the third party sees as the ''real issues'' (Peters, 1952; Simkin, 1971). Some writers argue for the effectiveness of MC techniques such as rewarding negotiators for making concessions (Wall, 1979), emphasizing the costs of nonagreement (Fogg, 1985; Carter, 1982) or threatening to quit (Shapiro, 1970; Stevens, 1963). Much of this literature consists of individual practitioner's anecdotes (see Ross, 1986, for a literature review). Researchers would better understand third-party procedures if they knew what techniques suggested by the Sheppard taxonomy were seen as effective by a variety of practicing mediators and arbitrators.

One CC technique appears to be particularly effective. Federal judges who also mediated saw ''channeling discussion to areas that have the highest probability of settlement,'' as the most effective of 40 techniques (Wall & Schiller, 1983). Similarly, Carnevale and Pegnetter (1985) reported that mediators sought to simplify the agenda when negotiators were involved in a multi-issue dispute. In a laboratory experiment, Ross (1986) found that mediators who narrowed the agenda had higher settlement rates than those who did not use this CC technique (80.0 vs. 60.9 percent). These findings are consistent with Fogg's (1985) recommendation that negotiators ignore intractable issues if they wish to make substantial progress on other issues.

There are several reasons why narrowing the agenda should be effective. First, the content of discussion may be broken into a manageable size, an approach similar to Fisher's (1969) technique of "fractionating" conflict. Second, it may create face-saving opportunities by allowing each party to do well on specific issues without conceding on other issues (Ilke, 1964). Third, an agreement on one or more issues may lower interpersonal hostility, increasing the likelihood of settling other issues (Holmes & Miller, 1976; Walton & McKersie, 1965).

Emphasizing the costs of nonsettlement appears to be a particularly effective MC technique. Hiltrop (1985) found that mediation was more likely to succeed when the threat of an impasse was salient to the disputants (76.5 vs. 58.2 percent). In one laboratory experiment, subjects who were to bargain were told that if bargaining failed, the parties would take the case to arbitration (Neale, 1983). The experimenter who emphasized the costs associated with the arbitration procedure affected the negotiation process relative to the experimenter who did not. Wall and Schiller (1983) reported that third parties saw several MC techniques, (for example, "Notes, to the lawyer, the high risk of going to trial") as effective. They used a select sample, namely, one hundred federal judges serving as pretrial mediators. It is important to consider evidence from other third parties (for example, labor-management mediators).

Together, these studies suggest that third parties should emphasize the costs associated with nonsettlement. By using this form of motivational control, the third party can make these contingent costs salient to the negotiators. If the parties are aware of the costs of a failure to agree (for example, costs associated with adjudication, strike costs), then the deterence value of such actions is enhanced, causing negotiators to more actively seek dispute resolution.

BARGAINING POWER

Several writers (see Rubin & Brown, 1975) have noted the influence of situational factors upon bargaining. One situational factor that several authors report as having a substantial influence upon bargaining is the *power* of the disputants. However, the Sheppard model has not adequately addressed the role of situational factors such as bargaining power. If bargaining power also affects third parties' choice of intervention strategies, then the model might benefit from appropriate revision.

One way to assess power is to note what each party anticipates receiving in the event of an impasse. Thibaut and Kelley (1959) call this a "comparison level for alternatives" (CLalt). They suggest that if the rewards obtainable through bargaining fall below the CLalt (that is, the level of rewards available from opportunities outside of the relationship), the disputant will leave the relationship.

Thibaut and Kelley suggest that a disputant with a high CLalt has power over an opponent with a low CLalt because the high CLalt limits the range of outcomes through which the party can be moved. Researchers have found that disputants whose CLalts are equal in value have a higher probability of agreeing than when one disputant has a relatively highly attractive CLalt (Rubin & Brown, 1975). Therefore it is hypothesized that third parties believe that equal bargaining power, in the form of equal CLalts, increase the likelihood of a settlement. Note that previous research has studied this form of power only in the context of either dyadic negotiation or coalition formation (Komorita, 1984); it is not clear how a mediator or an arbitrator might vary his or her strategy when the CLalts are equal or unequal.

Sheppard's taxonomy contains very broad categories. The theory has intuitive appeal; however, empirical evidence for the scheme is sparse. The taxonomy will receive strong empirical support if practitioners' responses to diverse third-party techniques are classified into categories corresponding to the taxonomy. A classification that does not correspond to the Sheppard model may suggest important revisions for the model.

The taxonomy is offered as a general model for classifying techniques used by third parties in diverse procedures and contexts—labor mediators, arbitrators, judges, divorce counselors, and so on. Sheppard (1983) presents evidence that the taxonomy is useful for understanding behavior when managers intervene in disputes among their subordinates. However, further testing is needed if the generality of the taxonomy is to be accepted.

Based upon the above considerations, the present research had two goals. The first goal was to determine whether the Sheppard taxonomy provided a reasonable classification scheme. A diverse set of PC, CC, and MC techniques were employed to test the following hypothesis:

Hypothesis 1: Third parties classify Process Control, Content Control, and Motivational Control techniques such that the results correspond to the three categories of the Sheppard model.

A second goal was to determine whether Sheppard's taxonomy generalized across diverse third-party procedures. The following hypothesis was tested:

Hypothesis 2: Mediators, arbitrators, and those who both mediate and arbitrate, as separate groups, classify strategies in ways similar to the Sheppard taxonomy.

Previous research suggested that CC and MC techniques are effective. However, the perceived effectiveness of such techniques under equal and unequal bargaining power had not been tested. Consequently, the following hypotheses were tested:

Hypothesis 3: Mediators, arbitrators, and those who both mediate and arbitrate believe that they will use content control techniques when presented with a specific, multi-issue dispute.

Hypothesis 4: Mediators, arbitrators, and those who both mediate and arbitrate believe that they will use motivational control techniques when presented with a specific, multi-issue dispute.

Hypothesis 5: Third parties believe that unequal bargaining power, in the form of unequal CLalts, decreases the likelihood of a settlement.

METHOD

Subjects

Subjects were 530 members of the Society of Professionals in Dispute Resolution (SPIDR) operating in the United States. Most SPIDR members mediated or arbitrated labor and business disputes, but many dealt with other types of disputes (for example, community disputes).[1]

Measurement

A questionnaire was constructed to measure a variety of third-party techniques. Each item was written to correspond to Sheppard's PC, CC, or MC categories. The questionnaire consisted of three parts. In Part I, respondents indicated how *generally* effective or ineffective they thought specific third-party techniques were likely to be, using nine seven-point bipolar rating scales.

In Part II, respondents were asked whether unequal CLalts generally made a settlement more likely or less likely. The specific item was, "One of the two parties has very favorable opportunities outside of the relationship; the other party does not." Respondents indicated their belief using a seven-point bipolar rating scale.

In Part III, respondents read an abbreviated version of a three-issue business contract dispute (Ross, 1986) involving two parties with little bargaining experience. Briefly, the parties had to resolve two issues if there was to be a new contract; otherwise, an important customer would take both parties to court. The third issue represented an older dispute. Although it was not necessary to resolve it, each party wanted a favorable settlement to the older issue.

Power was also varied in Part III of the questionnaire. In one-half of the questionnaires the disputants had equal CLalts. In the other half the CLalts were unequal.

After reading the case respondents reported the likelihood of using each of nine techniques, chosen to exemplify Sheppard's taxonomy of PC, CC, and MC (compare this procedure to Bazerman & Farber, 1985). These ratings were made using five-point bipolar rating scales. There were also three seven-point bipolar ratings asking respondents how effective or ineffective they generally believed PC, CC, and MC techniques would be if used with the dispute described in Part III.

Questionnaires were mailed, following Dillman's (1978) prcoedure. Nonrespondents received a second questionnaire three months later.

Analyses

In order to test the hypotheses, a principle-axes factor analysis was performed, using SPSS-X. Mean responses were substituted for missing data and squared multiple regression values provided initial communality estimates.[2] A "scree" test revealed three factors ("elbow excluded"). Orthogonal, varimax rotation was then performed upon these three factors. The factor analysis revealed whether the respondents organized the various third-party strategies in a way similar to the Sheppard taxonomy. Hypothesis 1 would be supported if diverse third-party techniques produced a rotated factor matrix corresponding to the Sheppard taxonomy.

The Sheppard taxonomy is designed to apply to a variety of third-party procedures. However, dispute resolution professionals may have different perceptions of third-party techniques, based upon their experiences with various procedures. Consequently, separate factor analyses of mediators and arbitrators were performed, testing Hypothesis 2.

A 2×3 Factorial Multivariate Analysis of Variance (MANOVA) was also computed on Part III items using the following independent variables: equal vs. unequal alternatives and whether the respondent was a mediator ($n = 78$), an arbitrator ($n = 112$), or both a mediator and an arbitrator ($n = 92$). Following the MANOVA, scales were created measuring the likelihood of third parties using PC, CC, and MC techniques for a specific dispute. These scales were created using Part III items with loadings above .40 on the appropriate factor in the initial factor analysis (there was only one exception to this rule: one CC item with a loading of .38 was included in the CC scale). Follow-up ANOVAs on the total scale scores provided further comparisons of these three groups, testing Hypotheses 3 and 4. Hypothesis 5 was tested by simply inspecting the overall mean for the rating of the CLalt item.

RESULTS

Of the 530 questionnaires mailed, 321 were returned for a response rate of 61 percent. Two were from widows of former mediators. Of the 319 remaining, 37 were from persons who were not professional third parties (for example, researchers). This left 282 questionnaires for analysis.

Factor Analysis of Third-Party Strategies

The questions in the survey included a variety of strategies designed to exemplify three types of control: PC, CC, and MC, as identified in Table 16.1. Factor analysis revealed whether the respondents organized the various third-party strategies in a way similar to Sheppard's taxonomy.

The results showed a strong correspondence with Sheppard's model and support Hypothesis 1. Factor 1 was composed of MC items, as shown in Table 16.1.

Factor 2 reflected CC. Factor 3 reflected PC, with most items dealing with whether the parties should be separated. Many factor loadings were greater than .40 on the appropriate factor (almost all loadings were greater than .30 on the appropriate factor) and below .30 on other factors, thus approximating simple structure (Hair, Anderson, & Tatham, 1987).

This factor structure was quite stable. Factor analyses of Part III items only (not shown here) yielded three similar factors. Factor analysis of Part I items only (containing CC and MC items and only one PC item) yielded two factors, corresponding to these CC and MC items. Finally, very similar factors (not shown here) emerged from the responses of those who only mediated or arbitrated disputes, supporting Hypothesis 2. These findings indicate that various third parties' beliefs about technique use and effectiveness are organized in a structure similar to the Sheppard taxonomy of third-party behaviors.

Comparisons Between Mediators and Arbitrators

The responses of mediators, arbitrators, and those who both mediated and arbitrated were compared using a 2 × 3 Factorial MANOVA. The results indicated that there was a significant effect (Wilk's Lambda = .696; multivariate $F = 2.14$; $p < .001$). Only the first of three canonical variables was significant, correlating .84 with the type of third party.

Because the MANOVA results were significant, univariate (ANOVA) follow-up tests were performed on Part III PC, CC, and MC scale scores (the items used both five- and seven-point rating scales, so they were converted to Z-scores prior to analyses). One difference emerged between the three groups. As shown in Table 16.2, persons who both mediated and arbitrated indicated that they were more likely than those who only arbitrated or mediated to use CC techniques (M's $= 0.81$, -0.17, and -0.69, respectively; $F(2,240) = 11.25$, $p < .001$, Eta$^2 = .090$). Similar results were obtained if factor scores were used rather than scale scores.

Although there were relative differences in the ratings provided by various types of third parties, all three groups were somewhat likely to use CC techniques for this dispute. For example, respondents gave the item, "Propose a solution to the representatives," an overall average rating of 3.24 ($SD = 0.97$) on a five-point scale. Other items received similar ratings and together these findings provide moderate support for Hypothesis 3.

The various third parties also indicated that they would use PC techniques with this dispute. For example, they indicated that they would ask each side to privately "try out" proposals before presenting them to the opponent $M = 3.89$; $SD = 1.02$).

Respondents were likely to use MC techniques to resolve this type of dispute. For example, they were likely to privately inform each side of the customer's threatened legal action ($M = 3.49$; $SD = 1.10$). Such responses support Hypothesis 4.

Table 16.1
Factor Analysis of Third-Party Techniques (N = 282)

Variable (type) [a]	Factor Loadings		
	Factor 1 Motivational Control	Factor 2 Content Control	Factor 3 Process Control
Q19 Privately inform each side that the customer is threatening legal action if they do not agree. (m)	.53	.05	.33
Q5 Tell each side that if no progress is made, you will quit. (m)	.52	.09	-.15
Q18 Remind the parties that if they don't settle the dispute, they will miss an opportunity to make a lot of money. (m)	.51	-.03	.24
Q22 Some techniques (for example, making threats, offering side payments, or stressing the costs of not agreeing) provide motivation to the parties to reach agreement. Generally, how effective are these techniques with this type of dispute? (m)	.50	.11	.06
Q4 Make the parties aware of the costs they will have to pay should they fail to reach an agreement. (m)	.49	-.09	.07
Q17 Tell each side that if no progress is made, you will quit. (m)	.49	.02	-.15
Q7 If you control additional rewards, promise some of these if they settle the dispute. (m)	.30	.18	-.04
Q6 Convince the parties that if they settle, they will have higher status (for example, "your agreement will be a model for others"). (m)	.27	-.05	-.15

	2.25 (10.7%)	1.65 (7.9%)	1.28 (6.1%)
Q14 Privately ask one side for a specific concesion on an issue. (c)	.08	.64	.29
Q2 Tell the parties what issues they should discuss. (c)	-.03	.63	-.09
Q3 Privately ask one side for a specific concession on an issue. (c)	.12	.62	.16
Q16 Propose a solution to the representatives. (c)	-.03	.38	.11
Q21 Some techniques (for example, suggesting that the parties discuss a specific issue) refer to your control over WHAT will be discussed. Generally, how effective are these types of techniques for this type of dispute? (c)	-.05	.31	-.02
Q9 Tell the parties not to discuss minor issues. (c)	.02	.28	-.03
Q15 Suggest that the parties postpose discussion of the third issue (the oldest issue). (c)	.03	.20	.11
Q8 Suggest that they discuss more than one issue at a time. (c)	.05	.18	.00
Q1 Talk to each side separately to learn what each wants. (p)	-.09	.11	.59
Q12 Talk to each party separately to discover what each wants. (p)	.00	.02	.57
Q11 Ask each side to privately "try out" their proposals with you before presenting them to the other side. (p)	.01	.16	.55
Q20 Some techniques (for example, separating the two sides) specify ways that you control HOW the issues will be discussed. Generally, how effective are these types of techniques for this dispute? (p)	-.02	.10	.37
Q13 Keep the parties together at the bargaining table, "until the dispute is settled." (p)	-.05	.21	-.36
Final Eigenvalue--after Varimax rotation (Percentage of Variance)	2.25 (10.7%)	1.65 (7.9%)	1.28 (6.1%)

a Letters in parenthesis refer to the following types of control: p = process,   c = content,   and   m = motivational.

217

Table 16.2
Analysis of Variance

Dependent Variable	Source of Variance	df	Mean Square	F
Process Control (N = 247)	Power (A)	1	8.351	1.95
	Type of third party (B)	2	0.139	0.03
	A x B	2	8.115	1.89
	Error	241	4.284	
Content Control (N = 246)	A	1	1.394	0.38
	B	2	41.043	11.25*
	A x B	2	8.231	0.11
	Error	240	3.650	
Motivational Control (N = 244)	A	1	5.382	0.72
	B	2	3.223	0.43
	A x B	2	15.123	0.14
	Error	238	7.483	

* $p < .001$

Ratings of Unequal Power

Third parties reported that unequal CLalts generally made a dispute more difficult to resolve ($M = 3.19$, $SD = 1.62$) on a seven-point rating scale. This finding supports Hypothesis 5. However, when presented with the dispute in Part III, third parties reported using the same approach whether the disputants had equal or unequal power.

DISCUSSION

The present research had two goals. The first goal was to evaluate frequently used intervention techniques suggested by prior research in order to obtain evidence of the efficacy of Sheppard's taxonomy of third-party techniques. A second goal was to determine the generalizability of Sheppard's framework to different third-party procedures. These two goals were pursued by surveying professional third parties.

Mediator and arbitrator responses indicated that they believed CC techniques to be effective. This is consistent with the recent work of Carnevale and Pegnetter (1985) who found that mediators were likely to simplify the agenda.

Third parties also said that they would use MC and PC techniques. The active participation of most third parties is similar to the approach used by those state public-sector mediators described as "dealmakers" (Kolb, 1985).

Ratings of various techniques yielded three factors corresponding to Sheppard's CC, MC, and PC. Wall (1985) obtained similar factors (although he used different factor labels). The factor analysis results suggest that different types of third parties group various techniques in ways that are consistent with the Sheppard model. However, the MANOVA and ANOVA results indicate that these groups have somewhat different attitudes toward CC techniques.

Third parties reported that unequal CLalts lowered the probability of an agreement. Such results have three implications. First, new practitioners should attend to these situational factors when intervening, as these factors influence practicing third parties' evaluations of disputes. Second, future research should study how the use of third-party techniques varies as the situation varies. Third, mediator, and arbitrator choices should be studied under well-defined conditions, as was done in the present study.

The present findings are consistent with previous studies. However, certain features may limit the generalizability of the results. First, almost all MC items discussed punishments. Punishments often produce undesirable side effects. Further research must compare mediator and arbitrator use of rewards and punishments; different effects may indicate that the Sheppard model should be revised to distinguish these MC strategies.

Second, respondents reported what they would do in a specific situation, not what they actually did. Fortunately, the results are consistent with attorneys' reports of judges' actual mediation behavior (Wall & Schiller, 1983).

In conclusion, the present study suggests that many mediators and arbitrators view several PC, CC, and MC techniques as effective and reported that they would use these in a specific dispute (including narrowing the agenda and emphasizing the costs of nonsettlement). Further, although most third parties reported that unequal CLalts made dispute resolution more difficult, they did not report that they would use different techniques. Finally, the Sheppard taxonomy appears to be an appropriate way to classify techniques for both mediators and arbitrators. Further research is still needed to determine whether the Sheppard model requires specific modification to better fit the dynamics of mediation and arbitration.

17

A Taxonomy of Effective Mediator Strategies and Tactics for Nonlabor-Management Mediation

Tricia S. Jones

A great deal has been written about mediators' tactics. Some authors have presented taxonomies of general mediator strategies while others have focused on isolated behaviors. The majority of this literature comes from a labor-management view of mediation which does not adequately address the responsibilities of mediators involved in alternative dispute resolution mediation.

This chapter reviews taxonomies of mediator strategies from the labor-management perspective, critiques those taxonomies in terms of their adequacy for non-labor-management mediation, presents a new taxonomy of mediator strategies, and explicates the purpose of specific mediator tactics comprising those strategies. The potential utility of this chapter is fourfold: (1) it provides a synthesis of previous conceptualizations of effective mediator behavior, (2) it extends that work by focusing on mediation as a general dispute resolution mechanism not restricted to labor-management contexts, (3) it provides a rationale for the significance of specific tactics within general strategies, and (4) it serves as a behavioral outline for effective intervention that may prove useful to theorists, researchers, and practitioners.

A LABOR-MANAGEMENT VIEW OF EFFECTIVE MEDIATOR BEHAVIOR

Mediator strategies have traditionally been viewed as either content or process interventions. Content interventions emphasize the third party's role in the substantive decision-making process, while process interventions focus on establishing communication and a cooperative relationship between the disputants (Bartunek, Benton, & Keys, 1975). In this bifurcated view, content interventions are preferred when the major barrier to resolution is disagreement about substantive issues in dispute; and process interventions are preferred when the barrier is the interpersonal relationship of the conflicting parties (Burton, 1969). However, more recently, theorists have recognized the interdependence of both interventions in facilitating effective mediation (Felstiner, 1975). Therefore, most taxonomies of mediator behavior include both content and process interventions, although not always with equal emphasis.

Kochan and Jick (1978) suggest that mediators employ three general strategies: noncontingent, contingent, and aggressive. *Noncontingent* strategies are process-oriented and serve a variety of functions including: gaining the trust and confidence of the parties; and gathering information regarding the dispute, the disputants' relationship, internal distributions of power, and the relationship between the disputants and their constituencies. *Contingent* strategies are content-oriented behaviors which directly involve the mediator in the decision-making process. Some examples of contingent strategies include: making suggestions for resolution, pressuring parties to alter bargaining positions or expectations, and criticizing the disputants for intransigent behavior. *Aggressive* strategies are a more extreme form of contingent strategies, as is apparent in Kochan and Jick's (1978) description of aggressive strategies as: directive behavior that pressures a party to change position, suggestions for alternatives to settlement, and statements which bring the parties' assumptions in line with "reality." The key distinction between contingent and aggressive strategies may be the vehemence of the mediator's behaviors and willingness to impose his or her view of "reality" on the disputants.

Kressel (1977) also presents a taxonomy of three general strategies: reflexive, directive, and nondirective. *Reflexive* strategies, similar to noncontingent strategies, consist of behaviors that orient the mediator to the dispute, for example: explaining the mediator's role, discovering the issues in dispute and the nature of the disputants' relationship, identifying power relationships, and providing supportive behavior to increase trust. *Directive* strategies are equivalent to contingent, and possibly, aggressive strategies. Directive strategies actively promote a specific solution by pressuring or manipulating the parties. Discovering areas of compromise, making the parties face "reality," making suggestions for settlement, and applying pressure to induce settlement, are classified as directive behaviors. The *nondirective* strategies are process-oriented and focus heavily on the agenda-building function of the mediator. Behaviors comprising a nondirective strategy include: producing a favorable climate, forming an agenda, pacing the negotiations, prioritizing issues, and educating the parties about negotiation and mediation.

Perhaps the best-known classification system is provided by Simkin (1971), who argues for three strategies: communication tactics, substantive tactics, and procedural tactics. *Communication* tactics aid the parties in communicating with one another, and as such, are process-oriented. These tactics include: serving as a conduit of information, presenting a party's positions and rationales to the other, distorting the party's position to interject the mediator's views, raising points of clarification, and making direct requests for information. *Substantive* tactics are similar to contingent and directive strategies. They are specific, usually mediator-initiated, input concerning the issues in dispute and include: calculating the cost of demands, identifying deviation of demands from standard practice, indicating the ''reasonableness'' of a demand, and making suggestions for resolution. *Procedural* tactics, obviously process-oriented, include: structuring the format and sequencing of meetings, arranging joint or separate meetings, developing an agenda, and threatening to withdraw from mediation.

A fourth taxonomy worthy of examination is provided by Sheppard (1984). Extending Thibaut and Walker's (1975) examination of types of third-party intervention, Sheppard developed a taxonomy of control strategies used by third parties to explicate the similarities of these interventions across different types of conflicts and contexts. This taxonomy is not limited to mediation or to mediation in a labor-management dispute. However, it is illustrative of potential mediator strategies in both labor-management and non-labor-management situations.

There are four general control strategies in Sheppard's taxonomy: process control, content control, control by request, and motivational control. *Process control* attempts to direct the manner in which the disputants and other parties interact but does not address what the topics or substantive aspects of interaction should be. General process controls include using caucuses, establishing an agenda, acting as an advocate of one position, acting as a conduit, counseling parties, controlling access to information, establishing time limits, and establishing particular rules of order. *Content control* involves the direction of substantive issues in the dispute. For example, a mediator may refute or attack a particular point, present his/her own opinions, disallow certain content, interpret or clarify content, or withhold content from one or all parties. *Control by Request* may involve any of the behaviors already discussed as process or content controls. The difference is that the third party uses these behaviors in response to a direct request for such intervention from one or more parties. Finally, *motivational control* is the third party's source of power or influence that allows the direction of content and process concerns. When using motivational control, a third party may provide the parties with incentives or disincentives to perform certain actions, may change the power distribution between the parties, may use persuasive arguments, may invoke legitimate authority, or may even use physical force.

A comparison of these taxonomies, the three taxonomies from a labor-management perspective and Sheppard's (1984) general taxonomy of third-party intervention behaviors, reveals certain similarities and differences. (1) All four share an emphasis on content interventions (specifically, the contingent/aggressive, directive, substantive, and content control strategies). One tactic common to the labor-management taxonomies is making suggestions/recommendations for resolution. To some extent, this tactic is included in Sheppard's behavior of providing the third party's opinions on the issues in dispute. (2) All four taxonomies emphasize the information-exchange focus of process interventions. The common tactic here is the active search for information regarding the nature of the dispute. (3) Three of the four (Kressel, 1977; Sheppard, 1984; Simkin,

1971) include reference to procedural strategies directed at agenda building and arrangement of joint versus separate (caucus) meetings. (4) However, these four taxonomies differ in terms of the specific tactics included within the general strategies.

A TAXONOMY OF EFFECTIVE MEDIATOR STRATEGIES AND TACTICS FOR NON-LABOR-MANAGEMENT MEDIATION

In the past two decades, the application of mediation to non-labor-management contexts has increased significantly (Bethel & Singer, 1982; Blumrosen, 1972; Chalmers, 1948; Coulter, 1979; Danzig & Lowy, 1975; Nader, 1979; Sviridoff, 1980). The growth of mediation in alternative dispute resolution necessitates a view of effective mediator strategies and tactics that considers the nature of the disputants and conflicts in these, as well as more traditional, mediation situations.

Disputants in non-labor-management mediation are characteristically different from experienced labor-management representatives. These disputants are often emotionally and substantively involved in the dispute, are usually ignorant of the nature of mediation, and are ego-invested in alternatives for resolution (Riskin, 1982). Although Rubin and Brown (1975) note that negotiators in labor-management conflicts are also involved in the nature of the dispute and may be inexperienced, there is still a qualitative difference that needs to be addressed. While disputants in labor-management situations may be acting for themselves, they are also representing a constituency, that to some extent, controls their orientation to the dispute and aids in the decision-making process. This is rarely true of disputants in non-labor-management mediation. Similarly, although labor-management disputants may be inexperienced, they are usually provided with a general understanding of the mediation process before entering extended negotiations and often receive coaching from more experienced negotiators. Again, this is rarely true for disputants in non-labor-management mediation. Finally, the ego investment of disputants in labor-management is probably not as extreme as that of disputants in non-labor-management mediation. For example, a decision concerning pay increases or cost-of-living adjustments, while significant, is less likely to produce ego investment than a decision concerning which parent receives custody of a child.

Similarly, the nature of the conflicts in nontraditional mediation differs from labor-management mediation. Mediation as an alternative dispute resolution method usually involves recurring conflicts between persons in relatively intense and long-term relationships (Garafalo & Connelly, 1980). Moreover, these disputes are more likely to involve the resolution of a previous agreement or condition that has ceased to operate effectively. In contrast, labor-management mediation is more often concerned with the construction of an agreement in the form of a contract, and is as such, more interest-based than non-labor-management mediation (Simkin, 1971). As a result, effective non-labor-management mediation not only addresses the conflict proper, but also seeks to improve the disputants' relationship and to decrease the potential for future conflict. Therefore, the mediator may need to place more emphasis on allowing disputants to fully express their positions (Smith, 1978), to educate the other party about the nature of the dispute or relationship difficulties (Fraser & Froelich, 1979), and to assess the feasibility of solutions in light of future relational goals (McEwen & Maiman, 1982).

The distinctive nature of non-labor-management mediation and the evaluation of similarities and differences in previous taxonomies of mediator behavior suggest areas of improvement in conceptualizations of effective mediator strategies and tactics. (1) Working from the strengths of the previous taxonomies, a revision of general strategies is in order. Instead of concentrating on content versus process interventions, the taxonomy should focus on major mediator functions, specifically, facilitating communication between the parties, engaging in substantive-directive decision making, and providing for procedural efficacy. (2) Disputants' ignorance of the mediation and negotiation process necessitates greater emphasis on instructive tactics within the communication-facilitation strategy. (3) Similarly, relational tension between the disputants, coupled with ignorance of mediation, indicates the importance of supportive tactics to facilitate communication. In other words, in order to reestablish effective communication between the parties, the mediator must first reduce their defensiveness and increase their trust in the mediator and in the process. (4) Since the nature of power resources in interpersonal and community disputes may differ significantly from those in labor-management conflicts, a more thorough delineation of pressuring and power-balancing tactics in the substantive-directive strategy is needed. Although these tactics are mentioned in previous taxonomies, the behavioral descriptions of these tactics are vague. (5) The significance of procedural effectiveness, especially with inexperienced, emotionally involved disputants, indicates a need to extend the formulation of agenda-related behaviors including the appropriate use of caucuses in mediation.

The following pages present a taxonomy of mediator strategies and tactics derived from the review of previous taxonomies and recognition of possible areas of development. Three general strategies—communication-facilitation, substantive-directive, and procedural—and their composite tactics are discussed.

Communication-Facilitation

The Communication-facilitation strategy consists of three tactics: search for information, supportive communication, and instruction. Each tactic serves a variety of purposes.

The *search for information* enables the parties to define the dispute consensually, vent emotion, counteract attributional biases, and identify an operative negotiation range. In general, information exchange facilitates constructive behavior (Krauss & Deutsch, 1966).

Disputants often have different ideas about the nature of the conflict, the causes of conflict, and the appropriate outcome (Gulliver, 1973). Achieving a consensual definition of the dispute affects the entire mediation process (Felstiner, Abel, & Sarat, 1980–1981; Scheff, 1967). If this understanding is not achieved, misinterpretations of subsequent behavior is likely, and the consequences may be destructive (Louis, 1977). Access to information reduces discrepancies in perceptions of the situation (Sillars, 1980).

In interpersonal and community mediation, highly charged emotions are more often the rule than the exception. A search for information provides an opportunity for parties to vent emotions, which if repressed, may increase the chances for perpetuation of differentiation (Folger & Poole, 1984). As Douglas (1957) has argued, vehemence in initial stages of negotiation may serve as a catharsis critical for conflict resolution.

A third purpose of the search for information is the counteracting of attributional biases, or the inaccurate assignment of qualities or attributes to the other (Ross, 1977). Contexts common in interpersonal mediation are more likely to increase attributional biases than contexts common in labor-management mediation (Sillars & Scott, 1983). Such biases negatively affect the definition of the situation (Thomas & Pondy, 1977), interpretations of another's actions (Deutsch, 1969), and the attributer's behavior. Attributional biases increase the potential for competitive behavior (Wilson, 1969) and retaliatory escalation of conflict (Sillars, 1981). Fortunately, attributional biases can be counteracted through exchange of information (Miller, Brehmer, & Hammond, 1970). As Felstiner et al. (1980–1981, p. 648) summarize, "Attributions are not fixed. As moral coloration is modified by new information . . . attributions are changed."

The search for information also aids in identifying possible negotiation ranges since initial information often contains indications of the degree of commitment to desired outcomes. Using Thibaut and Kelley's (1959) terminology, information exchange aids interactions in identifying operative comparison levels and comparison levels for alternatives, thereby indicating a potential negotiation range.

Four behaviors are employed in the search for information: requests for information, requests for clarification, paraphrasing statements, and summarization statements. Requests for information and clarification are effective in generating information in a nonthreatening manner (Waln, 1984) and enable the mediator to maintain control of the interaction (Lieberman, 1979). Paraphrasing and summarization behaviors clarify the accurate perception of information and stimulate contribution of additional information. Both have proven effective in reducing defensiveness and thus in reducing conflict (Alexander, 1979; Fitzgerald & Dickens, 1980–1981).

The second communication-facilitation tactic, *supportive communication,* increases the parties' trust in the mediator, decreases defensiveness, and decreases the need for face-saving behaviors. The need for supportive behaviors is greater in hostile than in nonhostile conflict situations (Landsberger, 1955), and thus is more often necessary in alternative dispute resolution mediation. The purposes of supportive communication are accomplished through the use of: explanation of the mediator's impartiality, expressions of empathy, confirmation, and appropriate use of humor.

A major tenet of mediation is impartiality of the mediator (Young, 1972). Mediators who lose impartiality contribute to the use of destructive negotiation behaviors (Van de Vliert, 1981) and decrease the potential for resolution (Brookmire & Sistrunk, 1980). Impartiality assures disputants of equal treatment and contributes to the disputants' trust of the mediator.

Statements that communicate empathy for another's position are obviously supportive. Empathic statements reduce defensiveness (Gibb, 1961) and increase the disputants' use of constructive problem-solving behaviors (Kogler-Hill & Courtright, 1981).

Confirmation is accepting a person's definition of himself or herself. According to Sieburg's (1969) conceptualization, a behavior is confirming if it expresses an awareness of the worth of the other person, accepts the experience of the other as valid, or expresses an appreciation for the other as an individual in a relationship. In Goffman's (1956) terms, confirmation is "giving face" to another. In interpersonal mediation, disputants have often suffered significant face loss prior to mediation. In order for the mediator to facilitate communication, he or she must first work to restore the face of the disputants.

A final supportive communication technique is the appropriate use of humor. Humor is supportive by reducing tension and promoting a relaxed and informal relationship between the mediator and the disputants. While the effectiveness of humor is a function of its appropriateness for the situation (Emerson, 1969), it can increase concession making, increase the disputants' liking of the task, and decrease tension (O'Quin & Aranoff, 1979).

Instruction educates the parties about the mediator's role, the nature of mediation, and constructive negotiation behaviors. Disputants unfamiliar with mediation often confuse it with arbitration and expect the mediator to render a decision (Pearson, Thoennes, & Vanderkooi, 1982). Correcting this misperception increases the probability that the parties will adopt a problem-solving rather than an adversarial stance.

Instruction in constructive negotiation behaviors can be accomplished through the use of suggestions for, rewards for, and criticisms of certain behaviors. Suggestions for behaviors often come in the form of ground rules for behavior stated in the beginning of mediation. Rewarding behaviors serve as positive reinforcement valued by disputants (Berkowitz, Goldstein, & Indik, 1964) and promote concessions and agreements (Wall, 1979). Criticisms should be reserved until other options have failed since they may increase defensiveness and reduce the potential for resolution (Deutsch, 1969).

Substantive-Directive

The Substantive-directive strategy consists of four tactics: discussing solutions, pressuring, power balancing, and formalizing agreement. This strategy directly involves the mediator in the decision-making process.

Discussion of solutions involves mediators in presenting their own or another party's ideas for solutions and evaluating the feasibility of the offered solutions. This tactic encourages problem-solving behaviors and reduces the face-saving needs of the disputants.

As a mediator considers information presented by the disputants, he or she often recognizes potentially acceptable solutions. Offering these ideas may move disputants into a problem-solving orientation, especially if the disputants are unaware of the function of mediation to encourage this development (Wall, 1979). More important in interpersonal and community mediation is the ability of the mediator to save face for the disputants by offering and evaluating solutions. The mediator's use of this tactic allows the parties to entertain compromise positions without appearing weak (Young, 1972) and without losing face for future disputes (Pruitt, 1971).

Pressuring can be an effective means for moving disputants from unreasonable and extreme positions, although pressuring may also antagonize a disputant and decrease trust in the mediator (Lovell, 1952). Three behaviors used to pressure are invoking social norms, detailing the costs of disagreement, and threatening to withdraw from mediation. When invoking social norms, the mediator advocates change on the basis that currently held positions violate some common value, such as reciprocity, fairness, or equity (Rubin & Brown, 1975). Detailing costs of disagreement usually involves explaining the disadvantages of moving to a more adversarial system of intervention, such as arbitration or adjudication (Moore, 1983). As a last resort, the mediator may threaten to withdraw from mediation, usually after detailing the costs of disagreement.

Power balancing attempts to equalize power resources between disputants to prevent the dominance of one party (Wiseman & Fiske, 1980), to avoid an untenable solution (Moore, 1983), and to produce more effective negotiation behaviors (Donohue, 1978). In interpersonal mediation, disputants often have unequal power resources (Bahr, 1981). To reverse this imbalance, the mediator "provides the necessary power underpinnings to the weaker negotiator—information, advice, friendship—or reduces those of the stronger. If he cannot balance the relationship, the mediator can bargain with or use his power against the stronger negotiator to constrain the exercise of his power" (Wall, 1981, p. 167).

Formalization of agreement involves clear and specific indications of agreement through stages of negotiation using four behaviors: statement of interval agreements, statement of final agreement, discussion of the implementation of agreement, and discussion of future disputes. Throughout mediation, disputants often form interval agreements on specific issues which translate into components of the final agreement package. The clarity provided by the mediator in these behaviors is critical as Manson (1958, p. 762) suggests: "The experienced mediator takes great pains to forestall later trouble by spotting and correcting loosely-drawn terms of agreement." Discussion of implementation and future disputes is especially necessary in alternative dispute resolution mediation where disputants are often unaware of mechanisms necessary for implementation or avenues of recourse if difficulties with implementation arise in the future.

Procedural

The procedural strategy is designed to maintain the mediator's control over interaction. The three tactics comprising this strategy are: establishment of environment, agenda setting, and use of caucuses.

Establishment of environment involves creating a private, informal, and comfortable arena for negotiation. In moderation, all three factors can contribute to effective mediation by reducing tension and defensiveness.

Agenda setting reduces confusion for the disputants and prevents issue proliferation (Walton, 1969). While agenda setting is primarily a process-oriented behavior, it is also content-oriented since it may indicate the importance of issues by the order of discussion or even omission of some issues. A mediator uses three behaviors to establish an agenda: indicating the order of information presentation, setting the order of issues for discussion, and deciding on the number of sessions necessary to complete resolution. Perhaps the most important of these behaviors is the order of issues for discussion. This order may facilitate agreement by focusing on the least volatile issues first, thus creating a pattern of cooperative negotiation in initial stages of mediation (Donohue, Diez, & Weider-Hatfield, 1984). Further, this order enables the mediator to refocus interaction on specific issues if the disputants have wandered from productive discussion (Warren & Bernstein, 1949).

The *use of caucuses,* or private meetings with each disputant, is most helpful in cases involving problems with the relationship between parties, problems with the negotiation process, and problems with the substantive issues under discussion (Moore, 1983)—all problems that commonly occur in nontraditional mediation. While a caucus increases the mediator's control of negative information exchange (Wall, 1981), increases the negotiators' perceptions of the mediator's empathy (Bethel & Singer, 1982), prevents inflammatory statements from affecting the mediation process (Herrman, McKenry, & Weber, 1979), and reduces extreme positions (Haman, Brief, & Pegnetter, 1978), it may also be disadvantageous in that it may create distrust in the party excluded from the caucus.

CONCLUSION

Taxonomies of effective mediator behaviors from a labor-management perspective present helpful but not exhaustive advice for mediators in non-labor-management conflicts. The nature of disputants and conflicts in alternative dispute resolution mediation requires a refocusing of attention on other mediator strategies and tactics. This chapter presents a taxonomy of effective mediator behavior targeted for nontraditional mediation. Three mediator strategies—communication-facilitation, substantive-directive, and procedural—and their composite tactics incorporate critical mediator behaviors for non-labor-management mediation.

18

Incorporating Idiosyncratic Family System Characteristics in the Development of Agreements: Toward an Expanded Understanding of "Success" in the Mediation of Child Custody Disputes

E. Joan Hunt
Elizabeth J. Koopman
Laurie S. Coltri
Francine G. Favretto

Traditionally, the conflictual issues surrounding the parenting of children subsequent to parental separation and divorce have been viewed as immediate, short-term disputes between contending individuals, for which the solution was either legal negotiation or legal adjudication, the respective foci being to "strike a deal" or "determine a winner." Customarily, attorneys negotiated for their clients, and usually this negotiation took place between the two attorneys. Otherwise attorneys argued on behalf of their clients before a judge. Rarely did divorcing parents negotiate with each other, face to face. In these instances the time frame was short-term, that is, terminated by a single adjudication of disputed issues.

More recently, the advocates of divorce and child custody mediation have sought to reframe such disputes as ones in which the parents have a joint interest, and for which the solution is mediator-assisted parental negotiations in which the focus is on "getting an agreement." Studies of the outcomes of divorce mediation commonly ask the questions, "Did the parties reach agreement?" (short-

The authors thank the University of Maryland Graduate School for its support in the preparation of this manuscript.

term success) and ''Were the participants satisfied with the outcome?'' (success in meeting joint interests) (Pearson & Thoennes, 1984).

It is the belief of the authors that neither the original competition/win-lose concept nor the more recent parental joint-interest negotiation model adequately conceptualizes the goals, processes, and outcomes of successful mediation of child custody disputes. We suggest that the two fundamental dimensions of concern be (1) the viable post-divorce *family system* and (2) ongoing *long-term* relationships, and that in each mediation case to address these dimensions adequately both the mediation process and the mediated agreement must incorporate the multiple idiosyncratic characteristics of the particular family. Thus the purpose of this chapter is to stimulate a reconceptualization, both theoretically and functionally, of child custody mediation. Through an explication and integration of (1) Thomas' model of conflict management, (2) critical variables affecting children's well-being in the post-divorce family, and (3) important idiosyncratic familial characteristics, a more comprehensive and relevant understanding of ''successful'' child custody mediation can emerge.

THE THOMAS MODEL

Thomas (in press [a]) suggested that a functional model of conflict management should incorporate two essential dimensions defined by (1) the scope of the social group being served, that is, the individual/''partisan,'' the bipartisan/''joint interest'' or the multi-party/''systemic'' social units and (2) the temporal focus, that is, short-term or long-term. As shown in Table 18.1, this conceptualization is useful and enlightening when applied to the field of child

Table 18.1
Thomas' Model Applied to Child Custody Mediation

CLIENT FOCUS	TEMPORAL FOCUS	
	SHORT TERM	**LONG TERM**
Partisan/ Disputing Parent Focus	Typical adversarial model for custody disputes (Goals: to negotiate a deal; to adjudicate a decision)	
Joint Interest/ Disputing Parents Focus	Traditional Divorce Mediation (Goal: to reach an agreement)	
Systemic/ Family System Focus		Proposed Child Custody Mediation Model (Goal: to jointly create a post divorce parenting plan)

custody disputes. In Thomas' terms, the traditional adversarial mode of divorce litigation or negotiation falls into the partisan/short-term category; the modal model of divorce/child custody mediation falls into the joint-interest/short-term category; and the authors' proposed model of mediating child custody disputes falls into the "systemic/long-term category.

VARIABLES PREDICTIVE OF CHILD ADJUSTMENT IN THE POST DIVORCE PERIOD

Clinical observations, research findings, and personal experiences all evidence the fact that for many parents, children, and other family members the post-divorce stage of life is filled with persistent and deep residues of anger, conflict, hostility, fragile standards of living, and other strong evidences of individual and familial "failure to thrive" (Hetherington, Cox, & Cox, 1978; Wallerstein & Kelly, 1980; Weitzman, 1985). Indeed, the emergence of the field of divorce/child custody mediation has been largely due to the realization that this failure is not only a catastrophic outcome but an unnecessary one. Increasingly for many mediation practitioners the basic purpose of the field is the creation of viable, that is, "successful," post divorce families, and the mediation focus is upon the creation of agreements that are both equitable and functional for each individual family as it enters into and cooperatively creates the plans and blue-prints for this new stage of life (Girdner, 1986; Koopman, 1985).

It is important in child custody mediation to define "success" in terms of the factors that best predict viable post-divorce families and positive developmental outcomes for children. In a comprehensive compilation and analysis of research findings on children's adjustment following divorce, Felner and Terre (1987) cited evidence that five contextual factors are associated with children's post-divorce well-being: (1) the levels of interparental conflict, (2) the quality of the relationship between the child and each parent, (3) the degree of stability and change in the child's daily life, (4) the emotional well-being of the parents, and (5) the level of economic stress in the child's residential household(s). Thus, the mediator and parents are faced with the task of creating an agreement which will restructure what has been a conflictual and fragile family system into what will be a viable and functional post-divorce family. It is essential then that the process become one in which the parents incrementally move from the stance of situationally bound contending spousal partisans to farsighted, problem-solving parental collaborators (Pruitt, 1986; Thomas, in press [a]).

When examining the five factors identified by Felner and Terre (1987), it becomes clear that some of them may lend themselves to other types of family services in addition to mediation. For example, parental emotional maladjustment may necessitate psychiatric or other mental health services. While a more complete discussion of professional boundary distinctions can be found in the literature (Folberg & Taylor, 1984; Kelly, 1983; Koopman & Hunt, 1983), for the present purposes the following critical distinctions between a mediative intervention and a therapeutic intervention may suffice: in child custody mediation the primary tasks of the parents and the mediator are (1) to identify the needs and interests of each child, (2) to articulate the nature of the family (resources, needs, interests, relationships), (3) to formulate the specifics of an appropriate parenting plan, taking into account those mutually determined resources, needs, interests, and relationships, and (4) to plan for the exigencies of the future (Koopman, 1987). In light of the rather specific and limited nature of these tasks, it is clear that a mediator does not stress a fundamental modification of, much less the treatment of, individual and family characteristics or incapacities. Of critical importance, however, is the capacity of the mediator to identify, recognize, and validate such characteristics and to help the parents incorporate them into the content of an appropriate, workable agreement. When truly dysfunctional familial characteristics are apparent, a referral to other types of services may be indicated, instead of or in addition to mediation.

As in all human service work, practitioners must acknowledge the human and contextual limitations to their outcomes. In child custody mediation one must ask: What is the best that mediation can accomplish at this time, given these circumstances, these people, these resources, and these children, who have these needs? Nonetheless, given these constraints one can achieve a reasonable measurement of success by ascertaining whether, via the mediation process and agreement, parental conflicts were lowered, ongoing nurturing parent-child relationships were strengthened, predictability, continuity, and stability in the child's life were enhanced, the incidences of potentially damaging circumstances, such as the undue overburdening of one parent, or dysfunctional parental interactions were lowered, and the equitable sharing of both the parental fiscal and caretaking responsibilities were addressed, even if, in the specific court system in which the mediation took place, child support amounts were not actually being mediated.

VARIATIONS IN CLIENT CHARACTERISTICS

If one is adequately to understand and address the realities of long-term, family system, post-divorce phenomena, it is vital to articulate the idiosyncratic individual and familial characteristics that affect the mediation process and that must be taken into consideration in formulating the kind of agreement that will facilitate, as well as possible, long-term familial functioning. As is the case in every mediation sector, one needs to understand the persons involved, the issues encountered, and the context within which decisions are to be made and implemented. In the family sector the number of client characteristics are extraordinarily great and the dynamic interactions among them complex indeed. Nonetheless, their nature and importance may be illustrated by organizing them into six generalized categories of information which describe and define the idiosyncratic characteristics of each family and its members: (1) information regarding significant characteristics of individual family members, both adults and children; (2) information about familial relationships, patterns, and roles; (3) information about familial and societal resources; (4) information about geographic location of family members; (5) information regarding important subcultural values and characteristics; and (6) information about the potentiality for change in familial characteristics over time.

Characteristics of the Individual Family Members

This constellation of factors includes, among others, variations in health, emotional stability, skills, interests, age, maturity, and intellectual functioning of the parents, the children, and extended family members. The characteristics of each individual in the family system will impact upon both the process of mediation and the nature of the resulting parenting agreement. For example, the emotional instability of an extended family member may necessitate specialized agreements. The special needs of a child with physical, mental, or emotional handicaps may similarly require an idiosyncratic solution for the family. The young child requires arrangements quite different from those appropriate for children of more advanced years. Parents for whom abstract intellectualization is a preferred mode of thinking often incorporate formulaic or philosophic decision structures in their agreements, whereas agreements determined by less intellectualizing parents may reflect a more concrete type of thinking utilizing discrete dates, times, events, and amounts as determinants of agreements.

Additionally, the differences among family members will also be significant in determining the types of agreements that can be most helpful. Variations in specific parental skills and interests may be incorporated into different, yet complementary parenting roles and responsibilities. For example, in a family where the parents have significantly disparate intellectual capacities, a functional parenting plan might be constructed to reflect an allocation of parenting responsibilities requiring greater intellect to the parent with the greater intellectual ability. Likewise, in determining responsibility for religious upbringing, the parents may choose to make the parent with the greater religious interest primarily responsible for the children's religious training.

Variations in Family Relationships, Patterns, and Roles

These characteristics comprise the range of family relational behaviors, and include the behavioral patterns and personal conflict styles of the parents, their individual roles and responsibilities, and the roles and influence of children, extended family, and significant others.

Traditionally, the study of such characteristics has focused on the extent to which such characteristics promote or preclude the ability of the participants to reach mediated agreements. However, it is the belief of the authors that even families with relational characteristics thought to be antithetical to the success of mediation can benefit greatly from mediated agreements that validate and accommodate such characteristics.

Variations in the Separation and Divorce Process

This category of characteristics includes variations in the stages of emotional separation or divorce of each family member, variations in the stages of legal processes (such as the stage of the legal divorce in which the mediation is occurring, the types of legal processes used in the pursuit of the divorce, the filing of other actions such as domestic violence petitions, and the absence of a legal divorce, as in never-married parents), and the characteristics of other professionals involved in the process, such as attorneys, judges, therapists, and mediators.

In addition to considering this set of factors as it impacts on the capacity of each family member to adjust to specific postdivorce or postseparation family arrangements, the discrepancies in the stages of divorce or separation of the parents influence the mediation process as well. For example, every skilled mediator is personally familiar with the profound effect on decision making of parents who are at disparate points in the emotional divorce process, for example, when one party believes reconciliation is both possible and desirable, while the other party has accepted the end of the relationship and wishes to proceed with the separation and divorce process.

Variations in Available Resources

These factors include variations in the family's material assets and wealth, as well as variations in the availability of existing or potential societal or institutional resources. Examples of the latter may run the gamut from proximity to schools, parks, and public libraries to the availability of free or inexpensive family counseling, subsidized housing, health care services, or day care centers, to the more global and subtle resource paucity inherent in rural and urban subcultures of poverty.

Variations in Geographic Proximity of Family Members

Of course, characteristics relating to geographic location and distance affect the immediate substantive decisions the parents make about where children will live, how often the children's residence will change, and the timing of visitations with extended family members. Additionally, families with unusual or problematic geographic characteristics often benefit from making agreements with a flexible temporal component; for example, parents who live a great distance apart often benefit from interim or experimental agreements which do not have the crushing finality of the traditional custody award.

Variations in Important Subcultural Characteristics

Subcultural client characteristics, for example, those associated with important religious, ethnic, or regional factors, affect all of the foregoing idiosyncratic categories and add their own unique factors as well. For example, the dual traumas of divorce and societal prejudice may create special needs for participants who are members of an ethnic minority, and the mores of certain groups necessitate agreements which accommodate and foster subcultural values.

In addition, the interests of extended family members and the extent of their involvement may vary as a function of ethnic traditions and recency of immigration. On many occasions in Afro-American, Hispanic, and Asian communities the involvement of extended family members in both the mediation process and the implementation of the agreement accommodates important ethnic and subcultural values (Saposnek, 1983).

Changes in Any Characteristic Over Time

It is a great failing of our legal system when it treats our families as essentially static entities, with custody determination often viewed as a terminal event (Koopman and Hunt, unpublished manuscript). Mediation gives families an opportunity to surmount this obstacle when it allows for the development of temporally flexible agreements. Both the unique and changing qualities of certain families and the inherently developmental nature of families in general can be addressed. Flexible agreements with built-in modification mechanisms can both facilitate thoughtful modifications and prevent unnecessary future conflicts. Families usually need to change a parenting arrangement as their children grow and their families change. Successful agreements address this developmental need.

VARIATIONS IN AGREEMENT CHARACTERISTICS

In all types of mediation, the successful agreement must be appropriate to the needs and interests of the parties. In light of the complexity of client characteristics in the family mediation sector, it is especially important for clients and mediators to be prepared to think in creative yet focused ways about what kind of agreement might best serve the particular family. Surely, a "one size fits all" mentality is unsuited to the formulation of successful parenting plans. The content of child custody agreements must vary, and the variations must depend on the issues that are important to the individual families. Some issues are resolved more easily than others, and the differing needs, values, and interests in given families give rise to variations in values, suitable procedures, and differing parental roles. By considering the variety of agreements that may be formulated, one can understand a general framework within which each uniquely tailored agreement may be created. Agreements can be understood in terms of variation in (1) values components, (2) substantive parenting roles and responsibilities, (3) procedural mechanisms, and (4) temporal considerations.

Variations in the Values Component of Agreements

Very frequently parents in the midst of divorce have difficulty in problem solving, focusing, and even thinking about their fundamental values and hopes.

In these instances, the mediation process can assist in the formulation of a set of parenting values. These values function as guiding principles upon which substantive parenting decisions are formulated. Such ''agreements in principle'' include general statements such as, ''We agree that our children need and love us both, and we both are committed to responsibly fulfilling those needs.''

Often general parenting values and principles function as critical underpinnings in more comprehensive agreements, yet they can also represent a ''successful milestone'' in the management of family conflict. In some cases an agreement in principle represents the first time estranged parents have been able to discuss mutually important matters affecting their children. For these parents, even when they are unable to operationalize their values in a more specific parenting plan, such an agreement reflects a limited yet significant achievement previously unattained. Other parents can build on such values in creating agreements with more specific details about parenting. For example, ''Since we agree that our children need our love, our attention, and continued contact with both of us, we agree to. . . .'' Seen from these perspectives, the articulation of values often serves both to direct and focus the decision-making process and to consolidate a ''successful'' comprehensive agreement.

The articulation of ethnically or religiously linked family values may be important to some families. For example, in one Afro-American family, the father suggested that the parenting plan provide for his five-year-old son the opportunity to experience persons from a wide range of ethnic groups. This father explained that he wanted his son to be a part of the demise of the racism of which he himself had been a victim and believed that this goal could be facilitated by such a broadening experience for his son. This family's parenting plan included a list of parenting principles, of which this principle was a prominent one, and included specific activities which could help achieve this valued outcome.

Variations in Substantive Parental Roles and Responsibilities Articulated in Agreements

As parents articulate substantive parenting arrangements they face a complex set of choices concerning the appropriate content of a parenting plan. Those matters which are traditionally thought of as comprising a custody arrangement (living arrangements, visitation arrangements, and primary costudial responsibilities) are not the only substantive parenting issues of relevance to parents. Even parents who have already agreed on such matters, or have had them imposed by judicial decree, are well served by a variety of substantive agreements. Parents need to define jointly what parental tasks are important to them and their children, to agree upon an appropriate allocation of these responsibilities, and then to incorporate these considerations into the content of their agreement.

One aspect of defining parental roles and responsibilities which varies widely is the degree of specificity. Variations in specificity are often a function of either the parents' needs for well-defined understandings of their respective obligations or the children's needs to understand specific details of the parenting arrangements. The following examples illustrate such variations: In making plans for their children's higher education, one mother and father agreed "to share in the cost of our children's higher education," while another set of parents agreed to "contribute in a ratio reflecting our respective gross incomes at the time of our child's college entrance, the amounts not to exceed the tuition and fees charged at our state university for a full class load." In articulating scheduling agreements one family agreed that "our children will spend every other weekend with mother," while in another, the parents agreed that "father will pick up Sally at 5:00 P.M. on the second and fourth Fridays of each month and return her to mother's residence at 6:00 P.M. on the following Sunday."

Thus mediators and parents need to consider and explore a great range of possible variations in the contents and wording of agreements regarding parental roles and responsibilities. When individual parents define and delineate their parental tasks and obligations to match their own family needs, values, and traditions, they put in place an important component of success.

Variations in Procedural Mechanisms Articulated in Agreements

Substantive parenting issues, whether comprehensive or limited in scope, are only part of the content question. "Procedural agreements" may be useful in deciding issues that the parents do not resolve, in providing an effective mechanism for reducing the level of future conflict, and in ensuring the continued viability and workability of parenting arrangements. When the parents have achieved a partial agreement in which some, but not all, of the pertinent issues have been resolved, the achievement of a comprehensive agreement can be made possible through the use of procedural agreements that address the unresolved issue. For example, when the custodial label is particularly difficult for parents to decide, a successful agreement might request the court to make the custody determination. Another example of a facilitative procedural agreement is an agreement to abide by the recommendations of a mental health professional in determining the solution that best serves the children's needs. Such mutually determined agreements to allocate specific decision making to a trusted third party reflect significant and conciliatory resolution of those particular conflicts.

Likewise, including a procedure to return to mediation to modify or reevaluate the parenting agreement provides for a nonadversarial modification mechanism in the future. Such procedural agreements reflect the cooperative resolution of conflict on the part of the parents and help to assure compliance in the future. Moreover, these procedural agreements facilitate the continued viability of parenting arrangements throughout the family's development and change.

Variations in the Temporal Component of Agreements

Skilled mediators assisting families to restructure after a divorce are concerned not only with the immediate issues but also with familial growth, development, and change over time. They recognize that differences such as children's varied maturational levels, time-limited or short-term exigencies, and sensitive relational or personal characteristics that are in a state of flux may necessitate special temporal considerations. Temporal variations in agreements may be time-linked, event-linked or developmentally linked, and can serve either to accommodate changes in the family or to satisfy the need to experiment with and test various parenting options.

Mediators and parents need to recognize that such differences as children's varied developmental levels may require special attention to factors of timing and scheduling. The fact that the preschooler is quite different from the adolescent requires that the immediate plan appropriately address not only the given developmental stage but also the future need for change and modification as the child grows. Just as children, parents and issues change over time, so parenting plans need to be changed and adapted.

"Short-term agreements" can accommodate time-limited, time-dependent needs and situations. An example is a changing work schedule that interferes with visitation. A short-term agreement might be in effect for a few weeks until schedules stabilize. Another example is a parenting plan that is in effect for a short time to give parents an opportunity to develop a more permanent arrangement. Such time-limited agreements address immediate needs yet assist parents with a framework to modify and solve problems in the near future. Agreements may also be event limited. For example, parents may make an agreement that a particular schedule of living arrangements "shall terminate upon the child's graduation from high school," or that support payments "shall terminate upon the marriage of the child."

Time and event-linked agreements can serve a vital evolutionary need. Often what parents and children need is an opportunity to test out a living arrangement that may seem threatening at first glance. Arrangements made for a trial period might prove to be optimal over a long period of time but may not be tried of perceived as a definitive and "final solution." Family members thus have time to test out a possible plan and/or the parents have time to fine tune a particular arrangement without fear of a premature or unsuitable decision.

For parents whose overriding issue is mistrust, time can be used as a valuable ally. "Incremental agreements" are often effective for parents whose overriding issue is that of trust. Parents who agree to minor or limited short-term agreements may gradually experience, as a result, the restoration of confidence in the other parent and develop an increasingly civil and businesslike parenting relationship which gradually replaces the former one of hostility and mistrust.

The incremental making of small agreements may offer additional benefits for children. Since developmentally children change over time, incremental agreements are often optimal. For example, the plan for the infant who is attached to a primary caregiver can be changed as he/she is able to spend longer periods of time away from one or the other parent. For older children, "experimental agreements" can be used to evaluate how well various residential options fit educational requirements and special peer and recreational needs, interests, and opportunities. As in all successful parenting agreements, the most important considerations are, primarily, the children and the issues affecting them, and, secondarily, the workability of the agreement for the parents.

When one reflects upon the temporal aspect of parenting agreements, the concept of a "final agreement" merits reconsideration. In a sense a "final agreement" merely connotes the best parenting plan that *these* parents concerned about *these* issues at this time can develop. Even "final" agreements need not be considered permanent when they include a reevaluation mechanism to assess whether the plan is still working for these children and for these parents at some future time. A "procedural agreement" to return to mediation for future changes accomplishes the need for an orderly evolution of the family system over time. In a real sense there may never truly be such a thing as a "permanent" agreement for one feature of a successful parenting plan is that not only is it well suited to the current needs of the children and the family but that it also contains provisions for flexibility and appropriate modification over time.

DISCUSSION

The premises of this chapter are that it is desirable in child custody mediation to emphasize the long-term/family system dimensions articulated by Thomas (in press [a]), to incorporate in both process and outcome idiosyncratic familial characteristics, and to evaluate success against criteria shown to affect children's post-divorce adjustment. Given these premises the common utilization of client satisfaction or "getting an agreement" are inappropriate measures of success. Indeed, the world is full of both orders and agreements that have either continued or exacerbated the predivorce chaos of many families (Weitzman, 1985; Wheeler, 1980). When, as is often the case, such continued conflict results in relitigation, the result is not only damaging to the family but burdensome to the court.

The authors have participated in court-connected child custody mediation services during the past three years and have helped parents create a varied array of parenting agreements. Each mediation process and each mediated agreement has reflected the unique characteristics of the individual persons, the specific family, and the societal contexts within which the family transitions occurred.

While space constraints preclude the inclusion of complete cases and texts of agreements made by parents, some striking contrasts between two selected families serve to illustrate how different parents (here, the Does and the Jones) made significant improvements in their post-divorce families.

While the limited emotional, intellectual, and financial capacities of both Mr. and Mrs. Doe had been noted in voluminous social worker notes, Mrs. Doe's initiation of a divorce and the parents' subsequent separation triggered increasingly hostile interpersonal exchanges and repeated angry visits to the court with multiple filings of pleadings and motions by Mr. Doe. These were followed by Mrs. Doe's refusal of visitation between their daughter, Sally, and Mr. Doe. The court granted sole custody to Mrs. Doe and referred them to mediation for determination of a mutual agreement regarding visitation. Early mediation sessions were marked by highly volatile outbursts by Mr. Doe who was sure he had "lost little Sally forever." However, after several sessions, including one in which mother, father, and child had a "play session" together so that the mediator was able to observe parent-child interactions, the Does were able to reach an agreement. The agreement consisted largely of the articulation of a plan by which Mrs. Doe would bring three-year-old Sally to McDonald's each Friday noon to have lunch with her father, and Mr. Doe agreed to buy Sally some shoes and jeans. They also agreed to return to mediation if the plan was not working for them.

The Jones, by contrast, were highly educated, upper-middle-class parents with successful independent careers. Mr. Jones' "mother killer" lawyer (his reputation in legal and societal circles) had refused to negotiate with the other attorney and had exasperated everyone, including the judge who had ordered them to mediation. During the mediation sessions these parents decided on an agreement in which there was almost equal sharing of parental roles and responsibilities. They, too, agreed to return to mediation if their plan ceased to be functional for their family.

Largely because of the modification clauses, there was an opportunity to follow up on these families. Mr. Doe requested a return due to a disagreement over the delivery of his Christmas presents to Sally. A two-hour Christmas afternoon visit at Mrs. Doe's home was quickly agreed upon at an expediently scheduled mediation session. At the session both parents reported that otherwise things were working out quite amicably most of the time, and that Sally seemed to be getting along fine. Mr. and Mrs. Jones requested another session about a year after their original mediation when they were unable to agree about how they would make changes in their parenting arrangements when Mr. Jones was to be overseas for a sabbatical leave. They agreed to consult with the children's school personnel and their therapists, and subsequently agreed in mediation that the children would spend three summer months abroad with Mr. Jones and return for the fall semester to live with Mrs. Jones. Both Mr. and Mrs. Jones acknowledged that they were both actively involved in their children's lives, had reduced the frequency and intensity of their bickering over scheduling and "luxury purchases" for the children, and were moving in emotionally independent ways from one another.

Based upon all information currently available to the authors, in both families the level of overt interparental hostility has been significantly reduced, the parent-child relationships have been both nurtured and maintained, and the children have undergone a minimum of uprooting and change. Considering the critical factors predictive of post-divorce child adjustment, there are strong indices of some real success. Idiosyncratic familial characteristics were actively incorporated into the nature of the mediation process and into the nature of the agreements while the mediation focus remained on long-term family functioning. For these families the modification clauses were essential to the maintenance of long-term developmental planning.

Currently, the authors are conducting a structured, longitudinal research study, designed to examine and assess empirically the variables of (1) level of parental conflict and (2) parent-child contact in the adjustment of children whose parents have formulated mediated agreements in court settings. (Koopman, Hunt, & Favretto, 1987) When such empirical data are added to the pool of existing empirical and anecdotal data, both theoretical and clinical assumptions may be better tested, and recommendations regarding theory, practice, and evaluation in the child custody mediation field be made with greater relevance and confidence. By construing the purpose of child custody mediation as being the creation of a strengthened and functioning post-divorce family and by recognizing the necessity of utilizing idiosyncratic familial characteristics, the essence of custody mediation practice and the real meaning of success in this mediation sector can be recognized and validated.

PART V

Integrating Perspective

Introduction

M. Afzalur Rahim
Evert van de Vliert

About two decades ago, Fink (1968) in his extensive review of conflict literature noted that the literature was badly in need of integration. Subsequently, Thomas (1976), after reviewing the literature on conflict and conflict management, expressed his concern that the theory and research were largely specialized and segmented. He stressed the desirability of developing integrative and, consequently, more complex models. Today the literature on conflict is still very specialized, as the chapters in this volume amply illustrate. There is a need for continued integration of the literatures on organizational conflict, conflict in communication, bargaining and negotiation, mediation, arbitration, and international conflict.

It was suggested by Thomas (1976) that integration stands for (a) the clarification of the theoretical ties between different insights in the scattered literature, and (b) the search for generic variables that appear helpful in understanding the various manifestations of conflict. We want to extend Thomas' description of integration by considering it as the last phase of theory development which attempts to reconcile initially different or even incompatible positions. It is very similar to Hegel's dialectic process, which consists of a movement from thesis to antithesis and finally to synthesis. The dialectical method essentially effects a synthesis of opposites. The synthesis in turn becomes a new thesis and the dialectical process continues until a fully developed synthesis (the Absolute Idea) is reached. Each stage in this process relates back to the previous ideas but results in broadened knowledge. The literature on conflict is greatly in need of synthesis.

The three chapters in this section have been selected because they cut across different specialized areas of conflict theory and research. The authors have made a commendable effort to provide some integration of the diverse literature on conflict.

Johnson, Johnson and Smith, in Chapter 19, "Controversy within Decision-making Situations," are concerned with the process by which controversy among group members increases the quality of decisions. They have developed an integrative process model of how conflict among ideas, perspectives, and conclusions result in high quality decisions. The model states that group members will initially conclude what the decision should be, present their position and rationale to the group, be challenged by opposing views, experience conceptual conflict and uncertainty followed by a search for new information. Ultimately the participants reconceptualize their conclusions based on an accurate understanding of the opposing perspectives, by incorporating opponents' information and reasoning into their position, and by using higher-level reasoning strategies. Controversies tend to be constructive when the situational context is cooperative and when there is some heterogeneity among informed and socially skilled group members.

A salient feature of the chapter is the emphasis placed on the notion of reconceptualization of one's position. Johnson et al. appropriately distinguish among the indices of reconceptualization, and two major dependent variables, productivity and positive attitudes. It is interesting to note that the section on reconceptualization refers predominantly to the literature on developmental and educational psychology, while the section on productivity is based primarily on work and organizational psychology, and the section on positive attitudes rests mainly on social psychological insights.

In his critical review, "Norms as an Integrative Theme in Conflict and Negotiation: Correcting Our 'Sociopathic' Assumptions" (Chapter 20), Thomas contrasts the rational-instrumental paradigm of the economists and the "normative" behavioral assumptions of clinical psychologists, sociologists and anthropologists. Conflict researchers have been strongly influenced by the economic approach, either ignoring norm-related behavioral phenomena, or treating these as nonrational "noise." Recent interest in the topic of justice, along with normative considerations in the Fishbein-Ajzen motivation/behavior model, induce Thomas to present a strong case for an integrated "rational-normative" of conflict management. This revised paradigm includes time perspective as a synthesizing factor. Contingency theories have tended to provide answers to the short-term question of which behaviors will work best under a given set of current conditions. In contrast, normative theories deal with desirable circumstances that improve a system's functioning in the long run. The two time horizons appear to reconcile the contradictions between the two theoretical positions.

Norm-related conflict phenomena lead the researcher out of the laboratory into real world situations of disagreement and obstruction. Although Thomas does not mention social role theory, his specific suggestions for future research could be phrased in terms of role senders, role expectations, and role enactment. First, there is a need for the study of violations of role expectations as another form of conflict in addition to interest and cognitive conflicts. Second, we need to know more about how conflict parties establish mutual role expectations, evoke existing role expectations, and try to enforce such prescriptions concerning proper styles of handling conflict, justice, appeals to third parties, and so on. Third, the role conceptions of distinct intervening parties, including their role expectations for the other parties' behaviors, are yet another fruitful area for research.

Chapter 21, "Third Party Intervention: A Theoretical Framework," by Kaufman and Duncan, focuses on similarities and differences in the mechanisms by which intervenors achieve results in decision situations involving conflict. An essential difference among mediators, go-betweens, auditors, counselors, ombudsmen, elected representatives, managers, brokers, judges, and law enforcement officers is the mandate (set of formal and informal role prescriptions) under which they operate. This mandate is analyzed according to whether the intervenor is expected to transfer information, inform choices, promote choices, make choices, or implement choices. Here empirical data would be most welcome. The actual intervention process is supposed to be characterized by who initiates intervention, who selects the intervenor, who controls the process, who enforces outcomes, who evaluates the intervention, and what criteria are used for evaluation. It is shown how these features of the intervention process discriminate among the many types of intervenors. The authors state that the parties' choice processes are potentially affected along three perceptual dimensions: available options, outcome probabilities, and valences of outcomes. They pay special attention to the mediation mode, an intervention style that relies solely on persuasion when altering the parties' solution space, subjective probabilities, or preferences for outcomes.

Because role expectations and role enactment play an important part in the framework of conflict intervention, role transition might be one of the concepts that can advance the search for an integrating perspective. For example, a manager may become a ombudsman, a lawyer may become arbitrator, and a parent may have to assume any of these intervenor roles. Kaufman and Duncan's detailed classifications imply a complex pattern of more and less overlapping roles among the third parties, which may be related to the relative ease of certain transitions.

To conclude, both theory and research in the specialized areas of conflict, as well as integration of these specialized literatures, are essential for the development of theories and models on conflict and conflict management. It appeared to us that any constructive integration of different conflict theories and models is very difficult to achieve, and it may not be possible for an individual scholar to perform such a task effectively. A mission to accomplish such a challenging task should possibly be attempted by a group of interdisciplinary scholars in conflict.

19

Controversy within Decision Making Situations

David W. Johnson
Roger T. Johnson
Karl Smith

INTRODUCTION

Decision making typically involves considering several possible alternatives and choosing one. By definition, all decision-making situations involve some conflict as to which of several alternatives should be chosen. Such conflict is known as controversy, and may be differentiated from conflicts-of-interest and other types of conflict that occur in decision-making groups (Johnson & Johnson, 1987). The management of the disagreement among individuals' ideas, theories, expertise, conclusions, and perspectives is a critical and often ignored aspect of effective decision making. Within decision-making groups controversy is often avoided, suppressed, and ignored. Yet controversy is the source of creative and high quality decisions based on high-level reasoning and a thorough examination of all alternatives. The objectives of this chapter are to define decision making and controversy, detail the process by which controversy affects the quality of decision making, and discuss the conditions that mediate the effectiveness of controversy.

DECISION MAKING

Decision making typically involves considering possible alternatives and reaching agreement as to which of several courses of action is most desirable for achieving the organization's goals (Johnson & Johnson, 1987). Most important group decisions involve more than one source of expertise and, as Tversky and Kahneman (1981) note, most decision makers are normally unaware of alternative perspectives and frames of reference and of their potential effects on the relative attractiveness of options. Thus, two different group members, with different information and perspectives, can make directly opposing decisions without recognizing the limitations of their frames of reference. Since individuals are capable of all sorts of rationalizations enhancing the importance of their expertise, any decision made by a single group member is suspect. When group members with different information and perspectives come together to make a joint decision, conflict and disagreement result. Such controversy is an essential part of group and organizational decision making.

THE NATURE OF CONTROVERSY

Within decision-making situations, group members can engage in controversy, debate, concurrence-seeking, or individualistic efforts. The type of conflict most important for high quality decision making is *controversy*, the situation that exists when one person's ideas, information, conclusions, theories, and opinions are incompatible with those of another, and the two seek to reach an agreement. An example of controversy is when a decision is to be made about whether more or less regulations are needed to manage the disposal of hazardous wastes and two members are given the position that fewer regulations are needed and the other two members are given the position that more regulations are needed, and the group has to prepare a group report reflecting consensus among group members. In effect, advocacy subgroups are formed, present their positions to the best of their ability, listen carefully to opposing points of view, and then drop their advocacy to arrive at a consensus on a decision. Within a controversy there are both positive goal interdependence (come to a consensus on the decision) and resource interdependence (different members have different information). Whenever more than one alternative is being considered within a decision-making situation, a controversy exists. Controversies, therefore, are an inherent part of and inevitable within any organizational decision-making situation.

In contrast to controversy, *debate* exists when group members argue for positions that are incompatible with one another and a judge declares a winner on the basis of who presented their position the best. In a debate group members compete to see who is best in presenting their position. An example of debate is when two or more advocacy subgroups present their positions to the best of their ability and the chair of the group decides which alternative to adopt.

Concurrence seeking occurs when group members inhibit discussion to avoid any disagreement or arguments and emphasize agreement. An example of concurrence seeking is when a decision making group is assigned the task of formulating recommendations concerning hazardous waste regulation with the stipulation that they do not argue but rather compromise quickly whenever opposing opinions are expressed. Most decision-making situations are dominated by concurrence seeking (Walton, 1987). Concurrence seeking is close to the *groupthink* concept of Janis (1982), in which members of a decision-making group set aside their doubts and misgivings about whatever policy is favored by the emerging consensus so as to be able to concur with the other members. The underlying motivation of groupthink is the strong desire to preserve the harmonious atmosphere of the group on which each member has become dependent for coping with the stresses of external crises and for maintaining self-esteem.

Individualistic decision making occurs when each member of a decision-making group independently makes his or her decision without interacting with others or discussing the information on which the decision is being made. Isolated individuals independently decide on a course of action without any interaction or consultation with each other. An example of individualistic decision making is when the group has to formulate recommendations concerning hazardous waste regulation and each member is asked to consider the issue on his or her own, without discussing it with other members, and the independent decisions are then combined into a group decision.

A key to the effectiveness of conflict procedures is the mixture of cooperative and competitive elements within the procedure. The greater the cooperative elements and the less the competitive elements, the more constructive the conflict (Deutsch, 1973). Cooperative elements alone, however, do not ensure high quality decisions. Both cooperation and conflict are necessary. Controversy is characterized by positive goal interdependence, resource interdependence, and conflict. Debate is characterized by resource interdependence, negative goal interdependence, and conflict. Within concurrence-seeking groups there is only positive goal interdependence, and within individualistic situations there is neither interdependence nor conflict.

The hypothesized process by which controversy sparks higher quality decisions than do debate, concurrence seeking, and individualistic efforts is outlined in Figure 19.1. It consists of six steps leading to increased quality of decision making. The steps and their validating research are discussed in detail in the following sections.

STEP 1: ORGANIZING INFORMATION AND DERIVING CONCLUSIONS

High quality decision making begins with group members categorizing and organizing their present information and experiences so that a conclusion is derived. Individuals' interaction with the world always involves categorization or conceptualization, the forming or being aware of concepts (Johnson, 1979). Concepts are then systematized into coding systems or conceptual structures that organize related concepts from the very specific to the generic, which promotes retention of information and its transfer and application. Conclusions are then derived based on the principles of scientific inquiry and deductive and inductive logic.

A manager may structure a controversy by holding a group discussion about a decision in which a number of alternatives are identified. Each group member is then assigned to a advocacy pair and given the responsibility to prepare the "best case" for the alternative assigned. All available relevant information is then gathered and organized in order to advocate that alternative to the whole group. An *advocacy subgroup* is a task force that prepares and presents a particular policy alternative to the decision-making group. An example is when the president of a company, faced with a decision of whether to buy or build a manufac-

Figure 19.1
Process of Controversy

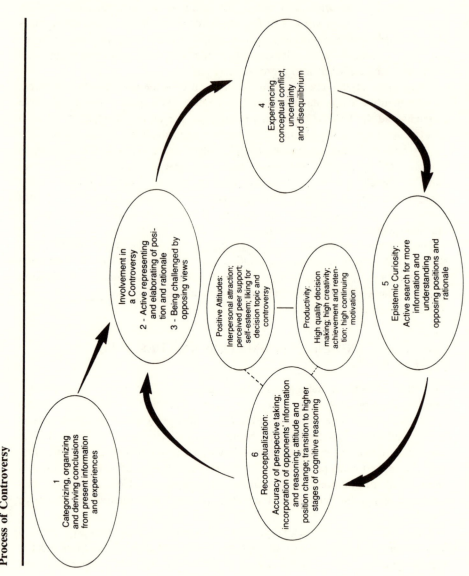

turing plant, established two advocacy groups. The "buy" team was instructed to present the best case for purchasing a manufacturing plant and the "build" team was told to present the best case for building a new manufacturing plant near the national headquarters of the company. The "buy" team identified a large number of existing plants that would meet the company's needs, narrowed the field down to 20, further narrowed the field down to three, and then selected one plant as the ideal plant to buy. The "build" team contacted dozens of engineering firms and after several months of consideration, selected a design for the ideal plant to build. Nine months after they were established, the two teams presented their best case with well worked out details about cost to the top management. From the presentations it was apparent that the two options would cost about the same amount of money and, therefore, the "build" option was selected as it allowed the plant to be conveniently located near company headquarters.

STEP 2: PRESENTING AND ADVOCATING POSITION

A central aspect of controversy is having individuals advocate their position to the rest of the group. Advocating their position and reasoning and defending it against refutation requires engaging in considerable (a) searching for facts, information, and evidence to support their position, (b) organizing what is known into a coherent and reasoned position, and (c) presenting a position forcefully, sincerely, and persuasively while keeping an open mind. This results in considerable cognitive rehearsal and elaboration of the position and its rationale. A number of research studies have found that decision makers engaged in controversy (compared with those engaged in debate, concurrence seeking, and individualistic study) contributed more information to the discussion, more frequently repeated information, shared new information, elaborated the material being discussed, presented more ideas, presented more rationale, made more higher-level processing statements, made more comments aimed at managing their efforts to make high quality decisions, made fewer intermediate level cognitive processing statements, and made more statements managing the group's work (Johnson & Johnson, 1985; Johnson, Johnson, Pierson, & Lyons, 1985; Johnson, Johnson, & Tiffany, 1984; Lowry & Johnson, 1981; Smith, Johnson, & Johnson, 1981, 1984). Nijhof and Kommers (1982) found that the presence of controversy in cooperative groups increased the oral participation of group members. Disagreements within a group have been found to provide more information and a greater variety of facts as well as changes in the salience of known information (Anderson & Graesser, 1976; Kaplan, 1977; Kaplan & Miller, 1977; Vinokur & Burnstein, 1974).

When decision makers know that they will have to present the best case possible for "Alternative A" to the group as a whole, and try to convince the other group members to decide to adopt "Alternative A," they tend to understand more thoroughly the alternative they represent, to use higher-level reasoning strategies more frequently, to conceptualize it at a higher level, and become more committed to its implementation (Johnson & Johnson, 1979, 1983; Murray, 1983; Nel, Helmreich, & Aronson, 1969).

STEP 3: BEING CHALLENGED BY OPPOSING VIEWS

In controversy (and debate), individuals' conclusions are challenged by others who present opposing positions. After all advocacy teams have presented their positions, members of the decision-making group must evaluate and criticize the advocated alternatives. Members attack each other's positions in attempts to weaken or even discredit the alternatives being advocated. The members then rebut the attacks while arguing why the alternative they are advocating is the most desirable one. Hearing other alternatives being advocated and having one's position attacked and refuted results in considerable conceptual conflict and uncertainty results.

STEP 4: CONCEPTUAL CONFLICT AND UNCERTAINTY

When decision makers are challenged by information that is incompatible with and does not fit with their conclusions, conceptual conflict can result. The evidence indicates that the greater the disagreement within a decision-making group, the more frequently disagreement occurs, the greater the number of people disagreeing with a person's position, the more competitive the context of the controversy, and the more affronted the person feels, the greater the conceptual conflict and uncertainty the person experiences (see Johnson, Johnson, & Smith, 1986).

STEP 5: EPISTEMIC CURIOSITY

Epistemic curiosity is reflected in individuals' (a) active search for more information and (b) seeking to understand the position and its supporting rationale of the opposing persons. Conceptual conflict motivates an active search for more information (often called epistemic curiosity) in hopes of resolving the uncertainty. Lowry and Johnson (1981) found that individuals involved in controversy, compared with persons involved in concurrence seeking, read more relevant material, reviewed more relevant materials, more frequently gathered further information during their free time, and more frequently requested information from others. Smith et al. (1981) found that controversy, compared with both concurrence seeking and individualistic decision making, promoted greater use of relevant materials and more frequent giving up free time to gather further information. Johnson and Johnson (1985) and Johnson, Johnson, and Tiffany (1984) found that controversy, compared with debate and individualistic decision making, promoted greater search for more information outside of class. Johnson, Brooker, Stutzman, Hultman, and Johnson (1985) found that individuals engaged in controversy had greater interest in learning more about the subject being discussed than did persons engaged in concurrence seeking or individualistic efforts.

Individuals engaged in controversy have been found to be motivated to know others' positions and to develop understanding and appreciation of them (Tjosvold & Johnson, 1977, 1978; Tjosvold et al., 1980; Tjosvold, Johnson, & Lerner, 1981). Individuals involved in a controversy developed a more accurate understanding of other positions than did persons involved in noncontroversial discussions, concurrence-seeking discussions, and individualistic efforts (Smith et al., 1981; Tjosvold & Johnson, 1977, 1978; Tjosvold et al., 1980).

STEP 6: RECONCEPTUALIZATION, SYNTHESIS, INTEGRATION

The purpose of structuring overt controversy within a decision-making situation by identifying alternatives and assigning members to advocate the best case for each alternative is not to choose the best one. The purpose is to create the situation in which a synthesis of the best reasoning and conclusions from all the various alternatives may be made. *Synthesizing* occurs when decision makers integrate a number of different ideas and facts into a single position. It is an intellectual bringing together of ideas and facts and engaging in inductive reasoning by restating a large amount of information into a conclusion or summary. It is a creative process involving seeing new patterns within a body of evidence, viewing the issue from a variety of perspectives, and generating a number of optional ways of integrating the evidence. The dual purposes of synthesis are to arrive at the best possible decision and to find a position that all group members can agree and commit themselves to. The quality of individuals' reconceptualization, synthesis, and integration depends on the accuracy of their perspective taking, their incorporation of others' information and reasoning into their own position, their attitude and position change, and their transition to higher stages of cognitive reasoning.

Accuracy of Perspective Taking

In order to arrive at a synthesis that is acceptable to all group members, the issue must be viewed from all perspectives. Understanding the facts being presented by other advocacy teams is not enough. The perspective from which the members are speaking must also be clearly understood. Group members need to be able to both comprehend the information being presented by their opposition and to understand the cognitive perspective their opposition is using to organize and interpret the information. A *cognitive perspective* consists of the cognitive organization being used to give meaning to a person's knowledge, and the structure of a person's reasoning. Tjosvold and Johnson (1977, 1978) and Tjosvold et al. (1980) conducted three experiments in which they found that the presence of controversy promoted greater understanding of another person's cognitive perspective than did the absence of controversy. Individuals engaging in a controversy were better able subsequently to predict what line of reasoning their opponent would use in solving a future problem than were persons who interacted without any controversy. Smith et al. (1981) found that individuals engaged in a controversy were more accurate in understanding their opponents' perspective than were persons involved in concurrence-seeking discussions or individualistic efforts. D. W. Johnson et al. (1985) found that individuals in the controversy condition were better able to take the opposing perspective than were individuals participating in concurrence-seeking discussions.

Perspective-taking skills are of great importance for exchanging information and opinions within a controversy (see Johnson, Johnson, & Smith, 1986). When individuals are competent in taking the other's perspective, more information (both personal and impersonal) is disclosed, messages are phrased so that they are easily understood by others, other people's messages are comprehended more accurately, opponents' information and perspective are understood better and retained longer, more creative and higher quality solutions are developed, more accurate problem solving results, and more positive perceptions result of the information exchange process, fellow problem solvers, and the problem-solving experience.

Incorporation of Others' Information and Reasoning

A more accurate understanding of the opponents' position, reasoning, and perspective has been posited to result in greater incorporation of the opponent's reasoning into one's own position. There is evidence that participation in a controversy, compared with participating in noncontroversial or concurrence-seeking discussions or individualistic efforts, resulted in greater incorporation of opponents' arguments and information (Johnson & Johnson, 1985; Johnson et al. 1984; Tjosvold et al. 1981). These findings, however, are limited to conditions where the overall context is cooperative and individuals have the skill of disagreeing while confirming their opponents' competence. Tjosvold and Johnson (1978) found that when the context was cooperative there was more open-minded listening to the opposing position. When controversy occurred within a competitive context, a closed-minded orientation was created in which individuals comparatively felt unwilling to make concessions to the opponent's viewpoint, and closed-mindedly refused to incorporate any of it into their own position. Within a competitive context the increased understanding resulting from controversy tended to be ignored for a defensive adherence to one's own position. Lowin (1969) and Kleinhesselink and Edwards (1975) found that when individuals were unsure of the correctness of their position, they selected to be exposed to disconfirming information when it could easily be refuted, presumably because such refutation could affirm their own beliefs. Van Blerkom and Tjosvold (1981) found that individuals selected to discuss an issue with a peer with an opposing position more frequently when the context was cooperative rather than competitive, and that individuals in a competitive situation more often selected a less competent peer with whom to discuss an issue. Tjosvold (1982) and Tjosvold and Deemer (1980) found that when the context was competitive, participants in a controversy understood but did not use others' information and ideas, but when the context was cooperative, the information and ideas provided by opponents were used. Tjosvold et al. (1980) and Tjosvold et al. (1981) found that when individuals involved in a controversy have their personal competence disconfirmed by their opponent, a closed-minded rejection of the opponent's position, information, and reasoning results. The amount of defensiveness generated influenced the degree to which individuals incorporated the opponent's information and reasoning into their position, even when they understood accurately their opponent's position.

Attitude and Position Change

Disagreements within a group have been found to provide a greater amount of information and variety of facts, and a change in the salience of known information, which in turn resulted in shifts of judgment (see Johnson et al., 1986). A number of studies have found that controversy promoted greater attitude change than did concurrence seeking, no-controversy, and individualistic efforts (Johnson & Johnson, 1985; C Johnson et al., 1985).

Transition from One Stage of Cognitive Reasoning to Another

Cognitive development theorists (Kohlberg, 1969; Piaget, 1948, 1950) have posited that it is repeated interpersonal controversies in which individuals are forced again and again to take cognizance of the perspective of others that promote cognitive and moral development, the ability to think logically, and the reduction of egocentric reasoning. Such interpersonal conflicts are posited to create disequilibrium within individuals' cognitive structures, which motivate a search for a more adequate and mature process of reasoning. There is considerable evidence to support these propositions (Johnson et al., 1986). Thus, it may be expected that when controversy is deliberately structured and conducted within decision-making groups, higher-level reasoning in analyzing the decision will result.

PRODUCTIVITY

Within decision-making groups, greater productivity and higher-quality decisions result when members are assigned to advocacy teams and they (1) organize information into a coherent and reasoned position, (2) actively present and advocate their position, (3) defend their position from refutation while criticizing the positions of the other advocacy teams, (4) reassess the validity of the position they are advocating, (5) search for additional information about the issue, and (6) reconceptualize the issue based on synthesizing and integrating the information and perspectives of all the advocacy teams. The purpose of controversy within a group is to arrive at the highest quality decision that is possible. There is evidence that the occurrence of controversy within a group (see Johnson et al., 1986)

1. Enhances the quality of the group's decision.
2. Creates insight by influencing individuals to view a problem from different perspectives and reformulate a problem in ways that allow the emergence of new orientations to a solution. Controversy:
   a. Increases the number of ideas, quality of ideas, feelings of stimulation and enjoyment, and originality of expression in creative problem solving.
   b. Results in more creative problem solutions, with more member satisfaction.
   c. Encourages group members to dig into a problem, raise issues, and settle them in ways that show the benefits of a wide range of ideas being used.
3. Results in a high degree of emotional involvement in and commitment to solving the problems the group is working on.
4. Results in greater mastery and retention of the information being discussed.
5. Results in better generalization of the principles learned to a wider variety of situations (Inagaki & Hatano, 1968, 1977).

POSITIVE ATTITUDES

The six steps of the controversy process and the resulting high productivity result in positive attitudes toward the work being done, the topic being discussed, the other individuals, oneself, and the controversy process. Individuals who engaged in controversies liked the decision topic better than did persons who engaged in concurrence-seeking discussions or individualistic learning (D. W. Johnson et al., 1985; Lowry & Johnson, 1981; Smith et al., 1981).

It is often assumed that the presence of controversy within a group will lead to difficulties in establishing good interpersonal relations and will promote negative attitudes toward fellow group members (Collins, 1970). Within controversy and debate there are elements of disagreement, argumentation, and rebuttal that could result in individuals disliking each other and could create difficulties in establishing good relationships. It is often assumed that arguing leads to rejection, divisiveness, and hostility among peers. Conflicts have been hypothesized potentially to create positive relationships among participants (Deutsch, 1962; Johnson & Johnson, 1987), but in the past there has been little evidence to validate such a hypothesis. It may be posited that when conflict takes place within a cooperative context and facilitates the achievement of one's goals, a positive cathexis results that generalizes to one's attitudes toward the other individuals in the situation, oneself, the subject area, and the process of controversy (Deutsch, 1962; Johnson & Johnson, 1979). Within the research on controversy there is consistent evidence that controversy promoted greater liking among participants than did debate, concurrence seeking, no-controversy, or individualistic efforts (Johnson & Johnson, 1985; Johnson et al., 1985; Lowry & Johnson, 1981; Smith et al., 1981; Tjosvold, 1982; Tjosvold & Deemer, 1980; Tjosvold & Johnson, 1978; Tjosvold et al., 1980; Tjosvold et al., 1981). Concurrence seeking and debate promote greater interpersonal attraction among participants than do individualistic efforts. The more cooperative the context, the greater the cooperative elements in the situation, and the greater the confirmation of each other's competence, the greater the interpersonal attraction.

It is often assumed that low ability individuals' task-related self-esteem will be damaged by participating in controversies with more capable peers. Not being as persuasive in presenting arguments and in rebutting the opponent's position has been assumed to result in lowered task self-esteem. There is considerable evidence, however, that the task-related self-esteem of high-, medium-, and low-ability individuals is higher in cooperative than competitive or individualistic situations (Johnson & Johnson, 1983). Since controversy is basically a cooperative activity, it may be hypothesized that the experience of disagreeing with others and deriving a joint position that reflects the best reasoning of all individuals results in higher self-esteem. Johnson and Johnson (1985) did in fact find that controversy promoted higher task self-esteem than did debate or individualistic efforts, and debate promoted higher task self-esteem than did individualistic efforts, and Johnson et al. (1985) found that controversy promoted higher task self-esteem than did concurrence seeking. Smith et al. (1982) found that controversy promoted greater task self-esteem than did individualistic work.

There is considerable evidence that conflict is perceived negatively and generally avoided (Johnson & F. Johnson, 1987). Yet individuals involved in controversy (and to a lesser extent, debate) liked their experiences better than did persons working individualistically (Johnson & Johnson, 1985), and participating in a controversy consistently promoted positive attitudes toward the experience (Johnson et al., 1985; Johnson et al., 1984; R. Johnson et al., 1985; Lowry & Johnson, 1981; Smith et al., 1981, 1984).

CONDITIONS DETERMINING THE CONSTRUCTIVENESS OF CONTROVERSY

Although controversies can operate in a beneficial way, they will not do so under all conditions. As with all types of conflicts, the potential for either constructive or destructive outcomes is present in a controversy. Whether there are positive or negative consequences depends on the conditions under which controversy occurs and the way in which it is managed. The conditions required for controversy to be constructive are for the overall climate of the group to be cooperative, for the group to be heterogeneous, for members to have relevant information, for members to be skillful in managing conflicts, and for the canons of rational argument to be followed.

Deutsch (1973) emphasizes that the context in which conflicts occur has important effects on whether the conflict turns out to be constructive or destructive. There are two possible contexts for controversy: cooperative and competitive. Tjosvold and Johnson (1978) found that a cooperative context promoted more open-minded reception to the opponent's position as well as greater liking for the opponent and the opponent's ideas and arguments than did a competitive context. Van Blerkom and Tjosvold (1981) found that participants in a controversy within a cooperative context sought out individuals with opposing opinions to test the validity of their ideas and reap the benefits of controversy, while participants in a controversy within a competitive context attempted to strengthen their opinions either by choosing a more competent partner with the same opinion or a less competent discussant with an opposing view. Tjosvold and Deemer (1980) and Tjosvold (1982) found that controversy within a cooperative context induced (a) feelings of comfort, pleasure, and helpfulness in discussing opposing opinions; (b) expectations of the other being helpful; (c) feelings of trust and generosity toward the opponent; (d) uncertainty about the correctness of the opponent's position; (e) motivation to hear more about the opponent's arguments; (f) more accurate understanding of the opponent's position; and (g) the reaching of more integrated positions where both one's own and one's opponent's conclusions and reasoning are synthesized into a final position. Controversy within a competitive context promoted closed-minded disinterest and rejection of the opponent's ideas and information. Avoidance of controversy resulted in little interest in or actual knowledge of opposing ideas and information and the making of a decision that reflected one's own views only.

Differences among group members in personality, sex, attitudes, background, social class, reasoning strategies, cognitive perspectives, information, ability levels, and skills lead to diverse organization and processing of information and experiences, which, in turn, begin the cycle of controversy. Such differences have been found to promote learning (Fiedler, Meuwese, & Oonk, 1961; Johnson, 1977; Torrance, 1961; Webb, 1977). The greater the heterogeneity among group members, the more time spent in argumentation (Nijhof & Kommers, 1982).

If controversy is to lead to high quality decision making, participants must possess information that is relevant to the decision they are making. The more information participants have about an issue, the higher quality their decision tends to be (Johnson & Johnson, 1987). Having relevant information available, however, does not mean that it will be utilized. Participants need the interpersonal and group skills necessary to ensure that all individuals involved contribute their relevant information and that the information is synthesized effectively.

In order for controversies to be managed constructively, participants need a number of collaborative and conflict management skills (Johnson, 1986; Johnson & Johnson, 1987; Johnson, Johnson, & Holubec, 1986). Three of the more important are as follows. Disagreeing with others while simultaneously confirming their personal competence results in being better liked and in the opponents being less critical of one's ideas, more interested in learning more about one's ideas, less committed to their own ideas, and more willing to incorporate one's information and reasoning into their own analysis of the problem (Tjosvold, 1974; Tjosvold et al., 1981). To obtain a creative synthesis of all positions in a controversy, group members must obtain a clear understanding of all sides of the issues and an accurate assessment of their validity and relative merits. In order to do this fully, they must accurately perceive the perspective from which a colleague is viewing and analyzing the situation and problem. Finally, participants should ensure that there are several cycles of differentiation (bringing out differences in positions) and integration (combining several positions into one new, creative position) (Johnson & Johnson, 1987).

During a controversy participants have to follow the canons of rational argumentation. They should generate ideas, collect and organize relevant information, reason logically, and make tentative conclusions based on current understanding.

SUMMARY

Decision making typically involves considering possible alternatives and choosing one. By definition, all decision-making situations involve some conflict as to which of several alternatives should be chosen. Within decision-making groups that conflict takes the form of controversy. Controversy exists when one individual's ideas, information, conclusions, theories, and opinions are incompatible with those of another, and the two seek to reach an agreement. Within the research on decision making, controversy has been contrasted with debate, concurrence seeking, and individual decision making. Controversy may be structured within decision-making situations by identifying the alternative solutions to the issue being discussed; assigning advocacy teams to prepare, present, and advocate the "best case" for each of the alternatives; and then to synthesize the best reasoning from all perspectives into the group's decision. The research evidence indicates that within decision-making situations, the presence of controversy results in decision makers' (1) finding facts, information, and evidence and organizing it into a coherent and reasoned position, (2) presenting and advocating their position forcefully, sincerely, and persuasively, (3) defending their position from refutation while criticizing the positions of the other advocacy teams, (4) feeling uncertain about and reassessing the validity of the position they are advocating, (5) searching for additional information about the issue, and (6) reconceptualizing the issue by synthesizing and integrating the information and perspectives of all the advocacy teams. The purpose of controversy within a group is to arrive at the highest quality decision possible. The evidence indicates that it does so, promoting high quality and creative decisions to which members are highly committed to implementing. In addition, controversy promotes positive attitudes toward the decision, other group members, oneself, and the controversy process. Not all controversies, however, will result in these outcomes. Controversies tend to be most effective when the situational context is cooperative, there is some heterogeneity among group members, information and expertise is distributed within the group, members have the necessary conflict skills, and the canons of rational argumentation are followed.

20

Norms as an Integrative Theme in Conflict and Negotiation: Correcting Our "Sociopathic" Assumptions

Kenneth W. Thomas

Sociopath: . . . psychopath

(Merriam-Webster, 1986).

Psychopathic personality: . . . state characterized by clear perception of reality except for the individual's social and moral obligations . . .

(Merriam-Webster, 1986).

This chapter is based upon impressions gathered during a review of the literature on conflict and negotiation (Thomas, in press [b]), as an update of an earlier review (Thomas, 1976). One of the most fundamental issues which surfaced during the current review concerned the behavioral assumptions which underlie our research. My strong impression is that we have tended overwhelmingly to assume that individuals are calculating means/end thinkers who are attuned to power realities and motivated predominately by self-interest. They are only occasionally concerned with the welfare of others (for example, when in a good mood or dealing with a friend). Furthermore, they are only influenced by social expectations when monitored by others who have some power over them, and then only out of fear of sanctions. To be sure, I have stated these assumptions more starkly and explicitly than I have found them in the literature. However, this formulation seems to capture the behavioral assumptions or axioms which have provided the foundation for most of our theory.

My concern is not that these assumptions do not capture important causal dynamics in conflict/negotiation behavior—for there is strong empirical evidence that they do. Rather, my concern is that they omit other important dynamics which involve internalized concerns about social/normative issues. In short, *they portray individuals as bright sociopaths*. As indicated in the definitions at

Preparation of this paper was supported by the Foundation Research Program of the Naval Postgraduate School.

the beginning of this paper, "sociopath" is regarded here as a synonym for "psychopath." The word sociopath, however, conveys somewhat less lurid connotations and also highlights the social focus of this disorder. Just as sociopaths are considered by society to be deficient with respect to normative concerns, then, so do our behavioral assumptions appear to be deficient in the same way.

The recent growth of research on social justice norms in the negotiation literature seems to represent a deviation from these traditional assumptions (see, for example, Levinthal, 1976; Lamm, 1985; Tyler, 1986). The same is true for a smaller body of research on ethics within that literature (for example, Lewicki, 1982). In the broader organizational behavior literature, likewise, the increased attention given to organizational culture signals a growing recognition of the importance of norms and their internalization by individuals (for example, Deal & Kennedy, 1982; Schein, 1985). My hope is that these recent developments will serve as a beachhead or fulcrum for a more explicit and systematic paradigm shift in our behavioral assumptions.

THE PROBLEM

The Hegemony of Economic Assumptions

Many of the behavioral assumptions at issue can be traced to the discipline of economics. Economic theorists have historically played a central role in the analysis of conflict and negotiations (for example, Siegel & Fouraker, 1960; Boulding, 1963). Moreover, economic axioms have also played a very prominent role in organizational behavior approaches to motivation and behavior, due in large part to an impressive body of early work by organizational researchers at what is now Carnegie-Mellon University (see Simon, 1957; March & Simon, 1958; Cyert & March, 1963; Vroom, 1964). In general, this work brought an impressive precision and explicitness to the developing field and allowed nontrivial conclusions to be derived from a relatively simple set of behavioral assumptions.

The influence of the economic approach, however, has meant that much of the growth in our understanding of behavior has been, and will continue to be, associated with modifying or transcending conventional economic assumptions. In the 1960s, for example, Schein (1965) argued that organizational psychology had moved beyond "rational-economic" assumptions about the content of human motives to include a variety of higher order motives as well.

Here, I am concerned about two remaining rational-economic assumptions: self-interest and rational-instrumental (or means-ends) reasoning. A brief description of each of these assumptions follows, contrasted with the more complex views suggested by other behavioral disciplines.

Self-interest. This assumption involves the issue of whose welfare the individual attempts to satisfy. Traditionally, economics tends to assume a set of separate actors pursuing self-interest. The "self" in "self-interest," moreover, tends to be conceptualized rather narrowly, so that there is no intrinsic interest in the welfare of the other actors. Within these assumptions, other actors take on only occasional, instrumental value for the individual insofar as they help the actor reach personal goals.

In contrast, clinical psychologists, along with sociologists and anthropologists, tend to assume that individuals are more fundamentally "social" creatures. As such, they define their identity partly in terms of their membership in relationships and groups. As they identify with people, groups, and other social abstractions, their caring or emotional investment extends "beyond their skin" to include the welfare of those entities. Accordingly, individuals also derive pleasure or satisfaction from contributing to the welfare of individuals and groups with whom they identify.

Rational-instrumental Reasoning. This assumption involves the manner in which individuals make decisions. Economic axioms stress rational decision makers, with rationality defined in terms of choosing actions that are perceived to produce desired outcomes. Within these axioms, then, actions are accepted or rejected only insofar as they are believed to provide the means to desired ends. These assumptions, for example, form the basis of expectancy theory (see, for example, Vroom, 1964; Lawler, 1973), which is still the dominant motivational paradigm within the larger organizational behavior literature.

In contrast, the other disciplines mentioned above tend to view individuals as also engaging in an additional kind of reasoning. In Freudian terms, economics tends to glorify the id and the ego, while neglecting the superego. As social beings, individuals are subject to the social expectations that are the building blocks of groups and societies. In general, these expectations act to moderate the potential ruthlessness implicit in rational/instrumental decision making (where "the ends justify the means") by discouraging specific kinds of actions that are regarded as destructive to a social unit. As individuals come to identify with a given unit, its expectations regarding these actions become invested with a normative quality of good/bad, proper/improper, or right/wrong which attaches to the actions themselves in different contexts. Thus, individuals are also assumed to consider the "goodness" or propriety of an action itself in deciding upon that action.

TOWARD A REVISED BEHAVIORAL PARADIGM

My perception is that the economic assumptions described above, through their omissions, have had far-reaching consequences upon conflict theory and research. In terms of descriptive theory, they appear to have neglected or downplayed some of the most important, unifying forces toward intrasystem cooperation. Conflict phenomena are, a priori, among the most potentially threatening to a group or society. Thus, one would expect norms and cohesion/identification forces to be far more central to our field than they appear to have been. Likewise, whole classes of norm-related behavioral phenomena appear to have been largely ignored, or treated as nonrational "noise."

These economic assumptions or axioms play such a central role in guiding conflict/negotiation research and theorizing that they need to be explicitly challenged and tested in the real world. Toward that end, there is a need for an explicit, alternative model or paradigm which incorporates normative reasoning and which can be tested against the rational-economic assumptions. The material in this and the following section explores such a model and its implications for the field of conflict and negotiations. The interested reader is referred to Thomas (in press [b]) for a more extensive treatment of these issues.

The Fishbein Model

In the larger literature on motivation/behavior, the model developed by Fishbein (1967) and subsequently researched by Fishbein & Ajzen (1975; Ajzen & Fishbein, 1980) seems to provide a promising point of departure. Briefly, this model views behavior as intentional and reasoned. Behavior, then, results from the formulation of an intention to perform a given act. This intention, in turn, is shaped by the additive effects of *two* different kinds of reasoning. The first of these is essentially a set of *rational-instrumental* considerations, equivalent to expectancy theory. Here, intention to perform an act is based upon the perceived instrumentalities of the act for achieving various outcomes, weighted by the valences of those outcomes for the individual. The second set of considerations is a *normative* assessment of the perceived propriety of the act itself. Here, intention to perform an act is a function of the individual's perception that salient reference groups or individuals would endorse the act, weighted by the individual's identification with those groups or individuals. The rational-instrumental and normative factors are combined additively in a standard regression equation. (For the full mathematical representation of the model, see Fishbein & Ajzen, 1975.)

Although the Fishbein model has not, to my knowledge, been used to predict conflict or negotiation behavior, it has been extensively tested in a variety of other contexts. Evidence has been generally quite supportive (Fishbein & Ajzen, 1975; Ajzen & Fishbein, 1980). Interestingly, the normative portion of the model has explained most of the variance in behavior in some situations, while the rational/instrumental portion has dominated in others.

The Fishbein model may require modification, or at least qualification, for some applications to conflict and negotiation. For example, the model assumes reasoned behavior, so that it does not explicitly allow for forces that may distort or truncate the reasoning process under the stresses of the conflict process. Nevertheless, the Fishbein model would seem to provide a promising beginning point for for theory and research which explicitly incorporates normative considerations into conflict-negotiation behavior.

COROLLARY IMPLICATIONS

A combined, "rational-normative" paradigm of behavior provides a mechanism for explaining and predicting the manner in which social justice norms influence behavior. However, its impact would be considerably more extensive. It can serve to draw attention to a number of other important causal events and conditions in which normative dynamics influence behavior, and can serve to integrate these phenomena into a coherent view of conflict and negotiation. Some rather direct implications for the field are briefly discussed below. This list is not intended to be complete, but rather to illustrate some of the widespread implications of this paradigm.

Types of Conflict. Our current attention to types of conflict appears to be rather narrowly focused upon rational-instrumental factors. The predominant focus of conflict-negotiation research has been upon "interest" conflicts, in which conflict results from different outcome preferences (valences). A smaller, but still sizable, literature has involved "cognitive" conflicts in which parties differ about the probable consequences (instrumentalities) of an action or, more generally, draw different conclusions about objective reality from facts (see, for example, Hammond, Todd, Wilkins & Mitchell, 1966; Mason, 1969; Tjosvold, 1984). "Normative" conflicts need to be recognized and studied as a third, distinct form of elemental conflict, triggered by perceived violations of normative expectations.

While a complex, "molecular" conflict may include all three elemental types of conflict issues, normative conflict issues need to be recognized for their important contributions to conflict dynamics. Normative conflict issues appear to generate distinct dynamics, involving such emotional reactions as disapproval, blame, and anger, as well as punishments to extract retribution for violations. These dynamics play an important role in conflict escalation (see Glasl, 1982), and are difficult to understand in terms of traditional economic assumptions. Moreover, some conflicts (including many grievances) appear to be predominantly of a normative type (see, for example, Bouwen & Salipante, 1986).

Influence Strategies and Tactics. The combined, rational-normative paradigm implies that the intentions of the parties in all types of conflict (including interest and cognitive conflicts, as well as normative conflict) are likely to be shaped in part by normative considerations. Thus, the paradigm implies that a broad range of the influence strategies and tactics adopted by conflict parties will be predominately normative in nature (that is, aimed at influencing the other's normative reasoning). Such strategies are likely to go far beyond the invocation of justice norms, to include a wide variety of other norms regarding proper conflict or negotiation behavior—for example, acceptable levels and forms of assertiveness, collaborativeness, appeals to third parties, and so on. My perception at this point is that we simply do not know very much about how conflict parties establish norms, evoke existing norms, and try to enforce them during conflict or negotiation episodes—let alone how successful different normative tactics are likely to be. This appears to be a fruitful area for theory and research.

Conflict Management. The paradigm suggests that normative considerations will play a key role in conflict management within any social system. Consider their role in the process interventions and structural interventions of third parties. Briefly, *process interventions* refer to the third party becoming directly involved in the ongoing events of a conflict episode, attempting to steer that episode toward a desirable outcome. Here, the paradigm provides a more systematic way of appreciating the neutral third party's role in "setting a tone" for the negotiations, clarifying "ground rules," acting as referee, and otherwise serving to evoke and enforce constructive norms during the episode. In contrast, *structural interventions* are longer-term attempts to change the relatively stable parameters of the social system—the context which shapes the system's conflict processes (Kilmann & Thomas, 1978). Here, the paradigm underscores the importance of building the cohesiveness and norms necessary to channel intrasystem conflict behaviors in ways that will be constructive (or at least not destructive) for the system.

In this context, I now believe that the work of Blake and Mouton (1964) and Likert and Likert (1976) was significantly misinterpreted by myself and other conflict researchers. Rather than advocating collaboration as a universally effective strategy for individuals to handle conflicts, it seems clear now that these authors were largely proposing ways of creating organizational *cultures* which would tend to channel intraorganizational conflicts in ways that would be constructive for an organization.

"Normative" Theory. My perception is that the term "normative theory" has developed negative connotations within parts of the conflict negotiation literature, perhaps because it is seen as outside the prevailing (that is, economic) paradigm and thus "unscientific" in some way. "Normative" also implies a "one-best-way" approach to prescriptive theory, which appears to be inconsistent with the contingency theories in our field. In contrast, the combined rational-normative paradigm seems to imply the legitimate need for such theories. It underscores the importance of norms in shaping behavior and, accordingly, the social system's need for such norms. Thus, there is an applied, real world need for researcher/theorists to address the issue of which norms will be constructive for an organization or other social system.

In addition, it seems important to realize that this kind of "normative" theory would *not* be inconsistent with the kinds of contingency theories that have been developed by conflict researchers. As shown in Table 20.1, contingency theories have tended to deal with the short-term issue of which behaviors will work best under a given set of contextual conditions. In contrast, normative theories tend to involve the longer-term issue of what contextual conditions to create in order to *improve* a system's functioning. This latter sort of theory necessarily requires some explicit notion of ideal or improved system behavior as a goal for change, and thus implies behavioral norms. Thus, rather than contradict each other,

Table 20.1
Comparison of Contingency and Normative Theories

Properties	Type of Theory	
	Contingency	Normative
Time horizon	Shorter-term: coping with the here and now	Longer-term: building desirable futures
Context assumption	Contextual variables are given	Contextual variables are changeable
Goal	Local optimum: best achieveable in present situation	Global optimum: excellence
Recommendations	What actions to take under present circumstances	What circumstances to create
Flavor	Pragmatic/realistic	Idealistic/visionary

Note. Adapted from Thomas, K. W. (in press). Conflict and conflict management: Reflections and update, Journal of Occupational Behavior.

normative and contingency theories appear to supplement each other by dealing with two different applied issues—short-term coping and long-term improvement.

In the case of conflict-handling modes, for example, contingency theories have recognized that collaborating, competing, accommodating, and so on, will each be necessary under appropriate circumstances (see, for example, Thomas, 1977; Derr, 1978; Rahim, 1986a), while normative theories (see Blake & Mouton, 1964; Likert & Likert, 1976; Brown, 1983) have tended to consider the potential organizational benefits of collaborative processes and the issue of how to create the norms and other circumstances necessary to increase intrasystem collaboration. These are different issues which address separate, critical aspects of conflict management. *Both* need to be studied.

Methodology. Finally, the paradigm suggests yet another reason to interpret the external validity of laboratory experiments with great caution. Economic assumptions have encouraged laboratory researchers to focus on the importance of some experimental variables that fit the economic paradigm (for example, payoff matrices) at the neglect of social-normative conditions. To control these latter "exogenous" variables, moreover, such experiments tend to use strangers, with very little chance for socialization, except through the norm-setting implicit in the experimenter's instructions (for example, ''Win as much as you can''). Thus, it is unclear to what extent the results of these studies generalize to established relationships or organizations outside of the laboratory. For a review of other threats to external validity in laboratory studies of conflict and negotiation, see Greenhalgh (1986).

CONCLUSIONS

Paradigms serve, in part, to direct research attention to some phenomena and to determine the centrality or importance of different issues. My perception is that the prevailing economic paradigm in the conflict field has directed attention away from the norm-related phenomena and issues discussed above. Moreover, it appears to have relegated the work that has been done on these topics to a kind of ''miscellaneous'' category of less central phenomena which do not quite fit into the primary categories of variables within the paradigm.

As Kuhn (1962) noted, the accumulation of many of these miscellaneous cases provides a signal to researchers that a paradigm shift is needed and provides an impetus for such a shift. The dramatic growth of research on social justice norms has provided a very viable case. Adding this topic to the other norm-related phenomena discussed above, it now seems to me that there is sufficient evidence of the need for a major shift toward a combined, ''rational-normative'' paradigm of behavior.

A rational-normative paradigm would serve a number of functions. It would avoid a ''sociopathic'' portrayal of individuals (and help explain such behavior, when it does occur, as a special case). It would legitimate the study of norm-related issues, and bring them into the mainstream of conflict-negotiation research. In so doing, it would serve to direct attention to some of the mechanisms which seem especially crucial to constructive conflict management within organizations and other social systems. Finally, it would also encourage us to explicitly examine the complex ways in which self-interest interacts with consideration for others in real world settings, and the manner in which means-ends reasoning interacts with normative reasoning.

21

Third Party Intervention: A Theoretical Framework

Sandra Kaufman
George T. Duncan

A complex decision process typically involves multiple actors who separately contribute to its evolution and share in its consequences. Their actions may be individually conceived or the product of joint resolution. The consequences to them as stakeholders are the result of the ensemble of all their actions. Disagreement exists whenever one stakeholder's preferred outcome does not coincide with the outcome most preferred by some other stakeholders. The situation moves from this passive state to the active state of conflict when the disagreeing stakeholders, now *disputants,* act according to their individual preferences, and the outcome depends jointly on their actions. Examples of this transition to conflict include a couple seeking a divorce settlement, sites being chosen for hazardous waste disposal, labor and management disputing wage settlements, or countries negotiating disarmament proposals. In such conflict situations, an *intervenor* is a person, or group, not initially a stakeholder, but brought in by law, special mission or role, or at some (or all) of the disputants' request. An intervenor enters the decision situation with his or her own goals, knowledge, expectations, and beliefs. The intervenor's actions to change the situation include: applying physical force or credible threats of using it (Tedeschi & Bonoma, 1977); invoking some rule, law, or tradition that the disputants will, or can be made to abide by (Aubert, 1967); persuading the disputants that it is in their best interest to behave as the intervenor desires (Pruitt & Lewis, 1977).

This chapter establishes a theoretical framework, focusing on a class of intervention modes that rely on persuasion, such as mediation, and identifying key dimensions of the decision-making process susceptible to such intervention. The chapter complements that of Sheppard (1984), who provides a literature review on conflict intervention research, offering a recognition that conflict is not necessarily bad, identifying some recent innovative approaches to conflict intervention, and stressing cross-situational similarities.

An intervenor who does not use force or the authority of rules must persuade, that is, influence the parties' choices through information and resources. In the negotiations following the 1973 Middle East war, Henry Kissinger transferred information between the parties and promised resources (supplied by his sponsor, the United States). He made resource transfer contingent upon suitable choices by the parties. When information is the only means of persuasion, as with mediators, the only decision factors affected are the parties' current beliefs (facts, values, actions available and their consequences) and their preferences for outcomes.

First, we focus on the intervenor's mandate, which limits some intervenors to persuasion. Then we examine other key features of intervention and their relation to the parties' decision process. We conclude with a discussion of intervention mechanisms identified using the resulting theoretical framework. Throughout, *we focus on mediators,* since they epitomize reliance on persuasion through information, a mode also used by many of the other intervenors. We give examples of mediation in small claims disputes that came before the Brookline, Massachusetts, Municipal Court in 1985. We also illustrate mediation with an environmental dispute over Foothills, Colorado, mediated by Congressman Tim Wirth in 1978.

MANDATE

As illustrated in Table 21.1, the *mandate,* the rules authorizing intervenors' actions, is key in differentiating between intervention modes, and therefore in developing a taxonomy of intervenors. Mandate is often equivalent to the intervenor's role, as for arbitrators. At times however, others, such as firm managers (Lax & Sebenius, 1986), chairpersons, or parents take mediation or arbitration roles although their mandate allows them to dictate the conflict outcome. Some mandates derive formally from laws and rules, or are upheld by traditions; other mandates, more informal, draw on the intervenor's position, resources, specialized knowledge, or support from a sponsor.

Transactionists (matchmakers, brokers, and others) form a special group: They cannot force parties into agreement, but can accommodate each separately. The stakeholders are, in a sense, replaceable. A real estate agent who cannot close a transaction between a seller and a buyer can often find other matches for each. Information transferers cannot take their information elsewhere than to the intended recipient (without infringing upon some rules); a marital counselor does not usually provide alternative partners for a couple in conflict (matchmakers will); a parent cannot substitute siblings in a squabble.

The mediator's mandate (transfer information and inform choices) is common to several intervenors, from lawyers to conflict consultants. Parties sometimes restrict mediation to information transfer, and, indeed, some mediators believe this their only role. In a survey conducted during negotiation experiments, all participants agreed that mediators should improve communication between parties, and no other suggested activity met with such approval. Cross (1977) mentions lack of communication among mediation triggers. Sometimes medi-

Table 21.1
Mandates of Intervenors

Individuals	Transfer information	Inform choices	Promote choices	Make choices	Implement choices
Go-between	*				
Fact-finder	*				
Auditor	*	*			
Lawyer	*	*			
Dispute analyst, counselor, intermediary	*	*			
Ambassador	*	*			
Ombudsman	*	*			
Special envoy, trouble-shooter	*	*			
Mediator	*	*			
Clergy, elected representative	*	*		*	
Manager		*	*	*	*
Auctioneer			*		
Broker, agent, matchmaker			*		
Arbitrator, umpire, judge				*	
Parent				*	*
Dictator				*	*
Law enforcement officer					*

ators monitor the implementation of agreements, but they can enforce agreements only with mandate derived elsewhere than in this role.

The extent mandate authority is actually used is largely up to the intervenor. Mediators underuse their mandate when merely facilitating communication instead of also supplying information to help make choices; special envoys overstep their mandate when suggesting and even pressing solutions on feuding countries, while their mission is to supply and transfer information. We call *active* an intervenor who uses mandate authority to the fullest extent or even oversteps it. In contrast, a *passive* intervenor limits activities by choice to a subset of those allowed by the mandate. An active/passive distinction emerged first in connection with observed mediation styles (Kolb, 1983; Raiffa, 1982). The passive mediator may, in fact, have a more risk-taking attitude, since he or she chooses to rely on the disputants rather than on direct actions to promote settlement. There may be a consistent difference in attitudes toward risk among passive and active intervenors, which is a hypothesis for further investigation. We might also expect that the intervenor's subjective probability for the parties settling through negotiation may affect style, with the less sanguine intervenor attempting to compensate for this pessimism by using or overusing mandate.

At times, disputants think that intervenors have either a less or a more powerful mandate than in actuality; this misassessment affects how parties evaluate consequences of their choices. A case the first author mediated involved a

Korean dry cleaner whose customer, displeased with the service, had taken his garment out of the shop without paying. The cleaner asked for his money ($2.50), a fight ensued, and the customer, who beat the cleaner thoroughly, then sued the cleaner for medical expenses from hernia surgery undergone after the fight. This conflict was about wounded pride rather than the minor sum of money: the customer said the foreigner did not belong in this country, while the cleaner was paying a lawyer and neglecting his business to clear his name. He would only settle out of court if the mediator recognized he was right, which was not hard to do. This was mandate overstepping, due to one disputant's misperception of the mediator's role.

Since parties' choices are affected by how they assess the intervenor's mandate, intervenors can correct perceptions or preserve errors to suit their goals. Dictators may project a mandate exceeding what they can actually enforce; as a result, in dictatorial regimes people sometimes reduce their options, appearing irrational to an observer aware of the dictator's real capability. In contrast, a psychotherapist often seeks to give parties confidence in solving their own problems although they might well accept a settlement handed them by the therapist.

FEATURES OF THE INTERVENTION PROCESS

In this section, we identify other intervention characteristics and examine how they affect the parties' decision making. The intervenors' roles, and the intervention process itself, vary with the outcome sought, be it information transferred among parties, an agreement on a joint action, a transaction, or a verdict. How do intervenors become third parties to a decision situation? What triggers their intervention? When do they join? At whose request? And who selects them? We compare the intervenors of Table 21.1 along these aspects, and then examine who controls the process in each case, who enforces outcomes and who evaluates the intervention (see Table 21.2).

Initiation of Intervention and Choice of Intervenor

Intervention is triggered by various mechanisms, including some rule or law calling for intervention when certain outcomes or behaviors are observed; some or all parties' need for services that an outsider to the decision situation can provide; some group, not directly involved, incurring externalities of a conflict; as part of the duties of an employee to the employer; self-appointment. Laws and rules can bring in intervenors who diagnose, give verdicts, or settle disputes. In such a case, the disputants do not generally have the option of refusing intervention or selecting the intervenor. Auditors, umpires, and judges are law-triggered or rule-triggered intervenors: Observable events call for their intervention, and options then are also specified by law or rule.

Individuals or groups experiencing spillover effects of a conflict situation in which they are not directly participants may themselves intervene or may seek a third party's help. For example, to avoid service disruption, taxpayers pay state mediators to intervene in labor disputes involving public transit workers. Taxpayers also maintain law enforcement services triggered by rules and laws which also specify the outcome (as opposed to a mediation service, where outcomes are the disputants' choice). Courts use mediators to ease small claims load and reduce processing costs to the community: in Quincy, Massachusetts, mediation is mandatory; in Shaker Heights, Ohio, a mediator screens all cases before they reach the court referee. A troubleshooter is sent by a country whose interests are at stake if some international conflict erupts. Managers, parents and dictators appoint themselves as intervenors when their feuding ''subjects'' threaten their well-being.

All transactionists (brokers, agents) are called jointly or separately by stakeholders who need their skills and information. A couple enlists a marital counselor jointly. Parents intervene at a child's request. Priests intervene at the request of community members. Countries appeal to the institutional ''judge'' of the U.N. Security Council. Depending on the intervenor's mandate, the parties subsequently may or may not abide by the advice or ruling requested: children have to obey their parents, but countries will only abide by those U.N. Security Council resolutions which promote their interests, plans, and policies (Roling, 1966).

When intervenors lack choice and enforcement mandate, abidance by the outcome of a decision situation is up to the disputants. Is this abidance affected by the way in which intervention is initiated? We might expect that acceptance of the intervenor by all parties, or, at the very least, a selection process acceptable to all, would increase the likelihood of abidance due to the perception that a jointly selected intervenor is evenhanded—why would any party go along with an intervenor known to work in the opponent's favor? Appointed intervenors also appear evenhanded, being expected to act in the spirit of the sponsoring agency (Simkin, 1971), while self-appointed intervenors lack this appearance and their goals may be more closely scrutinized by parties. However, intervenors are sometimes accepted despite, or even due to perceived preference for one party, as was reportedly the case with Henry Kissinger in the 1973 disengagement talks in the Middle East (Touval, 1975), or with Tim Wirth in the Foothills dispute. Evenhandedness, or fairness, is mentioned in the literature as a desirable characteristic for mediators (Cormick, 1982; Susskind, 1981), but actually there is no operational definition (Rapoport, 1973; Kochan & Jick, 1978) or agreement on how a mediator should behave fairly. We suggest that what makes intervenors ultimately acceptable is the parties' expected outcome with the intervenor, regardless of perceived fairness, compared to the outcome expected in the intervenor's absence. Up-front bias may also be tolerated by parties who prefer a certain, known attitude, to self-professed but uncertain evenhandedness.

Time of Intervention

Timing is considered in the mediation literature as one of the reasons for a mediator's success or failure (Simkin, 1971; Susskind et al., 1984). Timing is

Table 21.2
The Nature of the Third Party Intervention

Issue	Initiation — a.law,sponsor b.disputants c.intervenor			Choice — a.law,sponsor b.disputants c.self-appoint.			Timing — a.outset b.incident c.end			Process Control — a.laws b.disputants c.intervenor			Locus of Choice — b.sponsor c.disputant d.intervenor		
	a	b	c	a	b	c	a	b	c	a	b	c	b	c	d
Go-between, messenger		b		a									b		
Fact-finder	a				b			b			b			c	
Auditor		b		a				b		a			b	c	
Lawyer		b			b			b		a			b		
Dispute analyst, counselor, intermediary		b			b			b		a	b			c	
Ambassador		b		a				b			b		b	c	
Ombudsman		b		a				b			b			c	
Special envoy		b		a				b		a			b		
Mediator		b			b			b		a	b			c	
Clergy, elected representative		b	c		b	c		b		a	b			c	
Manager		b	c		b	c		b				c		c	d
Auctioneer		b		a			a					c		c	d
Broker, agent, matchmaker	a	b		a	b		a			a		c		c	d
Arbitrator, umpire, judge		b	c	a	b				c			c		c	d
Parent		b	c			c		b				c		c	d
Dictator			c			c		b				c		c	d
Law enforcement officer	a	b	c	a	b			b		a					d

Issue	End Product					Enforce Choices			Evaluation Done By				Evaluation Outcome			
	a.action	b.verdict	c.choice	d.fact determ.	e.info. transfer	a.law,sponsor	b.voluntary	c.intervenor	a.sponsor	b.disputants	c.peers	d.oneself	a.payoffs	b.efficiency	c.equity	d.durability
Go-between, messenger					e		b			b				b		
Fact-finder				d			b		a	b				b	c	
Auditor				d		a			a					b	c	
Lawyer			c			a	b			b	c	d	a	b	c	d
Dispute analyst, counselor, intermediary			c				b			b	c	d	a	b		d
Ambassador					e		b		a	b	c	d	a	b		d
Ombudsman				d			b		a	b	c	d	a	b	c	d
Special envoy					e		b		a	b	c	d	a	b	c	d
Mediator			c				b		a	b	c	d	a	b	c	d
Clergy, elected representative			c		e		b		a	b	c	d	a	b	c	d
Manager		b	c						a	b			a	b		
Auctioneer			c			a			a	b	c		a	b		
Broker, agent, matchmaker		b				a			a	b	c	d	a	b		d
Arbitrator, umpire, judge		b				a		c	a	b	c	d	a	b	c	d
Parent	a							c				d	a			d
Dictator	a							c				d	a			d
Law enforcement officer	a							c	a				a		c	

279

generally not an issue for the intervenors authorized consensually by parties, such as transactionists, village elders, some mediators, matchmakers and brokers, and some lawyers. Nor do judges, compulsory arbitrators, or auditors struggle with timing: They enter the scene at a time predetermined by law (some at the end of the dispute, some at impasse). Contract embellishers, as proposed by (Raiffa, 1982), would intervene only after conclusion of an agreement, which they would try to improve with the assurance that any changes can only pass unanimously.

Timing matters only to those intervenors who control it by appointing themselves or who have the ability to take actions when they see fit. For instance, in labor disputes with mandatory mediation at impasse, the appointed mediator can call a meeting or, as one mediator expressed it, "let them stew" for a time before acting. International troubleshooters and family therapists can do the same. This respite is meant to let the parties revise overoptimistic assessments of likelihood of succeeding without concessions; to introduce some uncertainty as to the effectiveness of alternatives to negotiations (such as strikes or military attacks); and to remove some of the hostility accumulated during negotiations.

Process Control

The choice process encompasses agenda, sequence of moves by disputants (offers, negotiations, court appearances), timing, rules and procedures for interaction, and even the physical environment. Some or all aspects may be controlled by laws, traditions, or by rules laid out by the sponsor of intervention. This happens in judication, with priests and with umpires. In many other cases, process control is shared in various proportions by the parties and intervenors. Sheppard (1984) in his framework focuses on the forms of control available to third parties in conflict intervention.

Intervenors control the choice process if it is part of their mandate, as for dictators and arbitrators. Ombudsmen, auditors, auctioneers and croupiers also have process control, given them by a sponsor. In many other instances, although the parties have control, they informally award some to intervenors, in recognition of some perceived quality, or exchange for some benefit. The special knowledge of agents, dispute analysts, lawyers, and marital counselors, or the personality of some mediators, managers, intermediaries, priests, matchmakers, and elected representatives buys them process control. So does the perception of resource availability that an ambassador, a special envoy, or a dictator can convey.

Whether relinquished by parties for a benefit or due to misperceptions, control may be used by the intervenor to affect beliefs based on which parties make their choices. A labor mediator observed that in labor disputes mediators have more control when "unsophisticated" negotiators are involved. Haynes (1984) suggests this also happens in divorce mediation.

Since people may rely on proxies (Bazerman, 1986) to assess the competency of an intervenor, the Harvard name, a priest's robe, a name famous not necessarily for intervention skills, can all secure some process control. That such proxies make a perceptual difference is seen in this example: In the Brookline, Massachusetts, Court, the clerk reading the day's small claims list asks who will accept mediation, often without providing any information on it, and at such times few disputants choose mediation; sometimes the judge has opened with "We are fortunate today to have help from the Harvard Mediation Program . . . ," prompting a higher number of disputants to try mediation. Although overt claims or resort to legal knowledge are discouraged, trainees are advised to make no great effort to dispel such misperceptions, thereby taking advantage of them to establish and maintain control (without actively pursuing deception).

Process control provides influence over the outcome content. Most third parties find more influence desirable, whether to serve a reputation or because of a direct interest in the outcome. Although effects may be similar, process control is not what separates active from passive intervenors. Intervenors may be active in the sense discussed in the mandate section without controlling the process, or be passive while exercising process control. In small claims, the plaintiff's initial monetary claim provides an anchor: the defendant tries to bring the claim down, and the plaintiff tries to keep the settlement as close to the claim as possible. Such *positional* bargaining, where one party's loss is the other's gain, sometimes obscures solutions more satisfactory to at least one party. The passive mediator may allow positional bargaining, arguing that, as long as parties are communicating, the mediator's function is accomplished. The active mediator may replace this "haggling" mode with other negotiating procedures and even suggested solutions. Both actions may be taken while exercising various degrees of process control.

In a case where a priest sold a defective car to one of his seminary students, the parties agreed to split the repair cost. The plaintiff produced an estimate of $300; the defendant offered $100, hoping for an exchange of offers and counteroffers between $100 and $150 that would bring his share down. The disappointed plaintiff showed signs of backing out. The mediator insisted that the principle agreed upon be upheld, and offered to obtain an estimate, which lay outside the mediator's responsibility. The disputants complied and settled on the figure supplied by a repair shop. The passive approach would have been to allow settlement through distributive bargaining.

Locus of Decisions

The locus of choice in a decision process resides with whomever controls the decisions leading to the outcome. If the intervenor has no choice mandate, the locus of choice varies: With dispute analysts/consultants and ombudsmen, the sponsor of intervention has the final say; in other instances, as with mediators, the parties choose.

Some instances suggest that when parties make their own choices, or at least believe they did, they may uphold the agreement more readily than if the agreement was forced on them by an arbitrator, judge, or umpire. For example, records from some Massachusetts Municipal Courts show that 80 percent of small claims mediated agreements were implemented, whereas only 60 percent of the judge verdicts were carried out. Bigoness (1976) observed in an experiment that more concessions are made by negotiators expecting arbitration than by those expecting mediation if they fail to settle.

We could explain in several ways this observed disputants' preference for making their own choices. People may trust themselves: An intervenor is an outsider to their interests and history of the conflict and appears to have lower stakes, not having to bear consequences or shoulder responsibility for the decisions. With dictated choices, parties believe that given the freedom they would have acted differently (which is why choices had to be forced on them). A stakeholder with a constituency may find that imposed choices are more difficult to justify, and carry some loss of clout and status. There is likely also a cultural component: societies differ in preferences over the decision-making process, reflected in the variety of political processes they have developed. Some cultures have a pride factor: having to do what an outsider decided is not as commendable as deciding on one's own. Intervention techniques have to be tailored to accommodate cultural differences.

End Product

The end product of intervention can be an action, a verdict, a party's choice, a fact determination or transfer of information between parties or between them and a sponsor or a constituency. A law enforcement officer takes an action; judges, dictators, or umpires give verdicts; auditors and ombudsmen determine facts that can help settle a dispute; go-betweens and ambassadors transfer messages. Only jointly agreed choices are made by the disputants, although intervenors may supply the necessary information. Transactionists, counselors, decision analysts or mediators have no direct control over the end products of their effort, although, they do have preferences over results, and are rewarded and evaluated by them.

End product control influences the intervention process: those without direct end product control use different strategies to reach goals, influencing the choice process through the components of decision making they can provide and alter (Young, 1975). Arbitrators, agents, firm managers, union leaders, committee chairpersons, are also required at times to promote a choice they are unable to impose. Their recourse too is to steer the choice in their preferred direction by persuading the decision makers that it is the best; that other alternatives have undesirable consequences of which they were not aware; that the probability of benefits materializing from the other options is smaller than they thought; or that they should value more some benefits accruing from the choice favored by the intervenor.

Enforcement of Choices

Choice enforcement derives from mandate: most intervenors who cannot dictate choices cannot enforce them, with the exception of law enforcement officers. Parents and dictators enforce directly their own choices. Laws and rules ensure recourse for a party if the other fails to abide by the judge's, arbitrator's, umpire's, or regulatory agency's decision. The community punishes dissension from priests' or intermediaries' decisions. But with other intervenors, choice enforcement is up to the parties.

With voluntary abidance, a party defaults on an agreement when its outcome is no longer preferred, which may occur for several reasons. When negotiations and implementation unfold in stages over time, a once attractive outcome may become undesirable if some external factors affecting it change. Environmental and international disputes follow this pattern. Default may also be caused by new information altering the parties' perception of the outcome's costs and benefits. This information may be external to the negotiation process; or, parties come to think they have been misled by the other parties or the intervenor.

Should enforceability of an outcome be a criterion in its design? We consider this question first from the intervenor's and then from the disputants' point of view.

From the intervenor's perspective, enforceable agreements are more durable (hence more personally satisfying) and can result in higher direct payoffs. Elected representatives, parents, or groups who sponsor mediation to avoid conflict externalities get direct rewards from durable agreements. Reputation for most transactionists, arbitrators, mediators, contract embellishers, and marital counselors constitutes an incentive to promote a durable outcome. Dictators are also concerned with their reputation (besides deriving utility from the outcome itself). In their case, as with managers, parents, judges, and law enforcement officers, failure to enforce an imposed outcome diminishes their effectiveness in other cases by reducing the perceived threat for nonabidance.

The means to ensure outcome durability can be external to the outcome or built into it. By external we mean devices applied, at the intervenor's will or request, when default on the settlement is observed. A dictator, parent, judge, or umpire have access to such means. This access has its limits: Umpire decisions can be contested, judge verdicts appealed. Parents who overuse their dictatorial capability may drive children to rebel, while their failure carries loss of credibility in future encounters. Even dictators are sometimes overthrown.

Internal enforcement means are an intrinsic part of a settlement, such as contingence of each party's task upon performance of the other party's share of the agreement. This strategy was used in the Foothills final agreement, making the Water Board's payment to the opposing environmentalists' group contingent on their not suing the Board for at least a year. To make a settlement robust to external changes, other strategies are necessary, such as including a periodic review *process* (with possible renegotiation provisions) in agreements spanning a relatively long time. These provisions, called by Lee (1982) "mechanisms for coping with change," are used in organizational and community long-range plans.

Evaluation of Intervention

The contribution of third parties to decision situations is evaluated by those who fund intervention (sponsor, constituency), the direct users (disputants) and by the intervenors themselves and their peers. The evaluation is fashioned by the needs it serves, such as disputants' concern with future use of intervention or face-saving needs, or the preservation by intervenors of a collective image that may be hurt by the activities of a particular intervenor.

Sheppard (1984) gives criteria for choosing or evaluating an intervention procedure. For both qualities of the procedure itself and qualities of the outcome related to the procedure, he identifies fairness, participant satisfaction, effectiveness, and efficiency as central.

Funders and users of intervention focus on outcomes, evaluating by payoffs to parties, equity, efficiency, and durability, as well as costs of reaching the settlement (time spent in a courtroom, mediation service fee, and so on). Users also evaluate intervenors for later use, by the handling of the process (respect of trust, adherence to rules, intervenor's personality). Intervenors and their peers are more concerned with the quality of performance, as for instance the success/failure record, adherence to mandate, and effectiveness in reaching a durable settlement. They evaluate for purposes of allocating reputation and rank, for the ability to recommend the appropriate intervenor for a decision situation, as well as to learn from each other's experience and ensure conformity with formal and informal rules of behavior.

The same intervention may be judged differently by peers and disputants: peers may think an intervenor who failed to settle a dispute acted correctly, or as they would under similar circumstances; and disputants accept outcomes deemed unsatisfactory by other intervenors for reasons such as overstepping the mandate, inefficiency, the use of deceptive tactics or breach of trust.

The provision of face-saving outlets appears important in stakeholders' evaluations, supporting the hypothesis that they derive utility from both outcome and process. Brown (1968) has explored experimentally the role of face saving in bargaining, and Raiffa (1982) mentioned the catering to face-saving needs of the opponent as a good negotiation strategy. In the Foothills conflict some disputants (who had agreed to the joint choice) declared that they had been "beaten over the head" (Susskind et al., 1984). In a dispute over rent payment, described earlier, the plaintiff, after agreeing to settle, declared mediation to be a "sell-out." In both cases, the apparently dissatisfied disputant needed to disclaim responsibility for the agreement. However, as the judge in this case put it, the settlement must have satisfied some of the disputants' needs since they adhered to it voluntarily.

For intervention modes with established structure, rules, and tradition, there is agreement at least on the evaluation process (if not on its outcome), as with judication. In contrast, for modes such as mediation excepting labor disputes (Simkin, 1971), evaluation is hindered by a lack of consensus on rules of behavior, on process and on criteria (Kochan & Jick, 1978; Cormick, 1980). Besides the direct consequences themselves, *fairness, efficiency* and *durability of the outcome* are often mentioned as desirable (see, for example, Susskind, 1981).

While people disagree about how to measure fairness (Rapoport, 1973), there is moral consensus that it is desirable and therefore its mention in the midst of a conflict is apt to get attention and serve the party claiming it has been wronged. However, lack of fairness is the complaint when parties feel the outcome fell short of their expectations, or when they predict this will happen; parties whose expectations are met or exceeded seldom complain about lack of fairness. So fairness of an outcome, a process, or an intervenor, as evaluated by parties, may be a proxy for the gap between expectations and outcome. Both perceptions can be affected by intervenors, to narrow this gap.

The fairness and even the size of payoffs are subjective criteria, manipulable and prone to misassessment; another candidate criterion is outcome efficiency, a concern to disputants, sponsors and peers alike. In terms of Lax and Sebenius's (1986) distinction between creating and claiming joint value during negotiations, an efficient outcome is one that has exhausted the joint value (regardless of how it is claimed by the disputants). However, only sometimes is it possible to determine the outcome efficiency of a decision situation in this sense. Fairness is a criterion for evaluating both the outcome of intervention and the intervenor. We distinguish here between fairness of the outcome, and process fairness of two kinds: how the intervenor treats the disputants—*procedural evenhandedness*—and how the intervenor weighs own goals against those of the disputants—*evenhandedness of objectives*.

Durability is the only mentioned criterion directly observable and, as discussed earlier, desirable to all participants in the decision situation, if for different reasons. Therefore we suggest that outcome durability is the most useful criterion examined here (in the case of voluntary abidance), encompassing equity and efficiency since, were the outcome not acceptable on those counts, it would not endure.

Some intervenors are evaluated chiefly for abidance by the rules, as for instance, go-betweens, umpires, and law enforcement officers. Where confidentiality of information is involved, as with auditors, lawyers, priests, mediators, respect of trust is an important criterion. It is a component of reputation sensitive to even a single incident of breech of trust. The relationship to parties has several components, such as use or abuse of mandate, appearance of evenhandedness (when the intervenor is not one-sided), ability to communicate, the amount of effort parties think has been expended to help them.

An intervenor is procedurally evenhanded if his/her management of the negotiation process does not give one disputant any advantages above those inherent in the problem structure. In small claims, it means giving disputants equal attention in joint sessions and caucuses. As they hear the story, mediators may feel that one disputant is ''right''; procedural evenhandedness requires that opinion not to affect their behavior toward the parties. In the case of the homeowner who could not get the workman to finish painting his house—and would not pay him—one mediator felt that the workman's behavior would have tried any patience: During the job, he was jailed for three months for drunken driving, he would work for only a few hours each day and drink during that time, and he disappeared for days. The co-mediator felt that the workman had many personal problems of which the homeowner was taking advantage to get the job done for less money. If the disputants could have correctly allocated opinions among the co-mediators, we might conclude that procedural evenhandedness has been violated.

Procedural evenhandedness can be practiced in spite of preferences over solutions, which partly explains why intervenors known to favor one disputant are nonetheless acceptable to all: the assurance of procedural evenhandedness may be more valuable to disputants than self-professed fairness, since the former is observable. Brookmire and Sistrunk (1980) observed in one experiment that the mediator's perceived personal stand had no effect on the outcome: A known bias may be tolerable, as long as parties trust the intervenor procedurally.

INTERVENTION MECHANISMS IN THE MEDIATION MODE

The matrix of Tables 21.1 and 21.2 displayed various intervention modes with their similarities and differences. We identified a *mediation mode,* characterized by a mandate that limits activities to altering the choice process, with no direct control over choices and outcomes. Several intervenors, besides mediators, operate at times in this mode, such as lawyers, elected representatives, priests, counselors, contract embellishers, managers, and even arbitrators. Parties negotiate only as long as giving in to the opponent, or making other unilateral choices seems less preferable (Rapoport, 1973). The mediation mode requires this perception to be sustained, and only through information supply and persuasion.

In order to help in decision situations, intervenors have to identify and alter the beliefs that currently block agreement. From the perspective of subjective expected utility theory (see Edwards, 1961), blocks to agreement relate to three perceptual categories (regardless of the specific context): beliefs about what choices are available; beliefs about the likelihood that certain consequences will follow their choices; beliefs about what consequences are valuable, and to what extent. Further elaboration of the role of these concepts in motivation is contained in expectancy-instrumentality-valence theory (see, for example, Campbell & Pritchard, 1976). Reference is also made to the work of Thomas (1988) in this volume; Thomas exposits what he calls ''The Fishbein Model'' (see Fishbein & Ajzen, 1975).

We illustrate the meaning of each dimension of perception susceptible to intervenor persuasion with examples from mediated small claims disputes, especially suitable because they are simple in most respects that make other disputes difficult to describe and resolve: They have usually only two parties, small stakes, a short time span, in many cases a nonrecurrent relationship, rarely require specialized knowledge of the issue, and can be resolved through mediation. In what follows, we recount briefly the dispute; we show how the mediator attempted to solve it working on some of the three choice influencing ingredients hypothesized as susceptible to the ''mediation mode.''

Altering the Solution Space

One of three co-tenants in an apartment sued another for half a month rent, since the latter had moved out without a month due notice. The third co-tenant, present as witness, also planned to sue the defendant for his share of the rent. One way out of this dispute, if seen as a ''fixed pie,'' was to find a point between zero and the half month rent, acceptable to both disputants. But the plaintiff was sure of his court case while the defendant did not wish to pay the whole rent (as he would end up doing if he agreed to pay each co-tenant his half). The mediator suggested that the defendant pay the plaintiff's full claim, on condition that the other co-tenant renounce his suit (sparing himself another day in court, which he admitted to dread). The plaintiff accepted because he needed money soon for a vacation. The defendant accepted, having had lower expectations. This outcome was not among the alternatives the co-tenants thought they faced, and all three preferred it to both litigation and any other option they thought they had.

Altering Subjective Probabilities

The plaintiff bought from the defendant a used car that broke down shortly after the transaction. Although anyone, including the judge, might have felt he had been wronged, the plaintiff had failed to complain within the time limit (seven days) set by the law for such incidents. He had, therefore, a weaker court case than he thought. The mediator persuaded him to settle by alerting him of his overassessment of court success probability. The settlement compensated him only partly for his loss but exceeded what the judge would (likely) have awarded him, or so he thought.

Altering Preferences for Outcomes

An elderly cable TV user sued the cable service for overcharging his bills, a claim unsubstantiated by records. Since, as a rule, payment cannot be withheld for a service rendered, the plaintiff's court case appeared weak. It became clear during negotiations that the plaintiff neither understood the billing nor wished to be proved wrong. Since the cable service could be blamed for failure to explain the billing procedure, the mediator persuaded the defendant to make concessions for the plaintiff to save face, arguing that the cable service reputation could be damaged otherwise. The defendant agreed to several of the mediator's suggestions (not included in the initial set of alternatives), such as providing some free service in exchange for full payment of the disputed bill, and even apologizing in writing for the misunderstanding. But the case went before the judge despite the defendant's allowances. As the plaintiff acknowledged in private conversation with the mediator, his goal was vindication: He resented the inconvenience and humiliation of being wrong and wished to punish the defendant by subjecting him to the court procedure (he attached utility to the defendant's waste of time). The mediator failed to convince the plaintiff that he should value the benefits offered by the defendant and to value less the defendant's loss from a day in court. The plaintiff's preferences blocked settlement.

In a dispute involving an elderly disabled veteran who owed payment to a car rental firm, the mediator tried to persuade the firm's representative to reduce the debt or ease the payment burden in recognition of the defendant's circumstances. Using the "put yourself in the other's shoes" technique, the mediator obtained a payment schedule acceptable to the defendant. However, although the sum involved was negligible to the firm, and payable in $5 monthly installments for four years, the representative refused to waive or reduce the debt, out of concern with precedent, which was also mentioned by the cable TV firm as an argument against waiving the $38 debt.

A disputant may not have thought of a possible alternative outcome, but at the intervenor's suggestion the disputant can judge it acceptable; a disputant may not have realized that a favored outcome has some undesirable consequences, but when informed, a disputant may lower the value of this outcome accordingly; a disputant may have thought that the likelihood of an outcome was very high, but if some evidence to the contrary is supplied, it may be accepted. Altering the way disputants value their payoffs (and those of the opponent) can give results, as in the cases of the cable TV firm and that of the disabled veteran, but it seems more difficult to alter valuations than, for instance, to enlarge the set of alternative choices (the co-tenants' case) or to consequences stakeholders overlooked or misassessed (the case of the lemon car). One reason may be that the way people value outcomes is part of an "internal" system, rooted in interconnected personal values rather than in external, observable, or verifiable events; trying to alter parts of this system may create dissonance that is difficult to resolve (Festinger, 1957).

Event probabilities seem to be the more malleable choice factor, possibly because subjective probabilities are sensitive to information, especially if made credible either by direct observation or by trust in the source. The intervenor's credibility when he/she offers arguments to alter subjective probabilities depends on the disputants' perceptions of the intervenor's level of competence and knowledge and of the intervenor's incentives. As mentioned, the fact that the Brookline mediators are part of the Harvard Law School program projects an image of knowledge of the law making it easier for the mediator to alter expectations of court verdicts, which happen to be the most common block to settlement in small claims disputes.

The effect of suggesting new alternatives for settlement—or removing some options from consideration—is difficult to predict. For example, Deutsch and Krauss (1962) found in one experiment that enlarging the space of options increases the likelihood of agreement. Examples can be found, however, where this is not the case. For instance, the mediator may suggest a new option with possible increased payoffs to all parties, who then are unable to agree on how the new surplus should be allocated among them (Lax & Sebenius, 1984).

CONCLUSION

This chapter establishes a theoretical framework for third-party intervenors who seek to resolve conflicts. The central role of the mandate, the rules authorizing intervenors' actions, is identified and provides a taxonomy of intervenors. These mandates are analyzed on dimensions of information transfer, choice delineation, choice promotion, choice making, and choice implementation. Special attention is paid to mediation, as an intervention mode that relies on persuasion. This persuasion is examined from a decision theoretic point of view of altering disputants' solution space, altering disputants' subjective probabilities, and altering disputants' preferences for outcomes. Intervention characteristics are examined on dimensions of initiation of intervention and choice of intervenor, time of intervention, process control, locus of intervention, end product, enforcement of choices, and evaluation of intervention.

References

Abelson, R. P. (1983). Whatever became of consistency theory? *Personality and Social Psychology Bulletin, 9,* 37–54.

Abelson, R. P. (1981). The psychological status of the script concept. *American Psychologist, 36,* 715–729.

Abelson, R. P. (1976). Script processing in attitude formation and decision making. In J. S. Carroll & J. W. Payne (Eds.), *Cognition and social behavior* (pp. 33–45). Hillsdale, NJ: Erlbaum.

Ajzen, I., & Fishbein, M. (1980). *Understanding attitudes and prediction social behavior.* Englewood Cliffs, NJ: Prentice-Hall.

Albert, S. (1977). Temporal comparison theory. *Psychological Review, 84,* 485–503.

Alexander, E. R. (1979). The reduction of cognitive conflict: Effects of various types of communication. *Journal of Conflict Resolution, 23,* 120–138.

Anderson, N., & Graesser, C. (1976). An information integration analysis of attitude change in group discussion. *Journal of Personality and Social Psychology, 34,* 210–222.

Argyris, C., Putnam R., & Smith, D. M. (1985). *Action science.* San Francisco: Jossey-Bass.

Argyris, C. & Schon, D. (1978). *Organizational learning: A theory of action perspective.* Reading, MA: Addison-Wesley.

Aubert, V. (1967). Courts and conflict resolution. *Journal of Conflict Resolution, 11,* 40–51.

Averill, J. R. (1982). *Anger and aggression: An essay on emotion.* New York: Springer-Verlag.

Bacharach, S. B., & Lawler, E. J. (1980). *Power and politics in organizations.* San Francisco: Jossey-Bass.

Bacharach, S. B., & Lawler, E. J. (1981). *Bargaining: Power, tactics, and outcomes.* San Francisco: Jossey-Bass.

Bahr, S. J. (1981). An evaluation of court mediation: A comparison in divorce cases with children. *Journal of Family Issues, 2,* 39–60.

Baldwin, D. A. (1978). Power and social exchange. *American Political Science Review, 72,* 1229–1242.

Bandura, A. (1986). *Social foundations of thought and action: A social cognitive theory.* Englewood Cliffs, NJ: Prentice-Hall.

Bargh, J. A. (1984). Automatic and conscious processing of social information. In R. S. Wyer, Jr., & T. K. Srull (Eds.), *Handbook of social cognition, Vol. 1* (pp. 1–43). Hillsdale, NJ: Erlbaum.

Bargh, J. A. & Pietromonaco, P. (1982). Automatic information processing and social perception: The influence of trait information presented outside of conscious awareness on impression formation. *Journal of Personality and Social Psychology, 42,* 437–449.

Barkowitz, M., Goldstein, B., & Indik, B. (1964). The state mediator: Background, self-image, and attitudes. *Industrial and Labor Relations Review, 17,* 257–275.

Baron, R. A. (1977). *Human aggression.* New York: Plenum.

Baron, R. A. (1985). Reducing organizational conflict: The role of attributions. *Journal of Applied Psychology, 70,* 434–441.

Baron, R. A. (in press [a]). Attributions and organizational conflict: The mediating role of apparent sincerity. *Organizational Behavior and Human Decision Processes.*

Baron, R. A. (in press [b]). Negative effects of destructive criticism: Impact on conflict, self-efficacy, and task performance. *Journal of Applied Psychology.*

Bartlett, F. A. (1932). *A study in experimental and social psychology.* New York: Cambridge University Press.

Bartos, O. J. (1970). Determinants and consequences of toughness. In P. Swingle (Ed.), *The structure of conflict* (pp. 45–68). New York: Academic Press.

Bartunek, J. M. (1984). Changing interpretive schemes and organizational restructuring: The example of a religious order. *Administrative Science Quarterly, 29,* 355–372.

Bartunek, J. M., Benton, A., & Keys, C. (1975). Third party intervention and the bargaining behavior of group representatives. *Journal of Conflict Resolution, 19,* 532–557.

Bass, B. M. (1985). Leadership: Good, better, and best. *Organizational Dynamics, 13*(3), 26–40.

Bauer, R. (1961). Problems of perception and the relations between United States and Soviet Union. *Journal of Conflict Resolution, 5,* 225–229.

Baxter, L. A., & Shepherd, T. L. (1978). Sex-role identity, sex of other, and affective relationship as determinants of interpersonal conflict-management styles, *Sex Roles, 4,* 813–825.

Bazerman, M. H. (1983). Negotiator judgment: A critical look at the rationality assumption. *American Behavioral Scientist, 27,* 211–228.

Bazerman, M. H. (1986). *Judgment in managerial decision making.* New York: Wiley.

Bazerman, M. H., & Carroll, J. S. (1987). Negotiator Cognition. In B. M. Staw & L. L. Cummings (Eds.), *Research in organizational behavior, Vol. 9* (pp. 247–288). Greenwich, CT: JAI Press.

Bazerman, M. H., & Farber, H. S. (1985). Arbitrator decision making: When are final offers important? *Industrial and Labor Relations Review, 39,* 76–89.

Bazerman, M. H., & Lewicki, R. J. (1982). (Eds.). *Negotiating in organizations.* Beverly Hills, CA: Sage.

Bazerman, M. H., Magliozzi, T., & Neale, M. A. (1985). The acquisition of an integrated response in a competitive market. *Organizational Behavior and Human Decision Processes, 35,* 294–313.

Bazerman, M. H., & Neale, M. A. (1982a). Improving negotiation effectiveness under final offer arbitration: The role of selection and training. *Journal of Applied Psychology, 67,* 543–548.

Bazerman, M. H., & Neale, M. A. (1982b). Heuristics in negotiation: Limits to effective dispute resolution. In Bazerman, M. H., & Lewicki, R. J. (Eds.), *Negotiating in organizations.* (pp. 51–67). Beverly Hills, CA: Sage.

Bazerman, M. H., & Neale, M. A. (1983). Heuristics in negotiation: Limitations to effective dispute resolution. In M. H. Bazerman & R. J. Lewicki (Eds.), *Negotiating in organizations* (pp. 51–67). Beverly Hills, CA: Sage.

Bellman H. & Graham, H. (1974). A suggested remedy for refusal to bargain in the public sector: Final offer arbitration. *Journal of Collective Negotiations, 3,* 183–189.

Ben-Yoav, O., & Pruitt, D. G. (1984a). Accountability to constituent: A two-edged sword. *Organizational Behavior and Human Performance, 34,* 283–295.

Ben-Yoav, O., & Pruitt, D. G. (1984b). Resistance to yielding and the expectation of cooperative future interaction in negotiation. *Journal of Experimental Social Psychology, 20,* 323–335.

Benedict, R. (1946). *The chrysanthemum and the sword.* Tokyo: Charles E. Tuttle.

Benson, J. K. (1975). The interorganizational network as a political economy. *Administrative Science Quarterly, 20,* 229–249.

Bercovitch, J. (in press). Mediation in international disputes: From mortatory to explanatory analysis. In K. Kressel & D. G. Pruitt (Eds.), *The mediation of disputes.* San Francisco: Jossey-Bass.

Berger, C. R. (1977). The covering law perspective as a theoretical basis for the study of human communication. *Communication Quarterly, 25,* 7–18.

Berger, P. L., & Luckmann, T. (1967). *The social construction of reality.* Garden City, NY: Doubleday.

Berkowitz, M., Goldstein, B., & Indik, B. (1964). The state mediator: Background, self-image, and attitudes. *Industrial and Labor Relations Review, 17,* 257–275.

Berscheid, E. (1983). Emotion. In H. H. Kelley, E. Berscheid, A. Christensen, J. H. Harvey, T. L. Huston, G. Levinger, E. McClintock, L. A. Peplau & D. R. Peterson (Eds.), *Close relationships* (pp. 110–168). San Francisco: W. H. Freeman.

Bethel, C. & Singer, L. (1982). Mediation: A new remedy for cases of domestic violence. *Vermont Law Review, 7,* 15–32.

Bies, R. J. (1982, August). *The delivery of bad news in organizations: A social information perspective.* Paper presented at the annual meeting of the Academy of Management, New York, NY.

Bies, R. J. (1987a). *The delivery of bad news in organizations: Managerial strategies and tactics.* Unpublished manuscript, Kellogg Graduate School of Management, Northwestern University, Evanston, IL.

Bies, R. J. (1987b). The predicament of injustice: The management of moral outrage. In L. L. Cummings & B. M. Staw (Eds.), *Research in organizational behavior, Vol. 9* (pp. 289–319). Greenwich, CT: JAI Press.

Bies, R. J., & Moag, J. S. (1986). Interactional justice: Communication criteria of fairness. In R. J. Lewicki, B. H. Sheppard & M. H. Bazerman (Eds.), *Research on negotiation in organizations* (pp. 43–55). Greenwich, CT: JAI Press.

Bies, R. J., & Shapiro, D. L. (1987). *Voice and justification: Their influence on procedural fairness judgments.* Manuscript submitted for publication.

Bies, R. J., & Shapiro, D. L. (in press). Interactional fairness judgments: The influence of causal accounts. *Social justice review.*

Bies, R. J., Shapiro, D. L., & Cummings, L. L. (1987). *Bad news and subordinate support for the boss: A multi-theoretical perspective.* Manuscript submitted for publication.

Bigoness, W. J. (1976). Effects of locus of control and style of third party intervention upon bargaining behavior. *Journal of Applied Psychology, 61,* 305–312.

Birchler, G. R., Weiss, R. L., & Vincent, J. (1975). Multimethod analysis of social reinforcement exchange between maritally distressed and nondistressed spouse and stranger dyads. *Journal of Personality and Social Psychology, 31,* 349–360.

Blake, R. R., & Mouton, J. S. (1964). *The managerial grid.* Houston: Gulf.

Blake, R. R., & Mouton, J. S. (1970). The fifth achievement. *Journal of Applied Behavioral Science, 6,* 413–426.

Blake, R. A., & Mouton, J. S. (1984). *Solving costly organizational conflicts.* San Francisco: Jossey-Bass.

Blumrosen, A. W. (1972). Civil rights conflicts: The uneasy search for peace in our time. *Arbitration Journal, 27*(1), 35–46.

Bohannon, P. (Ed.) (1970). *Divorce and after: An analysis of the emotional and social problems of divorce.* Garden City, NY: Doubleday.

Boozer, R. W. (1987, June). *Jungian psychological types and conflict-handling styles: A comparison of dimensional and typological assumptions.* Paper presented at the International Conference of the Conflict Management Group, Fairfax, VA.

Bostrom, R. N. (1984). *Competence in communication.* Beverly Hills, CA: Sage.

Boulding, K. E. (1958). *The skills of the economist.* Cleveland: Howard Allen.

Boulding, K. E. (1963). *Conflict and defense: A general theory.* New York: Harper & Row.

Bouwen, R., & Salipante, P. (1986, July). *A kaleidoscopic model of conflict formulation.* Paper presented at the International Congress of Applied Psychology, Jerusalem, Israel.

Bower, G. H. (1981). Mood and memory. *American Psychologist, 36,* 129–148.

Brookmire, D. A. & Sistrunk, F. (1980). The effects of perceived ability and impartiality of mediators and time pressure on negotiation. *Journal of Conflict Resolution, 24,* 311–327.

Brown, B. R. (1968). The effects of need to maintain face on interpersonal bargaining. *Journal of Experimental Social Psychology, 4,* 107–122.

Brown, C. T., Yelsma, P., & Keller, P. W. (1981). Communication-conflict predisposition: Development of a theory and an instrument. *Human Relations, 34,* 1103–1117.

Brown, L. D. (1983). *Managing conflict at organizational interfaces.* Reading, MA: Addison-Wesley.

Burke, R. J. (1970). Methods of resolving supervisor-subordinate conflict: The constructive use of subordinate differences and disagreements. *Organizational Behavior and Human Performance, 5,* 393–411.

Burrell, G., & Morgan, G. (1979). *Sociological paradigms and organizational analysis.* London: Heinemann.

Burton, J. W. (1969). *Conflict and communication.* New York: Free Press.

Burton, J. W. (1987). *Resolving deep-rooted conflict.* Lanham, MD: University Press of America.

Campbell, D. J. (in press). Task complexity and strategy development: A review and conceptual analysis. *Academy of Management Review.*

Campbell, D. T. (1975). Degrees of freedom and the case study. *Comparative Political Studies, 8,* 178–193.

Campbell, J. P., & Pritchard, R. D. (1976). Motivation theory in industrial and organizational psychology. In M. D. Dunnette (Ed.), *Handbook of industrial and organizational psychology* (pp. 63–130). New York: Wiley.

Cantor, N., & Mischel, W. (1977). Traits as prototypes: Effects on recognition memory. *Journal of Personality and Social Psychology, 35,* 38–48.

Carnevale, P. J., & Isen, A. M. (in press). The influence of positive affect and visual access to the discovery of integrative solutions in bilateral negotiation. *Organizational Behavior and Human Decision Processes.*

Carnevale, P. J. D., & Isen, A. M. (1986). The influence of positive affect and visual access on the discovery of integrative solutions in bilateral negotiation. *Organizational Behavior and Human Decision Processes, 37,* 1–13.

Carnevale, P. J. D., & Pegnetter, R. (1985). The selection of mediation tactics in public-sector disputes: A contingency analysis. *Journal of Social Issues, 41,* 65–82.

Carnevale, P. J. D., Pruitt, D. G., & Britton, S. C. (1979). Looking tough: The negotiator under constituent surveillance. *Personality and Social Psychology Bulletin, 5,* 118–121.

Carnevale, P. J. D., Pruitt, D. G., & Seilheimer, S. D. (1981). Looking and competing: Accountability and visual access in integrative bargaining. *Journal of Personality and Social Psychology, 40,* 111–120.

Carter, J. (1982). *Keeping faith.* New York: Bantam.

Chalmers, W. E. (1948). The conciliation process. *Industrial and Labor Relations Review, 1,* 337–350.

Christopher, R. C. (1982). *The Japanese mind: A goliath explained.* New York: Simon and Schuster.

Clark, M. S., & Isen, A. M. (1982). Towards understanding the relationship between feeling states and social behavior. In A. Hastorf & A. Isen (Eds.), *Cognitive social psychology* (pp. 73–108). Amsterdam: North Holland.

Coker, D. A., Neale, M. A., & Northcraft, G. B. (1987). *Structural and individual influences on the process and outcome of negotiation.* Working paper, University of Arizona, Tucson.

Collins, B. (1970). *Social psychology.* Reading, MA: Addison-Wesley.

Coogler, O. J., Weber, R. E., & McKenry, R. C. (1979). Divorce and mediation: A means of facilitating divorce adjustment. *Family Coordinator, 28,* 255–259.

Cooley, J. W. (1986). Arbitration vs. mediation: Explaining the differences. *Judicature, 66,* 263–269.

Cormick, G. W. (1982, Winter). Intervention in self-determination in environmental disputes: A mediator's perspective. *Resolve,* 1–77.

Coser, L. A. (1956). *The functions of social conflict.* Glencoe, IL: The Free Press.

Cosier, R. A., & Ruble, T. L. (1981). Research on conflict-handling behavior: An experimental approach. *Academy of Management Journal, 24,* 816–831.

Coulter, R. T. (1979). Indian conflicts and nonjudicial dispute settlement. *Arbitration Journal, 34,* 28–31.

Craig, R. T. (1986). Goals in discourse. In D. G. Ellis & W. A. Donohue (Eds.), *Contemporary issues in language and discourse processes* (pp. 257–274). Hillsdale, NJ: Erlbaum Associates.

Craig, R. T., & Tracy, K. (1983). Conversational coherence. Beverly Hills, CA: Sage.

Crohn, M. (1985). Signs of cohesion in dispute resolution. *Negotiation Journal, 1,* 23–28.

Cross, J. (1969). *The economics of bargaining.* New York: Basic Books.

Cross, J. G. (1977). Negotiations as a learning process. *Journal of Conflict Resolution, 21,* 581–606.

Crowne, D. P., & Marlowe, D. (1960). A new scale of social desirability independent of psychopathology. *Journal of Consulting Psychology, 14,* 349–354.

Cyert, R. M., & March, J. G. (1963). *A behavioral theory of the firm.* Englewood Cliffs, NJ: Prentice-Hall.

Danet, B. (1980). Language and the legal process. *Law and Society Review, 14,* 445–564.

Danzig, R., & Lowy, M. J. (1975). Everyday disputes and mediation in the United States: A reply to Professor Felstiner. *Law and Society Review, 9,* 675–694.

Dawes, R. M., & Corrigan, B. (1974). Linear models in decision making. *Psychological Bulletin, 81,* 95–106.

Deal, T. E., & Kennedy, A. A. (1982). *Corporate cultures.* Reading, MA: Addison-Wesley.

DeNisi, A., Dworkin, J. B. (1979, August). *Final offer arbitration and the naive negotiator.* Paper presented at a special symposium of the annual meeting of the Academy of Management, Atlanta, GA.

Derr, C. B. (1978). Managing organizational conflict: Collaboration, bargaining, and power approaches. *California Management Review, 21*(2), 76–83.

Deutsch, M. (1949). A theory of cooperation and competition. *Human Relations, 2,* 129–151.

Deutsch, M. (1960). The effect of motivational orientation on trust and suspicion. *Human Relations, 13,* 123–140.

Deutsch, M. (1962). Cooperation and trust: Some theoretical notes. In M. Jones (Ed.), *Nebraska symposium on motivation* (pp. 275–319). Lincoln: University of Nebraska Press.

Deutsch, M. (1969). Conflicts: Productive and destructive. *Journal of Social Issues, 25*(1), 7–41.

Deutsch, M. (1973). *The resolution of conflict: Constructive and destructive processes.* New Haven, CT: Yale University Press.

Deutsch, M. (1980). Over fifty years of conflict research. In L. Festinger (Ed.), *Four decades of social psychology* (pp. 46–77). New York: Oxford University Press.

Deutsch, M., & Krauss, R. M. (1960). Studies in interpersonal bargaining. *Journal of Conflict Resolution, 6,* 52–76.

Devlin, A., & Ryan, J. P. (1986). Family mediation in Canada: Past, present, and future developments. *Mediation Quarterly, 11,* 93–108.

Dillman, D. A. (1978). *Mail and telephone surveys: The total design method.* NY: Wiley.

Dindia, K. (1986). Antecedents and consequences of awkward silence: A replication using revised lag sequential analysis. *Human Communication Research, 13,* 108–125.

Donohue, W. A. (1978). An empirical framework for examining negotiation processes and outcomes. *Communication Monographs, 45,* 247–257.

Donohue, W. A. (1981a). Analyzing negotiation tactics: Development of a negotiation interaction system. *Human Communication Research, 7,* 273–287.

Donohue, W. A. (1981b). Development of a model of rule use in negotiation interaction. *Communication Monographs, 48,* 106–120.

Donohue, W. A. (in press). Mediator communicative competence: A research program review. In K. Kressel & D. Pruitt (Eds.), *Research in mediation*. Hillsdale, NJ: Jossey-Bass.

Donohue, W. A., Allen, M., & Burrell, N. A. (1985). Communication strategies in mediation. *Mediation Quarterly, 10,* 75–90.

Donohue, W. A., Allen, M., & Burrell, N. A. (1986, November). *A lag sequential analysis of mediator intervention strategies*. Paper presented at the Speech Communication Association convention, Chicago, IL.

Donohue, W. A., Cushman, D. P., & Nofsinger, R. E. (1980). Creating and confronting social order: A comparison of rules perspectives. *Western Journal of Speech Communication, 44,* 5–19.

Donohue, W. A., Diez, M. E., & Hamilton, M. (1984). Coding naturalistic negotiation interaction. *Human Communication Research, 10,* 402–425.

Donohue, W. A., Diez, M. E., & Stahle, R. B. (1983). New directions in negotiation research. In R. N. Bostrom (Ed.), *Communication yearbook, 7* (pp. 249–279). Beverly Hills, CA: Sage.

Donohue, W. A., Diez, M. E., & Weider-Hatfield, D. (1984). Skills for successful bargainers: A valence theory of competent mediation. In R. Bostrom (Ed.), *Competence in communication* (pp. 219–258). Beverly Hills, CA: Sage.

Donohue, W. A., Diez, M. E., & Weider-Hatfield, D. (1984, May). *A valence theory of mediator competence*. Paper presented at the International Communication Association Convention, San Francisco, CA.

Douglas, A. (1957). The peaceful settlement of industrial and intergroup disputes. *Journal of Conflict Resolution, 1,* 69–81.

Drake, B. H., Zammuto, R. F., & Parasuraman, S. (1982). *Five conflict styles: Factor structure and social desirability issues underlying the conflict MODE instrument*. Paper presented at the annual meeting of the American Institute for Decision Sciences, Boston.

Dubois, P. L. (Ed.). (1982). *The analysis of judicial reform*. Lexington, MA: Lexington.

Dyer, W. G., & Dyer, J. H. (1984). The m*a*s*h generation: Implications for future organizational values. *Organizational Dynamics, 13*(1), 66–79.

Earley, P. C., & Perry, B. C. (1987). Work plan availability and performance: An assessment of task strategy priming on subsequent task completion. *Organizational Behavior and Human Decision Processes, 39,* 279–302.

Earley, P. C., Wojnaroski, P., & Prest, W (1987). Task planning and energy expended: Exploration of how goals influence performance. *Journal of Applied Psychology, 72,* 107–114.

Easterbrook, J. A. (1959). The effect of emotion on cue utilization and the organization of behavior. *Psychological Review, 66,* 183–201.

Edwards, W. (1961). Behavioral decision theory. In P. R. Farnsworth (Ed.), *Annual review of psychology,* Palo Alto, CA: Annual Reviews.

Ehninger, D., & Brockriede, W. (1978). *Decision by debate*. New York: Harper & Row.

Einhorn, H. J. (1974). Expert judgment: Some necessary conditions and an example. *Journal of Applied Psychology, 59,* 562–571.

Einhorn, H. J. (1980). Overconfidence in judgment. *New Directions for Methodology of Social and Behavioral Sciences, 4,* 1–16.

Einhorn, H. J., & Hogarth, R. M. (1978). Confidence in judgment: Persistence of the illusion of validity. *Psychological Review, 85,* 395–416.

Eiseman, J. W. (1978). Reconciling "incompatible" positions. *Journal of Applied Behavioral Science, 14,* 133–150.

Emerson, J. (1969). Negotiating the serious import of humor. *Sociometry, 32,* 169–181.

Emery, D., & Ellis, D. (1980, November). *Relational control in marital dyads: A lag sequential analysis.* Paper presented at the Speech Communication Association Convention, New York, NY.

Esser, J. K., & Komorita, S. S. (1974). Reciprocal and non-reciprocal concession strategies in bargaining. *Research and Social Psychological Bulletin, 1,* 231–233.

Eysenck, H. J., & Eysenck, S. B. G. (1968). *Eysenck personality inventory.* San Diego, CA: Educational and Industrial Testing Service.

Fahs, M. L. (1981). The effects of self-disclosing communication and attitude similarity on the reduction of interpersonal conflict. *Western Journal of Speech Communication, 45,* 38–50.

Felner, R. D., & Terre, L. (1987), Child custody dispositions and children's adaptation following divorce. In L. A. Weithorn (Ed.), *Psychology and child custody determinations: Knowledge, roles, and expertise.* Lincoln, NE: University of Nebraska Press.

Felstiner, W. L. F. (1975). Avoidance as dispute processing: An elaboration. *Law and Society Review, 10,* 695–706.

Felstiner, W. L. F., Abel, R., & Sarat, A. (1980–1981). The emergence and transformation of disputes: Naming, blaming, and claiming. *Law and Society Review, 15,* 631–654.

Ferguson, T. J., & Rule, B. G. (1983). An attributional perspective on anger and aggression. In R. G. Geen & E. I. Donnerstein (Eds.), *Aggression: Theoretical and empirical review, Vol. 1* (pp. 41–74). New York: Academic Press.

Festinger, L. (1954). A theory of social comparison processes. *Human Relations, 1,* 117–149.

Festinger, L. (1957). *A theory of cognitive dissonance.* Evanston, IL: Row Peterson.

Feuille, P. (1975). Final offer arbitration and the chilling effect. *Industrial Relations, 14,* 302–310.

Fiedler, F., Meuwese, W., & Oonk, S. (1961). An exploratory study of group creativity in laboratory tasks. *Acta Psychology, 18,* 100–119.

Filley, A. C. (1975). *Interpersonal conflict resolution.* Glenview, IL: Scott, Foresman and Company.

Filley, A. C. (1978). Some normative issues in conflict management. *California Management Review, 21*(2), 61–65.

Fink, C. F. (1968). Some conceptual difficulties in the theory of social conflict. *Journal of Conflict Resolution, 12,* 412–460.

Fischhoff, B. (1982). Debiasing. In D. Kahneman, P. Slovic, & A. Tversky (Eds.), *Judgement under uncertainty: Heuristics and biases* (pp. 422–444). Cambridge: Cambridge University Press.

Fishbein, M. (1967). Attitude and the prediction of behavior. In M. Fishbein (Ed.), *Readings in attitude theory and measurement* (pp. 477–492). New York: Wiley.

Fishbein, M., & Ajzen, I. (1975). *Belief, attitude and behavior: An introduction to theory and research.* Reading, MA: Addison-Wesley.

Fisher, B. A. (1983). Differential effects of sexual composition and interactional context on interaction patterns in dyads. *Human Communication Research, 9,* 225–238.

Fisher, R. (1969). *International conflict for beginners.* NY: Harper & Row.

Fisher, R. (1981). Playing the wrong game? In J. Z. Rubin (Ed.), *Dynamics of third party intervention: Kissinger in the Middle East.* New York: Praeger.

Fisher, R., & Ury, W. (1981). *Getting to yes: Negotiating agreement without giving in.* Boston: Houghton Mifflin.

Fisher, R. J. (1972). Third party consultation: A method for the study and resolution of conflict. *Journal of Conflict Resolution, 16,* 67–94.

Fiske, D. W. (1961). The inherent variability in behavior. In D. Fiske & S. Maddi (Eds.), *Functions of work experience,* (pp. 213–231). Homewood, IL: Dorsey Press.

Fiske, S. T., & Linville, P. W. (1980). What does the schema concept buy us? *Personality and Social Psychology Bulletin, 6,* 543–557.

Fiske, S. T., & Taylor, S. E. (1982). Schema triggered affect: Applications to social perceptions. In M. S. Clark & S. T. Fiske (Eds.), *Affect and cognition: The 17th annual carnegie symposium on cognition* (pp. 55–78). Hillsdale, N.J.: Erlbaum.

Fiske, S. T., & Taylor, S. E. (1984). *Social cognition.* Reading, Mass.: Addison Wesley.

Fitzgerald, J., & Dickens, R. (1980–1981). Disputing in legal and non-legal contexts: Some questions for sociologists of law. *Law and Society Review, 15,* 681–706.

Fitzpatrick, M. A., & Indvik, J. (1982). The instrumental and expressive domains of marital communication. *Human Communication Research, 8,* 195–213.

Flavell, J. *et al.* (1968). *The development of role taking and communication skills in children.* New York: Wiley.

Fogg, R. W. (1985). Dealing with conflict: A repertoire of creative, peaceful, approaches. *Journal of Conflict Resolution, 29,* 330–358.

Folberg, J., & Taylor, A. (1984). *Mediation: A comprehensive guide to resolving conflicts without litigations.* San Francisco: Jossey-Bass.

Folger, R., & Martin, C. (in press). Relative deprivation and referent cognitions: Distributive and procedural justice effects. *Journal of Experimental Social Psychology.*

Folger, J. P., & Poole, M. S. (1984). *Working through conflict: A communication perspective.* Glenview, IL: Scott, Foresman.

Folger, R., Rosenfield, D., Rheume, K., & Martin, C. (1983). Relative deprivation and referent cognitions. *Journal of Experimental Social Psychology, 19,* 172–184.

Folger, R., Rosenfield, D., & Robinson, T. (1983). Relative deprivation and procedural justifications. *Journal of Personality and Social Psychology, 45,* 268–273.

Follett, M. P. (1924). *Creative experience.* New York: Peter Smith.

Follett, M. P. (1940). Constructive conflict. In H. C. Metcalf & L. Urwick (Eds.), *Dynamic administration: The collected papers of Mary Parker Follett* (pp. 30–49). New York: Harper.

Fraser, J. R., & Froelich, J. E. (1979). Crisis intervention in the courtroom: The case of the night prosecutor. *Community Mental Health Journal, 15,* 237–247.

Frei, D. (1976). Conditions affecting the effectiveness of international mediation. *Papers of the Peace Science Society (International), 26,* 67–84.

French, J. R. P., & Raven, B. (1968). The bases of social power. In D. Cartwright & A. Zander (Eds.), *Group dynamics* (3rd Ed. (pp. 259–269). New York: Harper & Row.

Frey, R. L., & Adams, J. S. (1972). The negotiator's dilemma: Simultaneous in-group and out-group conflict. *Journal of Experimental Social Psychology, 8,* 331–346.

Friedman, M. I., & Jacka, M. E. (1969). The negative effect of group cohesiveness on intergroup negotiation. *Journal of Social Issues, 25,* 181–194.

Froman, L. A., J. R. & Cohen, M. D. (1970). Compromise and logroll: Comparing the efficiency of two bargaining processes. *Behavioral Science, 15,* 180–183.

Fry, W. R., Firestone, I. J., & Williams, D. L. (1983). Negotiation process and outcome of stranger dyads and dating couples: Do lovers lose? *Basic and Applied Social Psychology, 4,* 1–16.

Galbraith, J. (1978). *Organization design.* Reading, MA: Addison-Wesley.

Gamson, W. A. (1961). A theory of coalition formation. *American Sociological Review, 26,* 373–382.

Gamson, W. A. (1964). Experimental studies in coalition formation. In L. Berkowitz (Ed.), *Advances in experimental social psychology, Vol. 1* (pp. 81–110). New York: Academic Press.

Garafalo, J., & Connelly, K. J. (1980). Dispute resolution centers part I: Major features and processes. *Criminal Justice Abstracts, 12,* 416–439.

Geen, R. G., & Donnerstein, E. I. (Eds.). (1983). *Aggression: Theoretical and empirical reviews.* New York: Academic Press.

George, A. (1972). The case for multiple advocacy in making foreign policy. *American Political Science Review, 66,* 751–785.

Gibb, J. (1961). Defensive communication. *Journal of Communication, 11,* 141–148.

Giles, H., Mulac, A., Bradec, J. J., & Johnson, P. (1987). Speech accommodation theory: The first decade and beyond. In M. L. McLaughlin (Ed.), *Communication yearbook, 10* (pp. 13–48). Beverly Hills, CA: Sage.

Gioia, D., & Manz, C. C. (1985). Linking cognition and behavior: A script processing interpretation of vicarious learning. *Academy of Management Review, 10,* 527–539.

Girdner, L. K. (1986). Family mediation: Toward a synthesis. *Mediation Quarterly, 13,* 21–29.

Gladwin, T. N. & Kumar, R. (1986, September). *The social psychology of crisis bargaining: Toward a contingency model.* Paper presented at the International Conference on Industrial Crisis Management, New York University.

Glasl, F. (1982). The process of conflict escalation and roles of third parties. In G. B. J. Bomers & R. B. Peterson (Eds.), *Conflict management and industrial relations* (pp. 119–140). Boston: Kluwer-Nijhoff.

Glass, A. J. (1955). *Psychological considerations in atomic warfare,* (Report No. 560). Washington, DC: Walter Reed Army Medical Center.

Goaux, C. (1971). Induced affective states and interpersonal attraction. *Journal of Personality and Social Psychology, 20,* 37–43.

Goffman, E. (1952). On cooling out the mark: Some aspects of adaptation to failure. *Psychiatry, 15,* 451–563.

Goffman, E. (1956). *The presentation of self in everyday life.* Edinburgh, Scotland: University of Edinburgh Press.

Golden, J. L., Berquist, G. F., & Coleman, W. E. (1983). *The rhetoric of western thought.* Dubuque, IA: Kendall/Hunt.

Gorry, G. A., & Krumland, R. B. (1983). Artificial intelligence research and decision support systems. In J. Bennet (Ed.), *Building decision support systems* (pp. 205–220). Reading, MA: Addison-Wesley.

Gottman, J. M. (1979). *Marital interaction: Experimental investigations.* New York: Academic Press.

Gouran, D. S., & Baird, J. E., Jr. (1972). An analysis of distributional and sequential structure in problem-solving and informal group discussion. *Speech Monographs,* *39,* 16–22.

Graham, J. L., & Sano, Y. (1984). *Smart bargaining.* MA: Ballinger.

Greenhalgh, L. (1986). *Negotiated outcomes of interpersonal conflicts in organizations.* Working paper, The Amos Tuck School of Business Administration, Dartmouth College, NH.

Greenhalgh, L., Neslin, S. A., & Gilkey, R. W. (1985). The effects of negotiator preferences, situational power, and negotiator personality on outcomes of business negotiations. *Academy of Management Journal, 28,* 9–33.

Griffit, W. B. (1970). Environmental effects on interpersonal affective behavior: Ambient effective temperature and attraction. *Journal of Personality and Social Psychology, 15,* 240–244.

Gruder, C. L. (1971). Relationships with opponent and partner in mixed-motive bargaining. *Journal of Conflict Resolution, 15,* 403–416.

Gruder, C. L. & Rosen, N. A. (1971). Effects of intergroup relations on intergroup bargaining. *International Journal of Group Tensions, 1,* 301–317.

Gulliver, P. (1973). Neogiations as a mode of dispute settlement: Towards a general model. *Law and Society Review, 7,* 667–691.

Gulliver, P. H. (1979). *Disputes and negotiation.* New York: Academic Press.

Hage, G. (1974). *Communication and organizational control.* New York: Wiley.

Hair, J. F., Jr., Anderson, R. E., & Tatham, R. L. (1987). *Multivariate data analysis with readings* (2nd ed.). New York: Macmillan.

Hall, J. (1969). *Conflict management survey.* Conroe, TX: Teleometrics International.

Haman, D. C., Brief, A. P., & Pegnetter, R. (1978). Studies in mediation and the training of public sector mediators. *Journal of Collective Negotiations in the Public Sector, 7,* 347–361.

Hamburg, J. (1985). Mandatory divorce mediation and joint custody agreements: The need for interprofessional cooperation and communication. *Conciliation Courts Review, 22,* 27–32.

Hamilton, V. L. (1980). Intuitive psychologist or intuitive lawyer? Alternative models of the attribution process. *Journal of Personality and Social Psychology, 39,* 767–772.

Hammock, G. S., Richardson, D. R., Pilkington, C., & Utley, M. (1987, June), *Measurement of conflict in close interpersonal relationships.* Paper presented at the International Conference of the Conflict Management Group, Fairfax, VA.

Hammond, K. R., Todd, F. J., Wilkins, M., & Mitchell, T. O. (1966). Cognitive conflict between persons: Application of the "lens model" paradigm. *Journal of Experimental and Social Psychology, 2,* 343–360.

Hare, R. (1985). *The philosophies of science.* Oxford: Oxford University Press.

Harsanyi, J. C. (1977). *Rational behavior and bargaining equilibrium in games and social situations.* London: Cambridge University Press.

Hart, L. B. (1981). *Learning from conflict: A handbook for trainers and group leaders.* Reading MA: Addison-Wesley.

Hart, R. P., & Burke, D. M. (1972). Rhetorical sensitivity and social interaction. *Speech Monographs, 39,* 75–91.

Hartnett, D., Cummings, L., & Hughes, G. (1968). The influence of risk-taking propensity on bargaining behavior. *Behavioral Science, 13,* 91–101.

Hastorf, A. H., & Cantril, H. (1954). They saw a game: A case study. *Journal of Abnormal and Social Psychology, 49,* 129–134.

Hawes, L. C., & Smith, D. H. (1973). A critique of assumptions underlying the study of communication and conflict. *Quarterly Journal of Speech, 59,* 423–435.

Hayes-Roth, R., & Hayes-Roth, F. (1977). Concept learning and the recognition and classification of exemplars. *Journal of Verbal Learning and Verbal Behavior, 16,* 321–338.

Haynes, J. M. (1981). *Divorce mediation.* New York: Springer Publishing.

Haynes, J. M. (1982). A conceptual model of the process of family mediation: Implications for training. *American Journal of Family Therapy, 10,* 15–16.

Haynes, J. M. (1984). Matching readiness and willingness to the mediators strategies. *Negotiation Journal, 1,* 1–11.

Henne, D., Levine, M. J., Usery, W. J. Jr., & Fishgold, H. (1986). A case study in cross-cultural mediation: The General Motors–Toyota joint venture. *Arbitration Journal, 41,* 5–15.

Herrman, M. S., McKenry, P. C., & Weber, R. E. (1979). Mediation and arbitration applied to family conflict resolution: The divorce settlement. *Arbitration Journal, 34,* 17–21.

Hetherington, E. M., Cox, M., & Cox, R. (1978). The aftermath of divorce. In J. H. Steven, Jr. & M. Matthews (Eds.), *Mother-child, father-child relations.* Washington, DC: National Association for the Education of Young Children.

Hewes, D. E. (1985). Systematic biases in coded social interaction data. *Human Communication Research, 11,* 554–574.

Hewitt, J. P., & Stokes, R. (1975). Disclaimers. *American Sociological Review, 40,* 1–11.

Higgins, E. T. (1987). Self discrepancy: A theory relating self and affect. *Psychological Review, 94,* 319–340.

Higgins, E. T., King, G., & Mavin, G. H. (1982). Individual construct accessibility and subjective impressions and recall. *Journal of Personality and Social Psychology, 43,* 35–47.

Higgins, E. T., Kuiper, N. A., & Olson, J. M. (1981). Social cognition: A need to get personal. In E. T. Higgins, C. P. Herman & M. P. Zanna (Eds.), *Social cognition: The Ontario symposium* (pp. 395–420). Hillsdale, NJ: Erlbaum.

Higgins, E. T., Strauman, T., & Klein, R. (1986). Standards and the process of self-evaluation: Multiple affects from multiple stages. In R. M. Sorrentino & E. T. Higgins (Eds.), *Handbook of motivation and cognition: Foundations of social behavior* (pp. 23–63). New York: Guilford.

Hills, F. S., & Mahoney, T. A. (1978). University budgets and organizational decision making. *Administrative Science Quarterly, 23,* 454–465.

Hiltrop, J. M. (1985). Dispute settlement and mediation: Data from Britain. *Industrial Relations, 24,* 139–146.

Hirschmann, A. O. (1970). *Exit, voice, and loyalty.* Cambridge, MA.: Harvard University Press.

Hocker, J. L., & Wilmot, W. W. (1984). *Interpersonal Conflict.* Dubuque, IA: W. C. Brown.

Hodges, W. F. (1986). *Interventions for children of divorce.* New York: Wiley.

Hoffman, Martin L. (1986). Affect, cognition and motivation. In R. M. Sorrentino, & E. T. Higgins (Eds.), *Handbook of motivation and cognition: Foundations of social behavior* (pp. 244–280). New York: Guilford.

Hogarth, R. M. (1981). Beyond discrete biases: Functional and dysfunctional aspects of judgmental heuristics. *Psychological Bulletin, 90,* 197–217.

Holden, L. T. (1977). Final offer arbitration in Massachusetts. *Arbitration journal, 32,* 26–35.

Holmes, J. G., & Miller, D. T. (1976). Interpersonal conflict. In J. W. Thibaut, J. T. Spence & R. C. Carson (Eds.), *Contemporary topics in social psychology* (pp. 265–308). Morristown, NJ: General Learning Press.

Hopmann, P. T. (1974). Bargaining in arms control negotiations: The Seabeds Denuclearization Treaty. *International Organization, 3,* 313–343.

Horai, J. (1977). Attributional conflict. *Journal of Social Issues, 33,* 88–100.

Hordijk, J. W., & Van de Vliert, E. (1983). *Communicatie en samenweking op de bouwplaats [Communication and cooperation on construction sites].* Rotterdam, The Netherlands: Stichting Bouwresearch.

Huber, V. L., & Neale, M. A. (1986a). Effects of cognitive heuristics and goals on negotiator performance and subsequent goal setting. *Organizational Behavior and Human Decision Processes, 38,* 342–365.

Huber, V. L., & Neale, M. A. (1986b). Effects of self-and competitor goals on performance in an interdependent bargaining task. *Journal of Applied Psychology, 72,* 197–203.

Ilgen, D. R., Fisher, C. D., & Taylor, M. S. (1979). Consequences of individual feedback on behavior in organizations. *Journal of Applied Psychology, 64,* 349–371.

Ilgen, D. R., Mitchell, T. R., & Fredrickson, J. W. (1981). Poor performers: Supervisors' and subordinates' responses. *Organizational Behavior and Human Performance, 27,* 386–410.

Ilgen, D. R., Peterson, R. B., Martin, B. A., & Boeschen, D. A. (1981). Supervisor and subordinate reactions to performance appraisal sessions. *Organizational Behavior and Human Performance, 28,* 311–330.

Ilke, F. C. (1964). *How nations negotiate.* New York: Harper & Row.

Inagaki, K., & Hatano, G. (1968). Motivational influences on epistemic observation. *Japanese Journal of Educational Psychology, 16,* 221–228.

Inagaki, K., & Hatano, G. (1977). Application of cognitive motivation and its effect on epistemic observation. *American Educational Research Journal, 14,* 485–591.

Infante, D. A. (1981). Trait argumentativeness as a predictor of communicative behavior in situations requiring argument. *The Central States Speech Journal, 32,* 265–272.

Infante, D. A., & Rancer, A. S. (1982). A conceptualization and measure of argumentativeness. *Journal of Personality Assessment, 46,* 72–80.

Ingleby, R. (1986). Out of court settlements: Policy, principle, practice and procedure. *Mediation Quarterly, 11,* 57–67.

Irving, H. H. (1981). *Divorce mediation: A rational alternative to the adversary system.* New York: Universe Books.

Isen, A. M., Shalker, T. E., Clark, M. S., & Karp, L. (1978). Affect, accessibility of material in memory and behavior: A cognitive loop? *Journal of Personality and Social Psychology, 36,* 1–12.

Jackson, E. (1952). *Meeting of minds: A way to peace through mediation.* New York: McGraw-Hill.

Janis, I. (1982). *Groupthink: Psychological studies of policy decisions and fiascocs.* Boston, MA: Houghton-Mifflin.

Janis, I., & Mann, L. (1977). *Decision making: A psychological analysis of conflict, choice and commitment.* New York: Free Press.

Jelinek, M., Smircich, L., & Hirsch, P. (1983). Introduction: A code of many colors. *Administrative Science Quarterly, 28,* 331–338.

Johnson, D. W. (1971). Role-reversal: A summary and review of the research. *International Journal of Group Tensions, 1,* 318–334.

Johnson, D. W. (1977). Distribution and exchange of information in problem-solving dyads. *Communication Research, 4,* 283–298.

Johnson, D. W. (1979). *Educational psychology.* Englewood Cliffs, NJ: Prentice-Hall.

Johnson, D. W. (1986). *Reaching out: Interpersonal effectiveness and self-actualization* (3rd ed.). Englewood Cliffs, NJ: Prentice-Hall.

Johnson, D. W., & Dustin, R. (1970). The initiation of cooperation through role reversal. *Journal of Social Psychology, 82,* 193–203.

Johnson, D. W., & Johnson, R. (1979). Conflict in the classroom: Controversy and learning. *Review of Education Research, 49,* 51–61.

Johnson, D. W., & Johnson, R. (1983). The socialization and achievement crises: Are cooperative learning experiences the solution? In L. Bickman (Ed.), *Applied social psychology annual 4.* Beverly Hills, CA: Sage.

Johnson, D. W., & Johnson, R. (1985). Classroom conflict: Controversy versus debate in learning groups. *American Educational Research Journal, 22,* 237–256.

Johnson, D. W. & Johnson, R. (1987). *Joining together: Group theory and group skills* (3rd Ed.). Englewood Cliffs, NJ: Prentice-Hall.

Johnson, D. W., Johnson, R. T., & Holubec, E. (1986). *Circles of learning: Cooperation in the classroom* (Rev. Ed.). Edina, MN: Interaction Book.

Johnson, D. W., Johnson, R. T., & Maruyama, G. (1983). Interdependence and interpersonal attraction among heterogeneous and homogeneous individuals. A theoretical formulation and a meta-analysis of the research. *Review of Educational Research, 53,* 5–54.

Johnson, D. W., & Johnson, R. T., Pierson, W., & Lyons, V. (1985). Controversy versus concurrence seeking in multi-grade and single-grade learning groups. *Journal of Research in Science Teaching, 22*(9), 835–848.

Johnson, D. W., Johnson, R. T., & Smith, K. (1986). Academic conflict among students: Controversy and Learning. In R. Feldman (Ed.), *Social psychological applications to education.* Cambridge University Press.

Johnson, D. W., Johnson, R. T., & Tiffany, M. (1984). Structuring academic conflicts between majority and minority students: Hindrance or help to integration. *Contemporary Educational Psychology, 9,* 61–73.

Johnson, D. W., Maruyama, G., Johnson, R. T., Nelson, D. & Skon, S. (1981). Effects of cooperative, competitive, and individualistic goal structures on achievement: A meta-analysis. *Psychological Bulletin, 89,* 47–62.

Johnson, P. E., Duran, A. S., Hassebrock, F., Moller, J., Prietula, M., Feltovick, P. J., & Swanson, D. B. (1981). Expertise and error in diagnostic reasoning. *Cognitive Science, 5,* 235–283.

Johnson, R., Brooker, C., Stutzman, J., Hultman, D., & Johnson, D. W. (1985). The effects of controversy, concurrence seeking, and individualistic learning on achievement and attitude change. *Journal of Research in Science Teaching, 22,* 197–205.

Johnson, T. E., & Rule, B. G. (1986). Mitigating circumstance information, censure, and aggression. *Journal of Personality and Social Psychology, 50,* 537–542.

Jones, E. E., & Nisbett, R. E. (1971). *The actor and the observer: Divergent perceptions of the causes of behavior.* Morristown, NJ: General Learning Press.

Jones, T. S. (1985). *"Breaking up is hard to do": An exploratory investigation of communication tactics and phases in child-custody divorce mediation.* Unpublished doctoral dissertation, Ohio State University.

Kabanoff, B. (1985). Potential influence structures as sources of interpersonal conflict in groups and organizations. *Organizational Behavior and Human Performance, 33,* 42–76.

Kabanoff, B. (1985, August). *Do feelings of cooperativeness and assertiveness affect the choice of conflict management mode?* Paper presented at the annual meeting of the Academy of Management, San Diego, CA.

Kabanoff, B. (1986). *The type of power, affect and preference for different conflict modes.* Unpublished manuscript. Australian Graduate School of Management, University of New South Wales, Kensington, Australia.

Kabanoff, B. (1987). Predictive validity of the MODE conflict instrument. *Journal of Applied Psychology, 72,* 160–163.

Kahneman, D., Slovic, P., & Tversky, A. (Eds). (1982). *Judgment under uncertainty: Heuristics and biases.* New York: Cambridge University Press.

Kahneman, D., & Tversky, A. (1982). Availability and the simulation heuristic. In D. Kahneman, P. Slovic, & A. Tversky (Eds.), *Judgment under uncertainty: Heuristics and biases* (pp. 201–208). Cambridge, UK: Cambridge University Press.

Kaplan, M. (1977). Discussion polarization effects in a modern jury decision paradigm: Informational influences. *Sociometry, 40,* 262–271.

Kaplan, M., & Miller, C. (1977). Judgments and group discussion: Effect of presentation and memory factors on polarization. *Sociometry, 40,* 337–343.

Katz, D., & Kahn, R. L. (1978). *The social psychology of organizations.* New York: Wiley.

Katz, J. M. (1978). *Discrepancy, arousal and labeling: Towards a psychosocial theory of emotion.* Paper presented at World Congress of Sociology, Uppsala, Sweden.

Kelley, G. A. (1955). *The psychology of personal constructs.* New York: Norton.

Kelley, H. H. (1984). Affect in interpersonal relations. In P. Shaver (Ed.), *Review of personality and social psychology* (pp. 89–115). Beverly Hills, CA: Sage.

Kelley, H. H. (1979). *Personal relationships: Their structure and processes.* Hillsdale, NJ: Erlbaum Associates.

Kelley, H. H. (1972). Attribution in social interaction. In E. E. Jones, D. Kanouse, H. Kelley, R. Nisbett, S. Valins, & B. Wiener (Eds.), *Attribution: Perceiving the causes of behavior* (pp. 179–191). Morristown, NJ: General Learning Press.

Kelley, H. H. (1965). Experimental studies of threats in interpersonal negotiations. *Journal of Conflict Resolution, 9,* 80–107.

Kelley, H. H., & Schenitzki, D. P. (1972). Bargaining. In C. G. McClintock (Ed.), *Experimental social psychology* (pp. 298–337). New York: Holt, Rinehart, and Winston.

Kelly, J. (1983). Mediation and psychotherapy: Distinguishing the difference. *Mediation Quarterly, 1,* 33–44.

Keough, C. M. (in press). The nature and function of argument in organizational bargaining research. *Southern Speech Communication Journal.*

Kiesler, D. J. (1983). The 1982 interpersonal circle: A taxonomy for complementarity in human transactions. *Psychological Review, 90,* 185–214.

Kiggundu, M. N. (1981). Task interdependence and the theory of job design. *Academy of Management Review, 6,* 499–508.

Kiggundu, M. N. (1983). Task interdependence and job design: Test of a theory. *Organizational Behavior and Human Performance, 31,* 145–172.

Kilmann, R. H., & Thomas, K. W. (1975). Interpersonal conflict-handling behavior as reflections of Jungian personality dimensions. *Psychological Reports, 37,* 971–980.

Kilmann, R. H., & Thomas, K. W. (1977). Developing a forced-choice measure of conflict-handling behavior: The "MODE" instrument. *Educational and Psychological Measurement, 37,* 309–325.

Kilmann, R. H., & Thomas, K. W. (1978). Four perspectives on conflict management: An attributional framework for organizing descriptive and normative theory. *Academy of Management Review, 3,* 59–68.

Kimmel, M. J., Pruitt, D. G., Magenau, J. M., Konar-Goldband, E., & Carnevale, P. J. D. (1980). Effects of trust, aspiration, and gender on negotiation tactics. *Journal of Personality and Social Psychology, 38,* 9–22.

Kleinhesselink, R., & Edwards, R. (1975). Seeking and avoiding belief-discrepant information as a function of its perceived refutability. *Journal of Personality and Social Psychology, 31,* 787–790.

Klimoski, R. J., & Ash, R. A. (1974). Accountability and negotiator behavior. *Organizational Behavior and Human Performance, 11,* 409–425.

Kochan, T. A., & Jick, T. (1978). The public sector mediation process: A theory and empirical examination. *Journal of Conflict Resolution, 22,* 209–240.

Kochan, T. A., & Verma, A. (1982). Negotiations in organizations. Blending industrial relations and organizational behavior approaches. In M. Bazerman & R. Lewiciki (Eds.), *Negotiating in organizations* (pp. 13–32). Beverly Hills, CA: Sage.

Kochan, T. A., & Verma, A. (1983). Negotiations in organizations: Blending industrial relations and organizational behavior approaches. In M. H. Bazerman & R. J. Lewicki (Eds.), *Negotiating in organizations* (pp. 13–32). Beverly Hills: Sage.

Kogler-Hill, S. E., & Courtright, J. (1981). Perceived empathy: Its relationship to selected interpersonal variables and student's interpersonal laboratory performance. *Western Journal of Speech Communication, 45,* 213–226.

Kohlberg, L. (1969). Stage and sequence: The cognitive-developmental approach to socialization. In D. A. Goslin (Ed.), *Handbook of socialization theory and research* (pp. 347–480). Chicago: Rand McNally.

Kolb, D. (1983). *The mediators.* Cambridge, MA: MIT Press.

Kolb, D. M. (1985). To be a mediator: Expressive tactics in mediation. *Journal of Social Issues, 41,* 11–26.

Kolb, D. M. & Sheppard, B. H. (1985). Do managers mediate, or even arbitrate? *Negotiation Journal, 1,* 379–388.

Komorita, S. S. (1984). Coalition bargaining. In L. Berkowitz (Ed.), *Advances in experimental social psychology, 18,* NY: Academic Press.

Koopman, E. J. (1985). The teaching of family dispute resolution in colleges and universities. *Proceedings of the 12th annual conference of the society for professionals in dispute resolution, 10,* 325–334.

Koopman, E. J. (1987, April). *Principles and practices in child centered mediation of custody disputes.* Symposium conducted at the meeting of the National Conciliation Council, Bath, England.

Koopman, E. J., & Hunt, E. J. (1983). Divorce mediation: Issues in defining, educating and implementing a new and needed profession. *Conciliation Courts Review, 21*(2), 25–37.

Koopman, E. J., & Hunt, E. J. *Relational restructuring: Applying concepts of divorce law and conflict resolution in mediating post divorce parenting agreements.* Manuscript submitted for publication.

Koopman, E. J., Hunt, E. J., & Favretto, F. G. (1987). *Custody mediation in court settings: An examination of selected critical variables.* Unpublished manuscript, Department of Human Development, University of Maryland, College Park.

Koopman, E. J., Hunt, E. J., & Stafford, V. (1984). Child related agreements in mediated and nonmediated divorce settlements: A preliminary examination and discussion of implications. *Conciliation Courts Review, 22*(1), 19–25.

Koren, P., Carlton, K., & Shaw, D. (1980). Marital conflict: Relations among behaviors, outcomes, and distress. *Journal of Consulting and Clinical Psychology, 48,* 460–468.

Kozan, K. (1986). *Conflict management styles of Jordanian managers.* Unpublished manuscript, Yamouk University, Jordan.

Krauss, R. M., & Deutsch, M. (1966). Communication in interpersonal bargaining. *Journal of Personality and Social Psychology, 4,* 572–577.

Kravitz, J. H. (1987, June). *Conflict management during crisis and noncrisis situations: An examination of managerial preferences.* Paper presented at the International Conference of the Conflict Management Group, Fairfax, VA.

Kremer, J. F., & Stephens, L. (1983). Attributions and arousal as mediators of mitigation's effect on retaliation. *Journal of Personality and Social Psychology, 45,* 335–343.

Kressel, K. (1977). Labor mediation: An exploratory survey. In D. Lewin, P. Feuille & T. Kochan (Eds.), *Public sector labor relations* (pp. 252–272). Glen Ridge, NJ: Horton.

Kressel, K. (1985). *The process of divorce.* New York: Basic Books.

Kressel, K., Jaffee, N., Tuchman, B., Watson, C., & Deutsch, M. (1980). A typology of divorcing couples: Implications for mediation and the divorce process. *Family Process, 19,* 101–116.

Kristof, W. (1969). Estimation of true score and error variance for tests under various equivalence assumptions. *Psychometrika, 34,* 489–507.

Kuhn, T. S. (1962). *The structure of scientific revolutions.* Chicago: University of Chicago Press.

Kuiper, N. A., & Derry, P. (1981). The self as a cognitive prototype: An application to person perception and depression. In N. Cantor & J. F. Kihlstrom (Eds.), *Personality, cognition and social interaction* (pp. 215–232). NJ: Erlbaum.

Lamm, D. (1985a). Justice considerations in interpersonal conflict. In H. W. Bierhoff, R. L. Cohen, & J. Greenberg (Eds.), *Justice in social relations.* New York: Plenum Press.

Lamm, D. (1985b). *The structure of scientific revolutions.* Chicago: University of Chicago Press.

Landsberger, H. A. (1955). Interaction process analysis of mediation in labor-management disputes. *Journal of Applied Social Psychology, 57,* 552–558.

Landy, F. J., & Farr, J. L. (1982). *The measurement of work performance.* New York: Academic Press.

Langer, E. J. (1978). Rethinking the role of thought in social interaction. In J. Harvey, W. Ickes, & R. F. Kidd (Eds.), *New directions in attribution research, Vol. 2* (pp. 35–58). Hillsdale, NJ: Lawrence Erlbaum Associates.

Larson, J. R., Jr. (1984). The performance feedback process: A preliminary model. *Organizational Behavior and Human Performance, 33,* 42–76.

Larson, J. R., Jr. (1986). Supervisors' performance feedback to subordinates: The impact of subordinate performance valence and outcome dependence. *Organizational Behavior and Human Decision Processes, 37,* 391–408.

Lau, R. R., & Sears, D. (Eds.), (1986). *Political cognition.* NJ: Erlbaum.

Lawler, E. E., III. (1973). *Motivation in work organizations.* Monterey, CA: Brooks/Cole.

Lawrence, P. R., & Lorsch, J. W. (1967). Differentiation and integration in complex organizations. *Administrative Science Quarterly, 12,* 1–47.

Lax, D. A., & Sebenius, J. K. (1984). *Negotiation and management: Some analytical themes,* Technical Report 84–34, Harvard Business School.

Lax, D. A., & Sebenius, J. K. (1986). *The manager as negotiator.* New York: Free Press.

Lee, K. N. (1982, Spring) Defining success in environmental dispute resolution. *Resolve,* 1–5.

Lentz, S. S. (1986). The labor model for mediation and its application to the resolution of environmental disputes. *Journal of Applied Behavioral Science, 22,* 1277–139.

Lusch, R. F. (1976). Sources of power: Their impact on interchannel conflict. *Journal of Marketing Research, 13,* 382–390.

Levinthal, G. S. (1976). Fairness in social relationships. In J. W. Thibaut, J. T. Spence & R. C. Carson (Eds.), *Contemporary topics in social psychology.* Morristown, NJ: General Learning Press.

Levy, M. A. (1985). Mediation of prisoner's dilemma conflicts and the importance of the cooperation threshold: The case of Namibia. *Journal of Conflict Resolution, 29,* 581–603.

Lewicki, R. J. (1982). Ethical concerns in conflict management. In G. B. J. Bomers & R. B. Peterson (Eds.), *Conflict management and industrial relations* (pp. 423–445). Boston: Kluwer-Nijhoff.

Lewicki, R. J., & Litterer, J. A. (1985). *Negotiation.* Homewood, IL: Irwin.

Lewicki, R. J., Weiss, S. E., & Lewin, D. (1987). *Models of conflict, negotiation and conflict intervention: A review and synthesis.* Working Paper No. 87102), Graduate School of Business Administration, Ohio State University.

Lewin, K. (1951). *Field theory in social science.* New York: Harper.

Lewis, S. A., & Fry, W. R. (1977). Effects of visual access and orientation on the discovery of integrative bargaining alternatives. *Organizational Behavior and Human Performance, 20,* 75–92.

Liden, R. C., & Mitchell, T. R. (1985). Reactions to feedback: The role of attributions. *Academy of Management Journal, 28,* 291–308.

Lieberman, M. (1979). *Bargaining*. Chicago: Teach 'Em.

Likert, R., & Likert, J. G. (1976). *New ways of managing conflict*. New York: McGraw-Hill.

Lingoes, J. C., & Roskam, E. E. (1973). A mathematical and empirical analysis of two multidimensional scaling algorithms. *Psychometrika, 38*, 4 (Monograph supplement).

Linville, P. W. (1982). The complexity-extremity effect and age-based stereotyping. *Journal of Personality and Social Psychology, 42*, 193–211.

Linville, P. W., & Jones, E. E. (1980). Polarized appraisals of outgroup members. *Journal of Personality and Social Psychology, 38*, 689–703.

Lissak, R. I., & Sheppard, B. H. (1983). Beyond fairness: The criterion problem in research on conflict intervention: *Journal of Applied Social Psychology, 13*, 45–65.

Littlejohn, S. W., & Shailor, J. (1986). *The deep structure of conflict in mediation: A case study*. Paper presented at the Speech Communication Association convention, Chicago, IL.

Locke, E. A. (1968). Toward a theory of task motivation and incentives. *Organizational Behavior and Human Performance, 3*, 157–189.

Locke, E. A., Latham, G. P., & Erez, M. (in press). The determinants of goal commitment. *Academy of Management Review*.

Locke, E. A., Shaw, K. N., Saari, L. M., Latham, G. P. (1981). Goal setting and task performance: 1969–1980. *Psychological Bulletin, 90*, 125–152.

Lord, R. G., & Kernan, M. C. (1987). Scripts as determinants of purposeful behavior in organizations. *Academy of Management Review, 12*, 265–277.

Louis, M. R. (1977). How individuals conceptualize conflict: Identification of steps in the process and the role of personal/developmental factors. *Human Relations, 30*, 451–467.

Lovell, H. G. (1952). The pressure lever in mediation. *Industrial and Labor Relations Review, 6*, 20–30.

Lowin, A. (1969). Further evidence for an approach-avoidance interpretation of selective exposure. *Journal of Experimental Social Psychology, 5*, 265–271.

Lowry, N., & Johnson, D. W. (1981). Effects of controversy on epistemic curiosity, achievement, and attitudes. *Journal of Social Psychology, 115*, 31–43.

Magenau, J. (1980, August). *A laboratory experiment on alternative impasse procedures in bargaining*. Paper presented at the annual meeting of the Academy of Management, Detroit, MI.

Maggiolo, W. A. (1985). *Techniques of mediation*. Dobbs Ferry, New York: Ocean Publications.

Mallick, S. K., & McCandless, B. R. (1966). A study of catharsis of aggression. *Journal of Personality and Social Psychology, 4*, 591–596.

Manson, J. J. (1958). Mediators and their qualifications. *Labor Law Journal, 9*, 755–764.

March, J. G., & Simon, H. A. (1958). *Organizations*. New York: Wiley.

Markowitz, J. R., & Engram, P. S. (1983). Mediation in labor disputes and divorces: A comparative analysis. *Mediation Quarterly, 2*, 67–78.

Markus, H., & Smith, J. (1981). The influence of self schemas on the perception of others. In N. Cantor & J. F. Kihlstrom (Eds.), *Personality, Cognition and Social Interaction* (pp. 233–262). Hillsdale, NJ: Erlbaum.

Markus, H., Smith, J., & Moreland, R. (1985). The role of self concept in the perception of others. *Journal of Personality and Social Psychology, 49,* 14944–1512.

Martin, J., Scully, M., & Levitt, B. (1986, August). Revolutionary visions of injustice and justice: Damning the past, excusing the present, and neglecting the future. In R. J. Bies & S. B. Sitkin (Co-Chairs), *Justification in organizations: Leadership through excuse-making.* Symposium conducted at the annual meeting of the Academy of Management, Chicago.

Mason, R. O. (1969). A dialectical approach to strategic planning. *Management Science, 15,* B403–B414.

Mayo, E. (1945). *The social problems of an industrial civilization.* Boston: Harvard University Press.

McEwen, C., & Maiman, R. (1982). Arbitration and mediation as alternatives to court. *Policy Studies Journal, 10,* 712–726.

McGillicuddy, N. B., Welton, G. L., & Pruitt, D. G. (1987). Third-party intervention: A field experiment comparing three different models. *Journal of Personality and Social Psychology, 53,* 104–112.

McGrath, J. E. (1966). A social psychological approach to the study of negotiation. In R. Bowers (Ed.), *Studies on behavior in organizations: A research symposium* (pp. 101–134). Athens, GA: University of Georgia Press.

McGrath, J. E., & Julian, J. W. (1963). Interaction process and task outcome in experimentally-created negotiation groups. *Journal of Psychological Studies, 14,* 117–138.

McIsaac, H. (1986). Toward a classification of child custody disputes: An application of family systems theory. *Mediation Quarterly, 14–15,* 39–50.

McKenry, P. C., Herrman, M. S., & Weber, R. E. (1979). Attitudes of attorneys toward divorce issues. *Conciliation Court Review, 16,* 11–17.

Mendenhall, A. (1968). *Introduction to linear models and the design and analysis of experiments.* Belmont, CA: Wadsworth.

Menninger, K. A. (1954). Regulatory devices of the ego under major stress. *International Journal of Psychoanalysis, 35,* 412–420.

Merriam-Webster. (1986). *Webster's ninth new collegiate dictionary.* Springfield, MA.

Merry, S. E. (in press). Mediation in small-scale societies. In K. Kressel & D. G. Pruitt (Eds.), *The mediation of disputes.* San Francisco: Jossey-Bass.

Mettetal, G., & Gottman, J. M. (1980, November). *Affective responsiveness in spouses: Investigating the relationship between communication behavior and marital satisfaction.* Paper presented at the Speech Communication Association Convention, New York, NY.

Meyer, B. S., & Schlissel, S. W. (1982). Child custody following divorce: How grasp the nettle? *New York State Bar Journal, 54,* 496–501.

Miller, C. E., & Wong, J. (1986). Coalition behavior: Effects of earned vs. unearned resources. *Organizational Behavior and Human Performance, 38,* 257–277.

Miller, G. R., & Berger, C. R. (1978). On keeping the faith in matters scientific. *Western Journal of Speech Communication, 42,* 44–57.

Miller, M., Brehmer, B., & Hammond, K. (1970). Communication and conflict resolution: A cross-cultural study. *International Journal of Psychology, 5,* 75–87.

Mills, J., Robey, D., & Smith, L. (1985). Conflict-handling and personality dimensions of project-management personnel. *Psychological Reports, 57,* 1135–1143.

Milne, A. (1978). Custody of children in a divorce process: A family self-determination model. *Conciliation Courts Review, 16,* 1–10.

Mintzberg, H. (1973). *The nature of managerial work.* New York: Harper & Row.

Moore, C. A. (1967). *The Japanese mind.* Hawaii: University of Hawaii Press.

Moore, C. W. (1983). *A general theory of mediation: Dynamics, strategies, and moves.* Unpublished doctoral dissertation, Rutgers University.

Moore, C. W. (1986). *The mediation process: Practical strategies for resolving conflict.* San Francisco: Jossey-Bass.

Moore, C. W. (1987). The caucus: Private meetings that promote settlement. *Mediator quarterly,* Whole Number 16, 87–101.

Morbasch, H. (1980). Major psychological factors influencing Japanese interpersonal relations. In N. Warren (Ed.) *Studies in cross cultural psychology, Vol. 2* (pp. 317–344). New York: Academic Press.

Morley, D. D. (1984). Corrections to lag sequential results in communication research: An introduction. *Human Communication Research, 11,* 121–123.

Morley, D. D. (1987). Revised lag sequential analysis. In M. McLaughlin (Ed.), *Communication yearbook 10.* Beverly Hills, CA: Sage.

Morley, D. D., & Shockley-Zalabak, P. (1986). Conflict avoiders and compromisers: Toward an understanding of their organizational communication style. *Group & organization studies, 11,* 387–402.

Morley, I., & Stephenson, G. (1977). *The social psychology of bargaining.* London: George Allen and Unwin, Ltd.

Murnighan, K. (1985). Coalitions in decision making groups: Organizational analogs. *Organizational Behavior and Human Decision Processes, 35,* 1–26.

Murray, F. (1983). *Cognitive benefits of teaching on the teacher.* Paper presented at the annual meeting of the American Educational Research Association Annual Meeting, Montreal, Quebec.

Musser, S. J. (1982). A model for predicting the choice of conflict management strategies by subordinates in high stakes conflicts. *Organizational Behavioral and Human Performance, 29,* 257–269.

Nader, L. (1979). Disputing without the force of law. *Yale Law Journal, 88,* 998–1021.

Nakamura, H. (1964). *Ways of thinking of Eastern peoples: India, China, Tibet and Japan.* Hawaii: University Press.

Nakane, C. (1970). *Japanese society.* Berkeley: University of California Press.

Nash, J. (1950). The bargaining problem. *Econometrica, 18,* 128–140.

Neale, M. A. (1983). *The effects of negotiation and arbitration salience upon bargainer behavior.* Unpublished paper, University of Arizona, Tuscon.

Neale, M. A. (1984). The effect of negotiation and arbitration cost salience on bargainer behavior: The role of arbitrator and constituency in negotiator judgment. *Organizational Behavior and Human Performance, 36,* 97–111.

Neale, M. A., & Bazerman, M. H. (1983). The role of perspective taking ability in negotiating under different forms of arbitration. *Industrial and Labor Relations Review, 36,* 378–388.

Neale, M. A., & Bazerman, M. H. (1985a). Perspectives for understanding negotiation: Viewing negotiation as a judgemental process. *Journal of Conflict Resolution, 29,* 33–55.

Neale, M. A., & Bazerman, M. H. (1985b). The effects of framing and negotiator overconfidence on bargainer behavior. *Academy of management journal, 28,* 34–49.

Neale, M. A., Huber, V. L., & Northcraft, G. B. (1987). The framing of negotiations: Contextual versus task frames. *Organizational Behavior and Human Decision Processes, 39,* 228–241.

Neale, M. A., & Northcraft, G. B. (1986). Experts, amateurs, and refrigerators: Comparing expert and amateur decision making in a novel task. *Organizational Behavior and Human Decision Processes, 38,* 305–317.

Neale, M. A. & Northcraft, G. B. (in press). Experience, expertise and decision bias in negotiation: The role of strategic conceptualization. In B. Sheppard, R. J. Lewicki & M. H. Bazerman (Eds.), *Negotiating in organizations.* Greenwich, CT: JAI Press.

Nel, G., Helmreich, R., & Aronson, E. (1969). Opinion change in the advocate as a function of the persuasibility of his audience: A clarification of the meaning of dissonance. *Journal of Personality and Social Psychology, 12,* 117–124.

Nesdale, A. R., Rule, B. G., & McAra, M. (1975). Moral judgments of aggression: Personal and situational determinants. *European Journal of Social Psychology, 5,* 339–349.

Nijhof, W., & Kommers, P. (1982, July). *Analysis of cooperation in relation to cognitive controversy.* Second International Conference on Cooperation in Education, Provo, UT.

Nisbett, R., & Ross, L. (1980). *Human inference: Strategies and shortcomings of social judgment.* Englewood Cliffs, NJ: Prentice-Hall.

Nobles, W. S. (1978). Analyzing the proposition. In D. Ehninger & W. Brockreide (Eds.), *Decision by debate* (2nd Ed.) (pp. 151–173). New York: Harper & Row.

Northcraft, G. B., & Neale, M. A. (1986). Opportunity costs and the framing of resource allocation decisions. *Organizational Behavior and Human Decision Processes, 37,* 28–38.

Northcraft, G. B., & Neale, M. A. (1987). Experts, amateurs, and real estate: An anchoring-and-adjustment perspective on property pricing decisions. *Organizational Behavior and Human Decision Processes, 39,* 84–97.

Norton, R. (1980). Nonmetric multidimensional scaling in communication research: Smallest space analysis. In P. R. Monge & J. N. Cappella (Eds.), *Multivariate techniques in human communication research* (pp. 309–331). New York: Academic Press.

Notz, W. W., & Starke, F. A. (1978). Final offer vs. conventional arbitration as means of conflict management. *Administrative Science Quarterly, 23,* 189–203.

O'Quin, K., & Aranoff, J. (1979, September). *Eliciting compliance: Humor as a technique of social control.* Paper presented at the annual convention of the American Psychological Association, New York.

O'Reilly, C. A., & Weitz, B. A. (1980). *Conflict styles and sanction use.* Unpublished manuscript. University of California, Los Angeles, CA.

Organ, D. W. (1971). Some variables affecting boundary role behavior. *Sociometry, 34,* 524–537.

Orvis, B. R., Kelley, H. H., & Butler, D. (1976). Attributional conflict in young couples. In J. H. Harvey, W. J. Ickes, & R. F. Kidd (Eds.), *New directions in attribution research Vol. 1* (pp. 353–386). Hillsdale, NJ: Erlbaum Associates.

Patterson, J. W., & Zarefsky, D. (1983). *Contemporary debate*. Boston, MA: Houghton Mifflin.

Pearce, W. B. (1976). The coordinated management of meaning: A rules-based theory of interpersonal communication. In G. R. Miller (Ed.), *Explorations in interpersonal communication* (pp. 17–35). Beverly Hills: Sage.

Pearce, W. B. (1978). The "ecumenical spirit": A reply to Miller & Berger. *Western Journal of Speech Communication, 42*, 276–280.

Pearce, W. B., & Cronen, V. E. (1980). *Communication, action and meaning*. New York: Praeger.

Pearson, J. (1981). Child custody: Why not let the parents decide? *Judge's Journal, 20*(1), 4–10.

Pearson, J., & Thoennes, N. (1984a). Mediating and litigating custody disputes: A longitudinal evaluation. *Family Law Quarterly, 17*, 497–524.

Pearson, J., & Thoennes, N. (1984b). The preliminary portrait of client reactions to three court mediation programs. *Mediation Quarterly, 3*, 21–40.

Pearson, J., Thoennes, N., & Vanderkooi, L. (1982). The decision to mediate: Profiles of individuals who accept and reject the opportunity to mediate contested child custody and visitation issues. *Journal of Divorce, 6*(1/2), 17–36.

Peters, E. (1952). *Conciliation in action*. New London: National Forman's Institute.

Peters, T. J., & Waterman, R. H. (1982). *In search of excellence*. New York: Harper & Row.

Pfeffer, J. (1981). *Power in organizations*. Marshfield, MA: Pitman.

Pfeffer, J., & Leong, A. (1977). Resource allocations in United Funds: Examination of power and dependence. *Social Forces, 55*, 775–790.

Pfeffer, J., & Moore, W. (1980). Power in university budgeting: A replication and extension. *Administrative Science Quarterly, 25*, 637–653.

Pfeffer, J., & Salancik, G. R. (1974). Organizational decision making as a political process: The case of a university budget. *Administrative Science Quarterly, 19*, 35–151.

Piaget, J. (1948). *The moral judgement of the child* (2nd Ed.). Glencoe, IL: The Free Press.

Piaget, J. (1950). *The psychology of intelligence*. New York: Harcourt.

Pilisuk, M., Kiritz, S., & Clampitt, S. (1971). Undoing deadlocks of distrust: Hip Berkeley students and the ROTC. *Journal of Conflict Resolution, 15*, 81–95.

Pondy, L. R. (1967). Organizational conflict: Concepts and models. *Administrative Science Quarterly, 12*, 296–320.

Posner, M. I., & Keele, S. W. (1968). On the genesis of abstract ideas. *Journal of Experimental Psychology, 77*, 353–363.

Posner, M. I., & Keele, S. W. (1970). Retention of abstract ideas. *Journal of Experimental Psychology, 83*, 304–308.

Prein, H. C. M. (1976). Stijlen van conflicthantering [Styles of conflict management]. *Nederlands tijdschrift voor de psychologie, 31*, 321–346.

Prein, H. C. M. (1984, August). *The use of conflict-handling modes*. Paper presented at the Organization Development World Congress, Southampton, England.

Provan, K. G., Beyer, J. M., & Kruytbosch, C. (1980). Environmental linkages and power in resource-dependent relations between organizations. *Administrative Science Quarterly, 25*, 200–225.

Pruitt, D. G. (1971). Indirect communication and the search for agreement in negotiation. *Journal of Applied Social Psychology, 1,* 204–239.

Pruitt, D. G. (1981). *Negotiation behavior.* New York: Academic Press.

Pruitt, D. G. (1983a). *Achieving integrative agreements. In M. Bazerman & R. Lewicki (Eds.), Negotiating in organizations* (pp. 35–50). Beverly Hills, CA: Sage.

Pruitt, D. G. (1983b). Strategic choice in negotiation. *American behavioral scientist, 27,* 167–194.

Pruitt, D. G. (1986). Achieving integrative agreements in negotiation. In R. K. White (Ed.), *Psychology and the prevention of nuclear war* (pp. 463–478). New York: New York University Press.

Pruitt, D. G., & Gleason, J. M. (1978). Threat capacity and the choice between independence and interdependence. *Personality and social psychology bulletin, 4,* 252–255.

Pruitt, D. G., Kimmel, M. J., Britton, S., Carnevale, P. J., Magenau, J. M., Peragallo, J., & Engram, P. (1978). The effect of accountability and surveillance on integrative bargaining. In H. Sauermann (Ed.), *Contributions to experimental economics Vol. 7* (pp. 310–343). Tübingen: Mohr.

Pruitt, D. G., & Kressel, K. (1985). The mediation of conflict: An introduction. *Journal of Social Issues, 41(2),* 1–10.

Pruitt, D. G., & Lewis, S. A. (1975). Development of integrative solutions in bilateral negotiations. *Journal of Personality and Social Psychology, 31,* 621–633.

Pruitt, D. G., & Lewis, S. A. (1977). The psychology of integrative bargaining. In D. Druckman (Ed.), *Negotiations: Psychological perspectives,* New York: Sage.

Pruitt, D. G., & Rubin, J. Z. (1986). *Social conflict: Escalation, stalemate and settlement.* New York: Random House.

Pruitt, D. G., & Syna, H. (1983). Successful problem solving. In D. Tjosvold & D. W. Johnson (Eds.), *Productive conflict management: Perspectives for organizations* (pp. 62–81). New York: Irvington.

Putnam, L. L. (in press). Reframing integrative and distributive bargaining: An interaction perspective. In B. H. Sheppard, M. H. Bazerman, & R. J. Lewicki (Eds.), *Research on negotiation in organizations, Vol. 2.* Greenwich, CT: JAI Press.

Putnam, L. L., & Geist, P. (1985). Argument in bargaining: An analysis of the reasoning process. *Southern Speech Communication Journal, 50,* 225–245.

Putnam, L. L. & Jones, T. S. (1982a). Reciprocity in negotiations: An analysis of bargaining interaction. *Communication Monographs, 49,* 171–191.

Putnam, L. L., & Jones, T. S. (1982b). The role of communication in bargaining. *Human Communication Research, 8,* 262–280.

Putnam, L. L., & Poole, M. S. (in press). Conflict and negotiation. In F. M. Jablin, L. L. Putnam, K. H. Roberts, & L. W. Porter (Eds.), *Handbook of organizational communication.* Beverly Hills, CA: Sage Publications.

Putnam, L. L., & Wilson, C. E. (1982). In: M. Burgoon (Ed.), *Communication yearbook, Vol. 6.* Beverly Hills, CA: Sage.

Putnam, L. L., Wilson, S. R., Waltman, M. S. & Turner, D. (1986). The evolution of case arguments in teachers' bargaining. *Journal of the American Forensic Association, 23,* 63–81.

Rahim, M. A. (1977). The management of organizational intergroup conflict: A contingency model. *Proceedings of the annual meeting of the Midwest American Institute for Decision Sciences* (pp. 247–249). Cleveland, OH.

Rahim, M. A. (1983a). *Rahim organizational conflict inventory-II: Form C*. Palo Alto, CA: Consulting Psychologists Press.

Rahim, M. A. (1983b). A measure of styles of handling interpersonal conflicts. *Academy of Management Journal, 26*, 368–376.

Rahim, M. A. (1983c). *Rahim organizational conflict inventories: Professional manual*. Palo Alto, CA: Consulting Psychologists Press.

Rahim, M. A. (1986a). *Managing conflict in organizations*. New York: Praeger.

Rahim, M. A. (1986b). Referent role and styles of handling interpersonal conflict. *Journal of Social Psychology, 126*, 79–86.

Rahim, A., & Bonoma, T. V. (1979). Managing organizational conflict: A model for diagnosis and intervention. *Psychological Reports, 44*, 1323–1344.

Raiffa, H. (1982). *The art and science of negotiation*. Cambridge, MA: The Belknap Press of Harvard University Press.

Rapoport, A. (1973). *Two-person game theory: The essential ideas*. Ann Arbor: University of Michigan Press.

Rapoport, A., & Chammah, A. (1965). *Prisoner's dilemma: A study in conflict and cooperation*. Ann Arbor, MI: University of Michigan Press.

Rasmussen, K., & DeStephen, D. (1978). Building cases. In D. Ehninger & W. Brockriede (Eds.), *Decision by debate* (pp. 174–201). New York: Harper.

Reed, S. K. (1972). Pattern recognition and categorization. *Cognitive Psychology, 3*, 382–407.

Rempel, J. K., Holmes, J. G., & Zanna, M. P. (1985). Trust in close relationships. *Journal of Personality and Social Psychology, 49*, 95–117.

Renwick, P. A. (1975). Perception and management of supervisor-subordinate conflict. *Organizational Behavior and Human Performance, 13*, 444–456.

Richardson, B. M., & Ueda, T. (1981). *Business and society in Japan*. New York: Praeger.

Rieke, R. D., & Sillars, M. O. (1984). *Argumentation and the decision making process*. Glenview, IL: Scott, Foresman.

Riker, W. (1962). *The theory of political coalitions*. New Haven, CT: Yale University Press.

Riskin, L. L. (1982). Mediation and lawyers. *Ohio State Law Journal, 43*, 29–60.

Robbins, S. P. (1978). Conflict management and conflict resolutions are not synonymous terms. *California Management Review, 21*(2). 67–75.

Roling, B. V. A. (1966). The role of law in conflict resolution. In de Reuck & Knight (Eds.), *Conflict in society*. Boston: Little Brown.

Roloff, M. E. (1976). Communication strategies, relationships, and relational change. In G. R. Miller (Ed.), *Explorations in interpersonal communication* (pp. 173–196). Beverly Hills, CA: Sage.

Roloff, M. E., & Campion, D. E. (1987). On alleviating the debilitating effects of accountability on bargaining: Authority and self-monitoring. *Communication Monographs, 54*, 145–164.

Roloff, M. E., Tutzauer, F. E., & Dailey, W. O. (1987). *The role of argumentation in distributive and integrative contexts*. Paper presented at the International Conference of the Conflict Management Group, Fairfax, VA.

Roseman, I. J. (1984). Cognitive determinants of emotion: A structural theory. In P. Shaver (Ed.), *Review of personality and social psychology, Vol. 5* (pp. 11–36). Beverly Hills, CA.: Sage.

Rosen, S., & Tesser, A. (1970). On the reluctance of communicating undesirable information: The MUM effect. *Sociology, 33,* 253–263.

Ross, L. (1977). The intuitive psychologist and his shortcomings. *Advances in experimental social psychology, 10,* 173–220.

Ross, W. H. (1986). *The effects of motivational and content control upon dispute mediation.* Unpublished doctoral dissertation, University of Illinois at Urbana-Champaign.

Rousseau, D. R. (1987). *The impact of psychological and implied contracts on behavior in organizations.* Manuscript submitted for publication.

Rubin, J. Z., Brockner, J., Eckenrode, J., Enright, M. A., & Johnson-George, C. (1981). Weakness as strength: Text of a "my hands are tied" ploy in bargaining. *Personality and Social Psychology Bulletin, 6,* 216–221.

Rubin, J. Z., & Brown, B. R. (1975). *The social psychology of bargaining and negotiation.* NY: Academic Press.

Ruble, T. L., & Thomas, K. W. (1976). Support for a two-dimensional model of conflict behavior. *Organizational Behavior and Human Performance, 16,* 143–155.

Rule, B. G., Dyck, R., & Nesdale, A. R. (1978). Arbitrariness of frustration: Inhibition or instigation effects on aggression. *European Journal of Social Psychology, 8,* 237–244.

Sackett, G. P. (1974). The lag sequential analysis of contingency and cyclicity in behavioral interaction research. In J. Osofsky (Ed.), *Handbook of infant development* (pp. 623–649). New York: John-Wiley.

Samuelson, W. F., & Bazerman, M. H. (1985). Negotiating under the winner's curse. In V. Smith (Ed.), *Research in experimental economics,* Vol. 3 (pp. 105–138). Greenwich, CT: JAI Press.

Saposnek, D. T. (1983a). Strategies in child custody mediation: A family systems approach. *Mediation Quarterly, 2,* 29–54.

Saposnek, D. T. (1983b). *Mediating child custody disputes.* San Francisco: Jossey-Bass.

Schank, R. C., & Abelson, R. P. (1977). *Scripts, plans, goals and understanding: An inquiry into human knowledge structures.* Hillsdale, NJ: Erlbaum.

Scheff, T. J. (1967). A theory of coordination applicable to mixed-motive games. *Sociometry, 30,* 215–234.

Schein, E. H. (1965). *Organizational psychology.* Englewood Cliffs, NJ: Prentice-Hall.

Schein, E. H. (1985). *Organizational culture and leadership.* San Francisco: Jossey-Bass.

Scherer, K. R., & Giles, H. (1982). *Social markers in speech,* Cambridge: Cambridge University Press.

Schulz, J. W., & Pruitt, D. G. (1978). The effects of mutual concern joint welfare. *Journal of Experimental Social Psychology, 14,* 480–492.

Scott, M. B., & Lyman, S. M. (1968). Accounts. *American Sociological Review, 33,* 46–62.

Scott, W. A. (1955). Reliability of content analysis: The case of nominal scale coding. *Public Opinion Quarterly, 19,* 321–325.

Shapiro, F. C. (1970). Mediator. *New Yorker, 46,* 36–58.

Shaver, K. G. (1985). *The attribution of blame: Causality, responsibility, and blameworthiness.* New York: Springer-Verlag.

Sheppard, B. H. (1983). Managers as inquisitors: Some lessons from the law. In M.

Bazerman & R. Lewicki (Eds.), *Negotiating in organizations* (pp. 193–213). Beverly Hills: Sage.

Sheppard, B. H. (1984). Third-party conflict intervention: A procedural framework. In Staw, B. M., & Cummings, L. L. (Eds.), *Research in organizational behavior, 6* (pp. 141–190). Greenwich, CT: JAI Press.

Sherif, M., Harvey, O. J., White, B. J., Hood, W. E., & Sherif, C. W. (1961). *Intergroup conflict and cooperation: The Robber's Cave experiment.* Norman, OK: University of Oklahoma Book Exchange.

Sherman, R. (1967). Individual attitude toward risk and choice between prisoner's dilemma games. *Journal of Psychology, 66,* 291–298.

Shrauger, J. S., & Patterson, M. B. (1974). Self evaluation and the selection of dimension for evaluating others. *Journal of Personality, 42,* 569–585.

Sieburg, E. (1969). *Dysfunctional communication and interpersonal responsiveness in small groups.* Unpublished doctoral dissertation, University of Denver.

Siegel, S., & Fouraker, L. E. (1960). *Bargaining and group decision making.* New York: McGraw-Hill.

Sillars, A. L. (1980). Attribution and communication in roommate conflicts. *Communication Monographs, 47,* 180–200.

Sillars, A. L. (1981). Attributions and interpersonal conflict resolution. In J. H. Harvey, W. J. Ickes, & R. F. Kidd (Eds.), *New directions in attribution research, Vol. 3* (pp. 281–300). Hillsdale, NJ: Erlbaum.

Sillars, A. L., Pike, G., Jones, T. S., & Redmon, K. (1983). Communication and conflict in marriage: One style is not satisfying to all. In R. Nostrom (Ed.), *Communication yearbook, 7* (pp. 414–431). Beverly Hills, CA: Sage.

Sillars, A. L., & Scott, M. D. (1983). Interpersonal perception between intimates: An integrative review. *Human communication research, 10,* 153–176.

Simkin, W. E. (1971). *Mediation and the dynamics of collective bargaining.* Washington, DC: Bureau of National Affairs.

Simon, . A. (1957). *Administrative behavior: A study of decision-making processes in administrative organization* (2nd Ed.). New York: Macmillan.

Slaiku, K., Culler, R., Pearson, J., & Thoennes, N. (1985). Process and outcomes in divorce mediation. *Mediation Quarterly, 10,* 55–74.

Slaiku, K., Luckett, J., & Costin-Meyers, F. (1983). *Mediation process analysis: A descriptive coding system.* Unpublished manuscript, University of Texas at Austin.

Slocum, J. W. & Sims, H. (1980). A typology for integrating technology, organization and job design. *Human Relations, 33,* 193–212.

Slovic, P., & Lichtenstein, S. (1971). Comparison of Bayesian and regression approaches to the study of information processing in judgement. *Organizational Behavior and Human Performance, 6,* 649–744.

Smircich, L., & Stubbart, C. (1985). Strategic management in an enacted world. *Academy of Management Review, 10,* 724–736.

Smith, D. N. (1978). A warmer way of disputing: Mediation and conciliation. *American Journal of Comparative Law, 26* (Supplement), 205–216.

Smith, K., Johnson, D. W., & Johnson, R. (1981). Can conflict be constructive? Controversy versus concurrence seeking in learning groups. *Journal of Educational Psychology, 73,* 651–663.

Smith, K., Johnson, D. W., & Johnson, R. (1984). Effects of controversy on learning in cooperative groups. *Journal of Social Psychology, 122,* 199–209.

Sondak, H., & Bazerman, M. H. (1987). *Matching and negotiation in quasi-markets.* Working paper, Northwestern University, Evanston, IL.

Starke, F. A., & Notz, W. W. (1981). Pre- and post-intervention effects of conventional vs. final offer arbitration. *Academy of Management Journal, 24,* 832–850.

Staw, B. M. (1976). Knee-deep in the big muddy: A study of escalating commitment to a chosen course of action. *Organizational Behavior and Human Performance, 16,* 27–44.

Staw, B. M., Bell, N. E., & Clausen, J. A. (1986). The dispositional approach to job attitudes: A lifetime longitudinal study. *Administrative Science Quarterly, 31,* 56–77.

Staw, B. M., Sandelands, L., & Dutton, J. (1981). Threat rigidity effects in organizational behavior: A multilevel analysis. *Administrative Science Quarterly, 26,* 501–524.

Stein, J. G. (1985). Structures, strategies, and tactics of mediation: Kissinger and Carter in the Middle East. *Negotiation Journal, 1,* 331–347.

Stevens, C. M. (1963). *Strategy and collective bargaining negotiations,* New York: McGraw-Hill.

Stevens, C. M. (1966). Is compulsory arbitration compatible with bargaining? *Industrial Relations, 5,* 38–52.

Stiles, W. B. (1981). Classification of intersubjective elocutionary acts. *Language in Society, 10,* 227–249.

Stimac, M. (1982). Strategies for resolving conflict: Their functional and dysfunctional sides. *Personnel, 59,* 54–64.

Strauss, G. (1962). Tactics of lateral relationships: The purchasing agent. *Administrative Science Quarterly, 7,* 161–186.

Subbarao, A. V. (1978). The impact of binding interest arbitration on negotiation and process outcome. *Journal of Conflict Resolution, 22,* 79–103.

Susman, G. (1976). *Autonomy at work: A sociotechnical analysis of participative management.* New York: Praeger.

Susskind, L. (1981). Environmental mediation and the accountability problem. *Vermont Law Review, 6*(1), 1–47.

Susskind, L., Bacow, L., & Wheeler, M. (Eds.) (1984). *Resolving environmental regulator disputes.* New York: Shenckman.

Sviridoff, M. (1980). Recent trends in resolving interpersonal, community, and environmental disputes. *Arbitration Journal, 35,* 3–9.

Taylor, F. W. (1916, December). The principles of scientific management. *Bulletin of the Taylor Society,* pp. 13–23.

Taylor, S. E., & Crocker, J. (1981). Schematic basis of social information processing. In E. T. Higgins, C. P. Herman, & M. P. Zanna (Eds.), *Social cognition: The Ontario symposium* (pp. 89–134). Hillsdale, NJ: Erlbaum.

Tedeschi, J. T., & Bonoma, T. V. (1977). Measures of last resort: coercion and aggression in bargaining. In D. Druckman (Ed.), *Negotiations: Psychological perspectives,* New York: Sage.

Theye, L. D., & Seiler, W. J. (1979). Interaction analysis in collective bargaining: An alternative approach to the prediction of negotiated outcomes. In D. Nimmo (Ed.),

Communication yearbook 3 (pp. 375–392). New Brunswick, NJ: Transaction-International Communication Association.

Thibaut, J., & Kelley, H. H. (1959). *The social psychology of groups*. New York: Wiley.

Thibaut, J., & Walker, L. (1975). *Procedural justice: A psychological analysis*. New York: Wiley.

Thibaut, J., & Walker, L. (1978). A theory of procedure. *California Law Review, 66,* 541–566.

Thoennes, N., & Pearson, J. (1985). Predicting outcomes in divorce mediation: The influence of people and process. *Journal of Social Issues, 41,* 115–126.

Thomas, K. W. (1976). Conflict and conflict management. In M. Dunnette (Ed.), *Handbook of industrial and organizational psychology* (pp. 889–935). Chicago: Rand McNally.

Thomas, K. W. (1977). Toward multi-dimensional values in teaching: The example of conflict behavior. *Academy of Management Review, 2,* 484–490.

Thomas, K. W. (1979). Organizational conflict. In: S. Kerr (Ed.), *Organizational Behavior*. Columbus, OH: Grid Publishing.

Thomas, K. W. (1988). Norms as an integrative theme in conflict and negotiations: correcting our "sociopathic" assumptions. In M. A. Rahim (Ed.), *Managing conflict: An interdisciplinary approach*. New York: Praeger.

Thomas, K. W. (in press, a). Conflict and conflict management: Reflections and update. *Journal of Occupational Behavior*.

Thomas, K. W. (in press, b). Conflict and negotiation processes in organizations. For M. D. Dunnette (Ed.), *Handbook of industrial and organizational psychology* (2nd Ed.). Chicago: Rand McNally.

Thomas, K. W., & Pondy, L. R. (1977). Toward an "intent" model of conflict management among principal parties. *Human Relations, 12,* 1089–1102.

Thomas, K. W., & Schmidt, W. H. (1976). A survey of managerial interests with respect to conflict. *Academy of Management Journal, 19,* 315–318.

Thompson, J. D. (1967). *Organizations in action*. New York: McGraw-Hill.

Thompson, L., & Hastie, R. (in press). Negotiator's perceptions of the negotiation process. In B. H. Sheppard, M. H. Bazerman, & R. J. Lewicki (Eds.), *Research on negotiation in organizations, Vol. 2*. Greenwich, CT: JAI Press.

Ting-Toomey, S. (1983). An analysis of verbal communication patterns in high and low marital adjustment groups. *Human Communication Research, 9,* 306–319.

Tjosvold, D. (1974). Threat as a low-power person's strategy in bargaining: Social face and tangible outcomes. *International Journal of Group Tensions, 4,* 494–510.

Tjosvold, D. (1977a). The effects of constituent's affirmation and the opposing negotiator's self-presentation on bargaining between unequal status groups. *Organizational Behavior and Human Performance, 18,* 146–157.

Tjosvold, D. (1977b). Low-power person's strategies in bargaining: Negotiability of demand, maintaining face, and race. *International Journal of Group Tensions, 7,* 29–42.

Tjosvold, D. (1979). Control strategies and own group evaluation in intergroup conflict. *Journal of Psychology, 100,* 305–314.

Tjosvold, D. (1982). Effects of the approach to controversy on superiors' incorporation of subordinates' information in decision making. *Journal of Applied Psychology, 67,* 189–193.

Tjosvold, D. (1983). Social face in conflict: A critique. *International Journal of Group Tensions, 13,* 49–64.

Tjosvold, D. (1984). Cooperation theory and organizations. *Human Relations, 37,* 743–767.

Tjosvold, D. (1985). Implications of controversy research for management. *Journal of Management, 11,* 19–35.

Tjosvold, D. (1986). *Working together to get things done: Managing for organizational productivity.* Boston: Lexington.

Tjosvold, D., & Deemer, D. K. (1980). Effects of controversy within a cooperative or competitive context on organizational decision making. *Journal of Applied Psychology, 65,* 590–595.

Tjosvolv, D., & Johnson, D. W. (1977). The effects of controversy on cognitive perspective-taking. *Journal of Educational Psychology, 69,* 679–685.

Tjosvold, D., & Johnson, D. W. (1978). Controversy within a cooperative or competitive context and cognitive perspective taking. *Contemporary educational psychology, 3,* 376–386.

Tjosvold, D., & Johnson, D. W. (Eds.). (1983). *Productive conflict management: Perspectives for organizations.* New York: Irvington.

Tjosvold, D., Johnson, D. W., & Fabrey, L. (1981). Effects of controversy and defensiveness on cognitive perspective-taking. *Psychological Reports, 47,* 1043–1053.

Tjosvold, D., Johnson, D. W., & Lerner, J. (1980). Effects of affirmation and acceptance on incorporation of opposing information in problem-solving. *Journal of Social Psychology, 114,* 103–110.

Torrance, E. (1961). Can group control social stress in creative activity? *Elementary School Journal, 62,* 139–394.

Touval, S. (1975). Biased intermediaries: Theoretical and historical considerations. *Jerusalem Journal of International Relations, 1,* 51–69.

Tulving, E., & Pearlstone, Z. (1966). Availability versus accessibility of information in memory for words. *Journal of Verbal Learning and Verbal Behavior, 5,* 381–391.

Tung, R. (1981). *Business negotiations with the Japanese.* Lexington, KY: Lexington Books.

Turner, R. H. (1956). Role taking, role standpoint and reference group behavior. *American Journal of Sociology, 61,* 316–328.

Tversky, A., & Kahneman, D. (1981). The framing of decisions and the psychology of choice. *Science, 211,* 453–458.

Tyler, T. R. (1986). When does procedural justice matter in organizational settings? In B. Sheppard & R. Lewicki (Eds.), *Negotiation in organizations.* Greenwich, CT: JAI Press.

Van Blerkom, M., & Tjosvold, D. (1981). The effects of social context on engaging in controversy. *Journal of Psychology, 107,* 141–145.

Van de Vliert, E. (1981). Siding and other reactions to a conflict: A theory of escalation toward outsiders. *Journal of Conflict Resolution, 25,* 1554–1560.

Van de Vliert, E. (1984). Conflict: Prevention and escalation. In P. J. D. Drenth, H. Thierry, P. J. Willems, & CH. J. de Wolff (Eds.), *Handbook of work and organizational psychology* (pp. 521–551) New York: Wiley.

Van de Vliert, E. (1985). Escalation intervention in small group conflict. *Journal of Applied Behavioral Science, 21,* 19–36.

Van de Vliert, E., & Hordijk, J. W. (1986). De cognitieve afstand tussen compro-misgedrag en andere stijlen van conflicthantering [The cognitive distance between compromising and other styles of conflict management]. *Nederlands tijdschrift voor de psychology, 41*, 134–139.

Veitch, R., & Griffit, W. (1976). Good news bad news: Affective and interpersonal effects. *Journal of Applied Social Psychology, 6*, 69–75.

Vinacke, W. E., & Arkoff, A. (1957). An experimental study of coalitions in the triad. *American Sociological Review, 22*, 406–414.

Vinokur, A., & Burnstein, E. (1974). Effects of partially shared persuasive arguments on group-induced shifts. *Journal of Personality and Social Psychology, 29*, 305–315.

Von Neumann, J., & Morgenstern, O. (1947). *Theory of games and economic behavior.* Princeton: Princeton University Press.

Vroom, V. H. (1964). *Work and motivation.* New York: Wiley.

Wagatsuma, H. (1984). Some cultural assumptions among the Japanese. *Japan Quarterly*, 371–379.

Walcott, C., & Hopmann, P. T. (1975). Interaction analysis and bargaining behavior. *Experimental Study of Politics, 4*, 1–19.

Walcott, C., Hopmann, P. T., & King, T. D. (1977). The role of debate in negotiation. In D. Druckman (Ed.), *Negotiations: Social-psychological perspectives* (pp. 193–211). Beverly Hills, CA: Sage.

Walker, G. B. (1985). Argumentation and negotiation. In J. R. Cox, M. O. Sillars, & G. B. Walker (Eds.), Argument and social practice: *Proceedings of the fourth SCA/AFA conference on argumentation* (pp. 747–769). Annandale, VA: Speech Communication Association.

Wall, J. A. (1979). The effects of mediator rewards and suggestions upon negotiations. *Journal of Personality and Social Psychology, 37*, 1554–1560.

Wall, J. A., Jr. (1981). Mediation: An analysis, review, and proposed research. *Journal of Conflict Resolution, 25*, 157–180.

Wall, J. A. (1985, April). *New mediation melodies.* Paper presented at the annual conference of the Midwest Division of the Academy of Management, Champaign, IL.

Wall, J. A., & Schiller, L. F. (1983). The judge off the bench: A mediator in civil settlement negotiations. In M. Bazerman, & R. Lewicki (Eds.), *Negotiating in organizations* (pp. 193–213). Beverly Hills: Sage.

Wallerstein, J. S., & Kelly J. (1980). *Surviving the breakup: How children and parents cope with divorce.* New York: Basic Books.

Waln, V. G. (1984). Questions in interpersonal conflict: Participant and observer perception. *Southern Speech Communication Journal, 49*, 277–288.

Walton, R. E. (1965). Two strategies of social change and their dilemmas. *Journal of Applied Behavioral Science, 1*, 167–179.

Walton, R. E. (1969). *Interpersonal peacemaking: Confrontations and third party consultations.* Reading, MA: Addison-Wesley.

Walton, R. E. (1987). *Interpersonal peacemaking.* Reading, MA: Addison-Wesley.

Walton, R. E., Dutton, J. M., & Cafferty, T. P. (1969). Organizational context and interdepartmental conflict. *Administrative Science Quarterly, 14*, 522–542.

Walton, R. E., & McKersie, R. (1965). *A behavioral theory of labor negotiations: An analysis of a social interaction system.* New York: McGraw-Hill.

Warren, E. L., & Bernstein, I. (1949). The mediation process. *Southern Economic Journal, 15*, 441–457.

Watson, C. D. (1987, August). *Resolving superior-subordinate conflicts of interest: An examination of the merits of different types of participative style.* Paper presented at the annual meeting of the Academy of Management, New Orleans, LA.

Watzlawick, P., Beavin, J. H., & Jackson, D. D. (1967). *Pragmatics of human communication.* New York: Norton.

Webb, N. (1977). *Learning in individual and small group settings.* Technical Report No. 1, School of Education, Stanford University, CA.

Weick, K. E. (1966). *The social psychology of organizing.* Reading, MA: Addison-Wesley.

Weider-Hatfield, D., & Hatfield, J. D. (1987, June). *Relationships among conflict management styles, levels of conflict, and reactions to work.* Paper presented at the International Conference of the Conflict Management Group, Fairfax, VA.

Weiner, B. (1986). Attribution, emotion and action. In R. M. Sorrentino & E. T. Higgins (Eds.), *Handbook of motivation and cognition: Foundations of social behavior* (pp. 281–312). New York: Guilford Press.

Weiner, B., Amirkhan, J., Folkes, V. S., & Verette, J. A. (1987). An attributional analysis of excuse giving: Studies of a naive theory of emotion. *Journal of Personality and Social Psychology, 52,* 316–324.

Weingarten, H. R. (1986). Strategic planning for divorce mediation. *Social Work, 3,* 194–200.

Weisinger, H., & Lobsenz, N. M. (1981). *Nobody's perfect: How to give criticism and get results.* New York: Warner.

Weiss, H. M., & Adler, S. (1984). Personality and organizational behavior. In B. M. Staw & L. L. Cummings (Eds.), *Research in organizational behavior, 6* (pp. 1–50). Greenwich, CT: JAI Press.

Weitzman, L. J. (1985). *The divorce revolution: The unexpected social and economic consequences for women and children in America.* New York: Norton.

Welton, G. L., Pruitt, D. G., & McGillicuddy, N. B. (in press). An exploratory examination of caucusing: Its role in community mediation. *Journal of Conflict Resolution.*

Wheeler, M. (1980). *Divided children: A legal guide for divorcing parents.* New York: Norton.

Wildavsky, A. (1968). Budgeting as a political process. In D. L. Sills (Ed.), *The international encyclopedia of Social sciences, 2* (pp. 192–199). New York: Crowell, Collier and Macmillan.

Wildavsky, A. (1979). *The politics of the budgeting process.* Boston: Little Brown.

Wilder, D. A. (1981). Perceiving persons as a group: Categorization and intergroup relations. In D. L. Hamilton (Ed.), *Cognitive processes in stereotyping and intergroup behavior.* Hillsdale, NJ: Erlbaum.

Williams, S. (1970). *The need for social approval and negotiation success.* Unpublished master's thesis, University of Minnesota, Minneapolis.

Wilson, S. R., & Putnam, L. L. (1986, November). *Interaction goals and argument functions as schemes for organizing research on argument in bargaining.* Paper presented to the annual meeting of the Speech Communication Association, Chicago.

Wilson, W. (1969). Cooperation and the cooperativeness of the other player. *Journal of Conflict Resolution, 13,* 110–117.

Wiseman, J. M., & Fiske, J. A. (1980). A lawyer-therapist team as mediator in marital crisis. *Social Work, 25*, 442–445.

Young, O. R. (1970). *Bargaining*. Princeton, NJ: Princeton Center of International Studies, Princeton University.

Young, O. R. (1972). Intermediaries: Additional thoughts on third parties. *Journal of Conflict Resolution, 16*, 51–65.

Young, O. R. (Ed.). (1975). *Bargaining: Formal theories of negotiation*. Chicago: University of Illinois Press.

Zeuthan, F. (1950). *Problems of monopoly and economic welfare*. London: Routledge.

Ziegelmueller, G. W., & Dause, C. A. (1975). *Argumentation: Inquiry and advocacy*. Englewood Cliffs, NJ: Prentice-Hall.

Zillman, D., & Cantor, J. R., & Day. (1976). Effect of timing of information about mitigating circumstances on emotional responses to provocation and retaliatory behavior. *Journal of Experimental Social Psychology, 9*, 282–293.

Zimmerman, M. (1985). *How to do business with the Japanese*. New York: Random House.

Index

About the Editor and Contributors

M. AFZALUR RAHIM. Dr. Rahim is a Professor of Management at Western Kentucky University. He holds M.Com. (Dacca, Bangladesh), M.B.A. (Miami, Ohio), and Ph.D. (Graduate School of Business, University of Pittsburgh) degrees. Dr. Rahim teaches courses on strategic management, organizational behavior, and research methodology. He is the author of over 60 articles and book chapters, 5 cases, and 3 instruments on power and conflict. He is the author of 4 books including *Managing Conflict in Organizations* (Praeger, 1986) and *Rahim Organizational Conflict Inventories: Professional Manual* and is the founder of the International Association for Conflict Management.

ROBERT A. BARON. Dr. Baron is Professor and Chair of the Department of Psychology and also Professor of Organizational Behavior in the School of Management at Rensselaer Polytechnic Institute. A University of Iowa Ph.D. (1968), he has held academic positions at Purdue University, Princeton University, the University of Minnesota, University of Texas, and University of South Carolina. He was a Visiting Fellow at the University of Oxford (1982), and served as a Program Director at the National Science Foundation (1979-1981). He is the author of more than 80 journal articles and the author or co-author of sixteen books. Dr. Baron's current research interests focus on techniques for managing organizational conflict, and self-presentation during employment interviews.

MAX H. BAZERMAN. Dr. Bazerman is a Professor of Organization Behavior at the J. L. Kellogg Graduate School of Management at Northwestern University. Professor Bazerman has a B.S.E. from the Wharton School at the University of Pennsylvania and a Ph.D. from the Graduate School of Industrial Administration at Carnegie-Mellon University. Prior to taking his position at Northwestern University, he was on the faculty of the Sloan School of Management at MIT. Professor Bazerman is the author or co-author of over forty articles on decision making and negotiation and of five books including *Negotiating in Organizations* (1983) and *Research on Negotiations in Organizations* (1988).

THOMAS J. BERGMANN. Dr. Bergmann is a Professor of Business Administration at the University of Wisconsin-Eau Claire. He holds an M.S.I.R. from Loyola University (Chicago) and a Ph.D. from the Industrial Relations Center of the University of Minnesota. His primary interests include the areas of human resource management in both the public and private sectors. He has published in the *Journal of Occupational Psychology, Compensation Review, Personnel, Personnel Psychology, Personnel Administrator,* and *Psychological Reports.*

ROBERT J. BIES. Dr. Bies (Ph.D., Stanford University) is an Assistant Professor of Organization Behavior at the J. L. Kellogg Graduate School of Management at Northwestern University. He has published in *Academy of Management Journal, Communication Research, Representative Research in Social Psychology, Social Justice Research,* and in the annual series on *Research in Organizational Behavior,* and *Research on Negotiation in Organizations.* His research interests include the use of accounts in conflict situations, procedural justice, and the delivery of bad news in organizations.

GABRIEL F. BUNTZMAN. Dr. Buntzman is an Assistant Professor of Management at Western Kentucky University. He holds a B.A. (Oakland University), and M.B.A. (Ohio University) and M.A. and Ph.D. degrees (University of North Carolina). Dr. Buntzman's teaching and research interests are in the areas of organizational behavior, strategic management, and human resources management. His research has been presented at national meetings of the Academy of Management and Association for Human Resource Management and Organizational Behavior.

LYNN M. CASTRIANNO. Lynn M. Castrianno currently attends the University of Nebraska-Lincoln Law/Psychology program. Her research interests include social sciences in law and social policy.

LAURIE S. COLTRI. Ms. Coltri received her J.D. degree from the University of Southern California in 1978 and is a member of the American Bar Association, the Maryland State Bar, and the California State Bar. In addition to being a lawyer, Ms. Coltri is also a doctoral student in the Department of Human Development at the University of Maryland and has done graduate work in the areas of conflict management theory, mediation, and the effects of divorce on families. Since 1984, she has limited her private practice to divorce mediation and is active in child custody mediation in the Circuit Court of Prince George's County, Maryland. Ms. Coltri also teaches courses on the divorce experience in an adult education setting. One of the major interests is the due process implications of court connected mediation practices.

WILLIAM O. DAILEY. Dr. Dailey is a Visiting Assistant Professor of Communication at Michigan State University. He received his Ph.D. from Northwestern University in 1987. His research interests include bargaining and negotiation, conflict and discourse processing.

WILLIAM A. DONOHUE. Dr. Donohue is an Associate Professor of Communication at Michigan State University in East Lansing, Michigan. Both his M.A. and Ph.D. were obtained from Ohio State University in Communication. Dr. Donohue has published over 30 articles and book chapters in the areas of interpersonal communication, labor-management negotiation and divorce mediation. His articles have appeared in *Human Communication Research, Communication Monographs, Human Relations, Mediation Quarterly, Conciliation Courts Review,* and *Western Journal of Speech Communication.*

GEORGE T. DUNCAN. Dr. Duncan is a Professor of Statistics at the School of Urban and Public Affairs, Carnegie Mellon University, where he is the Director of the Decision Systems Research Institute. He received his B.S. and M.S. degrees from the University of Chicago and his Ph.D. degree from the University of Minnesota. He has taught at the University of California at Davis and was the editor of the *Journal of the American Statistical Association.* His current research is focused on confidentiality issues, dispute resolution, and computer decision support systems in policy and management areas. His articles have appeared in such professional journals as *Journal of the American Statistical Association, Operations Research, Econometrica, Psychometrika, Biometrika, Technometrics, American Journal of Political Science,* and *Negotiation Journal.*

P. CHRISTOPHER EARLEY. Dr. Earley is an Assistant Professor of Management at the Karl Eller School of Management, University of Arizona. He holds M.A. and Ph.D. in industrial/organizational psychology from the University of Illinois. Dr. Earley is the author of over 30 articles and book chapters. His articles have appeared in professional journals such as *Journal of Applied Psychology, Journal of Personality and Social Psychology, Organizational Behavior and Human Decision Processes, Academy of Management Journal, Journal of Organizational Behavior.* Dr. Earley teaches courses on organizational behavior, work motivation, and intercultural aspects of organizational behavior.

FRANCINE G. FAVRETTO. Ms. Favretto received an M.Ed. in early childhood at the University of Maryland and is currently a Ph.D. candidate in the University's Institute for Child Study. Ms. Favretto has also been involved in organizing and conducting court connected child custody mediation pilot programs in Baltimore City and Prince George's County, Maryland. She has worked extensively with divorcing families as a child custody mediator as well as a parent educator. Ms. Favretto is presently engaged in research on the effects of divorce on young adults and the efficacy of court connected mediation services.

WILLIAM RICK FRY. Dr. Fry is an Associate Professor in the Psychology Department at Youngstown State University. His research interests include integrative bargaining, conflict escalation and de-escalation, mediation as well as procedural and distributive justice. He received both his Masters and Ph.D. degrees from Wayne State University (Detroit).

E. JOAN HUNT. Dr. Hunt, a faculty member in the Department of Human Develoment at the University of Maryland, College Park, holds an M.A. from Claremont Graduate School, Claremont, California and a Ph.D. from the University of Maryland. Her teaching and research emphasize conflict management particularly in educational setting, divorce, and family mediation. Dr. Hunt has been instrumental in developing court based child custody mediation programs in both Baltimore and Prince George's County, MD. She has co-authored papers in the area of divorce and family mediation and has been published in *Conciliation Courts Review, American Journal of Orthopsychiatry* and others.

CAROL A. IPPOLITO. Ms. Ippolito received her B.A. degree from the State University of New York College at Buffalo and is currently a graduate student in the doctoral program in social and organizational psychology at the State University of New York at Buffalo. Ms. Ippolito has recently completed a thesis on power-differentials in mediation for which she has earned an M.A. degree in social psychology.

DAVID W. JOHNSON. Dr. Johnson is a Professor of Educational Psychology with an emphasis in social psychology at the University of Minnesota. He has a masters and a doctoral degree from Columbia University. He has published 17 books and over 250 research articles in leading psychological journals. He received national awards for outstanding research from the American Personnel and Guidance Association (1972) and for outstanding research on intergroup relationships from the APA (1981). He is a practicing psychotherapist, and is a recent past-editor of the *American Educational Research Journal*.

ROGER T. JOHNSON. Dr. Roger T. Johnson is a professor in the Department of Curriculum and Instruction with an emphasis in science education at the University of Minnesota. He holds an M.A. degree from Ball State University and an Ed.D. from the University of California in Berkeley. He is the author or co-author of numerous articles, several book chapters, and two books. He has been the recipient of several national research awards.

TRICIA S. JONES. Dr. Jones is an Assistant Professor of Speech Communication at the University of Denver. She has a M.S. in organizational communication and organizational behavior from Purdue University and a Ph.D. from Ohio State University. Dr. Jones teaches in the areas of dispute resolution, negotiation, and mediation as well as qualitative and quantitative research methods. She has authored over 20 articles and book chapters, most pertaining to the examination of communication in interpersonal and organizational conflict. Her publications have appeared in such journals as *Human Communication Research, Communication Monographs, Southern Speech Communication Journal, Central States Speech Journal,* and *Perceptual and Motor Skills.*

SANDA KAUFMAN. Dr. Kaufman is Assistant Professor of Urban Studies at Cleveland State University. She holds degrees in architecture and in urban and regional planning (Israel Institute of Technology, Haifa) and a Ph.D. in public policy analysis (Carnegie-Mellon University, Pittsburgh). Dr. Kaufman's research in conflict management focuses on third party intervention, combining the work on a theoretical framework with the study of experimental results, and of actual environmental and urban disputes.

ELIZABETH JANSSEN KOOPMAN. Dr.Koopman is an Associate Professor in the Department of Human Development of the University of Maryland at College Park. She holds an M.A. from the University of Michigan and a Ph.D. from the University of Maryland. Over the past eight years her primary teaching, research, and service activities have been in the area of children and parents in non-marital families. She is the author of numerous chapters and articles concerning the education and training of family mediators, and on critical issues in the professional development of the family mediation field. Dr. Koopman's articles have been published in the *Journal of Divorce, Conciliation Courts Review,* and the *American Journal of Orthopsychiatry.*

RAJESH KUMAR. Dr. Kumar is a Ph.D. candidate at the Graduate School of Business Administration, New York University. His research interests are in the areas of strategic management and international business negotiations and conflict management in organizational settings. He has presented a number of papers, in national and international conferences, on industrial crisis management and cross-cultural negotiations.

NEIL McGILLICUDDY. Dr. McGillicuddy is a Program Manager at the Research Institute on Alcoholism in Buffalo, New York. He has an M.A. (University of Buffalo) and is close to receiving his Ph.D. in psychology. He is an author or co-author on seven articles in *Journal of Personality and Social Psychology, Journal of Conflict Resolution,* and *Personality and Social Psychology Bulletin.* He is currently conducting an experiment investigating the relative efficacy of two alternative methods of preventing substance abuse among developmentally disabled individuals.

MARGARET A. NEALE. Dr. Neale is an Associate Professor of Organization Behavior at the J. L. Kellogg Graduate School of Management at Northwestern University. She received her Ph.D. in business administration from the University of Texas. Prior to taking her position at Northwestern University, Professor Neale was on the faculty of the Eller Graduate School of Management of the University of Arizona. Professor Neale is the author of over thirty articles on negotiation and decision making.

GREGORY B. NORTHCRAFT. Dr. Northcraft is Associate Professor of Management and Policy at the University of Arizona. He holds undergraduate degrees from Dartmouth College and Oxford University, and M.A. and Ph.D. degrees in social psychology from Stanford University. Dr. Northcraft teaches courses on statistical decision making, organizational behavior, and human resources management. Dr. Northcraft has authored a variety of articles and book chapters on behavioral decision making, negotiation, and employee motivation which have appeared in professional journals such as *Organizational Behavior and Human Decision Processes, Academy of Management Review,* and *Decision Sciences.*

WILLIAM W. NOTZ. Dr. Notz is a Professor of Organizational Behavior at the University of Manitoba. He holds an M.B.A. (University of Denver) and Ph.D. (Northwestern University). His research has appeared in *American Psychologist, Administrative Science Quarterly, Journal of Applied Psychology, Academy of Management Journal, Academy of Management Review,* and *Human Relations.*

HUGO C. M. PREIN. Dr. Prein is an Associate Professor of Organizational and Social Psychology at the University of Utrecht, the Netherlands. He teaches courses in conflict management, third party intervention, group dynamics, intervention strategies, and organization development. He is the author of two books, one about third party intervention and one about training in conflict management and intervention. He wrote several articles, which have appeared in professional journals, such as *Group and Organization Studies, Human Relations,* and in Dutch Journals, such as *M & O, Nederlands Tijdschrift voor de Psychologie, Management Methoden en Technieken.*

DEAN G. PRUITT. Dr. Pruitt is Professor of Psychology at State University of New York at Buffalo. He got his Ph.D. from Yale University in 1957 and did post doctoral work in psychology at the University of Michigan and in international relations at Northwestern University. He specializes in the psychology of social conflict and does laboratory and field research on negotiation and mediation. He is the author of *Theory and Research on the Causes of War* (with Richard Snyder), *Negotiation Behavior, Social Conflict: Escalation, Stalemate and Settlement* (with Jeffrey Rubin), and the forthcoming *The Mediation of Disputes: Empirical Studies in the Resolution of Social Conflict* (with Kenneth Kressel).

CLEMENT O. PSENICKA. Dr. Psenicka is an Associate Professor and Chairman of the Department of Management at Youngstown State University. He has an M.A. in economics and a D.B.A. both from Kent State University. His area of teaching is management science and operations management. He is currently doing research in transportation modeling under a grant from the State of Ohio. Dr. Psenicka has published an article on conflict in *Psychological Reports.*

LINDA L. PUTNAM. Dr. Putnam is a Professor of Communication at Purdue University. She holds a Ph.D. from the University of Minnesota and an M.A. degree from the University of Wisconsin. Dr. Putnam teaches courses in negotiation and conflict management and in organizational communication. She is the author of over 45 articles and the co-editor of four books. She currently serves on the editorial boards of five journals and was the guest editor for two special issues on conflict in organizations in *Communication Research* and *Management Communication Quarterly*. Her articles have appeared in such publications as *Human Communication Research, Communication Monographs, Communication Yearbook 4, 5*, and *6, Small Group Behavior, Southern Speech Communication Journal, Journal of Business Communication*, and *Journal of the American Forensic Association*.

MICHAEL E. ROLOFF. Dr. Roloff is a Professor of Communication Studies at Northwestern University. He holds an M.A. and Ph.D. in communication from Michigan State University. Dr. Roloff teaches courses in persuasion, interpersonal communication, bargaining and negotiation, and interpersonal conflict management. He has written one book and co-edited three volumes. He has written numerous articles appearing in professional journals such as *Communication Monographs, Communication Quarterly, Communication Research*, and *Human Communication Research*

WILLIAM H. ROSS. Dr. Ross is an Assistant Professor of Management at the University of Wisconsin-La Crosse. He holds a Ph.D. in industrial/organizational psychology from the University of Illinois-Urbana. Dr. Ross teaches courses on labor-management relations and policy issues in personnel/human resource management. He has several published cases and book chapters. His articles appear in professional journals such as *Negotiation Journal, Academic Computing*, and *Journal of Management Case Studies*.

KARL A. SMITH. Dr. Smith is an Associate Professor of Civil and Mineral Engineering at the University of Minnesota. He earned an M.S. in metallurgical engineering from Michigan Technological University and a Ph.D. from University of Minnesota in educational psychology. He teaches courses in metallurgical engineering, computer application, and cooperative education. He has published over 25 articles in the areas of metallurgical engineering and engineering education.

FREDERICK A. STARKE. Dr. Starke is a Professor of Organizational Behavior at the University of Manitoba (Canada). He holds a B.A. and M.B.A. from Southern Illinois University, and a Ph.D. from Ohio State University. Dr. Starke teaches courses in organizational behavior, administrative theory, and decision making. He has co-authored three textbooks. His articles have appeared in journals such as *Administrative Science Quarterly, Academy of Management Journal, Journal of Applied Psychology,* and *Journal of Systems Management.*

KENNETH W. THOMAS. Dr. Thomas is Professor of Administrative Sciences at the Naval Postgraduate School, Monterey, California. He holds a B.A. in philosophy from Pomona College and a Ph.D. in administrative sciences from Purdue University. He has held previous faculty positions at UCLA, Temple University, and the University of Pittsburgh. He is best known for his theoretical and empirical contributions on the topic of organizational conflict and conflict management, although his recent research interests also include research usefulness and intrinsic work motivation. Key works on conflict include a theoretical synthesis in the *Handbook of Industrial and Organizational Psychology* (now updated for a second edition), and the *Thomas-Kilmann Conflict Mode Instrument.*

DEAN TJOSVOLD. After graduating from Princeton University, Dean Tjosvold earned his Ph.D. in the social psychology of organizations at the University of Minnesota in 1972, and is now, Professor, Faculty of Business Administration, Simon Fraser University, Canada. Before that he taught at Pennsylvania State University and was a visiting scholar at the National University of Singapore. He has published over a 100 articles on managing conflict, cooperation and competition, decision making, power, and other management issues. He is the author or co-author of three books including *Productive Conflict Management: Perspective for Organizations* (with David Johnson; 1983) and *Managing Conflict: The Key to Making an Organization Work* (1988).

FRANK TUTZAUER. Dr. Tutzauer is a Visiting Assistant Professor of Communication at the State University of New York at Buffalo. He holds a B.S. in mathematics (Southwestern, 1981), an M.A. in communication studies (Northwestern, 1984), and a Ph.D. in communication studies (Northwestern, 1985). His research pertains to bargaining and negotiation, social networks, and the mathematical modeling of behavioral phenomena. Recent publications include articles in *Behavioral Science, Social Networks,* and *Communication Yearbook.*

EVERT VAN DE VLIERT. Dr. Van de Vliert is a Professor of Organizational and Applied Social Psychology at the University of Groningen, The Netherlands. He holds a Ph.D. degree in the social sciences from the Free University in Amsterdam. His research interests include organizational interventions, role transitions, conflict, and conflict management. Dr. Van de Vliert is the author of over 75 articles and book chapters as well as the editor of three books. His articles have appeared in professional journals, such as *Academy of Management Review, Journal for the Theory of Social Behavior, Journal of Conflict Resolution, Journal of Social Psychology,* and *Journal of Applied Behavioral Science.*

ROGER VOLKEMA. Roger Volkema is an Assistant Professor of Organization Behavior at the American University in Washington, D.C. He holds a Ph.D. from the University of Wisconsin-Madison in industrial engineering. His primary research interest includes the study of conflict theory and behavior, third party dispute resolution, face-saving techniques, and other organizational behavior issues. He has published in such journals, such as *Management Science, Strategic Management Journal,* and *AEDS.*

GARY L. WELTON. Dr. Welton is a Visiting Assistant Professor of Psychology at the University of Missouri-Columbia. He holds a Ph.D. (Buffalo) degree in social and organizational psychology. Dr. Welton teaches courses on univariate and multivariate statistics. Along with his research on mediation, he has an active research program on social dilemmas. His articles have appeared in professional journals, including *Journal of Conflict Resolution, Journal of Personality and Social Psychology,* and *Personality and Social Psychology Bulletin.*

STEVEN R. WILSON. Mr. Wilson (MA, Indiana University, 1984) is a David Ross fellow and doctoral candidate in the Department of Communication at Purdue University. Mr. Wilson teaches courses in interpersonal communication, persuasion, and research methodology. He has authored articles appearing in *Human Communication Research, Central States Speech Journal,* and *Journal of the American Forensic Association.*

JO MACIAG ZUBEK. Ms. Zubek earned her B.A. degree summa cum laude from the State University of New York at Buffalo, where she received the Feldman-Cohen Award for achievement in psychology. Ms. Zubek is a member of Phi Beta Kappa and of the National Honor Society in Psychology. She is currently training in the doctoral program in social and organizational psychology at the State University of New York at Buffalo.